About Pearson

Pearson is the world's learning company, with presence across 70 countries worldwide. Our unique insights and world-class expertise comes from a long history of working closely with renowned teachers, authors and thought leaders, as a result of which, we have emerged as the preferred choice for millions of teachers and learners across the world.

We believe learning opens up opportunities, creates fulfilling careers and hence better lives. We hence collaborate with the best of minds to deliver you class-leading products, spread across the Higher Education and Test Preparation spectrum.

Superior learning experience and improved outcomes are at the heart of everything we do. This product is the result of one such effort.

Your feedback plays a critical role in the evolution of our products and you can contact us - reachus@pearson.com. *We look forward to it.*

WHAT RANK HOLDERS SAY

I have found Shiv Gupta Sir's book to be a must for UPSC aspirants. The book provides an easy, conceptual, and concise overview of World History through the various flowcharts, diagrams, timelines and revision. This book can be a single source of preparation for World History for CSE. I highly recommend this book to everyone who is interested or wants to score good marks in World History.

Shrutisha Patade
(AIR 281, CSE 2022)

Swapnil Patil
(IAS, AIR 55 2017)

I have found Shiv's book to be an invaluable resource for aspirants. It is comprehensive, well-written, and easy to understand. The book covers all the important topics related to World History that are likely to be tested in the exam, and it provides a clear and concise overview of each topic. World History is a vast and complex subject, but Shiv Gupta's book makes it easy to understand through the various flowcharts, schematic diagrams, timelines, and maps. The book is well-organized and easy to follow, and I highly recommend this book to anyone who is interested in learning about World History.

I got the opportunity to read a few chapters of World History by Shivlal Gupta. The book provides concepts, maps, pointers about reasons and outcomes of world events along with points to ponder and revision of main contents at the end. I found the chapters to be concise and conceptually planned from an exam point of view. I think it will give clarity to the students of World History. I wish Shiv a great success for this book and other upcoming endeavours.

Shraddha N. Pandey
(IPS 2017)

WORLD HISTORY

For UPSC and State Civil Services Examination

Second Edition

Shivlal Gupta

Pearson

Disclaimer

The maps published in this book where India boundaries are depicted are copyrights by Govt. of India 2026 is made on the basis of maps provided by SOI on its website (URL) under tab Maps and Data_ External Boundaries with all reasonable care and diligence.

ISBN 978-93-713-6715-8

First Impression

Published by Pearson India Education Services Pvt. Ltd, CIN: U72200TN2005PTC057128.

Head Office: 1st Floor, Berger Tower, Plot No. C-001A/2, Sector 16B, Noida – 201 301, Uttar Pradesh, India.

Registered Office: 6th Floor, Tower A, Unit A and B, International Tech Park, CapitaLand, 200 Feet Radial Road, Zamin Pallavaram, Old Pallavaram, Chennai – 600 117, Tamil Nadu, India.

Website: in.pearson.com, Email: companysecretary.india@pearson.com

Compositor: Saksham Printographics
Printed in India at Rajkamal Electric Press, Kundli, Haryana-131 028.

CONTENTS

PREFACE

Having taught history to the young ignited minds, aspiring for Civil Services, I have had my fair share of crests and troughs. But one question that has always troubled me is which book to recommend to the candidates that covers World History in totality. While there is so much material available, no single volume has been able to do justice to the exam requirement.

While the subject of History is pretty interesting, comparatively World History, is amongst the low-hanging fruits, which is not only interesting but easier to cover, yet the problem of the scarcity of good literature for the topic makes it difficult to prepare for the examination. This provoked me, to ponder and do something.

And hence, I decided to author a book on this subject. The motive was to provide a one-stop solution for all the problems that aspirants face while preparing for World History. Therefore, the book covers the entire syllabus of World History, along with diagrams for easier learning and understanding of the chronology of various events; quotes from Historians to understand various dimensions and depths of the topics; summary of the chapters for easy revision and retention; the previous years and probable questions for a detailed focus on a classical area for examination, and a supplementary workbook for answer writing practice along with the model answers to validate a candidate's learning. The book in its second edition is updated with 2024 and 2025 UPSC CSE Mains Questions along with the explanations.

Aspirants can read the Historian's quotes to create curiosity and depth of topics, following which they can read the paragraph and hence understand the same via a diagram. In fact, most paragraphs are followed by diagrams which will help aspirants to learn, understand and retain in a simplified manner. Once an aspirant completes the chapter, they can then revise all the topics through chapter-end summary and can finally practice answer writing through previous years and probable questions.

I sincerely hope this little effort will prove to be a small yet significant step in the impending success of many young minds to lead the nation.

I wish all my readers, all the very best!

Shivlal Gupta

ACKNOWLEDGEMENT

I would like to dedicate this book to my family, especially my wife, without whose support I could not have been able to write it.

I would also like to thank my professors, colleagues and friends

- Abhishiekh Saxena (Faculty of Public Administration, Governance & Social Justice) and Pankaj Dwivedi for their constant encouragement and motivation.
- Special thanks to Sherry A Singh from Pearson for coming up with this innovative project and providing constant support, including the idea for the workbook.
- I would also like to mention the immense contribution by Ruchira Dash who turned my vision into reality with her intuitive design and overall setting of the book.
- Lastly, Deya Bhattacharjee and the entire team of Pearson for their support and suggestions.

ABOUT THE AUTHOR

Shivlal Gupta, an IIM Bangalore alumnus, has been training and mentoring students for Civil Services exams for more than a decade. Being a MA in History and UPSC mains exam writer 6 times, he understands the demand and nuances of Civil Services and what it takes to crack it. He has successfully trained thousands of students in his career and under his mentorship many of his students have already cracked the Civil Services examinations.

In his professional life, he is teaching in various Civil Services academies since 2010 and has been teaching full time since 2014. Even though he did management from IIM, he is passionate about History as a subject and scored 290 plus marks in History as an optional subject in Civil Services exam. He continues to enlighten aspirants and has helped many to qualify Civil Services examination.

HOW TO USE THIS BOOK

QUOTATIONS

Quotations by various historians included to provide a holistic perspective of the topics

> *American Revolution was a 'dual revolution' that was the first question of home rule; the second was the question of who should rule at home.*
>
> ***—Carl Becker***

> *The spirit behind great reforms of Napoleon's Consulate at home was the transference of the methods of Bonaparte the general to the task of Bonaparte the statesman.*
>
> ***—David Thomson***

> *The Industrial Revolution was the transformation in the methods of production and transformation through the general substitution of power-driven machinery for hand labour.*
>
> ***—T.W. Ricker***

FLOWCHARTS

Summarize almost every topic for better understanding of the concepts and facts.

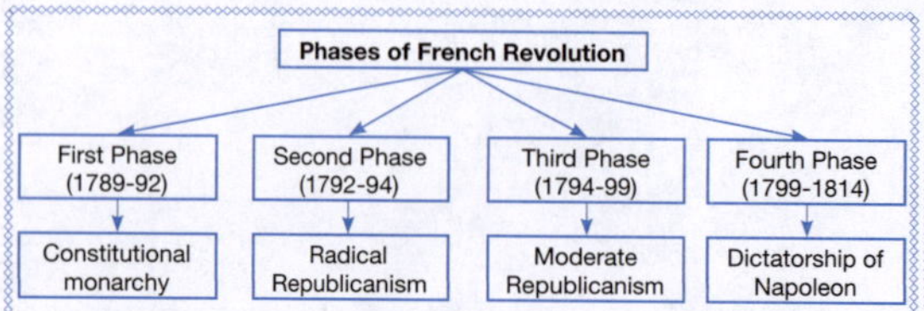

FIGURE 2.6: Various Phases of French Revolution

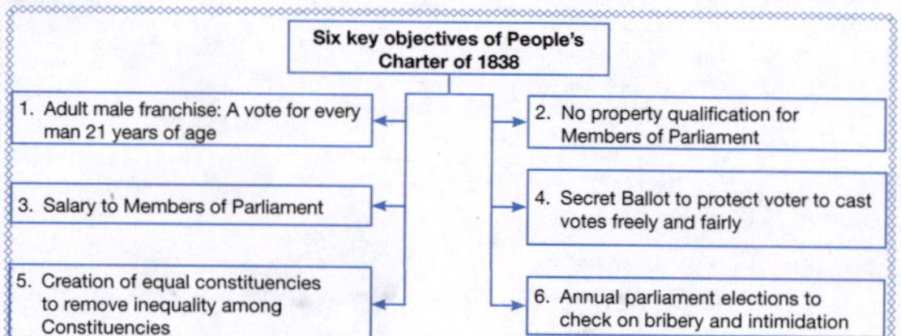

FIGURE 3.7: Six Key Objectives of People's Charter of 1838

POINTS TO PONDER BOXES

To provide students with useful/important information to reflect and focus apart from text

Points to Ponder

Approximately 400,000 English subjects were eligible to vote before the 1832 Reform Act was passed; after its enactment, that number rose to 650,000, an increase of more than 60%.

Points to Ponder

Fascism never seemed to take root in Italy as deeply as the Nazi system did in Germany.

Points to Ponder

Japan was significantly more powerful than most of Europe by 1930.

Points to Ponder

British economist John Maynard Keynes said, 'It was not blood and iron but iron and coal which made the unification of Germany possible.'

MAPS

The maps depict the most important and significant changes in the geography of the world, during the historical events and wars.

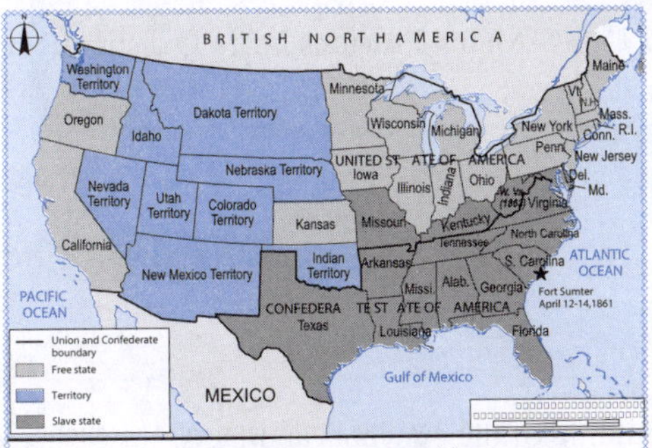

MAP 1.3: Division of America into Free and Slave States

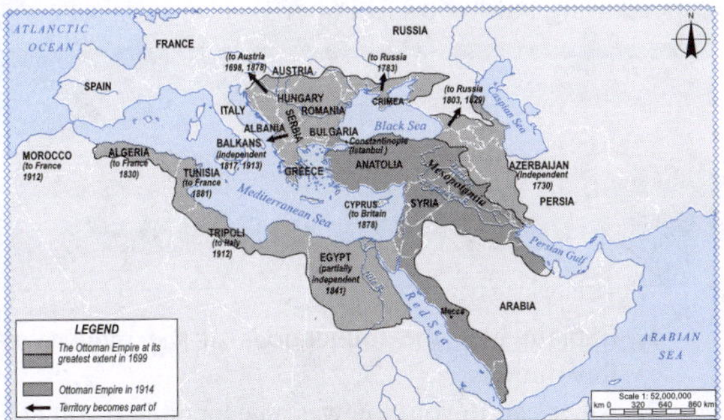

MAP 8.1: Ottoman Empire (1699–1914)

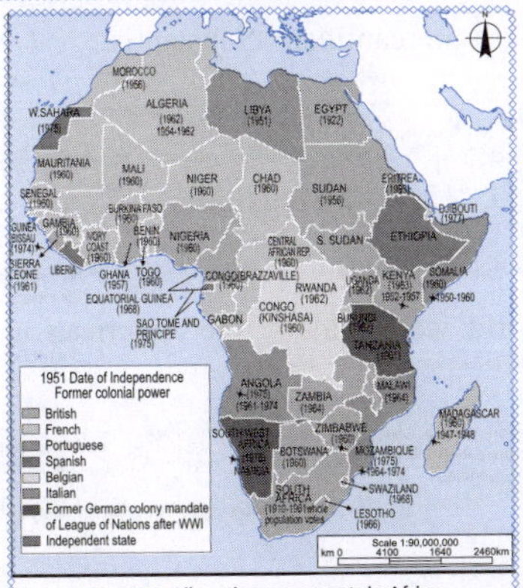

MAP 11.3: Liberation movements in Africa

MAP 5.2: Italy as Represented Geographically in 1815

▶▶ IN-TEXT CROSS-REFERENCING

All the figures and maps in the book are cross-referenced in a unique manner, with their corresponding texts, for better understanding and knowledge of the students.

that because Dred Scott was an African immigrant and not regarded as a citizen, he was not entitled to freedom. Additionally, the court argued that Congress lacked the authority to settle the slavery issue, rendering the Missouri Compromise illegal and securing the legality of slavery across all territories **(Refer Figure 1.7)**.

Source: Uncredited, Public domain, via Wikimedia Commons, accessed on 5th June 2023

FIGURE 1.7: Dred Scott

2. **Problems and composition of unreformed House of Commons:** Two types of constituencies, counties, and Boroughs, were used to elect the 658 members to the unreformed British parliament. The county represented feudal lords and landowners, whereas Borough represented the mercantile and trading community **(Refer Figure 3.3)**.

Points to Ponder

Boroughs

This term refers to a town or city that has its own elected representatives in parliament.

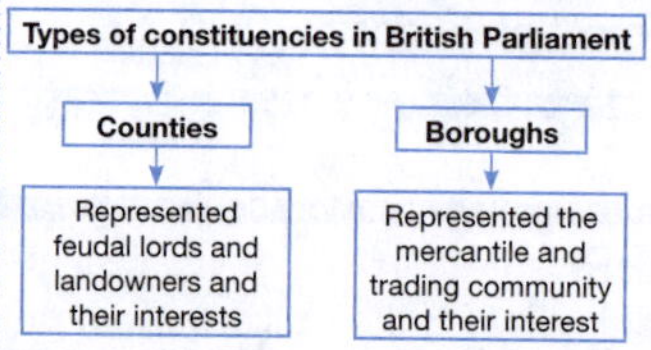

FIGURE 3.3: Types of Constituencies in British Parliament

▶▶ UPSC PREVIOUS YEAR'S QUESTIONS

Students can prepare, better with the chapter end UPSC Mains Previous Years Questions, pertaining solely to GS Paper I.

UPSC PREVIOUS YEARS' QUESTIONS

1. Explain how the foundations of the modern world were laid by the American and French Revolutions. **[15 Marks] [2019]**
2. American Revolution was an economic revolt against mercantilism. Substantiate. **[10 Marks] [2013]**

UPSC PREVIOUS YEAR QUESTION

1. Explain how the foundations of the modern world were laid by the American and French Revolutions. **[2019] (15 marks)**

▶▶ PROBABLE QUESTIONS

Every chapter has a set of Probable Questions at the end for the students to consolidate their knowledge, and frame correct possible answers for their examination.

PROBABLE QUESTIONS

1. With the introduction of assembly line factories, urbanization, and the emergence of the urban working class, the Industrial Revolution had significant social and political repercussions. Critically assess.
2. The Industrial Revolution brought about great changes in the social and economic life of Europe. Explain.
3. Why England became the harbinger of the Industrial Revolution? Explain. Also, throw light on its social consequences.

PROBABLE QUESTIONS

1. Explain the causes of the Second World War.
2. Was Czechoslovakia served on a dish to Hitler at Munich? What were its implications?
3. Hitler did not want the world war but rather a limited war in Poland. Critically examine.
4. One of the most important consequences of the Second World War was 'division of Europe', eastern and western. Comment.

▶▶ LET'S REVISE

Aspirants can quickly revise the entire chapter in the Let's Revise Section, wherein the chapter summary is provided in a crisp pointer format.

LET'S REVISE

Factors/ Causes Leading to American Revolution

1. Immediate Causes
   - (a) Seven Years' War and Consequent Events
2. Fundamental Causes
   - (a) American Capitalism vs British Capitalism
   - (b) Class interest behind Revolution
   - (c) Role of Philosophers
   - (d) Nature of American Population
   - (e) Constitutional issue in the American conflict

Reasons for American Success

1. Concept of the spirit of liberty and a group of gifted leaders

Significance of the American Revolution

1. Inspired a series of trans-Atlantic Revolutions.
2. War of Independence against colonial dominance.
3. First democratic government
4. New political, social, and economic setup
5. Bill of Rights
6. Inspired the French Revolution

Effects of the America Revolution

1. Effects on America
   - (a) Expulsion of Loyalists
   - (b) Societal Impacts of t Revolution
   - (c) Change in the status women

LET'S REVISE

The Factors for Unification of Germany

1. Role of Napoleon
   - (a) Provided Administrative Unity
   - (b) Spread of Ideals of the French Revolution
2. Cultural-Ideological factor
   - (a) Role of German philosophers like John Herder, Fichte, and Hegel
3. Economic-Industrial factor
   - (a) Coal and Iron Policy: Role of Zollverein (Custom union)
4. Political-Diplomatic Factor
   - (a) Blood and Iron Policy of Bismarck
   - (b) Role of William I

Consequences of Franco-Prussian War and Battle of Sedan

1. Completion of the unification of Germany
2. Completion of the unification of Germany
3. Third Republic in France
4. Rivalry between France and Germany
5. Indirect cause of World War I
6. Russia violated the Treaty of Paris

Comparison between the Unification of Italy and that of Germany

1. Similarity
   - (a) Role of Napoleon
   - (b) Vienna Congress

▶▶ TIMELINE

Chronologically designed, the Timeline of every chapter provides a student with the exact order of historical events occurred in the respective eras. It helps them to remember the details from the beginning to the end.

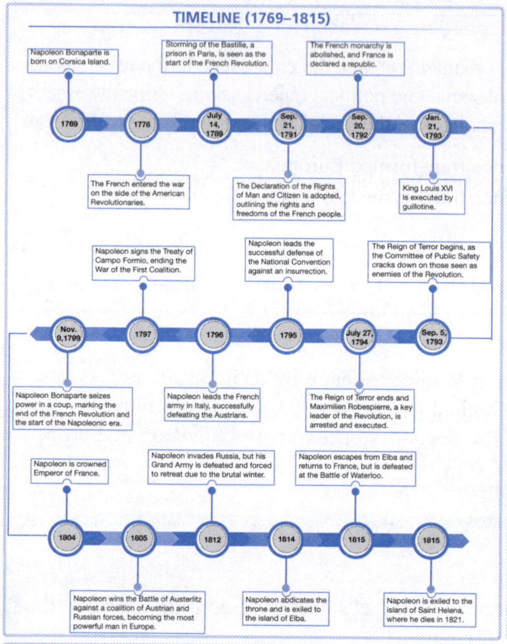

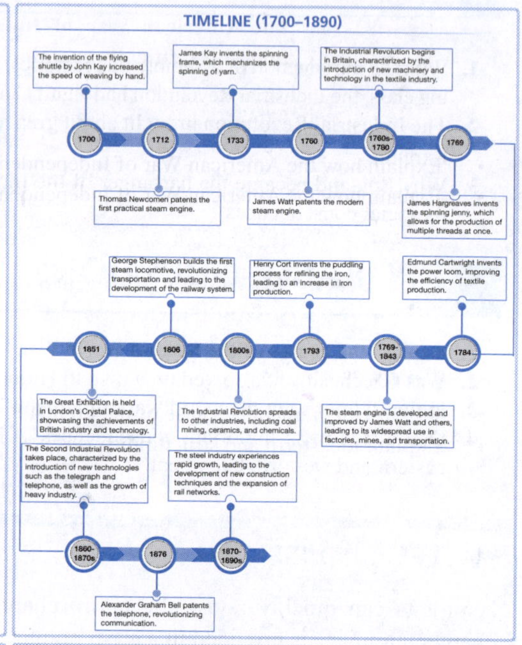

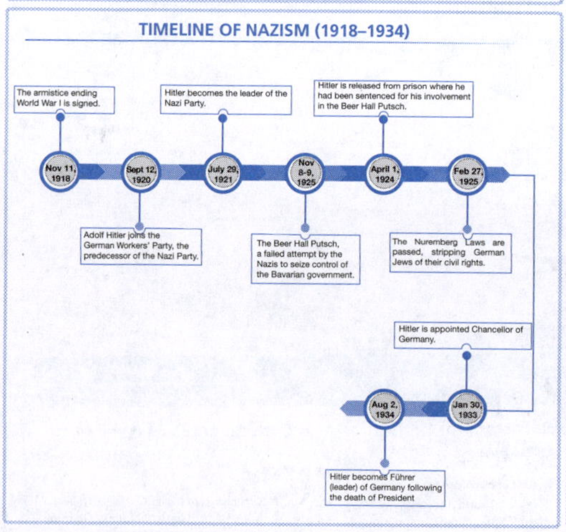

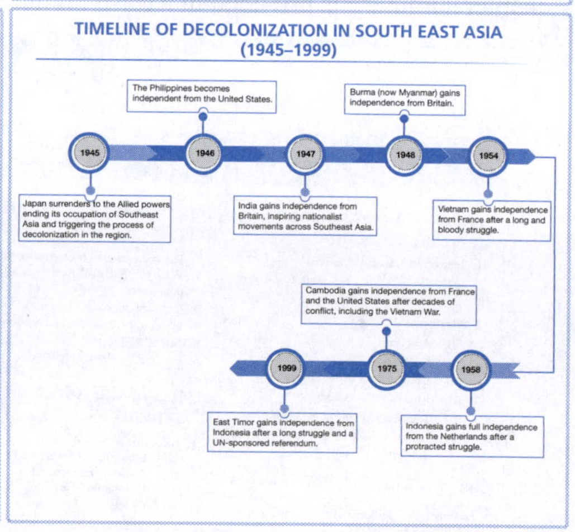

SUPPLEMENTARY WORKBOOK

Designed with model answer writing approach, the supplementary workbook is a one stop solution for the aspirants to evaluate their learning and prepare best for the examinations.

Model Answer

2. 'The American War of Independence transformed Europe as well as America.' Critically examine.

Approach

- Explain how the American War of Independence transformed Europe.
- Explain how the American War of Independence transformed America.

Model Answer

1. 'The causes of the French Revolution of 1789 included both long-term and structural factors, as well as more immediate events.' Critically examine.

Approach

- Explain the immediate cause of the French Revolution.
- Explain long-term and structural causes.

PREVIOUS YEAR CORNER

1. 'The French Revolution has enduring relevance to the contemporary world'.—Explain.

(UPSC Mains Exam 2025)

Introduction: The French Revolution of 1789 marks the beginning of the modern world.

Body:

1. Highlight some of the factors that led to the French Revolution in a concise manner.
2. Enduring Relevance to the Contemporary World
   - **(a)** The idea of democracy and popular sovereignty (Arab Springs)
   - **(b)** The concept of Equality, Liberty and Fraternity (the feminist 'Me too' and LGBT movements)
   - **(c)** The idea of constitutionalism
   - **(d)** The Idea of Liberalism and Freedom (Rise of Autocratic Government)
   - **(e)** The Idea of Secularism (ISIS)
   - **(f)** The Origin of major ideologies: capitalism, socialism, and liberalism

Conclusion: The American and French Revolutions led to the rise of the modern world. It also led to the rise of many modern ideas, which will always be relevant in contemporary society.

2. How far is it correct to say that the First World War was fought essentially for the preservation of the balance of power?

(UPSC Mains Exam 2024)

Introduction: Begin with the facts connected with the First World War.

Body:

1. The First World War was fought to preserve the balance of power.
   - **(a)** Creation of an alliance system (Triple Alliance and Triple Entente) to preserve the Balance of Power.
   - **(b)** Preservation of colonies and the Rise of Imperialism after the Unification of Germany and Italy.
   - **(c)** The rise of extreme Nationalism was a threat to the preservation of the empires, like the Austrian Empire and the Russian Empire.
2. The First World War was fought for other reasons.
   - **(a)** Eastern Question and Balkan Crisis
   - **(b)** **Economic Factors:** Rise of industrialisation led to the conflict between the industrialised nations for the creation of colonies.
   - **(c)** Militarism and Arms Race

Conclusion: The First World War was fought for many reasons, including the preservation of the balance of power. However, the First World War led to the change of the old order and the creation of the new order.

3. How far was the Industrial Revolution in England responsible for the decline of handicrafts and cottage industries in India? **(UPSC Mains Exam 2024)**

Introduction: Begin with the fact that the first Industrial Revolution took place in Britain.

Body:

1. The Industrial Revolution in England was responsible for the decline of handicrafts.
   - **(a)** Bombardment of cheap, machine-made industrial goods from Britain to India.
   - **(b)** The Industrial Revolution in England broke the linkage between agriculture and the cottage industry.
   - **(c)** British Trade and Tariff Policy
   - **(d)** India became the supplier of Raw material and the market for the finished goods.
   - **(e)** Change of the old ruling class with the new ruling classes, who were not interested in the goods of the cottage Industry.

Conclusion: Unlike the world, the decline of industry was not followed by the rise of modern industry and led to the colonisation of the Indian economy to the needs of the British industry.

4. Bring out the socio-economic effects of the introduction of railways in different countries of the world. **(UPSC Mains Exam 2023)**

Introduction: Give some facts about the introduction of the Railway and the Industrial Revolution

Body:

1. **Economic transformation:** It facilitated the movement of raw materials, agricultural produce and labour, supporting the growth of the economy.
   Britain: It led to the transformation of the British economy, such as the production of cheap goods and Britain's role as a supplier of manufactured goods.
   India: The Indian economy was transformed into a colonial economy as a supplier of raw materials and a market for the finished goods.
2. **Social Transformation:**
   - **(a)** Cultural exchange
   - **(b)** Urbanisation and population shift
   - **(c)** Rise of unemployment in the colonies due to the decline of the artisanal industry.
   - **(d)** Disruption of traditional society and social linkages.

Conclusion: The introduction of the railway led to both positive and negative economic and social changes in the world.

CHAPTER

1

Photo Credit: Patrimonio designs ltd / Shutterstock

AMERICAN REVOLUTION AND CIVIL WAR

> *American Revolution was a 'dual revolution' that was the first question of home rule; the second was the question of who should rule at home.*
>
> —*Carl Becker*

INTRODUCTION

The American Revolution of 1776 is one of the most significant event in human history because it opened the doors of the modern age for mankind. The American Revolution (1775–1783) began in 1775 primarily as a War of Independence between the united thirteen colonies and Great Britain. With the implementation of the Treaty of Paris that ended the war in 1783, the colonies won their independence from British Imperialism. The war began as a disagreement over how Great Britain treated the colonies versus the way the colonies felt they should be treated. The Americans felt they deserved all the rights of Englishmen. The British, on the other hand, felt that the colonies were created to be used in the way that best - suited the Crown and British parliament.

FACTORS LEADING TO AMERICAN REVOLUTION

The American Revolution or the American War of Independence was caused by a number of long-term as well as short-term factors, including the Seven Years' War, the Crown's Proclamation of 1763, the imposition of multiple taxes, the conflict between American and British capitalism, nature of American population, the revolution in the realm of ideas and many other factors **(Refer Figure 1.1)**.

Immediate Causes

The immediate causes of the American Revolution included the Seven Years' War along with the subsequent series of events thereafter.

Seven Years' War and Treaty of Paris (1763)

Points to Ponder

Seven Years' War (1756–1763)

War between Britain and France over issues left unresolved by the Austrian War of Succession (1740–1748).

> *England will soon repent of having removed the only check that could keep her colonies in awe.* **— *Vergennes (French writer)***

One of the most significant causes of the American Civil War was the Seven Years' War, which saw Great Britain defeat France and Spain and, as a result, drive France off the continent of North America. Despite Britain emerging victorious in this war but the financial cost of this victory was very high.

Additionally, the French presence in North America was a persistent threat to Americans. Thirteen American colonies were accordingly in need of protection, and were hence, dependent on Britain. However, after the Seven Years' War, French influence in North America was entirely eradicated. The removal of the French completely altered the relations between England and colonists and led to the 'reversal of alliances' (French from being an enemy became a friend of America while Britain from a friend became an enemy of America).

A French writer, Vergennes remarked: 'England will soon repent of having removed the only check (by conquering Canada from France after 7 years of war) that could keep her colonies in awe (as Britain offered protection to colonies from French invasion)'.

Additionally, the Seven Years' War with France put a heavy financial burden on the British people. Britain, therefore, demanded payment for the security it had given the Americans. Massive debts acquired by Britain in protecting

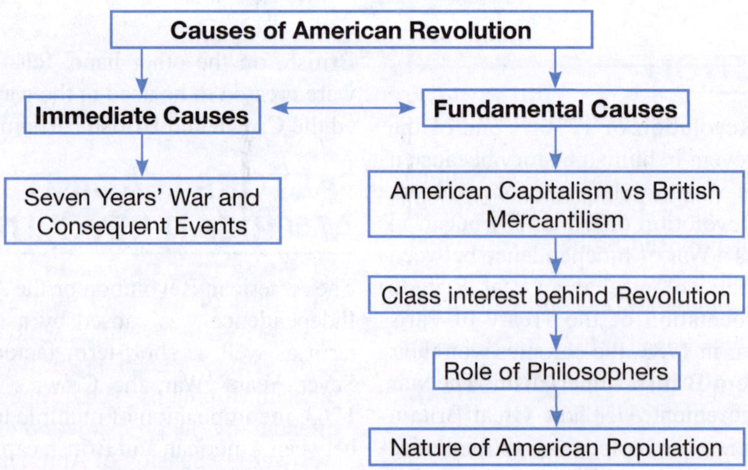

FIGURE 1.1: Factors of the American Revolution

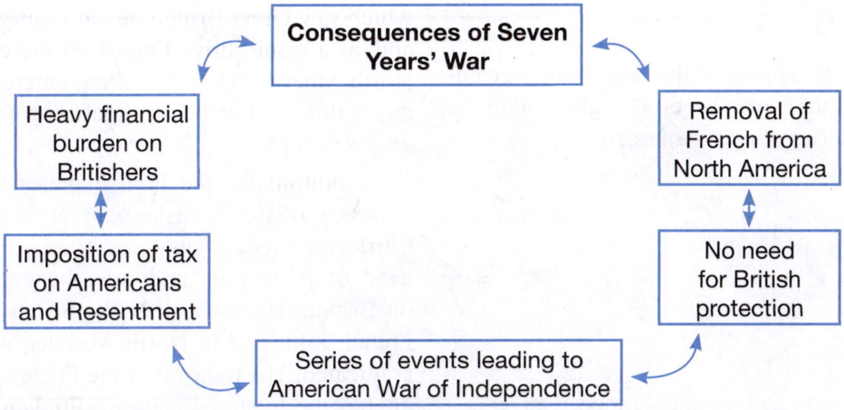

FIGURE 1.2: Consequences of Seven Years' War

MAP 1.1: British and French Colonies in America

American colonies were requested to be paid by colonists **(Refer Figure 1.2)**. As a result, the British Parliament imposed higher taxes, which were bitterly resented and opposed by the colonists. These taxes were opposed by the people in American colonies because they did not need British protection after 1763 as there was no threat of French invasion. All these set off a series of events that eventually led to the American War of Independence **(Refer Map 1.1)**.

Series of Events Leading to the American War of Independence

1. **Crown's Proclamation of 1763:** George Granville (PM of England) issued Crown's (King George III) Proclamation which prohibited the expansion of all settlement west of the Appalachian Mountains. The thirteen colonies were offended by the proclamation as it stopped the westward expansion of American colonies and their growing economy **(Refer Map 1.2)**.

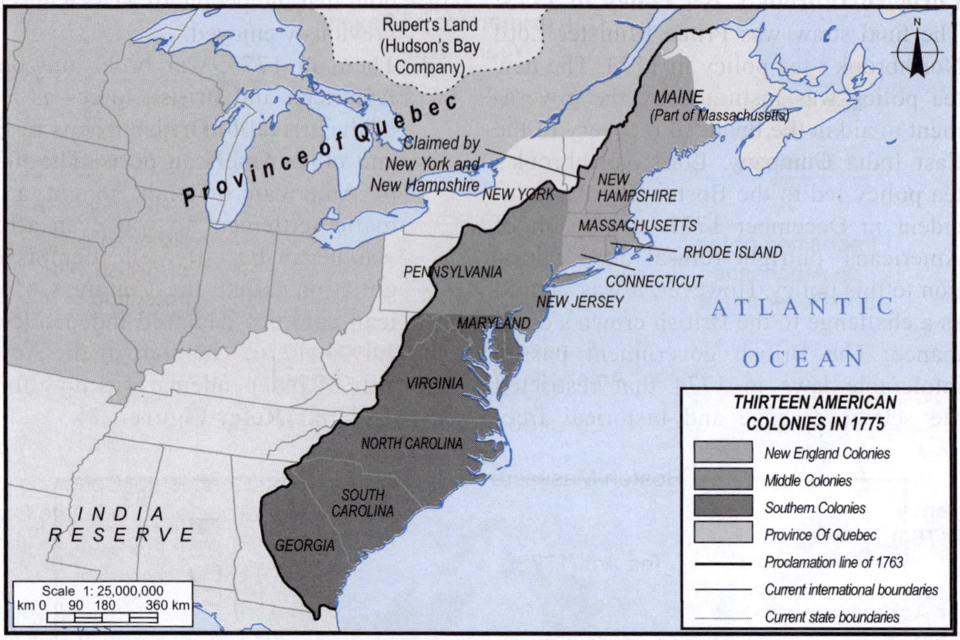

MAP 1.2: Thirteen American Colonies in 1775

After Seven Years' War, number of taxes were imposed by British Parliament which led to resentment by the Colonial. These were:

(a) **Currency Act (1764):** It forbade the use of paper money to settle any debts, but a strict monetary policy imposed by the British in America led to financial problems.

(b) **Sugar Act (April 5, 1764):** George Grenville, the prime minister of Great Britain, enacted the Stamp Act and the Sugar Act to levy taxes. It led to the end of the French and Dutch sugar smuggling trade, but it also saw a significant drop in American marine trade, harming Americans' economic interests.

(c) **Stamp Act (March 22, 1765):** The Stamp Act was the first direct tax levied by the British Parliament against America. All official documents were 'stamped' on paper. The Stamp Act was repealed by the British Parliament after the Americans' outright resentment and refusal of the Act.

(d) **Townshend Acts (1767):** It was a series of laws passed by the British parliament to assert authority. It led to the imposition of new import duties on British goods including paint, paper, lead, glass and tea. America signed the boycott pledge at Boston to put economic pressure on British merchants.

2. **Boston Massacre (1770):** The Townshend Acts prompted the arrival of British forces in Boston. Five civilians were killed after a British soldier was fired after being harassed. The entire incident was referred to as the Boston Massacre (the word Boston Massacre was coined by patriot Samuel Adams). The Boston Massacre had major, significant, and far-reaching consequences. These were:

   (a) Led to the unpopularity of the British and Armed rebellion throughout colonies.

   (b) Resulted in the 1773 Tea Act leading to Boston Tea Party on December 16, 1774, where more than 342 containers of tea (approximately £10,000 worth of tea) were dumped into the sea by Samuel Adams, John Hancock, and Paul Revere.

3. **Lord Northbrook's Tea Policy in 1773:** The final straw was Prime Minister Lord Northbrook's tea policy in 1773. The new tea policy was instituted by the government to aid in the financial recovery of the East India Company. Lord Northbrook's tea policy led to the Boston Tea Party incident in December 1773 as a result of Americans' outright refusal and opposition to this policy. However, it was viewed as a challenge to the British crown's dominance. The British government passed intolerable laws in 1774 that restricted the self-governance and historical freedom that the people of Massachusetts had previously enjoyed.
4. Then, in 1775, war broke out between American and British forces as a result of the arrival of British troops in Boston and other American ports. The majority of American officials sought a diplomatic settlement to war even after this war began but after all attempts of negotiation failed, the Congress of American colonies declared independence on July 4, 1776. The start of the American War of Independence was now formally declared **(Refer Figure 1.3)**.

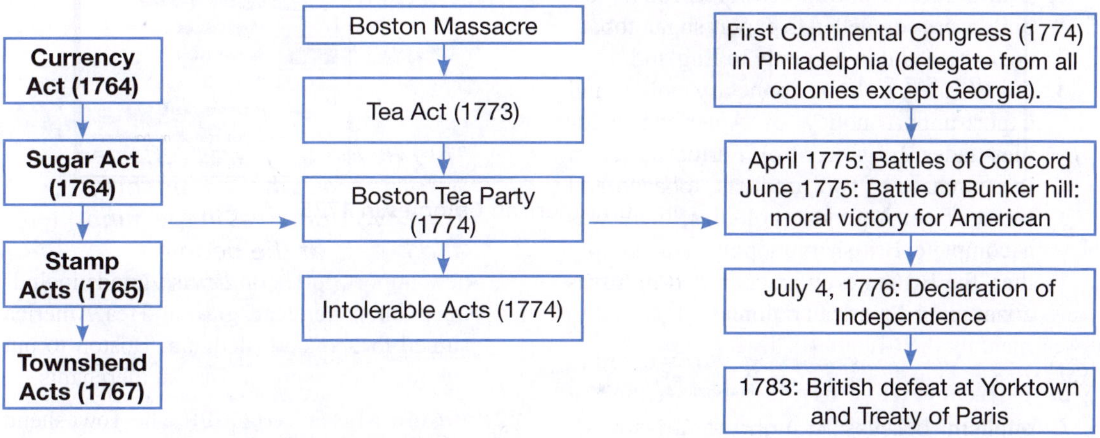

FIGURE 1.3: Series of Events Leading to the American War of Independence

Fundamental Causes

Some of the fundamental causes of the French Revolution included the conflict between the American capitalism and British mercantilism, nature of American population, influence of the philosophers and the class interest behind the revolution.

> *"The struggle was not over high-sounding political and constitutional concepts. It was over the survival or collapse of English mercantile capitalism.*
> ***—Andrews Hacker"***

The Conflict between American Capitalism and British Mercantilism

American Revolution was a conflict between British mercantilism and American capitalism. British mercantilism was inclined to bring the American economy under strict British colonial control. For this purpose following steps were taken:

1. **Navigation Acts:** It was introduced in the 17th century to promote the British shipping industry at the cost of American shipping. It had a provision that all sorts of exports to

and imports from American colonies could have been done or carried on only in British ships or in the ships in which at least 75% of employees should have been British.

Points to Ponder

Mercantilism is an economic doctrine based on the theory that a nation benefits by accumulating monetary reserves through a positive balance of 'trade, especially through promotion of exports and demotion of imports.

2. **Enumerated Commodities Act, 1660:** Colonies were compelled to export sugar, tobacco, cotton, and indigo only to England.
3. British tried to bring monetary policy and export-import policy of American colonies under British control. Furthermore, on the purchase of two products, tobacco and maize, from American colonies, there was a complete British monopoly. Not simply that, the British even discouraged industrialization in American colonies.

Points to Ponder

Capitalism believes in right to private property, complete freedom to engage in economic activity, doctrine of free hand, rule of law, individualism and democratic regime.

Moreover American economy was a fast-growing economy. American industry in general and the shipping industry in particular, could not thrive if the British control could not been relaxed. Americans realized that they could not go for industrialization in British presence. Therefore, the objective of the American slogan *'No Taxation without Representation'* lay in this capitalist ambition of American colonies.

Nature of American Population

Most of the Americans who fought the British during the American Revolution were of British descent. Approximately 90% of white colonists in America were originally from Britain; the remaining 10% were also from European countries like Spain, Portugal, Holland, and France. These Americans either immigrated to America from Europe against their will or were expulsed from the country by the authorities. Some of them relocated to avoid church retribution. Some emigrated as a result of financial hardships after learning about the abundance of resources in America. Others departed to enjoy a life of independence on their terms. Therefore, they didn't feel any love or affection for Britain.

Influence of Philosophers

> "*The Revolution was effected before the war commenced. The Revolution was in the minds and hearts of the people.*
> —***John Adams***"

Points to Ponder

Three important values which led to the American Revolution:

1. Preservation of life
2. Preservation of liberty
3. Pursuit of happiness

American Revolution was having some ideological inspiration as well. They were greatly inspired by enlightenment and British thinkers like John Locke, Thomas Paine, Thomas Jefferson, Benjamin Franklin, James Otis, and many more. Jefferson asserted the colonists' right to rebellion and encouraged their increasing desire for independence.

Thomas Paine

Among thinkers, one of the most important contributions was made by Thomas Paine who was known for his revolutionary thought, anti-monarchy, and pro-republican view, and the idea of natural rights. His famous work like '*Common Sense*' and '*Right of Men*' became popular among Americans and ignited them to make sacrifices for American Independence.

Thomas Paine in his book '*Common Sense*' wrote that, 'It was repugnant to reason to suppose that this continent can longer remain subject to any external power … there is something absurd in supposing a continent to be perpetually governed by an island'. Therefore, he argued that it was against common sense that a small island like Britain would rule a continent like America. Thus, Thomas Paine commented that it is common sense that the British must leave America.

No Taxation without Representation

In addition to Thomas Paine's '*Common Sense*', James Otis's statement, '*No Taxation Without Representation*,' gained popularity among Americans as a means of protesting the taxes and other laws that the British Parliament implemented upon them without the participation of American representatives. The colonial Americans treasured their representative legislatures and thought it was wrong to be subject to one located hundreds of miles away.

However, British Prime Minister George Grenville defended the absence of American lawmakers in the British Parliament by referring to the concept of 'virtual representation' which held that lawmakers, regardless of where they were first elected, served the interests of all British subjects worldwide.

Nevertheless, '*No Taxation Without Representation*' was more of a symbolic protest than anything else, notwithstanding the American colonists' desire for representation. Colonial American delegates in parliament would have been too less in number and politically powerless to make a significant impact. Instead, the colonists' rallying cry was founded on the principle, a straight forward declaration that they desired less interference from British Parliament and greater freedom and ability to run their provincial governments.

Influence of Writing of Adam Smith

The writing of Adam Smith like Wealth of Nations also helped the American cause. Adam Smith attacked the 18th century European economic system of mercantilism where each nation's goal was to increase exports to its colonies and other nations, and limit imports from them leading to a favorable balance of trade. He argued that:

1. Only a few privileged classes benefited from mercantilism and not all society members, and
2. Colonies had cost the British more than they gained for maintaining a monopoly of trade.

Thus, British Parliament should let American colonies peacefully go their own way. These thoughts of a free market economy (without British interference in American economy) greatly influenced American leaders as they moved towards war with England.

The Class Interest Behind the Revolution

Certain classes in American colonies were against the British presence in America and worked wholeheartedly for the American Revolution. These were:

1. Merchants moved for revolution as they were offended by Navigation Acts.
2. Smugglers were equally offended as the British government tried to enforce the 'Anti-smuggling Act' strictly.
3. Political leaders in American colonies visualized their bright future in independent America.
4. Students and intellectuals were inspired by republican ideas. That's why they supported the revolution.
5. Tobacco growers of Virginia were in search of fresh land that's why they were making a westward expansion, but their progress was checked by the British government.

Nevertheless, certain classes opposed the revolution as well. These were aristocrats, Red Indians as well as peasants from middle American regions.

Constitutional Issue in the American Conflict

A constitutional issue also existed between British and America. The British believed that the British parliament was a supreme institution to which all other institutions were just subordinates. However, according to Americans, men have certain natural rights that supersede all other rules, including parliamentary laws.

AMERICAN SUCCESS

American success in war could be ascribed to several factors. They were as follows:

1. The American Revolution was achieved by a concept of the spirit of liberty and a group of gifted leaders like Thomas Jefferson, George Washington, Benjamin Franklin, James Otis, etc., who rose to prominence between 1763 and 1775.
2. The American Revolution was not given much attention by the British authorities from the start, and they mostly used mercenary soldiers to put an end to it.
3. As H.R. Anderson correctly noted, 'Nature, Washington, and France were primarily responsible for the colonies' achievement of independence against overwhelming odds.
   (a) **Nature:** The Americans' triumph was aided by the isolation of the American continent and British ignorance of its topography.
   (b) **George Washington** provided exceptional military leadership, which helped the military succeed.
   (c) Thirdly, the situation benefited from outside assistance from other nations. France's proactive assistance was vital in guiding the Americans to victory **(Refer Figure 1.4)**.
4. English underestimated the strength of Americans.
5. Solid organization of American patriots and disorganization of loyalists.
6. Guerrilla warfare by American patriots.

> *The colonies won their independence against great odds was due mainly to three factors: **Nature, Washington, and France.***
>
> ***—H.R Anderson***

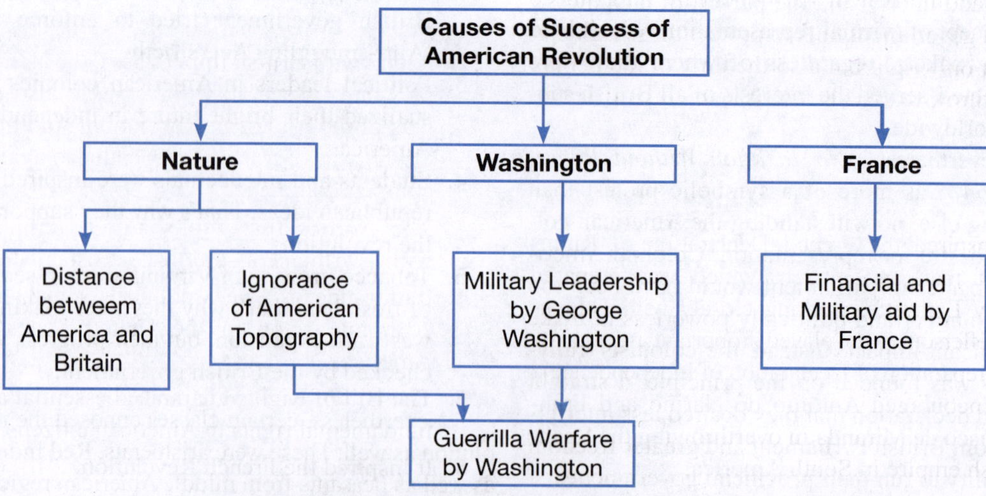

FIGURE 1.4: Causes of the Success of American Revolution by H.R Anderson

Declaration of Independence (1776)

Declaration of Independence (1776) was a political document, written largely by Thomas Jefferson and approved by Continental Congress in Philadelphia on July 4, 1776. The document stated reasons and justification for 13 American colonies for independence by listing:

> *King had a history of repeated injuries and usurpations, all having a direct object of the establishment of an absolute tyranny over these states.*
> ***—Declaration of Independence (1776)***

1. Colonial grievances against King George III
2. Asserting certain natural and legal rights, including the right of revolution.

The document also stated that 'All men are created equal and independent, that from that equal creation, they derive rights inherent and inalienable, among which are the preservation of life, and liberty, and the pursuit of happiness'. When a government fails to protect those rights, it was not only right but also the duty of the people to overthrow that government.

Significance of the Declaration of Independence

1. Inspired the French Declaration of Rights of man and citizen, which was prepared by Lafayette, working closely with Thomas Jefferson (who played important role in the preparation of Declaration of Independence) .
2. Encouraged Antonio de Nariño and Francisco de Miranda in overthrowing the Spanish empire in South America.
3. According to Abraham Lincoln, declaration helped in abolishing slavery in USA.
4. Inspired many other similar documents in the USA and other countries, e.g,. when the Universal Declaration of Human Rights stated that, 'Everyone has the right to life, liberty, and security of person,' it was influenced by the Declaration of Independence.

SIGNIFICANCE OF THE AMERICAN REVOLUTION

American Revolution is one of the most significant events in the history of mankind because the outbreak of this revolution opens the doors of modernization not only for Americans but also for the whole of the world.

1. The United States of America became free, sovereign, and republic as the American colonies gained their freedom. It triggered a series of transatlantic revolutions which transformed America as well as Europe. From America, the revolution spread to France in 1789 against the old regime. Irish Revolution of 1798, the Latin American nationalist Revolution during the first half of the 18th and the 19th century Spanish Revolution of 1820, and the European Revolution of 1830's and 1848 were part of the same.
2. Along with British Imperialism, the aristocracy and conservative forces were also targets of the American Revolution. Additionally, it was a War of Independence against colonial dominance.
3. The world's first democratic government with a written constitution was established.
4. It introduced a new political, social, and economic setup in the United States of America.
5. The Bill of Rights guaranteed essential and fundamental rights to American citizens.
6. It inspired the French Revolution.

EFFECTS OF THE AMERICAN REVOLUTION

The American Revolution had significant and widespread repercussions on both America and Europe.

> *The American War of Independence transformed Europe as well as America.*

Effects on America

The expulsion of loyalists were the immediate result of the American Revolution. Approximately 60,000–70,000 loyalists emigrated to Britain and North America. However, over 80% of loyalists stayed and became devoted and loyal citizens of America.

Societal Impacts

Some historians criticized the American Revolution as did not lead to as radical consequences as in French Revolution or revolutionary Russia.

> *The Revolution was essentially legal, peaceful, and conservative, a Revolution to preserve a social order rather than to change it.*
>
> ***—Charles Rossiter***

Some other historians criticize American Revolution as it did not lead to the empowerment of women and slavery. They argue:

1. American Revolution did not abolish slavery and empowerment of women.
2. American Revolution did not significantly change the structure of American society; rather, reinforced the political, economic, and social status quo.
3. American Revolution did not establish a truly democratic government. Nevertheless, no truly democratic nations in the late 18th century.
4. American Revolution did not create a new economic structure; rather kept capitalism to speed up the process of industrialization.

Nevertheless, some other historian argues that American Revolution and revolutionary spirit impacted every aspect of American life. The attitude of Americans changed forever. Some changes in the society were carried out immediately while some later like abolition of slavery and empowerment of women. Slavery was not abolished for another one hundred years but revolutionary spirit led to the organization of the abolitionist movement. Moreover, these historians argue that revolutionary spirit and ideas produced a new outlook among Americans which had huge ramifications for future.

Change in the Status of American Women

The democratic ideals of revolution inspired changes in the roles of women. The concept of republican motherhood was promoted, i.e., the essential role of instilling their children with republican values conducive to a healthy republic. The traditional husband-wife relationship became more liberal though not equal. Women were still subordinated, legally and socially, to their husbands and politically disfranchised. Nevertheless, some historians argue that the revolutionary spirit produced a new modern outlook, inspired by ideas of equality and liberty which had huge ramifications for the empowerment of women in the future.

Financial Impact on America

American War of Independence led to huge expenditures for Americans and the federal and states government faced too much difficulty in financing war. Later, war expenditure led to a number of economic crises in America for example the issue of non-payment of wages to army men after the war. It was not until 1781 when Robert Morris was made Superintendent of finance, the economic condition improved.

Effects on World

Inspiring the European and Freedom Movements

American Revolution led to three major events which had significant and far-reaching consequences on Europe and Liberation Movement. These were document of Declaration of Independence, implementation of ideas of enlightenment, and liberal and constitutional values in the US Constitution.

The significance of American Revolution lies in the fact that it was:

1. First successful revolution against a European empire.
2. First time a colony had rebelled successfully.
3. First republican form of democratically elected government.

The above facts inspired many European nations and colonies to revolt against the colonial empire and free the mother country from the clutches of colonial imperialism. American Revolution inspired:

1. Ireland to pursue armed rebellion against Britain.
2. Liberation Movement from Spanish and Portuguese colonial rule in South America under Simon Bolivar in 1820's.
3. French Revolution and French Declaration of Rights of Man and Citizen of 1789.

Inspiration for Political System

The United States Constitution became the first written constitution, and the country was the first secular state to grant the public the right to vote. Moreover, new political and constitutional experiments, including the republican form of government, the theory of checks and balances, the theory of separation of powers, the federal system etc. became models for many other nations and dealt a severe blow to Europe's political systems of absolute monarchy and aristocratic supremacy.

Change in British Attitude Towards Colonies

> *"The American War of Independence deprived Great Britain of one empire, but it strengthened the foundations of another."*

American War was the first blow at the British Policy of Colonialism. American War revealed the limitations of Britain's financial and military posture when Britain faced powerful enemies, with no allies. Britain realized that if an old aggressive colonial policy were continued, it would lose other colonies as well. Therefore, Britain changed its aggressive policy to a liberal and rational policy. It resulted into:

1. Dominion status to many white colonies like Australia, New Zealand, etc., in fear of losing them like America.
2. Some sort of economic and political independence to other colonies
3. Involvement of locals in various representative institutions to pacify their grievances.
4. England realized the modern concept of principles of free trade and commercial monopoly were opposed to each other. The monopoly was abolished, and new colonies were granted the right to trade free.

Thus, even though Britain lost thirteen colonies, it continued to grow its colonial dominance in Africa, Asia, and India, creating what is known as the 'Second British Empire.'

Additionally, Britain's influence in Europe was not decreased, and its diplomatic authority was soon restored. Britain was crucial in restraining the spirit of the French Revolution and in forging a European alliance against the Napoleonic Wars. Additionally, the loss of the American colonies allowed Britain to respond to the French Revolution more effectively than it otherwise could have. Therefore, it is true that all these liberal and rational policies prolonged colonial authority by consolidating British power and bringing colonies closer to the home nation.

LIMITATIONS OF THE AMERICAN REVOLUTION

1. The American Revolution was inspired by ideas of liberty, equality, and fraternity, but these ideas are applied only to the whites, women, and slaves in America who benefited nothing from it.
2. The majority of delegates in American Congress, which drafted the Constitution, were slave owners and only five out of thirteen colonies abolished slavery in 1787.
3. The American Constitution favoured the rich class by declaring the right to property as a sacred and inviolable fundamental right which was against the interest of comparatively poorer sections of the population.

DRAFTING OF THE AMERICAN CONSTITUTION

Factors Responsible in Drafting of the Constitution

American Constitution was enacted and adopted in 1787 by American Congress at Philadelphia. The process of drafting an American constitution was inspired by social cultural and economic outlook of Americans, the impact of ideas of enlightenment, and better experiences gained by Americans under British rule.

1. American Constitution was drafted by representatives of thirteen colonies. they came together voluntarily and were concerned about their independence and autonomy. Because of this, the Constitution's framers chose a federal system of government that grants each state the greatest amount of authority.
2. The American Constitution, which is heavily influenced by the separation of powers Theory of Montesquieu, the Social Contract Theory of Locke, the Notions of Democracy, the Rule of Law, Egalitarianism, Liberalism, etc., was inspired by enlightenment ideals.
3. Before achieving independence, Americans fought for almost ten years to end British colonial control. Because anti-British emotions were so pervasive among Americans, the American Constitution's delegates created a document that was exactly the reverse of the British system. These were:
   (a) American written constitution against British unwritten constitution,
   (b) American federal form of government against British unitary form of government,
   (c) American system of direct election of President as compared to British system of unelected hereditary Monarch,
   (d) American separation of power against British fusion of powers.
4. The British bitter experience convinced Americans that they needed to protect their freedom, therefore the American Constitution's framers included a system of checks and balances.
5. The liberal, progressive, and cosmopolitan nature of American society had an impact on a clause in the constitution. The freedom of religious thought and practice was guaranteed. It promoted autonomy, excellence, and accomplishments of the self.

Articles of Confederation (AOC)

On November 15, 1777, the Articles of Confederation (AOC), often referred to as the US's first constitution was enacted by the Second Continental Congress. AOC created the first provisional governmental framework by establishing a loose confederation of sovereign states with a weak central government that delegated most authority to state governments. Due to the necessity for a powerful federal government, the Federal government was thus too weak to oversee U.S. affairs. The constitutional convention eventually convened in Philadelphia and decided on the Philadelphia Convention in 1787 because of a chain of events. Members of Constitutional Convention signed the 2nd U.S. Constitution in 1787 in Philadelphia (Pennsylvania) and a new federal government came into existence in 1789.

Weaknesses of the Articles of Confederation (AOC)

1. The structure of the government proved to be defective and inadequate under the Articles of Confederation.
2. Congress could request funds and borrow money but could not lay taxes or collect tariffs.
3. They could declare war but could not raise armies.
4. They could not regulate interstate commerce.
5. They could negotiate treaties but lacked authority abroad.

The United States Constitution became the first written constitution and made it the first secular state to grant the whole people the right to vote. The Social Contract Theory, which was propounded by several philosophers of the Enlightenment Era, was also first applied in the American Constitution.

Main Features of the US Federal Constitution

1. **Peoples' sovereignty:** The famous phrase 'We the people of the United States formed the constitution for the USA' appears in the US Constitution, which grants peoples' sovereignty over their country.
2. **The Doctrine of separation of power:** The American Constitution was based on the Montesquieu doctrine of strict separation of powers, which is built on the three branches of government (executive, legislative, and judicial), as well as a system of checks and balances.
3. Principle of Check and Balance which was inspired by Newton's ideology.
4. **Bicameralism:** Constitution proposed the creation of two houses:
   - (a) **House of Representatives** (also called Lower House): Representation would be depended on the population of states.
   - (b) **Senate member:** (also called Upper House): Representation of 2 member from every state.
5. **Rigid Constitution:** In the American constitution, the amendment process was made rigid. Constitutional amendments required a two-third vote in Congress and ratification by three-fourths of states.
6. All power lies in President as he was the head of state and head of government. President and Vice President both are elected to serve an identical 4-year term.
7. **Concept of Dual Citizenship:** Citizenship of America and state.
8. **Independence of Judiciary:** Judiciary would be autonomous from Legislature and Executive and enjoy authority under the 'Doctrine of Judicial Review'.
9. **Bill of Rights:** It was the collective name for the first ten amendments to the US Constitution which guarantee several personal freedoms and also limit the government's power.

AMERICAN CONSTITUTION AS AN ECONOMIC DOCUMENT

Numerous scholars have studied the nature and character of the American constitution, and as a result, various interpretations of it have been made. Initially, American historian Charles Beard argued that the American Constitution was an economic document in his book '*An Economic Interpretation of the United States Constitution*' (1913) **(Refer Figure 1.5)**.

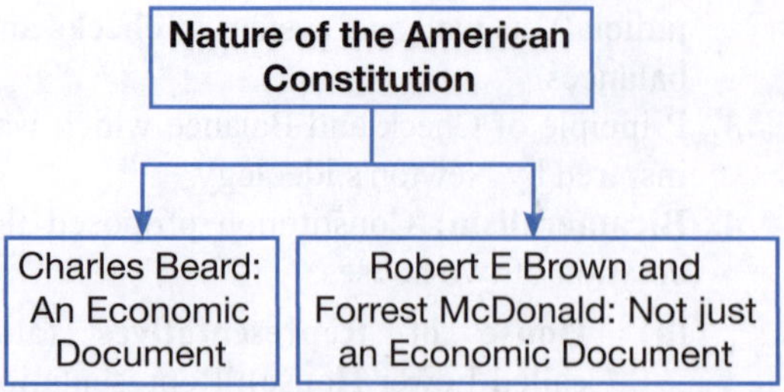

FIGURE 1.5: Nature of the American Constitution

Charles Beard's Arguments in Favour of Economic Document

1. There was not a single representative from the group of common artisans, craftspeople, peasants, or members of the general populace. Additionally, Beard discovered that, for one reason or another, more than three-fourths of the voters who belonged to the public were prohibited from voting in the process of choosing the delegates to the American constitution.
2. According to Charles Beard, a 'cohesive elite class' that sought to defend its personal property participated in and wrote the American Constitution. As a result, the right to property was converted into a fundamental right that could not be even violated by the government. Additionally, Beard highlights the property holdings of members of the constitutional convention. For example, George Washington belonged to the wealthiest landowner in the country and provided significant funding for revolution.
3. According to Beard, the American Constitution was a counter-revolution intended to counteract the radical democratic tendencies that the American Revolution had unleashed and that were intended to defend the interests of wealthy merchants and zamindars in opposition to farmers and planters.

American Constitution—Not an Economic Document

Charles Beard's view that American constitution is an economic document that was challenged by revisionist historians led by Forrest McDonald and Robert E Brown.

1. Revisionist historians argued that Beard had misinterpreted economic interests involved in writing the constitution. Instead of just two economic interests (economic interests of landlord vs peasant), there were many other economic and non-economic issues that were discussed during the constitution-making process.
2. Revisionist historians further argued that the constitution had many important non-economic clauses like:
   - **(a)** Bill of Rights (though it also had some economic clauses for eg: right to property but non-economic in nature).
   - **(b)** Separation of powers, and check, and balance.
   - **(c)** No property qualifications for members and voters.
   - **(d)** No property requirement to hold office
   - **(e)** Secular polity, freedom of religion, expression, belief, and practice.
3. Additionally, revisionist historians defend the constitution's economic provisions to build a strong country, which was necessary for the actual unification of states into a nation.

Accordingly, revisionist historians led by Forrest McDonald contend that the American Constitution was more than merely an economic constitution.

AMERICAN CIVIL WAR

The American Civil War was one of the bitterest civil wars in the world, which lasted from 1861 to 1865. Nearly 600,000 people died, and numerous others were injured. In January 1861, seven southern slave states individually declared their secession from the US on the issue of slavery and formed Confederate states of America

> *The greatest danger to American survival at mid-century, however, was neither class tension nor ethnic division. It was sectional conflict between North and South over the future of slavery.*
>
> **—James M. McPherson**

('Confederacy' or the 'South'). As soon as Fort Sumter was attacked by the southern states, consequently Abraham Lincoln declared war on them and the American Civil War started between North and South America. After 4 years of Civil War (1861–65) over 6 lakh soldiers were dead; Confederate states of America collapsed; slavery was abolished and national unity was restored.

Causes of American Civil War

The causes of the American Civil War were varied and included the problem of slavery, societal divisions between North and South America, and differences in the needs and conditions of North and South America's economies **(Refer Figure 1.6)**.

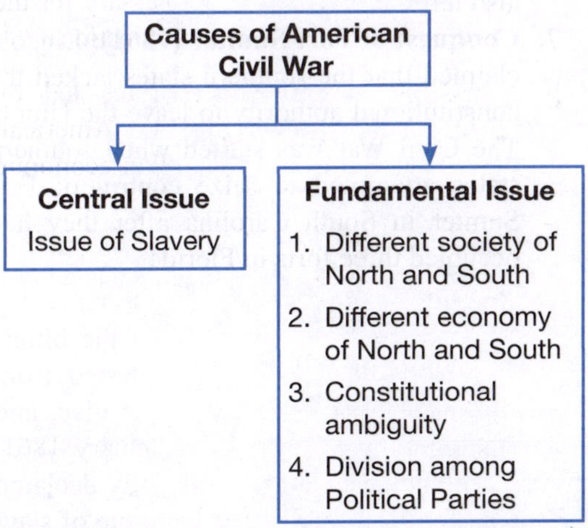

FIGURE 1.6: Causes of American Civil War

Issue of Slavery

The central issue for the American Civil War was the issue of slavery which was incompatible

> *Without slavery, the rebellion could never have existed; without slavery, it could not continue.*
>
> **—Abraham Lincoln**

with republicanism ideas of liberty and had been phased out in industrial North America, but expanding in agricultural districts of the south due to the expansion of agriculture and plantation, which was dependent on slaves.

Points to Ponder

Northwest Ordinance of 1787: Ordinance insured Northwest territory beyond Appalachian Mountains would be free territory.

Despite compromises of northwest ordinance 1787 and the Missouri Compromise of 1820 between North and South America, the slavery issue exploded in 1850s leading to the secession of seven southern slave states from the Union.

Points to Ponder

Missouri Compromise (1820): North of latitude 36°30′ was declared as free states.

The following are numerous series of activities related to the issue of slavery:

1. Controversy over admitting Missouri as a slave state. Because there were eleven free states and eleven slave states in the Senate, Missouri's application as a slave state disrupted the balance of power. The Missouri Compromise resulted in a temporary settlement, and these were:

   (a) North of latitude 36°30′ was declared as free states.

   (b) Missouri was admitted as a slave state and Maine as a free state to keep the balance of power in the Senate.

2. Issue of status of slavery in western territories acquired as result of Mexican American War.
3. Novel and play Uncle Tom's Cabin (1852) by abolitionist Harriet Beecher Stowe.
4. The Kansas-Nebraska Act, (1854) repealed the Missouri Compromise of 1820 and restored slavery north of 36° 30′ latitude. According to the Act, Nebraska would be split into the territories of Kansas and Nebraska. Whether Kansas and Nebraska will be a slave or free states will be decided by its citizens. The act left little space for compromise because Southerners backed the measure while Northerners saw it as a betrayal.
5. Supreme Court's Dred Scott decision (1857) ended Congressional compromise for popular sovereignty in Kansas. The Supreme Court's Dred Scott ruling (1857) put an end to the Congressional Compromise (Missouri compromise) to Popular Sovereignty. The U.S. Supreme Court concluded that because Dred Scott was an African immigrant and not regarded as a citizen, he was not entitled to freedom. Additionally, the court argued that Congress lacked the authority to settle the slavery issue, rendering the Missouri Compromise illegal and securing the legality of slavery across all territories **(Refer Figure 1.7)**.

Source: Uncredited, Public domain, via Wikimedia Commons, accessed on 5th June 2023

Figure 1.7: Dred Scott

6. The South perceived Lincoln as an abolitionist when he was in the White House. Secession was the only alternative, and it was legal, in the eyes of the southern states. South Carolina left the Union in 1860, and then in February 1861, Alabama, Florida, Texas, Georgia, Louisiana, and Mississippi also left.
7. **Conquest of Fort Sumter (1861):** Lincoln claimed that the southern states lacked the constitutional authority to leave the Union. The Civil War was started when southern states attempted to seize control of Fort Sumter in South Carolina after they had occupied three forts in Florida.

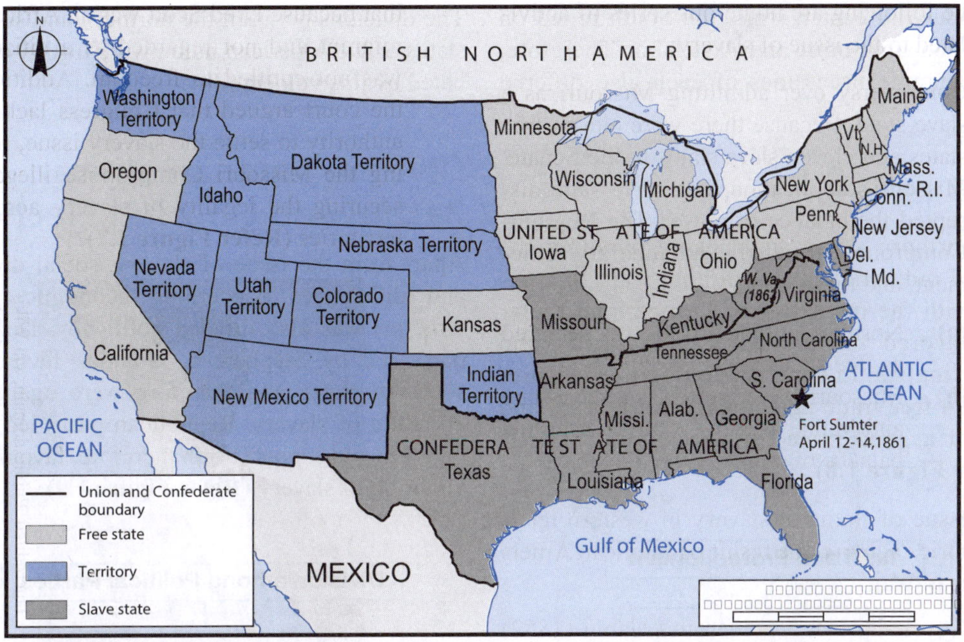

MAP 1.3: Division of America into Free and Slave States

FUNDAMENTAL FACTORS FOR THE AMERICAN CIVIL WAR

Social Factors

People in the North and South America came from different social backgrounds. North American society was urban and progressive, and South American society was the traditional stratified rural society. People therefore, had different opinions on the issue of slavery. These differences were:

1. Being a modern society, the industrialized north views slavery as being against republican values, i.e., the institution of slavery is contrary to the principle of liberty; all persons were created equal and have a right to pursue happiness.
2. Being a traditional orthodox society and belief in white supremacy, South American view the slavery as legitimate, natural, and essential for a civilized society. For example, slaves were present in 95% of southern states, whereas just 1% of families in northern states possessed slaves **(Refer Map 1.3)**.

Because of the diverse societal perspectives, both South and North Americans were highly rigid. As a result, the Civil War became inevitable.

Economic Factors

The American Civil War was also caused due to the economic factors such as role of slavery and tariff and protectionism.

Role of Slavery as an Economic Institution

Between 1800 and 1860, the disparities between the economics, social structures, and political values of the North and South America grew quickly. North America developed as urbanized and industrial center, while the South relied on plantation agriculture and slave labor. Therefore, the economic necessities of each also differed greatly.

Tariff and Protectionism

The northern states which were pursuing the path of industrialization, did not want to compete with the industries of Europe, and therefore favored the policy of high tariffs and protectionism. In contrast, southern states preferred a free trade agreement with Europe and desired a good price for agricultural exports **(Refer Figure 1.8)**.

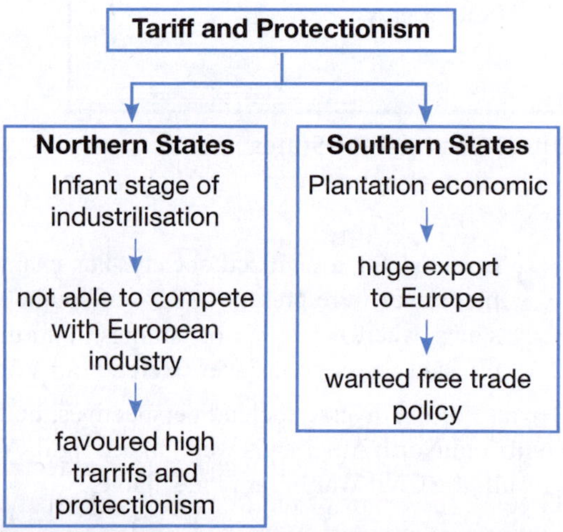

FIGURE 1.8: Difference of Opinion on Tariff and Protectionism

Constitutional Ambiguity

The right of a state to secede from the union was not addressed in the American constitution. The Constitution neither prohibited nor authorized a state's act of secession. The North American Union interpreted the constitution radically different than the southern slave states, who saw themselves as free to leave the union at any time. The divisions between the northern and southern states of the American union were further exacerbated by this vulnerability.

Division among Political Parties and Lincoln's Election

Apart from the issue of slavery, social division, and differences concerning economic policy, America was also divided politically. Democrat party led by Stephen A. Douglas favored the southern states and therefore were against the abolition of slavery. Republican party led Abraham Lincoln support north therefore, favoured the abolition of slavery **(Refer Figure 1.9)**.

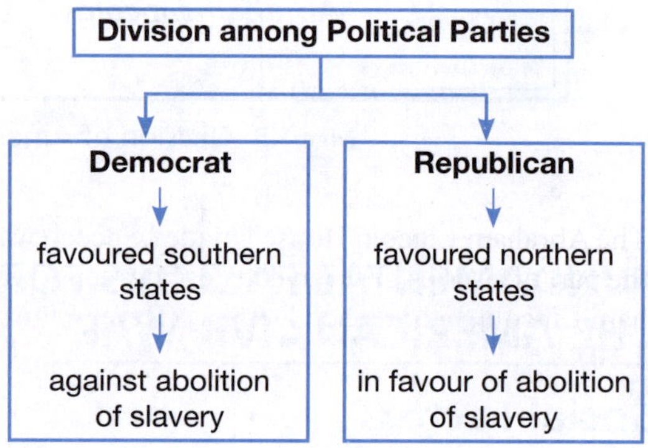

FIGURE 1.9: Division among Political Parties

In the circumstances, Abraham Lincoln's win in the election of November 1860—which he did without receiving a single vote from the South—acted as the catalyst for the secession of seven southern states from the union. Southern leaders feared that Lincoln, an abolitionist, would abolish the institution of slavery because southern slave states were now in the minority in the House of Representatives and might continue to be so in the senate. So, before Lincoln took office in March 1861, seven slave states officially announced their secession and founded the Confederacy.

LINCOLN'S HOUSE DIVIDED SPEECH 1858

> *A house divided against itself cannot stand. I believe this government cannot endure, permanently half slave and half free. I do not expect the Union to be dissolved - I do not expect the house to fall - but I do expect it will cease to be divided. It will become all one thing, or all the other.*
>
> ***—Abraham Lincoln***

The Abraham Lincoln House Divided Speech was the part of a series of seven debates between Abraham Lincoln and Stephen Douglas **(Refer Figure 1.10)**.

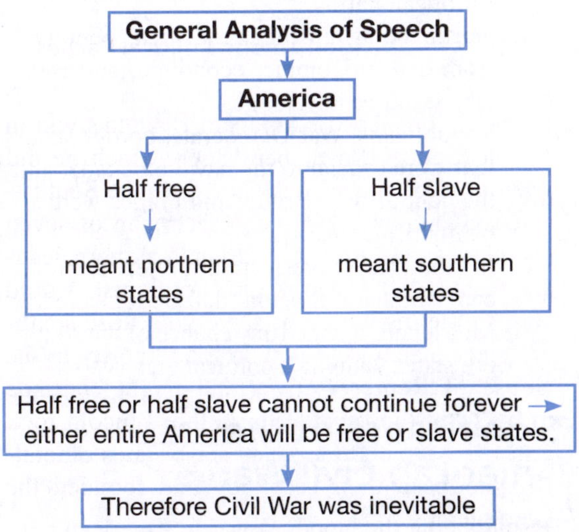

FIGURE 1.10: General Analysis of Lincoln's Speech

However, most historians argue that Lincoln's objectives were to set differentiate himself from Douglas rather than to cause the Civil War. Douglas was looking for a compromise on the issue of slavery and trying to create a common ground between the north and the south. But in his House Divided Speech, Abraham Lincoln argued that the Dred Scott decision had already made it possible for slavery to be legal in both the North and the South. Douglas's chosen choice of a midpoint had been eliminated, leaving him with only two options: either all slaves would be kept, or all would be set free. In effect, Lincoln was saying, 'I am on the side of the abolition of the institution of slavery and Douglas is on the side of slavery.'

Emancipation Proclamation

> *That all persons held as slaves are and henceforward shall be free.*
>
> ***—Abraham Lincoln***

Abolitionists urged Lincoln to issue the Emancipation Proclamation and to abolish the institution of slavery after the Civil War had begun. Horace Greeley, the editor of the Republican newspaper, claimed in effect that it would be 'preposterous and fruitless' to fight the Civil War without abolishing the institution of slavery.

Lincoln informed Horace Greeley that it was his duty as president to uphold the Union, not to keep or end slavery. Lincoln declared, 'If I could save Union without freeing any slave I would do it, if I could save it by freeing all slaves I would do it; and if I could save it by freeing some and leaving others alone, I would also do that.' Lincoln therefore made it clear that his responsibility as president was to defend the Union first (the main goal of the war), and that the abolition of slavery was the secondary goal.

Strategic Reason for Lincoln's Statements

Lincoln's statement had a strategic objective. Most southerners fought in the Civil War for the sole purpose of preserving slavery. On the other hand, northerners were divided between wanting to abolish slavery and keeping the Union together by preventing the secession of southern states. Lincoln's statement was intended to unite the various groups in the north together to maintain the Union so that the Confederacy might be defeated. Therefore, despite being a prime cause of the American Civil War, the abolition of slavery was not the war's main objective.

However, the scenario changed in 1862, when President Lincoln issued his Preliminary Emancipation Proclamation, one hundred days later when Civil War continued unabated. Emancipation Proclamation declaring that all persons held as slaves are, and henceforward shall be free. Remember that the Preliminary Emancipation Proclamation was also issued for tactical reasons. The prime goal was not to free slaves but rather to break up the solidarity among southern states and incite slave revolts.

Limitations of the Preliminary Emancipation Proclamation

1. Did not completely end slavery in the US.
2. Applied only to states who seceded from the Union and exempted parts of the Confederacy that already come under Union control.

REASONS FOR THE VICTORY OF NORTH AMERICA

1. Lincoln's pragmatic approach towards preserving the Union as the most important duty of the President led to unity among entire northern states therefore, a united front against southern states.
2. Confederate (Southern States) failed to get Europe involved in war militarily, particularly Britain and France. The southern states hoped that Great Britain and France would provide the Confederacy with military support because European industriesrely on the southern plantation economy (mostly cotton). To break up Lincoln's Atlantic and Gulf of Mexico naval blockade on Southern ports and cities, Southern states sorely needed the assistance of European powers. The European governments were persuaded not to intervene, nevertheless, by the availability of cotton and Britain's opposition to the system of slavery **(Refer Figure 1.11)**.

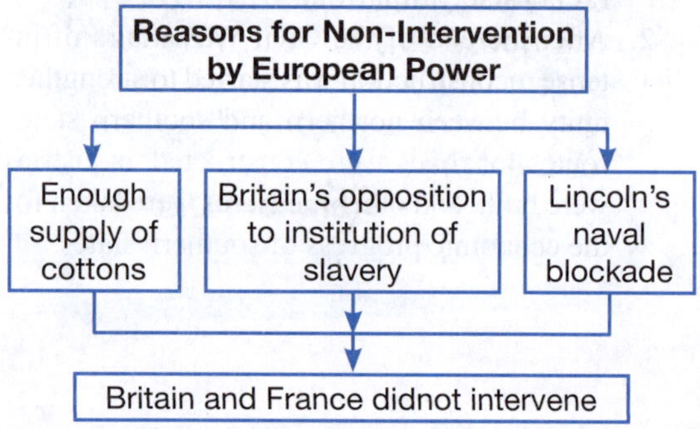

FIGURE 1.11: Reasons for Non-Intervention by European Power

3. Lincoln's naval blockade strategy eliminated any chance of involvement by a powerful European nation.
4. North, being an industrial area, benefited from a demographic, economic, and military resource advantage.
5. Republicans, War Democrats, border states that were crucial to the naval blockade, and the neutrality of Britain and France were all behind Lincoln.
6. In the 1864 presidential vote, Republican Abraham Lincoln defeated Democrat McClellan. It ended any chance of the southern states winning a political victory.

Significance of the American Civil War

Despite being the bloodiest war in American history, the American Civil War had a profound and far-reaching influence:

1. The emancipation of slaves was made possible by the American Union's triumph. President Lincoln issued the Emancipation Proclamation in 1862, and the 13th Amendment gave it constitutional status in 1865. The 14th and 15th Constitutional Amendment Acts were passed to give Black people more power. The 14th Amendment Act of 1868 increased federal legal protection for every American citizen, regardless of race, while the 15th Amendment separated voting rights from racial discrimination.
2. After the end of the Civil War affairs of intense reconstruction was started to strengthen unity between northern and southern states routes for roads were constructed, industries were built, and other measures were taken for the economic progress of southern states.
3. After the Civil War ended, significant reconstruction efforts were launched to strengthen the bond between the northern and southern states. Roads were built, industries were established, and other steps were made to advance the southern states' economies. Additionally, tariffs and protectionism were put on European trade, which sped up the industrialization of both the north and the south.
4. The American Constitution was amended to guarantee the indestructible unity of America. The state had no right to break away from the union, according to an amendment.
5. The American government had not given the Armed Forces much attention before to the Civil War, but the necessity of war forced them to do so, which boosted strengthening of American military and development of military technology.

LET'S REVISE

Factors/ Causes Leading to American Revolution

1. Immediate Causes
   (a) Seven Years' War and Consequent Events
2. Fundamental Causes
   (a) American Capitalism vs British Capitalism
   (b) Class interest behind Revolution
   (c) Role of Philosophers
   (d) Nature of American Population
   (e) Constitutional issue in the American conflict

Reasons for American Success

1. Concept of the spirit of liberty and a group of gifted leaders.
2. Not much attention by the British authorities.
3. 'Nature, Washington, and France'.
4. English underestimated the strength of Americans.
5. Solid organization of American patriots and disorganization of loyalists.
6. Guerrilla warfare by patriots.

Significance of the Declaration of Independence

1. Inspired French Declaration of Rights of Man and Citizen.
2. Inspired overthrowing of the Spanish empire in South America.
3. Helped in abolishing slavery in the USA.
4. Inspired many other similar documents in other countries.

Significance of the American Revolution

1. Inspired a series of trans-Atlantic Revolutions.
2. War of Independence against colonial dominance.
3. First democratic government
4. New political, social, and economic setup
5. Bill of Rights
6. Inspired the French Revolution.

Effects of the American Revolution

1. Effects on America
   (a) Expulsion of Loyalists
   (b) Societal Impacts of the American Revolution
   (c) Change in the status of American women
   (d) Financial impact on America
2. Effects on World
   (a) Inspiring the European and freedom movements
   (b) Inspiration for the political system
   (c) Changed in British attitude towards colonies

Limitations of the American Revolution

1. Women and black slaves not benefited
2. Majority of delegates were slave owners
3. Favoured the rich class

Main Features of the US Federal Constitution

1. People's Sovereignty
2. Doctrine of Separation of Power

3. Principle of Check and Balance
4. Bicameralism
5. Rigid Constitution
6. Concept of Dual Citizenship
7. Independence of Judiciary
8. Bill of Rights

Nature of the American Constitution

1. Charles Beard: An Economic Document
2. Robert E Brown and Forrest McDonald: Not just an economic document

Factors responsible in Drafting of Constitution

1. Concerned for the autonomy of states
2. Inspired by enlightenment ideals
3. Anti-British emotions
4. Protection of Freedom and Liberty
5. Liberal, progressive, and cosmopolitan nature of American society

Causes of the American Civil War

1. Central Issue: Issue of Slavery
2. Fundamental Issue
   - (a) Different societies of North and South
   - (b) Different economies of North and South
   - (c) Constitutional ambiguity
   - (d) Division among Political parties

Reasons for Victory of North America

1. Lincoln's pragmatic approach
2. Non-intervention by a European power
3. Lincoln's naval blockade strategy
4. Demographic, economic, and military resource advantage.
5. Defeat of Democrat McClellan in 1864

Significance of the American Civil War

1. Emancipation and empowerment of slaves.
2. Unity between northern and southern states.
3. Tariffs and protectionism for European trade.
4. No right to secession.
5. Military and development of military technology.

UPSC PREVIOUS YEARS' QUESTIONS

1. Explain how the foundations of the modern world were laid by the American and French Revolutions. **[15 Marks] [2019]**
2. American Revolution was an economic revolt against mercantilism. Substantiate. **[10 Marks] [2013]**

PROBABLE QUESTIONS

1. 'The American War of Independence transformed Europe as well as America.' Critically examine.
2. 'No taxation without representation.' Comment.
3. The American War of Independence 'deprived Great Britain of one empire, but it strengthened the foundations of another'. Comment.
4. Do you agree with the view that the 'Revolution of Idea (American Enlightenment) preceded the American War of Independence'.
5. 'The struggle was not over high-sounding political and constitutional concepts. It was over the survival or collapse of English mercantile capitalism.' Comment.
6. American Revolution 'became as much a war against the colonial aristocracy as a war for independence'. Comment.

TIMELINE (1756–1865)

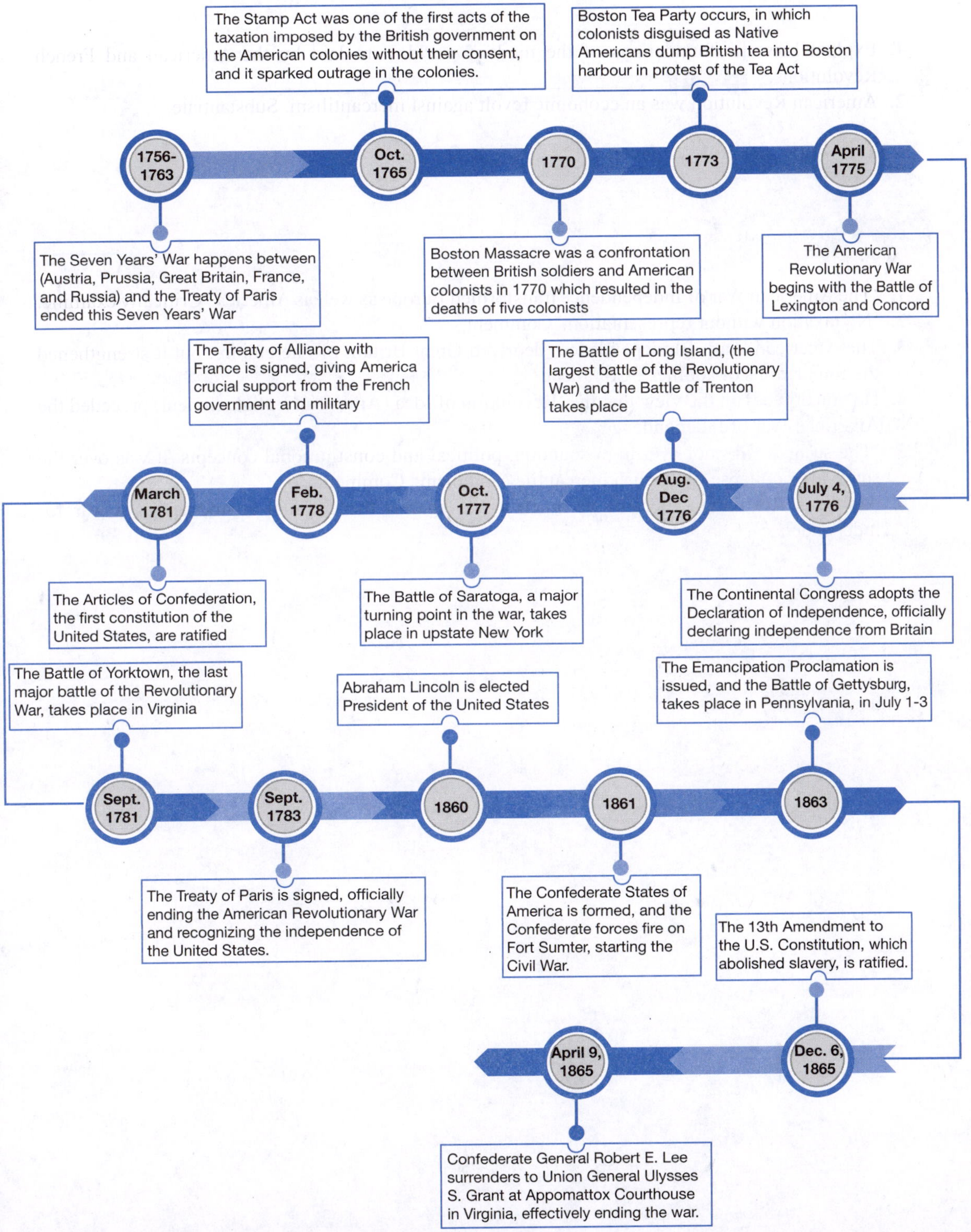

CHAPTER

2

Photo Credit: stefanocapra / Shutterstock, Andreas Horn / 123RF

FRENCH REVOLUTION AND RISE OF NAPOLEON

> *It was the best of times, it was the worst of times, it was the age of wisdom, it was the age of foolishness, it was the epoch of belief, it was the epoch of incredulity, it was the season of light, it was the season of darkness, it was the spring of hope, it was the winter of despair.*
>
> *—Charles Dickens on French Revolution*

INTRODUCTION

The French Revolution (1789–1815) was a social and political upheaval, that started in 1789 and was partially carried forward by Napoleon during the later expansion of the French Empire. The French Revolution resulted in the overthrow of the Bourbon monarchy, the establishment of a French republic, violent times of political unrest, and Napoleon's dictatorship, which swiftly spread many of its ideas throughout Western Europe and beyond. The French Revolution, which was greatly influenced by radical and liberal views, shook the whole of Europe. It changed the direction of modern world history by causing the republics to replace the absolute monarchies throughout the world. With the outbreak of the French Revolution, European history changed into the history of one country (France), one event (the French Revolution), and one man (Napoleon). It is, therefore, no surprise that historians around the world consider the French Revolution to be one of the most significant moments in human history.

FRENCH REVOLUTION AS AN INTELLECTUAL REVOLUTION

Many historians refer to the French Revolution as an 'intellectual revolution' since it led to the spread of modern ideas and resulted in:

1. Setback to established Feudal customs and institutions of Europe.
2. Spread of new Republican political ideas, leading to the decline of absolute monarchy.

> *"In my view, the French Revolution and the doings of Napoleon opened the eyes of the world. Nations knew nothing before, and people thought that kings were Gods upon the earth.* ***—Charles Dickens****"*

3. Global acceleration of the rise of republics and democracies.
4. Development of all modern political ideologies, i.e., liberalism, radicalism, nationalism, socialism, feminism, and secularism, among many others.
5. Almost all future revolutionary movements looked back to the French Revolution as their predecessor.
6. Creation of new social order that contrasts the privilege system and is based on the principles of liberty and equality.
7. Upholding rights of man based on the principle of equality, nationality and democracy.

Causes of French Revolution

The causes of the French Revolution are complex and are still debatable among historians. The foundation for the revolution has been attributed to several political, economic and social factors, which

> *"Chief among the causes of the French Revolution were the abuses and extravagances of the bourbon monarchy; the unjust privileges enjoyed by the nobility and the higher clergy; the wretched conditions of the poorer classes of the people and the revolutionary character and spirit of French philosophy and literature.*
> ***—David N. Myers****"*

among other things included growing social inequality, new political ideologies from the enlightenment, economic mismanagement, environmental factors that led to agricultural failure, an unmanageable national debt, and political mismanagement on the part of King Louis XVI **(Refer Figure 2.1)**.

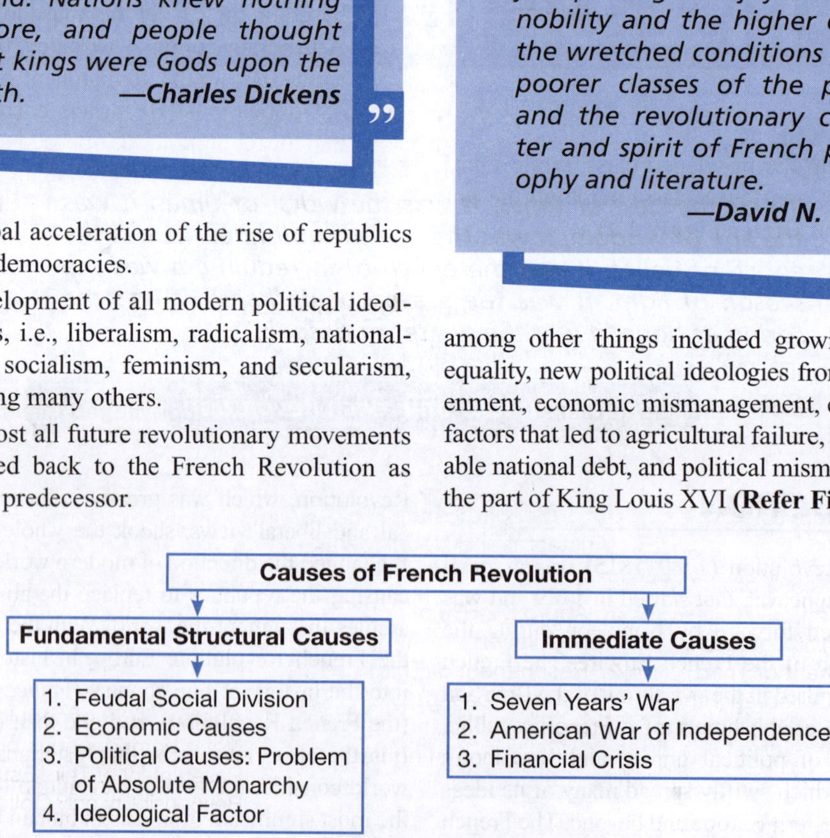

FIGURE 2.1: Causes of French Revolution

Fundamental and Structural Causes

The fundamental and structural causes of the French Revolution broadly included the feudal social division, the economic causes, political factors along with the ideological factors.

Feudal Social Division

French society was based on ancient regime, divided into the privileged and the unprivileged class. First Estate (clergy) and Second Estate (nobility) made up the privileged class, while Third Estate (middle and lower class) made up the unprivileged class **(Refer Figure 2.2).**

> "*The revolution was an outcome of a struggle between classes, of a movement for social equality by the bourgeoisie.*
>
> ***—Ricker***"

The social division based on privileged and unprivileged class was resented by the Third Estate (peasant, artisan, and bourgeoise) and French Revolution originated with Third Estate due to number of following factors:

Points to Ponder

Tithe

One-tenth of annual produce or earnings, formerly taken as a tax for the support of the Church and clergy.

1. Peasants were expected to pay several taxes, including the tithe (which represented a tenth of their earnings or harvest for the church), the taille (which represented a land tax for the state), 5% property tax, and the capitation tax (which represented a tax based on the size of the household).
2. Aristocrats continue to enjoy their feudal rights despite the abolishment of their feudal obligations. Historians correctly claim that the revolution was opposed to the 'effete survival of that Feudal system' rather than the feudal system itself.

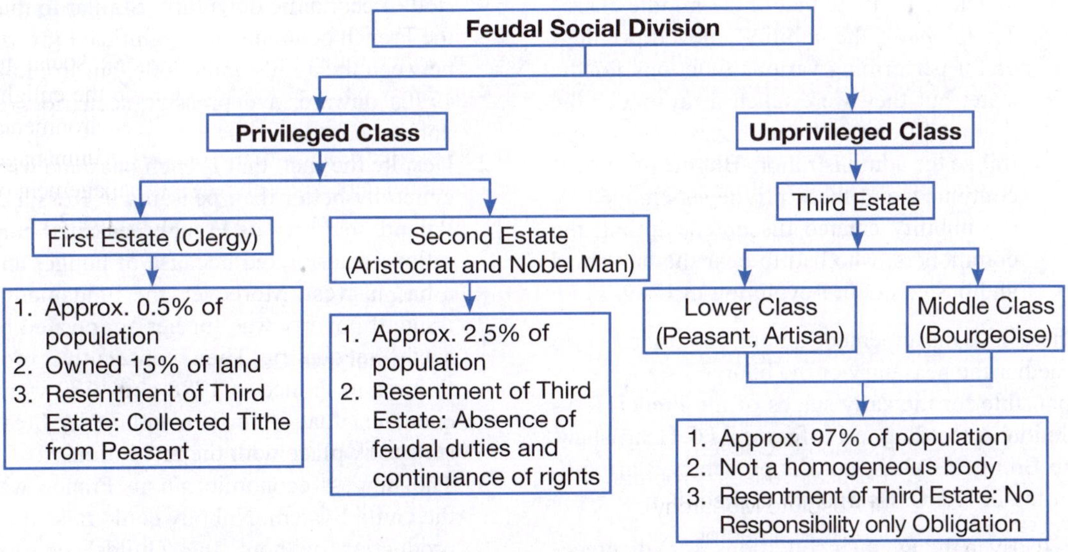

FIGURE 2.2: Feudal Social Division

3. The church held 15% control over all French resources, while the nobles held 20% control over them. The Third Estate with more than 98% of the population managed to survive just on 65% of the resources available.
4. The privileged class had all rights but were free from obligations, while the unprivileged classes had no rights but only obligations.
5. The First Estate and Second Estate enjoyed various sorts of economic and social privileges including not simply exemption from taxes but also the right to impose some taxes. Therefore, the privileged class had full or partial tax exemptions and held all official positions, whereas the unprivileged class were subjected to full taxation and was barred from all positions of power.
6. Although the economic situation of the middle class (Bourgeois class) had much improved, they were extremely unhappy with their social standing. In other words, in France, there was a major contradiction between economically effective class and the socially effective class.
7. Due to the heavy tax burden and harsh feudal exaction, even the lower classes suffered. As a result, it was looking to the middle class for leadership and prepared to attach its future to that of the middle class.
8. Traditionally, the nobility enjoyed privileges for performing various functions for the state, but they were taken away under the reigns of Louis XIII and Louis XIV to centralize the administration. But the privileges continued, and these privileges enjoyed by the nobility created discontent among the commoners, who had to bear the hardships and busted out in Revolution in 1789.

There is a disagreement among historians as to whether the peasantry or the bourgeoisie were responsible for the early stages of the French Revolution. According to Professor F.J.C Hearnshaw, the Bourgeois class, not the peasantry, started it. Professor F. J. C. Hearnshaw argued that,

1. Even though their conditions were disgraceful, French peasants fared better than those in Germany, Spain, Russia, and Poland. Their primary complaint was not being denied of political rights and employment in government positions, but rather excessively high tax burden.
2. On the other hand, the bourgeois class, which also paid the highest taxes, provided the majority of the loans to the French government. They, therefore, experienced bad administration more directly than any other class. They were highly educated, intellectual, and also enlightened by new concepts, popularized by the French philosophers like Montesquieu, Voltaire, and Rousseau.

Therefore because of the above point, Professor F.J.C. Hearnshaw argued that the enlightened middle-class started the French Revolution and peasants merely followed them.

Economic Causes: Decline

Several economic factors contributed to the French Revolution. These were:

1. The most favorable environment for a revolution is one in which a lengthy era of economic prosperity is followed by a short period of economic downturn. Similar to this, the French economy had significant growth between the 1730s and 1760s, but from the 1770s onward, a depressive scenario predominated.
2. Despite the fact, that French peasants were generally better than peasants in Russia or Poland, majority of French peasants' conditions deteriorated because of hunger and a bad harvest. Moreover, the fundamental issue of poverty was further aggravated by social inequality. Then consecutive crop failures in France in 1788 and 1789 worsened the situation further, and finally, bread riots took place with the revolutions.
3. The biggest economic sin in France was the Guild System. Nobody could raise their production without the Guilds' consent under the numerous economic operations

were carried out by the guilds. Without the Guild's consent, no one could even start a new profession. This approach contributed to the underfunding of the public treasury and prolonged underdevelopment of the French economy.

4. Moreover, the French Industrial Revolution did not begin until the 1780s, and the bulk of industry suffered from poor production while agriculture remained mired in a medieval era with most of the land controlled by feudal lords and minimal infrastructure development.
5. The taxation system was flawed, illogical, and unscientific because the privileged class were exempt from paying taxes. All taxes were paid by the general people, which made it difficult for the government to generate more revenue.

Political Causes: Problem of Absolute Monarchy

States-General (Feudal Representative assembly) were dissolved by Louis XIV, who declared himself 'The State, It Myself,' and the French political structure changed to a highly centralized monarchy and therefore needed a strong leader.

Points to Ponder

Estate General

Representative assembly of the three estates with power to decide on the levying of new taxes and to undertake reforms

> *"The causes of the French Revolution were economic and political, not philosophical and social.*
> ***—Morse Stephens"***

Louis XIV fought many wars which became one of the factors for financial bankruptcy. Nevertheless, he was a capable king. But Louis XV and Louis XVI were weak kings. Anybody could be imprisoned by warrants called 'letters de cachet'. Therefore, French government became corrupt, oppressive and arbitrary which led to widespread discontent among the French people.

Furthermore, in times of social unrest and economic catastrophe, only a capable leader could effectively manage the situation. But sadly, neither Louis XV nor Louis XVI (Louis XIV's successors), were capable of handling the situation. The bourgeois class criticized the feudal privileges and urged Louis XVI to abolish them. But he was afraid to confront the aristocracy. Because of this, social, and economic turmoil was permitted to intensify into a significant political crisis. Therefore, as Louis XVI was unable to resolve the issue of feudal privilege, the French Revolution began.

Immediate Cause: Financial Crisis

After Louis XIV's several wars, the Seven Years' War, the corrupt extravagance of Louis XV and Louis XVI, and the American Revolutionary War, the French government was heavily in debt and tried to improve its financial situation through controversial taxation methods **(Refer Figure 2.3).**

Louis XV, dissatisfied with Britain's success in the Seven Years' War, drew out a long-term strategy for a stronger navy and an anti-British alliance of allies, while Louise XVI entered France

> *"The immediate causes of the French Revolution of 1789 must be sought, not in the economic grievances of the peasants, nor in the political discontent of the middle class, but in the reactionary inspirations of the French aristocracy.*
> ***—Goodwin"***

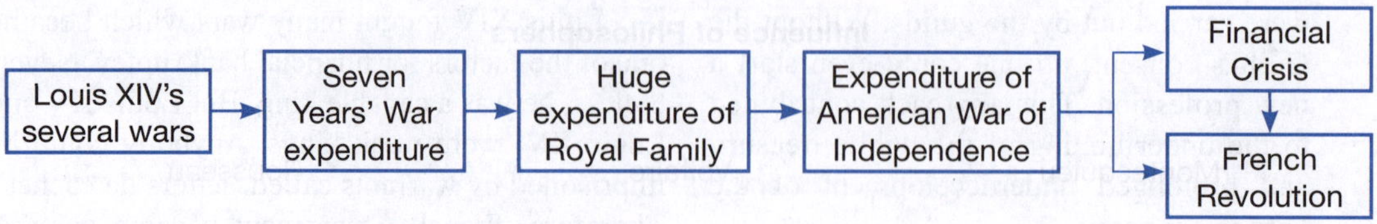

FIGURE 2.3: Financial Crisis and French Revolution

in the American War of Independence, sparking the financial crisis, mountain of debts and brought France nearer to bankruptcy.

Additionally, France had a flawed tax system where the assessment of taxes was plagued by the three evils of 'privilege, concession, and exemption' and the collection of taxes was plagued by the three evils of 'extravagance, waste, and corruption.'

The need for new taxes was necessary to cover the financial deficit. The Third Estate was already overburdened, while privileged classes were excluded from paying taxes. A change in the taxation structure would be required if looming insolvency could be avoided. Now French government was without credit and the treasury was empty. There was no prospect of replenishing it by taxation as the privileged class, which had money but enjoyed exemptions and would not pay, as well as the overtaxed middle and lower classes, were unable to pay.

The King appointed several talented ministers, like Necker, Brienne, Calonne, and others, to handle the financial crisis, but even they were unable to control the state's economy moving forward. Because the monarch disapproved of their proposal to tax the nobles, France became bankrupt.

The French government's financial crisis and its desperate efforts to find a solution led to the summoning of the Estate General (which had been in an animated state for the previous 175 years) as the First and Second Estates argued that only the Estate General had the authority to impose new taxes and not the French Monarch. But it was in Estate General on the issue of voting those differences among different classes took the form of a political crisis.

Finally, the representatives of the Third Estate boycotted the assembly of the Estate General and moved to Tennis Court Assembly. It is here they were joined by artisans of Paris and peasants of France popularly known as the 'Mob of Paris'. Thus, the revolution started.

Ideological Factor: Influence of Philosophers

An all-encompassing upheaval as the French Revolution cannot occur in the condition of the intellectual void. It is therefore, correctly argued by historians that the French Revolution was preceded by a revolution in the realm of ideas by French philosophers such as Voltaire, Montesquieu, Diderot, and Rousseau **(Refer Figure 2.4).**

> "*The Enlightenment undermined the ideological foundations of the established order.*
> ***—Albert Soboul***"

All these philosophers of the enlightenment criticized the absolute monarchy based on the Divine Theory, the stratified feudal social structure, feudal customs, norms, and institutions. Therefore, philosophers' criticisms of the existing feudal institutions, indirectly led to the French Revolution due to:

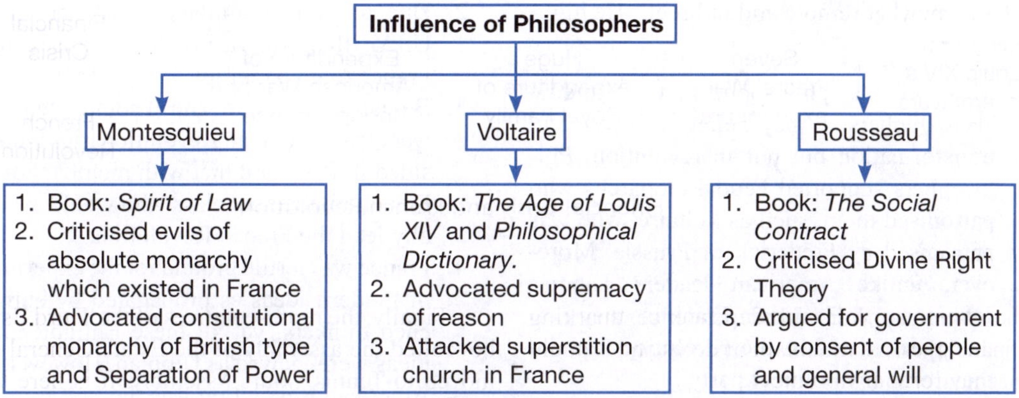

FIGURE 2.4: Influence of Philosophers

1. Deglorification of the institution of Absolute Monarchy based on the concept of Divine Theory. It led to the hostility of royal absolutism, criticism of the policy of Louise XVI, hate of Queen Marie-Antoinette, and anger towards oppressive and corrupt administration.
2. Highlighting malpractices, superstition, and wrongdoing in the Church. It resulted in dissatisfaction with the Catholic Church's control over public policy, as well as hostility among impoverished rural clergy of aristocratic bishops.
3. Recommending the creation of a modern society based on the 'Rule of Law', 'Equality', and 'Reason' instead of traditions. It encouraged the French people to strive for social, political, and economic equality as well as republicanism.
4. By creating one of the earliest forms of civil society, known as 'Club and Coffee Houses,' through which their ideas spread quickly.
5. Bringing the public's attention to the current state of political, economic, and social apathy.

While Voltaire's criticism aimed at destroying the existing institutions; Rousseau came forward with a plan of social reconstruction. Therefore, it was rightly commented by historian that while Voltaire had 'harnessed the horses of reason'; Rousseau 'unchained the tiger of emotion'. Voltaire aimed at destroying the existing institutions; whole Rousseau came forward with a plan of social reconstruction.

Limitations of Influence of Philosophers

There is debate among historians with respect to influence of philosophers on French Revolution. Renowned historian, David Thomson believed that connection between ideas of French philosophers and 'the outbreak of revolution in

> *"The connection between their (philosophers) ideas and the outbreak of revolution in 1789 is somewhat remote and indirect.*
>
> ***—David Thomson"***

1789 is somewhat remote and indirect'. He highlighted that:

1. Most of the philosophers were middle class thinkers so they believed in peaceful transformation but not in revolution. Philosophers supported Feudal monarchs who patronised them, such as Voltaire, who was patronised by Frederick of Prussia. Moreover, unlike American leaders Thomas Jefferson and Benjamin Franklin, they neither participated in the revolution nor did they form any political party.
2. Philosopher's teachings became more important only after the French Revolution. In the initial stages if philosophers had any influence, it was only to the extent of criticism and deglorification of monarchy and Church.

Therefore, historians argued that the long-term structural issues, together with mistakes of Bourbon dynasty, were the primary causes of the French Revolution. The Revolution was, nevertheless, indirectly influenced by these philosophers.

INFLUENCE OF THE AMERICAN REVOLUTION ON THE FRENCH REVOLUTION

Since the French monarchy took part in the American Revolution and there was only a 13-year gap between the two revolutions, most historians think that the American Revolution influenced the French Revolution. The influence of American Revolution can be highlighted in the following points:

1. Lafayette and other young Frenchmen took part in the American War of Independence. They returned with ideas of liberty, equality, fraternity, the rule of law, natural rights, separation of powers, popular sovereignty, and republicanism back to France and assisted in disseminating revolutionary ideas among the French population.
2. Due to French military assistance to the USA, the American Revolution caused France to go bankrupt.
3. Benjamin Franklin and Thomas Jefferson were two American Revolutionaries who resided in Paris and met with members of the French intellectual class who would eventually lead the French Revolution.
4. France was fertile ground for the experiment of modern ideas as propagated by enlightened thinkers, yet all these Enlightenment ideas were viewed as Utopian. However, the American Revolution was the first-time enlightened ideas were put into practice, proving the relevance of enlightenment ideals.

Objectives of the French Revolution

1. Equality, Liberty, and Fraternity
2. Constitutional monarchy in place of absolute monarchy
3. Popular sovereignty
4. Separation of powers
5. Recognition of the natural rights of man
6. Rule of law
7. Merit in jobs was recognized

REASONS FOR REVOLUTION IN FRANCE AND NOT IN OTHER EUROPEAN COUNTRIES

Historians disagree on not just the causes for the revolution, but also why it took place in France and not in other European countries. The French

> *"The ultimate cause of the revolution was the rise of the Bourgeois.*
>
> *—Lefebvre Henri"*

Revolution, according to historians, was caused by feudal social division, economic downturn, the issue of absolute monarchy and financial crises, to name a few.

Historians wonder that if all of the aforementioned factors were the causes, then other Western European nations appeared to have more favorable conditions for revolution than France, but it only occurred in France and not in other Western European nations. For example, the monarchies of Prussia and Russia were more despotic than Bourbon Dynasty; German, Polish, and Hungarian peasants, in contrast to those in France, were like slaves with no own plot of land, no freedom to marry, and no freedom to roam around; France had the most affluent, sophisticated, and progressive middle class after Great Britain. But unlike other European nations, France was the location of the revolution for a number of fundamental factors. These were: **(Refer Figure 2.5)**

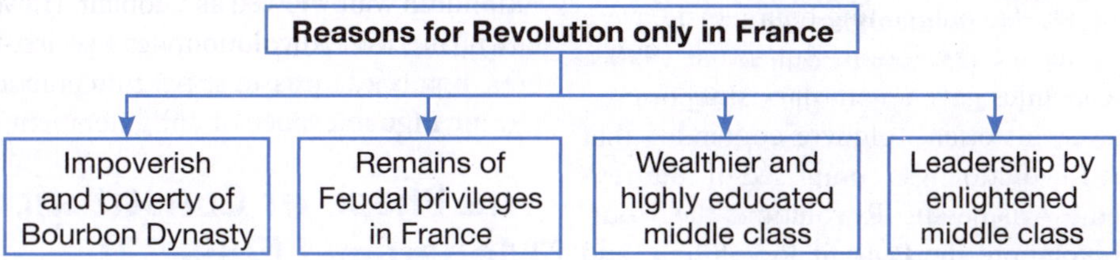

FIGURE 2.5: Reasons for Revolution in France and not in Other European Countries

1. The French monarchy was economically weaker than other European despots. Other kingdoms, unlike the Bourbon dynasty, were not as impoverished. In fact, French monarchy's poverty prompted the Estate General's assembly, which marked the beginning of the French Revolution.
2. Feudal lords in other European nations not only had certain privileges but also had responsibilities including providing the king with military support and maintaining law and order. However, in France, feudal lords merely enjoyed rights and privileges and no corresponding feudal obligations.
3. In comparison to other European countries, the French middle class was wealthier and more highly educated. Average Frenchmen's prosperity, the absence of slavery and serfdom, and people's enjoyment of some liberties led them to criticize the Church and the French absolute monarchy. The peasants in other European nations, such as Russia, Germany, Denmark, or Hungary, suffered under feudal serfdom and never thought and aspired for civil equality and liberty.
4. In contrast to other European nations, France had a prosperous, intelligent, and enlightened middle class. The enlightened middle class in France assumed leadership over workers and peasants who lacked the capacity for heroic action and were trapped in ignorance and superstition.

NATURE OF FRENCH REVOLUTION

The French Revolution has garnered a great deal of historical interest from historians and experts. Historians' points of view have been divided along ideological lines and disagree on the significance and key developments of the revolution. Historical perspectives range from popular uprising to part of the Atlantic Revolution to it being an anti-feudal and anti-autocratic Bourgeoisie Revolution.

While conservative Edmund Burke maintained that the revolution was the result of a few conspiratorial individuals who brainwashed the masses into overthrowing the old feudal order, historian Alexis de Tocqueville argued that the revolution was a manifestation of a more prosperous middle class becoming aware of its social importance.

Other historians, guided by Marxist ideas, have stressed the significance of artisans, rural workers, and urban peasants in portraying the revolution as a massive class struggle. Up to the 20th century, Marxist historians stressed class struggles as the revolution's primary motivating factor. This argument's main tenet was that the sans-culottes, who strove to overthrow the nobility, supported by the burgeoning bourgeoisie, were responsible for the revolution. But in the 1990's, western academics gave up on Marxist theories.

However, historian Lefebvre contended that the French Revolution was comprised of four revolutions: the Aristocratic Revolution, the Bourgeoisie Revolution, the Peasant Revolution, and the Sans-culottes Revolution, respectively.

Many historians claimed that the study of the French Revolution was in intellectual disorder by the year 2000. The outdated paradigm, which focused on class struggle, has fallen out of favor, and no new explanatory model has achieved general acceptance. However, as Spang has demonstrated, there is still a strong consensus that the French Revolution marked the transition from the premodern to the modern eras of western history.

VARIOUS PHASES OF THE FRENCH REVOLUTION

Traditionally, historians divide the French Revolution into four phases: the constitutional monarchy phase, the radical republican phase, the moderate republican phase, and the dictatorship phase **(Refer Figure 2.6).**

The Phase of Constitutional Monarchy (1789–92)

The middle class (Bourgeoise) was in charge of leading the revolution during its first phase, although they came under pressure from the lower class (Peasant).

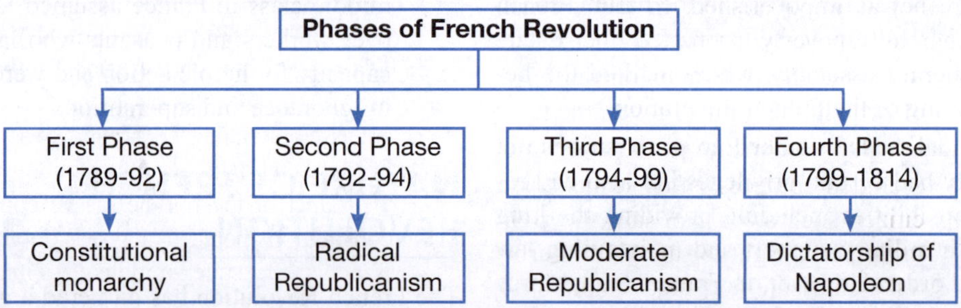

FIGURE 2.6: Various Phases of French Revolution

Timeline and Important Events During the 1st Phase

1. **Fall of Bastille:** The Paris mob attacked the Bastille on July 14, 1789. It was a royal prison that served as a representation of the absolutist character of the government.
2. **Abolition of feudalism in France:** On Aug 4, 1789, there was the abolition of feudalism in France. Some nobility renounced their feudal rights in front of the national assembly.

> *"French Revolution made an attack over privileges but not on the property"*

Consequences of abolition of feudalism are as follows:

(a) Class privileges were abolished in France. The privileges of feudal lords, such as imposing taxes on others, exemption from state taxes, and judicial rights, had to be given up. Nevertheless, nobles understood that they could only maintain their property rights, by sacrificing their privilege rights, and by doing so, they were able to maintain more significant, i.e., property rights.

(b) France transformed into a country of free peasants, which set it apart from other nations in Europe.

(c) Clergy had to surrender their right to impose the religious tax.

3. **Declaration of the rights of men and citizens on August 26, 1789:** It was a special and unique document since:

   (a) It was based on Rousseau's theory of 'General Will' by highlighting that sovereignty rests in the nation, not in the king or the Parliament.

   (b) Reflected the principles on the basis of which the future government of France was likely to be structured.

   (c) Included some essential rights for a citizen such as rule of law, the right to property, right to safety from arbitrary imprisonment, etc.

   (d) The Feudal System was abolished along with serf emancipation.

   (e) Property rights were proclaimed to be fundamental and unalienable.

   (f) All citizens had the right to acquire government offices without any discrimination.

   (g) Physical privileges and payment of taxes were abolished forever. Taxes were now to be collected from all citizens in the same manner.

Limitations of documents of declaration of the rights of men and citizen are as follows:

i. In line with the interests of the middle class (Bourgeoise), which is why the right to property was upheld but not the right to work or the right to food, which would have benefitted the lower class (Peasant).

ii. Declaration of rights of men but not of women.

iii. There was no emphasis on the fundamental right to vote.

iv. Finally, when the laborers began to organize their group after being encouraged by this declaration, it was forbidden. Therefore, their declarations were more abstract and symbolic than concrete.

4. On June 20 and 21, 1791, Louis XVI attempted to leave France. Due to the fact that the Queen of France was the sister of the King of Austria, the First Coalition of Spain, Persia, Britain, Austria, and Hungary had formed against France.

5. **Framing of new constitutions:** Since the National Assembly was also acting as a constituent assembly, a new constitution was created in September 1791. New constitution was clearly a product of the middle class's control. This constitution included a provision for limited franchise that suited middle-class interests and embraced Montesquieu's idea of the separation of powers. The voting criteria and the property criteria were also interlinked.

French Revolution targeted class privilege but not individual property

Most historians argue that the French Revolution made a target to class privilege but not to individual property. In fact, right from the very beginning, the middle class was completely opposed to the Feudal privileges which had been enjoyed by the aristocratic class. The middle class was in better economic condition but objected to aristocratic class enjoying such a higher social position. That is why, in the meeting of the Estate General, the main target of the middle class was social, feudal privileges being enjoyed by the clergy and aristocratic class.

The middle class was passionate about the protection of private property. So, even during the French Revolution, they always attempted to preserve it and preferred the peaceful transformation. That is why, even after the abolition of feudalism, the private property of the nobility and feudal lords were protected and enshrined the protection of private property in the 1791 constitution. Furthermore, middle class preferred to connect voting rights to property requirements. Therefore, the majority of historians are correct to note that, 'French Revolution made an attack over privileges but not on the property'.

The Phase of Radical Republicanism (1792–94)

On the basis of the Constitution of 1791, unicameral legislation was created in France. Numerous radical candidates, including Girondists and Jacobins, were elected to this legislature in the succeeding elections. Therefore, the French assembly was split into two groups: The Rightist (pro-monarchical elements) and the Leftist (Radical members)

The old European Feudal structure was now being threatened by the French Revolution as It was impossible for two Europe's to coexist after the French Revolution since France went ahead of Europe in the matter of ideology. The various European dynasties were now terrified that modern ideals would spread to their country and threaten their existence. It resulted in the building of a coalition in Europe to thwart the spread of ideas of the French Revolution. Therefore, throughout Europe, Revolution took the form of war.

Additionally, members of the National Convention, i.e., supporter of monarchy and radicals, both desired to start a war in order to achieve the desired result. In times of war, pro-monarchical forces hoped for the monarchy's restoration as war requires strong government; on the other hand, radicals believed that it would destroy the monarchical institution. Ultimately, the radical faction's desire come true, and on September 25, 1792, taking advantage of the war, radicals proclaimed France to be a republic.

Differences between Girondists and Jacobins

Following the declaration of a Republican France in 1792, radicals split, and disagreements emerged between Girondists and Jacobins.

1. As a matter of fact, Girondists and Jacobins constituted two distinct social classes. While Jacobians were considered lower class, Girondists represented the lower middle class.
2. According to Girondists, the French Revolution should have stopped after achieving its desired goal of establishing a republican

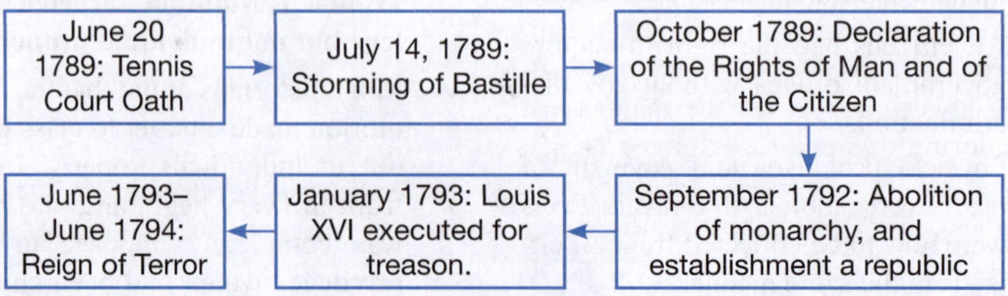

FIGURE 2.7: Timeline of Reign of Terror

government. However, Jacobins thought that the revolution ought to go forward. The aim of the Jacobins was to have the mob in Paris run the revolution.

Reign of Terror

Because Jacobians were far better organized than Girondists, they eventually overthrew them in June 1793, establishing a dictatorship that became known in French history as the Reign of Terror or Jacobians Terror **(Refer Figure 2.7).**

The lower class dominated the revolution and seized control of the government program during the period of radical republicanism. Between June 1793 and June 1794, Jacobian rule of the lower class persisted as a result of the revolution being bloody, deadly, and violent (more than 40,000 people were killed).

Early Jacobian leaders included Herbert, Dante, and Robespierre, among others, but Robespierre later executed the other leaders using the guillotine and formed a one-man dictatorship. Surprisingly, this autocratic regime under the Reign of Terror was established in the name of the 'General Will of Rousseau.'

Thermidorian Reaction

The Reign of Terror' came to an end in June 1794 when Robespierre's government fell apart and even Robespierre himself was executed by guillotine. This event was known as the 'Thermidorian Reaction'in French history.

The 'Reign of Terror' is characterized as the darkest phase as the French Revolution started to devour its own kids under Robespierre. The guillotine machine operated as a death machine and was employed throughout the period of brutality and tyranny in an effort to improve the situation of the lower classes, yet the majority of those killed during this period belonged to that lower class.

Nevertheless, the Robespierre regime instituted universal male suffrage, which was a significant accomplishment at the time. Similar to this, the Jacobean government encouraged the worship of reason in order to promote secularism. In addition, it instituted conscription or forced military service. Later, the strategy played a significant role in Napoleon Bonaparte's military triumph.

Moderate Republicanism (1794–99)

During the Moderate Republican phase, often known as the 'Rule by Directory,' the middle class rather than the lower class once again regained control of the government due to two factors:

1. The organization of lower-class people was weaker and not well structured.
2. Peasants were obliged to sell their grains at a lesser price, which was the major reason, Robespierre was overthrown. As a result, differences between artisans and peasants (both members of the lower class) emerged.

A new constitution was created in France in 1795 that included the provision of bicameral legislation. A group of five directors known as the 'Rule by Directory' held the executive power. Political party formation was actively prohibited in this regime, but no one realized at the time that this would eventually result in the establishment of a dictatorship under Napoleon Bonaparte.

Reasons for the Fall of the Rule of Directory

Directors were unable to reach a consensus with the legislature and between themselves. In addition, conspiracy, plans, and intrigues were frequently hatched in the legislature by both royalists and radicals. Additionally, the French people disliked and disapproved of the Directory's unprincipled domestic and foreign policies.

1. **Failure of Foreign Policy of Directory:**
   (a) Egypt's expedition ended in failure. Directory endured more humiliation and was seen to be the cause of the defeat rather than Napoleon's deed.

(b) Together with Austria and Russia, England established a new alliance of European powers. French was driven out of Germany and Italy due to the coalition's success everywhere. The directory was discredited by these reverses.

2. **Failure of Domestic Policy:** The directory alienated every social class and was authoritarian without being effective. The forced loan policy impacted capitalists, while laborers complained about the suppression of the Babeuf plot (an early Marxist conspiracy), and religious people objected to the persecution of Catholicism.

Together, Napoleon and Abbe Sieyes (one of the Directors) pulled out a coup d'état in November 1799. It signaled the end of Directory power and placed France under the control of three consulates, namely Abbe Sieyes, Ducos, and Napoleon Bonaparte, to draw a constitution and to carry on government **(Refer Figure 2.8).**

1792: France as republic → 1793–94: Reign of Terror → 1795–99: Rule of Directory → 1799–1802: Consulate Rule → 1802–1815: 1st Empire under Napoleon

FIGURE 2.8: Timeline of Various Government Rule in France

Formation of Dictatorship and the Age of Imperialism (1799–1814)

The fourth phase was marked by the rise of the dictatorship of Napoleon Bonaparte. Napoleon was educated in French military schools after being born in Corsica in 1769. At age 17, he joined the army as an artillery officer. He fought off a royalist uprising in 1795, which led to his eventual appointment as commander of Italy.

> *I found the crown of France lying on the ground and I picked it up with my sword.*
>
> ***—Napoleon Bonaparte***

On Napoleon's return after brilliant Italian campaigns, he was the forefront of public affairs. As a result of Austria's defeat, only England remained undefeated. Directory, therefore, prepared to invade England, but a direct invasion was impractical in the absence of a strong naval fleet. As a result, Napoleon advised Directory to send an expedition to conquer Egypt, which was vital to the East and would deal an indirect blow to England by undermining her authority in the region and destroying her trade. Directors agreed as they were afraid of predominance of Napoleon among French people and wanted Napoleon away from France.

Reforms of Napoleon Under Consulate (1799–1804)

Following the Treaties of Luneville (1801) and Amiens (1802), Napoleon focused on restructur-

> *The spirit behind great reforms of Napoleon's Consulate at home was the transference of the methods of Bonaparte the general to the task of Bonaparte the statesman.*
>
> ***—David Thomson***

ing the French government and establishing a solid foundation for social order **(Refer Figure 2.9).**

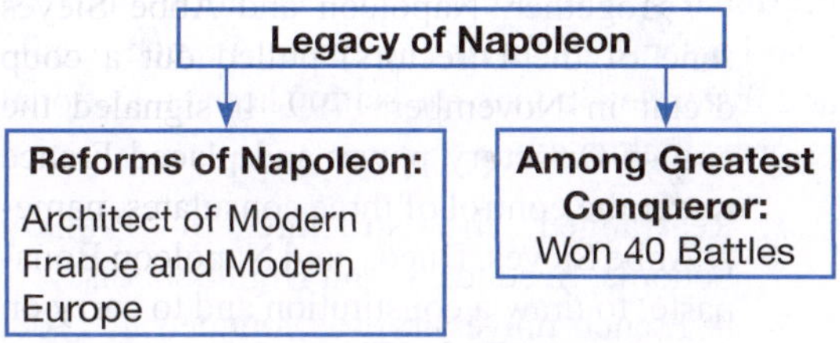

FIGURE 2.9: Legacy of Napoleon

REFORMS OF NAPOLEON

Napoleon's reforms can broadly be classified into socio-cultural, economic, educational and politico-administrative reforms.

Socio-Cultural Reforms

Napoleon also implemented a number of social and cultural reforms to heal the nation's wounds brought on by the social split of France between the Catholics, Radicals, Girondins, and Royalists **(Refer Figure 2.10).** These were:

1. Napoleon adopted the policy of conciliation to heal the nation's wounds and acquire the support and sympathy of all social classes by eradicating all distinctions. Under the policy of conciliation:

(a) Offices were open to all including Royalists and Girondists.

(b) **Reconciliation with Church (Concordat):** After the revolution, a system of priest election was put in place, which profoundly offended the feelings of the French Catholics who felt that granting non-Catholics the ability to vote to elect a Catholic priest was discriminatory.

Moreover, during the September Massacres in 1792, priests were killed and imprisoned, and during the Reign of Terror, clergy were tried in court. The Jacobean government abolished Catholicism deprived the Church of its power and promoted the worship of cult of reason in 1793. As a result, Catholics and non-Catholics became socially divided.

Napoleon signed an agreement with Pope in 1801 known as Concordat to heal the wounds caused to Catholics during the Reign of Terror.

Provisions of Concordat

(i) Catholicism was declared as the 'religion of the great majority of the French people'.

(ii) Pope agreed to the secularisation of public life, religious freedom for all, and the seizure of church property.

(iii) The State acquired responsibility for the maintenance of the clergy and bishops who would be appointed by the State but invested by the Pope.

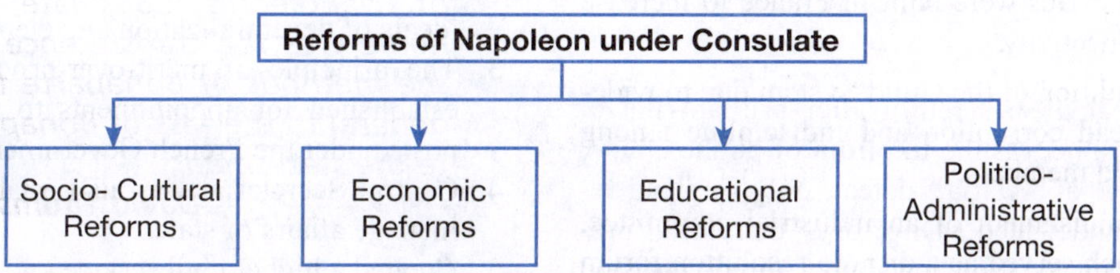

FIGURE 2.10: Reforms of Napoleon

Thus, Catholic Church was re-established in France but made dependent on State. At the same time, there was total religious tolerance for all faiths, and anyone could follow any religion they choose to. As a result, Napoleon, despite his atheism, gained the support and sympathy of both Catholics and non-Catholics.

(c) Napoleon established the Legion of Honour, a new aristocracy based on merit rather than a privilege. However, the new aristocracy were dependent upon Napoleon which later led to imperialism.

Economic Reforms

Financial management and taxation, which were important issues under the old regime and led to the French Revolution, were among the first to be reformed. These reforms included:

1. The Bank of France was established in 1800 to advance the French economy. It is one of the world's most reliable financial organizations, according to Hayes.
2. Tax collection was centralized and made more made efficient.
3. Machines from Britain and America were imported to speed up France's industrialization to increase employment opportunities.
4. Napoleon built infrastructure to boost trade and industry. For example, more than 299 new roads were built in France to increase connectivity.
5. Abolition of the Guild System due to widespread corruption and indiscipline among guild members.
6. Establishment of an industrial committee, which served as a dispute-resolution forum for business people and laborers.

Educational Reforms

Napoleon also concentrated on reforming the educational system. Reforms in education aimed to instill a sense of discipline among French people and foster devotion to the state. These educational reforms included:

1. Rearranged the structure of Primary Schools, Secondary, and High Schools.
2. A French university was founded in 1808, and colleges throughout France were affiliated with it.
3. Military schools called 'Lycée', and vocational schools were established to give students both military and vocational training.
4. If France were to have an intelligent, competent, qualified, and capable leader, Napoleon believes that Teachers must possess 'unique' qualities. Therefore, School of Higher Normal (Ecole Normale Superieure) was established in 1794 for training of teachers.

Politico-Administrative Reforms

Napoleon also carried out number of political reforms. These were:

1. Napoleon created a 'Modern State' based on principles of equality, rule of law and secularism.
2. **Centralization of Local Government:** Napoleon reduced the number of elected councils and placed departments and smaller administrative units (communes) under prefects, and sub-prefects, all of whom were appointed by Napoleon. It sought to increase municipal government efficiency but was against the French Revolution's ideals of decentralization and elections.
3. The principle of merit-over-privilege was established for appointments to all public posts under the French Government.
4. Central Secretariat was also established to manage affairs of state.
5. Created a higher civil service known as Anditeur in 1800.

NAPOLEON CODE OF 1804

Napoleon's Civil and Criminal Code, known as the Code of Napoleon, was perhaps his greatest and longest-lasting accomplishment in politico-administrative reforms. Code Napoleon included the Codes of Civil Procedure, Commercial Law (1807), Penal Code (1810), and Criminal Procedure (1808).

> *My true glory is not to have won 40 battles...Waterloo will erase the memory of so many victories...but...what will live forever, is my Civil Code.*
>
> ***—Napoleon Bonaparte***

There were many different types and a variety of laws governing pre-revolutionary France. According to the satirical remark made by French philosopher Voltaire that a man going across France would have to change as many laws as he would have to change his horse.

Napoleon saw the variety and number of existing laws as a serious issue and sought to establish a single, well-defined body of law. As a result, Code Napoleon, the first comprehensive body of laws, was created in 1804.

Code Napoleon abolished the system of privileges based on birth and established the principle of social equality in the legal system. It contained rights like freedom of expression, open courtrooms, freedom of religion, freedom to choose one's vocation, and government employment based entirely on merit, among other things. Because of Code Napoleon, the judicial system became efficient, and justice was delivered more quickly, affordably, and consistently. Moreover, Code Napoleon also enriched and strengthened the French Revolution by ensuring religious toleration to all and establishing the principle of social equality in law.

In most of the territories, Napoleon conquered, the Napoleon Code remained even after Napoleon's defeat at Waterloo in 1815. The Napoleonic Code laid the foundation for a modern nation-state and sped up the process of putting an end to feudalism in Western and Central Europe. More than seventy countries such as Italy, the Netherlands, Belgium, Spain, Portugal, Latin America, and others around the world like actually had their legal systems inspired by the Napoleonic Code. Therefore, Napoleon was correct, and his Code Napoleon of 1804 was his lasting legacy rather than a military triumph, which the Congress of Vienna overturned.

The Objective of Napoleon's Reform

1. Heal the nation's wounds caused by the social division of France between the Catholics, Radicals, Girondins, and Royalists.
2. Improve the efficiency of inefficient administration.
3. Promotion of the revolutionary concepts of social and financial 'Equality' while opposing the principle of 'Liberty.'

Limitation of Napoleon Code

Napoleon's code modeled after the Roman code of law, in which women were subordinate to men and the head of the family held excessive power.

Military Achievements of Napoleon

> *Tilsit, was, in a sense the turning point of his [Napoleon's] fortunes.*
>
> ***—Ricker***

Napoleon was regarded by historians as one of the greatest conquerors because of his forty wins. The military achievements of Napoleon were **(Refer Map 2.1)**:

1. The Italian campaign of 1796 to 1797 marked the rise of Napoleon in military aspects.
2. Napoleon defeated the second coalition against France when he coerced Britain to accept the Peace of Amiens in 1802, which recognized Napoleon's dominance over continental Europe. Britain also agreed to refrain from meddling in European issues.
3. In the Battle of Austerlitz in December 1805, Napoleon once more overcame the combined Austrian and Prussian forces after the third European coalition formed in 1803 to oppose him. Peace of Press burg was imposed on Austria under which:
   - **(a)** Holy Roman Empire was dissolved.
   - **(b)** Frankfurt Parliament was dissolved.
   - **(c)** The Rhine Confederation, which included thirty-nine states including Germany, was formed with Napoleon as its savior.
4. In the twin battles of Zena and Auerstedt in October 1806, Napoleon once more routed the combined troops of Austria and Prussia. Britain had already left the third coalition, and at this point, the only significant power not under Napoleon's control was Russia.
5. Napoleon defeated Russian forces in the Battle of Freedland in June 1807, and the Treaty of Tilsit was thereafter imposed on the Russian Czar. The Treaty of Tilsit was regarded by historians as the high-water mark of Napoleon's career and after 1808, the Napoleonic Empire began to experience setbacks.

Causes/Factors behind the Imperialistic Success of Napoleon Bonaparte

1. After researching his adversary's psychology, Napoleon formulated his strategy. He took use of every natural barrier after carefully

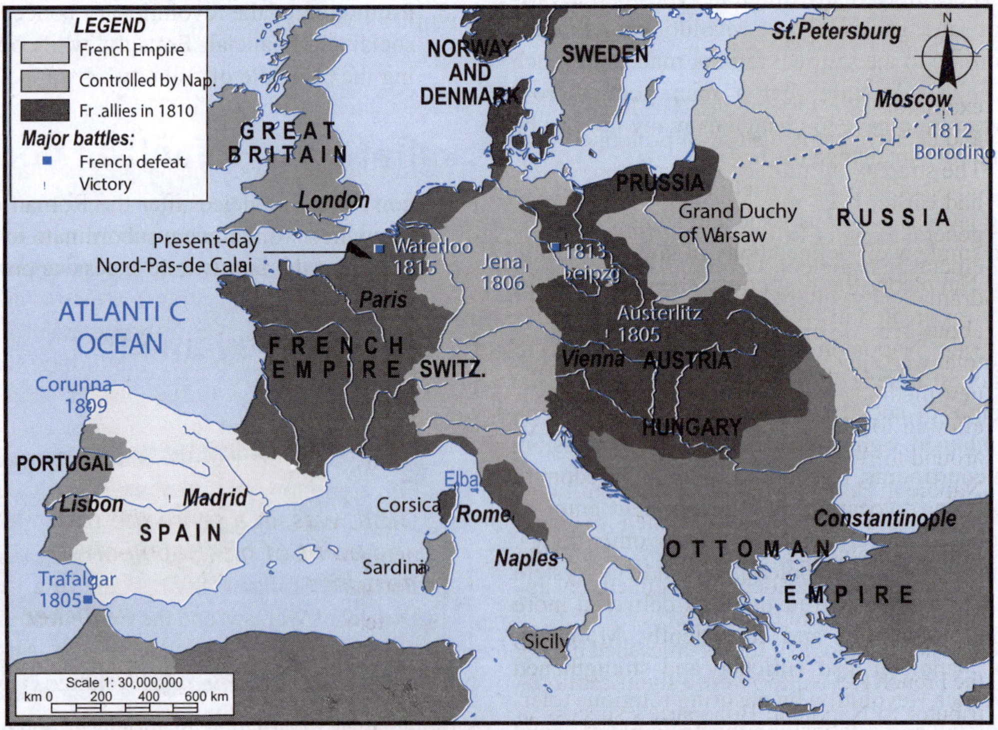

Map 2.1: Geographical Locations of Napoleon's Battles

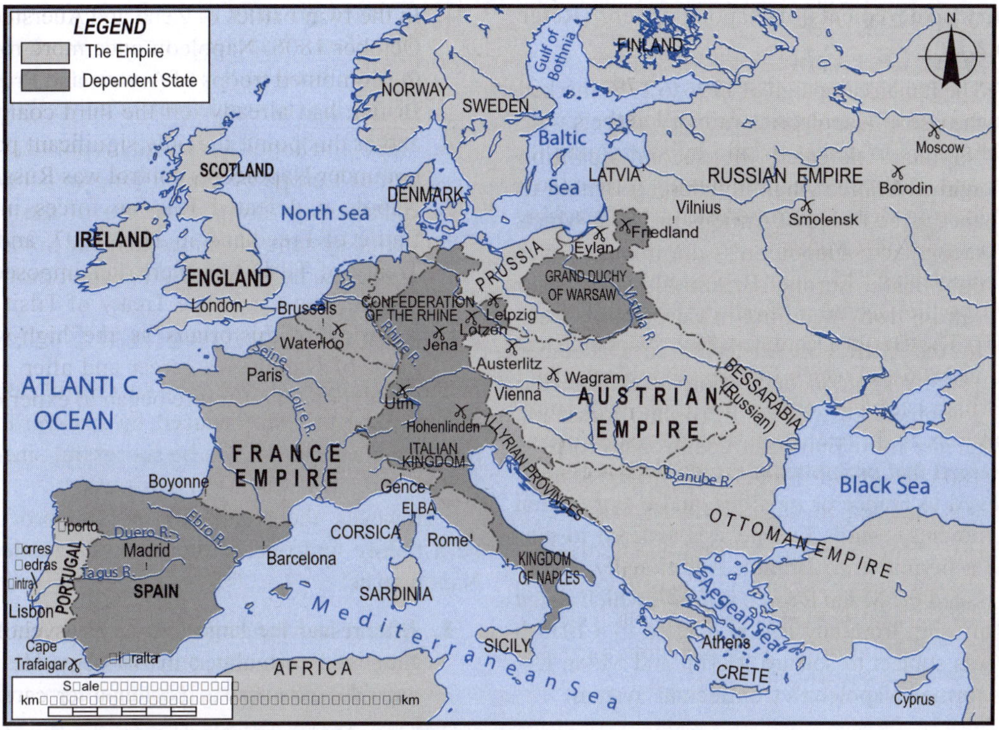

Map 2.2: Napoleon's Empire - 1812

examining the topography. He liked quick and decisive battle instead of prolonged war.

2. The strategy of military conscription, which had earlier been implemented by a military general named Carno, was one of the key elements in Napoleon's triumph. His approach dramatically altered how people thought about armies, and a new understanding of total war, and citizen's armies emerged. This new method greatly benefited Napoleon as it allowed for the vast army of France to have around thirteen lakh soldiers.
3. Napoleon Bonaparte was a brilliant military leader and officer. He obtained his new found knowledge of artillery from the French military academy and effectively applied it to the field of battle.
4. The new ideological forces unleashed during the French Revolution were a significant contributor to Napoleon Bonaparte's success in establishing his empire. The idea of the modern country first emerged during the French Revolution. It was the people's country, not the monarchies. Napoleon could have benefited from this contemporary nationalism concept, which would have allowed him to inspire the French people to construct an empire in a way that was truly unparalleled.
5. Napoleon was capable of building such a sizable empire in Europe that it served as an excellent model for the European Union. Apart from France, the primary region of his dominion was composed of Croatia, Dalmatia, Savoy, etc. At that point, the dependent states included Westphalia, Spain, Portugal, Holland, Switzerland, the Grand Dutchy of Warsaw, and the Confederation of the Rhine. Other than that, Prussia, Austria, and Russia developed close relations **(Refer Map 2.2)**.

CONTINENTAL SYSTEM OF NAPOLEON

Napoleon used a covert strategy called the Continental system to defeat Britain by sabotaging it's trade and commerce, strangulating of industry, and blocking British commodities from reaching the continent of Europe.

Napoleon's Continental System was established by the Decree of Berlin (1806) and Milan (1807). The Berlin Decrees, which Napoleon enacted in 1806 and which focused on a blockade of the British Isles and forbade any trade with continental Europe. In retaliation, Britain issued orders in Council that prohibited all trade with ports that belonged to France or its allies, and every neutral ship moving towards Europe was ordered to purchase a permit from Britain. Additionally, Napoleon issued the Milan Decree in 1807, which stated that any ship from any nation docked in a British port was subject to seizure. Berlin and Milan Decrees formed Napoleon's Continental System.

Reasons for Continental System by Napoleon

1. Disputes between Britain and France that have existed since the start of the French Revolution gave rise to the continental system. In addition, Britain participated in the first, second, and third coalitions, from which it eventually resigned, and fought continually against France from the outset.
2. By signing the Peace of Amiens, Britain pledged to acknowledge French domination in continental Europe, but when the third coalition developed in 1805, it joined. Napoleon sought to end the dominance of Britain across the continental system so that the Anglo-French rivalry might be resolved.
3. Napoleon's imperialistic aspirations gave rise to the continental system. He desired uncontested rule over all of Europe, but it was not possible until Britain was destroyed.
4. In 1805, Napoleon made an attempt to invade Britain, but Admiral Nelson of Great Britain defeated his navy at the Battle of Trafalgar. Therefore, Napoleon turned to economic warfare because it was now nearly impossible for him to invade Britain militarily.
5. Napoleon hoped to expand his political control of Europe by establishing an economic dictatorship through the use of the continental system. He aimed to make France the economic hub of the European economy.

Effects of Continental System

In the beginning, it was very successful because British exports were reduced by one-third. Napoleon's plan appeared to be successful since the British economy was in deep distress.

However, the continental system proved to be a failure and one of the greatest blunders of Napoleon as:

1. Britain had the largest naval navy and ruled the seas. In actuality, only British vessels were capable of transporting colonial commodities.
2. Despite facing significant disadvantages, trade and commerce in Britain continued as before because of Britain's colonies outside of Europe. Britain was a supplier of essential goods to continental Europe. However, the continental system destroyed trade in continental Europe, increased the cost of essential goods, and caused unhappiness among France's allies, who later adopted an aggressive policy that led to expensive wars with Napoleon and that became a significant factor in Napoleon's collapse.

Reasons for the Failure of Continental System

1. Britain supplied continental Europe with essential goods at lower costs, and the only way to receive colonial commodities was through British vessels. The Continental system increased the cost of essential goods and caused unhappiness among France's allies.
2. Britain had the largest naval fleet in the world therefore it was impossible for France

to control vast sea and European coast without a powerful fleet. In reality, the smuggling of goods became widespread throughout Europe, and Napoleon was powerless to stop it because of his weak navy.

3. The French industry could not fill the vacuum created by the prohibition from the entry of British goods. This system put the entire Europe against Napoleon.
4. Continental Europe experienced severe hardships as a result of a shortage of necessary goods and price increase. They started to reject the continental system, and Napoleon lost the support of the people. It had a cascading effect, making it challenging for some allies, like Russia, to continue with the continental system.
5. Napoleon was seen as the liberator and savior of the people prior to the introduction of the Continental system, but suddenly he was the cause of their suffering. His opponents, who are conventional monarchies, gained popularity when he lost the backing of the general population.
6. Napoleon used the policy of aggressiveness rather than diplomacy to enforce continental system, which resulted in expensive wars with Spain, Portugal, Russia, Austria, and subsequently a coalition of Europe led by Britain.

AGGRESSIVE WARS OF NAPOLEON

Spanish War, Peninsular War with Portugal the Moscow Expedition and also the war with coalition of Europe were some of the aggressive wars of Napoleon Bonaparte **(Refer Figure 2.11)**.

Spanish War

Napoleon wanted to rule over the Iberian Peninsula in order to successfully execute the Continental system. Napoleon requested that Portugal, an old

> “*It is the Spanish ulcer that ruined me.*
>
> ***—Napoleon Bonaparte***”

ally of England, restrict her ports to British trade because Portugal dominated the Iberian Peninsula, but the Portuguese responded diplomatically. Napoleon thus agreed to divide Portugal and its territories between France and Spain in a covert treaty that was made with Spain. Napoleon sent a French army and Spanish soldiers to seize Portugal. However, Napoleon's strategy against Portugal was a part of a bigger plan to conquer Spain along with the occupation of Portugal.

French army troops were sent to Spain with the intention of controlling Portugal, as a result, French army occupied some of the Spanish strongholds. Later, Charles IV of Spain and his son Ferdinand were involved in a succession dispute. Both were invited by Napoleon for meditation in Paris. Napoleon's goal was not to settle the succession conflict but to occupy Spain. Charles IV of Spain and his son Ferdinand were compelled to abdicate their claim.

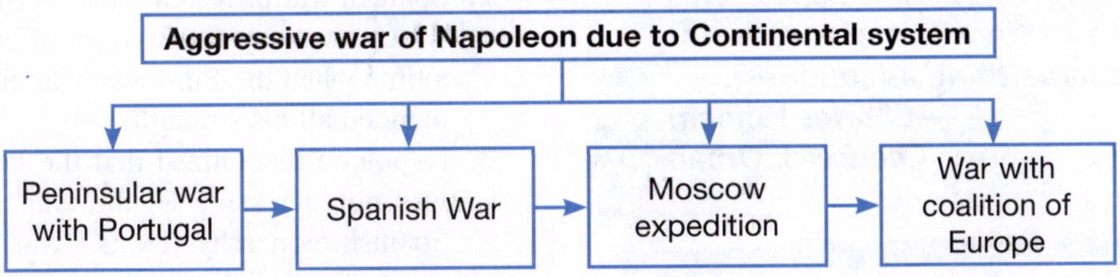

FIGURE 2.11: War of Napoleon to Enforce Continental System

Napoleon then made the catastrophic blunder of installing his brother Joseph on the Spanish Throne. This act of capturing the Spanish crown triggered widespread protests and revolts against the Napoleonic regime in Spain. People were mobilized by the nationalists. The Spanish rebels resorted to Guerrilla warfare and were supported by Britain which provided Spain with able commanders like John Moore, and Arthur Wellesley. Now Napoleon had to fight against not only the Spanish people but also national spirit since Spain had never accepted foreign rule, and this war subsequently turned into Napoleon's Spanish ulcer.

In the Spanish war, the unusual spectacle of a French army surrendering at Baylen in 1808 astounded all of the Europe. Although it was the Spanish nationalists' first triumph, the results were significant, profound, and far-reaching.

1. Napoleon's reign of invincible French army came to an end with the surrender of the French army.
2. Encouraged and inspired Spanish nationalists to continue their struggle, which subsequently turned into Napoleon's Spanish ulcer.
3. More significantly, it sparked nationalist movements in Central Europe.

Peninsular War

The Peninsular War begins with the landing of a British force led by Arthur Wellesley in Portugal.

> *Like so many other French generals in the Peninsula, he was soon to find that victory is not the same thing as conquest.*
>
> *—Charles William Chadwick Oman*

Causes of French Failure in Spain and Peninsular War

It is widely believed that the Peninsular War became the grave of the French military reputation. According to historians, a number of factors contributed to Napoleon's military loss in Spain and the Peninsular War. These were:

1. Napoleon launched so many theatres of war at the same time that he was unable to oversee every battle personally, resulting in a lack of cohesion and unity in the course of battle. Napoleon delegated most of the work to his generals and their animosity and rivalries kept them from working together at several crucial moments and frequently hampered coordinated action at key moments.
2. Napoleon's treachery sparked a sense of nationalism and national resistance. Napoleon underestimated the Spanish nation's struggle as a war against the monarchy. At this point, Napoleon's war was transformed into Spanish nationalist's war rather than a war against monarchy.
3. Napoleon's failure was also influenced by geographical factors and the physical characteristics of Spain. Spain was a mountainous country, making it difficult for the French army to supply and transport a sizable army. Additionally, it worked well for the Guerrilla warfare that nationalists favored.

Significance of the Spanish War

1. Napoleon's downfall began with the Spanish War. Additionally, Napoleon's need to maintain a sizable army in Spain which hindered his efforts elsewhere.
2. Spanish war proved to be a 'veritable ulcer' which ate away the strength of Napoleon at a time when the European war situation demanded all his strength.
3. Napoleon recognized that the People's war was not the same as the war against the Spanish monarchy. It was a war against the spirit of nationalism.

4. Nationalist movements, such as the one in Germany, rose as a result of the Spanish Nationalist War in territories that Napoleon had conquered.

Moscow Expedition

Although the Czar had signed the Treaty of Tilsit in 1807 to assist Napoleon's Continental government, the Continental system also resulted in Napoleon's Campaign against Russia.

Due to the history of Austria and Russia's rivalry, the Matrimonial alliance between Austria and Napoleon upset the Czar. Moreover, Russia suffered a severe financial loss as a result of the Continental system. As a result, in 1810, the Czar issued an edict amending allegiance to Continental System which completed the rupture between Napoleon and Czar. Napoleon followed the aggressive policy and decided to invade Russia with the largest army he had ever commanded.

Russian gradually retreated after adopting the strategy of avoiding battles and drawing the adversary deeper and deeper into a nation. Napoleon ultimately occupied Moscow after defeating the Russians at Bordino (1812). However, Russians abandoned the capital and set it on fire, forcing Napoleon to flee and causing hardships such as starvation and tiredness as well as a severe Russian winter and guerrilla attack.

Napoleon had originally anticipated that the Moscow campaign would be a short conflict, but when it turned out to be a drawn-out battle, he fled his troops and hastily returned to Paris. Napoleon's military might be destroyed by the disastrous Moscow campaign, which also inspired Central Europe to challenge his rule. The first to rise was Prussia.

Fourth Coalition against France

Britain, Russia, Prussia, and Austria formed the fourth coalition to fight France. Napoleon was defeated by the coalition at the Battle of Leipzig in 1813, and as a result, Napoleon's political order in the occupied territories disintegrated. Napoleon agreed to retire to the island of Elba under the Fontainebleau Treaty in 1814.

Napoleon's Escape from Elba and the Battle of Waterloo (1815)

Napoleon made his escape from Elba in February 1815 and landed close to Cannes. The locals welcomed him with open arms, and soldiers joined him. After learning of Napoleon's arrival in Paris, Louis XVIII left Paris. As soon as the coalition learned of Napoleon's escape, they put their differences aside and put a united front against Napoleon.

Napoleon's army was far smaller, so his only hope was to strike quickly and decisively. Napoleon was, nevertheless, trapped between two armies during the Battle of Waterloo. He escaped after losing the battle and made an attempt to reach America from Paris. Instead, he was sent into exile to St. Helena, where he passed away six years later, in 1821.

CAUSES OF NAPOLEON'S DOWNFALL

It is argued by some historians that internal contradictions caused Napoleon's empire to inevitably fall. They held that Napoleon found one of the most powerful empires in Europe, yet from its very inception, this empire had struggled with several fundamental contradictions **(Refer Figure 2.12).**

These internal contradictions were:

1. The fundamental inconsistency between the noble ideals of revolution and the realities of the Napoleonic Empire was the greatest contradiction. While the French Revolution proclaimed the lofty ideals of liberty, equality, and fraternity, Napoleon mercilessly pursued imperialistic policies elsewhere. Napoleon was initially hailed as a liberator by the people of Europe, but very quickly the imperialist nature of his authority was revealed in the light of the noble ideals of the revolution. Obviously, the people rebelled, and his hegemony over Europe was overthrown.
2. The French Empire was established via war, conquest, and dictatorship and was only maintained through force, not loyalty

or allegiance. However, only European submission out of fear was wholly dependent on Napoleon's strength. So, when Napoleon fell, his empire was destroyed.

3. Military conscription or the idea of the citizen's army was one of the key elements in France's military victory over Europe. France could surpass other European nations based on this premise. However, as a result of France's own inspiration, other European countries also adopted the military conscription approach, causing France to lose its advantage and allowing other European countries to outnumber its soldiers.
4. Napoleon dealt with each country in Europe on an individual basis. He had the foresight to avoid forming any European coalition so that European rulers would not have developed a common ground to build closeness with one another. However, as Napoleon deposed and humiliated the European monarchy, he unintentionally provided them with a platform for the growth of a sense of feelings. Therefore, European countries occasionally may form a coalition together to fight Napoleon Bonaparte.

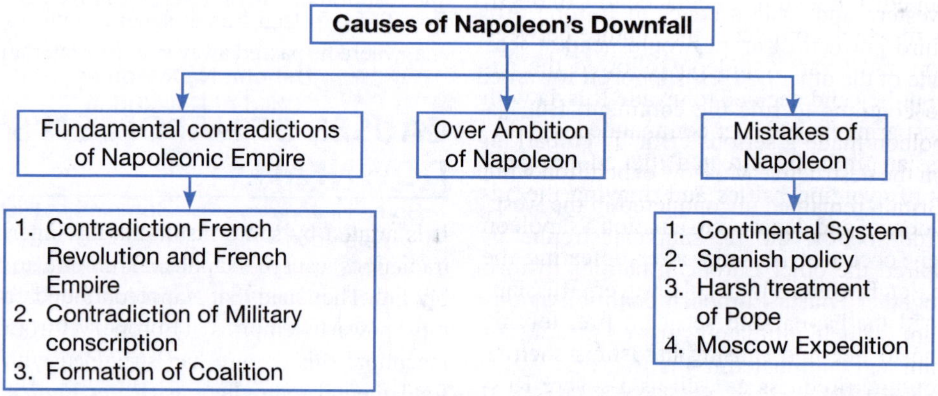

Figure 2.12: Causes of Napoleon's Downfall

Other Causes of Napoleon's Downfall

Some other reasons that led to the downfall of Napoleon Bonaparte included his overambitious nature, and several mistakes such as continental system, Spanish policy, etc.

Over Ambition of Napoleon

Napoleon's over-ambition was a major factor in his downfall. He was made emperor of France, but his true ambition was to rule all of Europe. It led to aggressive policy and numerous expensive wars, which rendered him incapable of judging what is realistic or not.

Mistakes of Napoleon

Napoleon's mistakes were a crucial factor in his downfall.

These were:

1. **Continental system:** Napoleon's Continental System, which sparked a series of wars, was his most catastrophic blunder. Napoleon's invasion of Portugal, treacherous seizure of the Spanish throne, dispute with the Pope, and conflict with the Tzar of Russia were all the results of his aggressive effort to impose the Continental System.
2. **Spanish policy:** The Napoleonic attempt to install his brother Joseph on the Spanish throne ignited national pride among the

Spanish people as well as in Prussia and Russia.

3. **Harsh treatment of Pope:** Napoleon's severe treatment of the Pope was another grave mistake. In order to enforce the continental system, Napoleon asked that Papal ports be closed to British ships, but the Pope responded by remaining neutral. Napoleon then detained the Pope and conquered his domains, which shocked Europe's Catholic population.
4. **Moscow expedition:** Napoleon Bonaparte made a big mistake with his Moscow expedition. A larger portion of his soldiers was lost on this expedition. In actuality, Britain and Russia were the two superpowers on the western and eastern edges of Europe. Any third power in Europe would need at least one of the other powers' support if it wanted to continue to rule the continent. But Napoleon made a serious error by embarking on the destructive Moscow expedition while Britain remained unconquered in the west. Additionally, the Russian catastrophe inspired the other European nations to form together Fourth European coalition against him, which ultimately proved deadly for him and culminated in the Battle of Waterloo in 1815.

Napoleon himself summed up the reasons for his demise in three words: Russian, Pope, and Spanish. To these must be added England's ongoing enmity and naval superiority, the Napoleonic empire's internal inconsistencies and contradiction, his excessive ambition, and his Continental system.

NAPOLEON AS A CHILD OF REVOLUTION

Napoleon adopted the principle of fraternity and 'equality' in social and financial affairs but rejected the principle of 'liberty,' which was one of the founding ideas of the French Revolution. By proclaiming 'I am the Revolution,' Napoleon referred to himself as a child of the revolution.

> "*The last of a series of benevolent despots, he was at the same time one of the first of great modern statesmen.*"

However, historians differ about whether or not, Napoleon was a child of the French Revolution. Napoleon Bonaparte is viewed by some historians as a child of the French Revolution, while other historians considers him as the product of the reaction against it **(Refer Figure 2.13).**

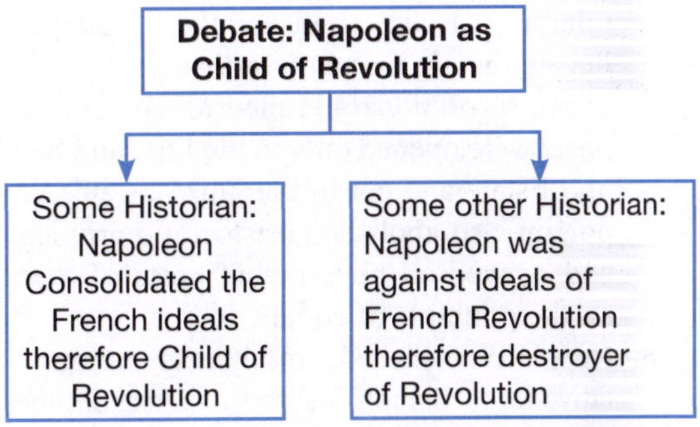

FIGURE 2.13: Debate of Napoleon as a Child of Revolution

Napoleon is termed as a child of revolution due to following factors:

1. The French Revolution opened the gate for the rise of talent and merit against pre-revolutionary birth-based privilege system. Napoleon Bonaparte's rise was made possible by the French Revolution itself; without revolution, a commoner like Napoleon would not have been able to advance to the position of military General of France.
2. By healing the Revolution's wounds, Napoleon brought peace and order back. By removing prohibitions against immigrants and harsh Jacobin regulations, Napoleon was able to regain the faith of the public.

3. Napoleon carried on the revolution's legacy even in the field of economics. Napoleon put a plan for the French national income survey into action and restored financial stability. Furthermore, he supported the notion of a trade exhibition show to advance business.
4. Napoleon was able to preserve certain revolutionary ideas in the religious sphere. He ended the excess of the Revolution (Reign of Terror) by signing the Concordat with the Pope, which healed division in the church and among people.
5. Napoleon was able to preserve certain revolutionary ideas in the social sphere as well. Feudalism was abolished and social equality was upheld under Napoleon's rule.
6. Napoleon's Code of 1804 was based on revolutionary ideals of equality and religious toleration. It also abolished the feudal privilege structure based on birth.
7. In pre-revolutionary France, all government posts were opened only to the First and Second Estate and not to the Third Estate. Napoleon also abolished aristocratic privilege and opened all government posts of merit on the principle of equality.
8. Napoleon positioned himself as the 'representative for revolution' and the 'architect of modern Europe' based on revolution's principles, therefore he welcomed and promoted revolutionary ideals even in conquered territory.
9. Napoleon Bonaparte's position was frequently justified by the revolution's objectives, even after Napoleon deviated from the revolution's predetermined trajectory.

NAPOLEON: NOT A CHILD OF THE REVOLUTION

Since Napoleon opposed several of the revolution's ideals, some historians view him as the revolution's destroyer rather than its child.

1. Napoleon undermined the republican ideals of the French Revolution by restoring the monarchy in a modified form in 1804 and even tying his legacy to earlier Bourbon kings (he referred to Louis XIV as 'mon-oncle' which means my uncle). He favored using his secret police to eliminate his opponents and carried out his work through a plebiscite while ignoring the legislative body which was against the ideals of democracy. Future dictators such as Hitler and Mussolini used this system frequently. Additionally, Napoleon reinstated a number of the unfair laws from the earlier Bourbon kings, including one that allowed for arrest even without a warrant.
2. Napoleon viewed liberty as a disruptive force that prohibited a state from functioning effectively. One of the principles of the revolution, the liberty of expression and the press, was curtailed by Napoleon. Even while he supported equality, for him equality means equal opportunity but not economic equality.
3. Napoleon preferred to separate the revolution from Rousseau's ideology and link it to Montesquieu and Locke in order to bring stability to France.
4. Napoleon removed the autonomy of local departments and imposed centralization via a prefect and a sub-prefect, all of whom were indirectly nominated by him. In this way, the principle of election, which was a revolutionary idea, was thus subordinated to the notion of selection.
5. Napoleon also opposed the ideals of nationality that were supported by the French Revolution. Napoleon not only restored the colonial empire that Louis XV had lost, but he was also fiercely anti-national towards other nations, particularly Germany and Spain.
6. The focus of the revolution had been on free trade, but Napoleon always followed mercantilist policy in the economic sphere; even his continental system was a reflection of the mercantilist policy. Napoleon always stressed mercantilist policy, and even his continental system followed the previous mercantilist policy, whereas the emphasis of the revolution had been on free commerce. Similarly, Napoleon placed greater emphasis on indirect tax than on direct tax, which had been ideals of the revolution.

7. Napoleon's Code was modeled after the Roman Code of Law, in which women were subordinate to men and the head of the family held excessive power.
8. Napoleon, especially outside of France, tended to represent the misguided and distorted ideas of the revolution.

Due to the centralized government, the curtailment of political freedom, the expansion of the Empire, opposition to the ideals of nationality, mercantilist continental policy, and the return to Louis XIV's methods, some historians view Napoleon Bonaparte as a 'destroyer of revolution rather than its child.'

Napoleon nevertheless encouraged the idea of equality by eliminating privileges and social barriers and by opening up jobs to merit. He established a centralized administration and was against the idea of liberty. Therefore, it was correctly remarked that historically Napoleon represented a period of transition. He was among the last of a series of benevolent despots, he was at the same time one of the first great modern statesmen.

Contribution of Napoleon Bonaparte to Europe

Though Napoleon got defeated in the Battle of Waterloo, he made a significant contribution to Europe.

1. Napoleon promoted the concept of nationalism and the ideals of the revolution. In fact, wherever Napoleon went, or his army went, they brought certain reforms. He abolished feudalism, put a check over the church, and introduced the so-called Napoleonic Code.
2. Due to the exploitative policy of Napoleon, some reaction set in against his policy and it took the form of nationalist resistance. In this way, he became an unconscious stimulator of nationalism in Europe.
3. In addition, he made some unique contributions to the cases of Germany and Italy. He reconstructed each of the regions geographically, becoming the harbinger of the future integration of Italy and Germany.

The Napoleonic Empire, it is said, proved ephemeral but his reforms were put on granite. Even after the fall of Napoleon Bonaparte, European reforms remained in place. It was because most of Napoleon Bonaparte's reforms served the interests of the middle class, and the 19th century was characterized by the rise of the middle class.

CONGRESS OF VIENNA, 1815

Under the direction of Austrian Chancellor Metternich, the fourth European alliance known as the 'great five' (Austria, France, Prussia, Russia, and Britain) against Napoleon created the Vienna Council. After Napoleon's downfall, Metternich was among the most powerful men in Europe. It began with the Fourth European Coalition's victory over Napoleon at the Battle of Leipzig. The Congress's initiatives were eventually encouraged following Napoleon's loss at the Battle of Waterloo in 1815.

Metternich

Metternich was at the centre of European politics as Austria's foreign minister beginning in 1809 and chancellor from 1821. He was forced to step down as a result of the 1848 revolution, which resulted in the destruction of the Vienna Congress and the political order it had established. He signed the Treaty of Fountainbleu and orchestrated Austria's inclusion in Napoleon's sixth coalition against France. The major goal of the Metternich system of international congresses was to achieve a balance of power in Europe.

Aims and Objectives of the Vienna Congress

1. The Vienna Congress was an assembly of leaders of the old regime. The Congress' primary objective was to eradicate modern concepts popularised by the French Revolution because they posed a danger to the established monarchical regime.
2. The Vienna Congress's organizers sought to reinstate the idea of royal absolutism-based semi-divine monarchy. They want to re-

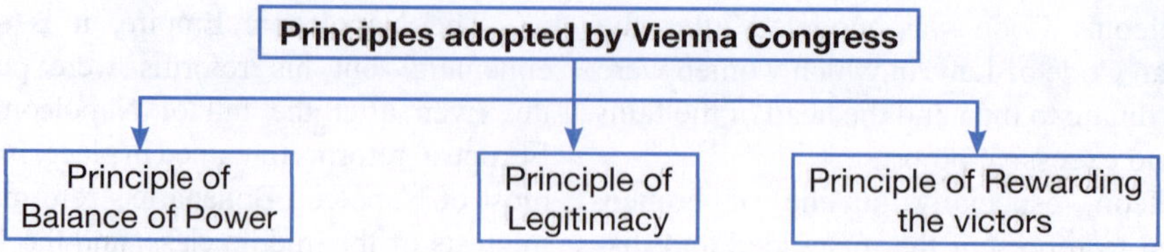

FIGURE 2.14: Principles Adopted by Vienna Congress

establish the old-style aristocratic system with its class privilege and other features of the old regime.

Principles Adopted by Vienna Congress

The Congress adopted three principles to restore the old regime **(Refer Figure 2.14).**

Principle of Balance of Power

Leaders of the Vienna Congress believed that the French Revolution's concepts had made France a major power and that this posed a threat to the stability and long-lasting peace of Europe. Therefore, the leaders decided to shrink France to its size in 1789 and surround it with a ring of powerful states in order to establish a balance of power. Under the policy of balance of power:

1. Prussia was given territories on the banks of the river Rhine.
2. Belgium was merged with Holland.
3. Austria was given to the Italian state of Piedmont and Sardinia.
4. Russia gained strength by retaining control over the Turkish territory it had taken.

Principle of Legitimacy

Congress of Vienna endorsed the principle of legitimacy. Under the principle of legitimacy, the traditional monarchy was restored which was earlier uprooted by Napoleon. These were:

1. Austrian dominance was re-established by restoring the Frankfurt parliament.
2. House of Savoy was reinstated in Piedmont and Sardinia.
3. The Bourbon dynasty was restored in France, Spain, Naples, Sicily.
4. House of Orange was re-established in Holland.
5. Netherlands was merged with the grand Dutchy.
6. Pope was restored as ruler of Central Italy.

Principle of Rewarding the Victors

1. Austria received the northern Italian provinces of Lombardy and Venetia. An Austrian prince's sovereignty was reinstated in the Italian provinces of Parma, Modena, and Tuscany.
2. Rhine Confederation's 39 states were unable to be restored to the original three hundred states. As a result, they came under Austrian control through the Frankfurt Parliament.
3. Norway was taken from Denmark and given to Sweden.
4. Finland was given from Sweden to Russia which also received Poland.
5. Swedish Pomerania was given to Prussia which also gained 60% of saxony and some parts of Poland.

Limitations of Vienna Congress

1. It had a reactionary outlook and was opposed to modern ideas of liberty, equality, and fraternity.
2. It was anti-democratic since it reinstated royal absolutism.
3. It opposed nationalism in general, but especially in Germany and Italy.
4. Territorial alliances were artificial for example- Austria and Holland.
5. It was the work of 'great five' (Austria, France, Prussia, Russia, and Britain) that seek to extract as much as possible from less developed countries.

LET'S REVISE

Causes of the French Revolution

1. Fundamental and Structural Causes
   - (a) Feudal Social Division
   - (b) Economic Causes
   - (c) Political Causes: Problem of Absolute Monarchy
   - (d) Ideological Factor
2. Immediate Causes
   - (a) Seven Years' War
   - (b) American War of Independence
   - (c) Financial Crisis

Objectives of the French Revolution

1. Equality, liberty, and fraternity
2. Constitutional monarchy in place of absolute monarchy
3. Popular sovereignty
4. Separation of powers
5. Recognition of the natural rights of man
6. Rule of law
7. Merit in jobs was recognized

Influence of the American Revolution on the French Revolution

1. Influence of American ideas
2. American Revolution caused France to go bankrupt
3. Role of American Revolutionaries
4. American Revolution as first successful experiment of enlightenments ideas

Limitations of influence of philosophers

1. Philosophers preferred transformation and not revolution
2. Only criticism and deglorification of monarchy and the Church

Reasons for Revolution in France and not in Other European Countries

1. Impoverish and poverty of the Bourbon Dynasty
2. Remains of Feudal privileges in France
3. Wealthier and highly educated middle class
4. Leadership by enlightened middle class

Course of the French Revolution

1. First Phase: (1789–92): Constitutional monarchy
2. Second Phase (1792–94): Radical Republicanism
3. Third Phase (1794–99): Moderate Republicanism
4. Fourth Phase (1799–1814): Dictatorship of Napoleon

Legacy of Napoleon

1. Reforms of Napoleon: Architect of Modern France and Modern Europe
2. Among Greatest Conquerors: Won 40 Battles

Reforms of Napoleon under Consulate (1799–1804)

1. Socio-Cultural Reforms
2. Economic Reforms
3. Educational Reforms
4. Politico-Administrative Reforms

Military Achievements of Napoleon

1. Italian campaign of 1796 to 1797
2. Napoleon defeated the second coalition in 1802
3. Battle of Austerlitz against combined Austrian and Prussian forces in 1805
4. Battles of Zena and Auerstedt in October 1806
5. Battle of Freedland in June 1807

Causes/factors behind the Imperialistic Success of Napoleon Bonaparte

1. Researching his adversary's psychology
2. Examination of the topography
3. Military conscription
4. Napoleon's personality and knowledge of artillery
5. New ideological forces

Reasons for Continental System by Napoleon

1. Long rivalry between Britain and the French
2. Britain did not honor the Peace of Amiens
3. Napoleon's imperialistic aspirations
4. Napoleon was defeated at the Battle of Trafalgar
5. Aspiration of economic dictatorship

Reasons for the Failure of Continental System

1. Britain supplier of essential goods
2. Britain had the largest naval fleet
3. French industry could not fill the vacuum
4. Continental Europe experienced severe hardships
5. People went against Napoleon
6. Series of War

Aggressive War of Napoleon Due to the Continental System

1. Peninsular war with Portugal
2. Spanish War
3. Moscow expedition
4. War with a Coalition of Europe

Causes of French Failure in Spain and Peninsular War

1. Many theatres of war at the same time
2. Napoleon's treachery sparked a sense of nationalism
3. Geographical factors and physical characteristics of Spain

Significance of the Spanish War

1. Beginning of Napoleon's downfall
2. Spanish ulcer
3. Rise of Nationalist movements

Causes of Napoleon's Downfall

1. Fundamental contradictions of the Napoleonic Empire
   - (a) Contradiction between French Revolution and French Empire
   - (b) Contradiction of Military conscription
   - (c) Formation of Coalition

2. Over Ambition of Napoleon
3. Mistakes of Napoleon
   (a) Continental System
   (b) Spanish policy
   (c) Harsh treatment of Pope
   (d) Moscow Expedition

Napoleon as a Child of Revolution

1. Some Historians: Napoleon Consolidated the French ideals, therefore, Child of the Revolution
   (a) Napoleon Bonaparte's rise
   (b) By healing the Revolution's wounds
   (c) Revolution's legacy in economics
   (d) Concordat with Pope
   (e) Feudalism was abolished
   (f) Napoleon Code of 1804
   (g) Open all government posts to merit
2. Some other Historians: Napoleon was against the ideals of French Revolution therefore the destroyer of revolution.
   (a) Restored monarchy
   (b) Plebiscite and secret police
   (c) Liberty as a disruptive force
   (d) Removed the autonomy of local departments
   (e) Opposed the ideals of nationality
   (f) Followed mercantilist policy

Contribution of Napoleon Bonaparte to Europe

1. Architect of Modern Europe
2. Promoted the concept of nationalism
3. Ideals of the Revolution
4. Unconscious stimulator to nationalism in Europe.

Principles Adopted by the Vienna Congress

1. Balance of power
2. Principle of legitimacy
3. Principle of rewarding the victors

UPSC PREVIOUS YEAR QUESTION

1. Explain how the foundations of the modern world were laid by the American and French Revolutions. **[2019] (15 marks)**

PROBABLE QUESTIONS

1. Privileged classes had rights but were free from obligations, while unprivileged classes had no rights but were saddled with galling obligations. Comment.
2. 'The causes of the French Revolution of 1789 included both long-term and structural factors, as well as more immediate events.' Critically examine.
3. Critically examine the statement that the French Revolution was not caused by the French philosophers but by the conditions of national life and by the mistakes of the government.
4. 'The multiple contradictions that quickly undermined the new edifice had been expressed even before the meeting of the Estate General in France. The internal conflict among Estates had manifested itself.' Critically examine.

5. 'If monarchical misrule ignited the French Revolution, lofty ideas both inspired and sustained it.' Comment.
6. 'The connection between the philosophers' ideas and the outbreak of the French Revolution (1789) is somewhat remote and indirect.' Critically evaluate.
7. 'To some extent, the American War of Independence inspired the French Revolution.' Comment.
8. Voltaire bad harnessed horses of reason, while Rousseau 'unchained the tiger of emotion'. Explain.
9. 'Napoleon showed himself at once the heir of the Revolution and the product of the reaction against it'. Comment.
10. 'The last of a series of benevolent despots, he was at the same time one of the first of great modern statesmen'. Explain the statement in light of Napoleon's reforms. Comment.

TIMELINE (1769–1815)

- **1769** — Napoleon Bonaparte is born on Corsica Island.
- **1778** — The French entered the war on the side of the American Revolutionaries.
- **July 14, 1789** — Storming of the Bastille, a prison in Paris, is seen as the start of the French Revolution.
- **Sep. 21, 1791** — The Declaration of the Rights of Man and Citizen is adopted, outlining the rights and freedoms of the French people.
- **Sep. 20, 1792** — The French monarchy is abolished, and France is declared a republic.
- **Jan. 21, 1793** — King Louis XVI is executed by guillotine.
- **Sep. 5, 1793** — The Reign of Terror begins, as the Committee of Public Safety cracks down on those seen as enemies of the Revolution.
- **July 27, 1794** — The Reign of Terror ends and Maximilien Robespierre, a key leader of the Revolution, is arrested and executed.
- **1795** — Napoleon leads the successful defense of the National Convention against an insurrection.
- **1796** — Napoleon leads the French army in Italy, successfully defeating the Austrians.
- **1797** — Napoleon signs the Treaty of Campo Formio, ending the War of the First Coalition.
- **Nov. 9,1799** — Napoleon Bonaparte seizes power in a coup, marking the end of the French Revolution and the start of the Napoleonic era.
- **1804** — Napoleon is crowned Emperor of France.
- **1805** — Napoleon wins the Battle of Austerlitz against a coalition of Austrian and Russian forces, becoming the most powerful man in Europe.
- **1812** — Napoleon invades Russia, but his Grand Army is defeated and forced to retreat due to the brutal winter.
- **1814** — Napoleon abdicates the throne and is exiled to the island of Elba.
- **1815** — Napoleon escapes from Elba and returns to France, but is defeated at the Battle of Waterloo.
- **1815** — Napoleon is exiled to the island of Saint Helena, where he dies in 1821.

CHAPTER

3

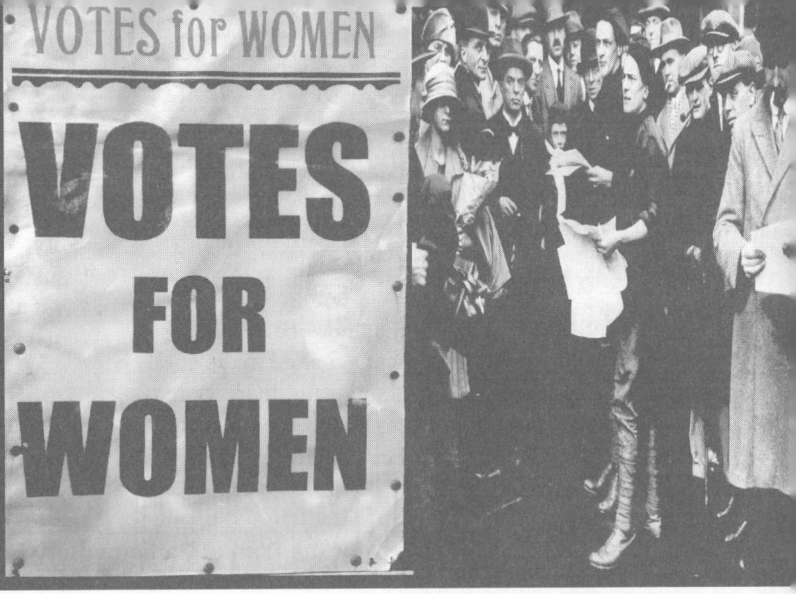

Photo Credit: jeff gynane / Shutterstock
Everett Historical / Shutterstock

BRITISH DEMOCRATIC POLITICS

> *During these years, the working people of England began to speak, and they began to act. They launched a movement for political reform, and they campaigned for better wages, working conditions, and rights for themselves and their families. They demanded a voice in the decisions that affected their lives, and they struggled to create a more democratic society.*
>
> ***—E.P. Thompson (British Historian)***

INTRODUCTION

British society underwent significant changes as a result of industrialization. As factories expanded, the nature of work was redefined and changed, resulting in the creation of new class dynamics and societal antagonisms. Workers were working for long hours at low wages in unhygienic conditions which led to serious public health crisis. Moreover, the crises in the countryside were engendered by agricultural depression and the Enclosure Movement. This led to the emergence of working-class consciousness in Britain by 1830.

REASONS/FACTORS FOR THE RISE OF PARLIAMENTARY REFORMS IN BRITAIN

Beginning of the early 19th century, British society endured a time of significant change in the societal and economic order. As a result, there were a variety of factors that necessitated the need for Parliamentary Reforms in Britain **(Refer Figure 3.1)**. These were:

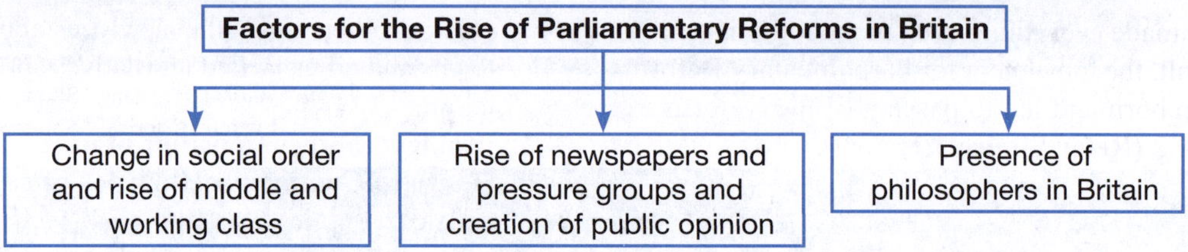

FIGURE 3.1: Factors for the Rise of Parliamentary Reforms in Britain

1. **Rise of newspapers and pressure groups and creation of public opinion:** The emergence of newspapers, various social organizations and pressure organizations had an impact on the formation of public opinion towards political reforms such as the expansion of voting rights, changes to election procedures, the abolition of Rotten Boroughs, etc.
2. **Presence of philosophers in Britain:** The liberal intellectual tradition in Britain contributed to the growth of philosophers who also favored political reforms. These were:
   (a) John Locke, who emphasized Parliament's shortcomings and promoted the Social Contract Theory, which promoted the natural rights to life, liberty, and property, also called for political improvements.
   (b) Charles Fox argued for political reforms such as the universal franchise and ballot voting in 1780.

   Later, the Society of Defence of the Bill of Rights and the Society for Constitutional Information were established in 1769 and 1780, respectively, to provide an organized framework for the British fight for political reforms and civic rights.
3. **Change in social order and rise of middle and working class:** The Industrial Revolution contributed to population growth and sustained economic prosperity throughout the 18th century. The old feudal order of clergy, feudal lords, and peasants were thus supplanted by a new socio-economic structure that was controlled by the middle and working classes. Therefore, they were opposed to Britain's unreformed political system and demanded political reforms.

REFORM ACT 1832

The Representation of People Act of 1832, often known as the First Reform Act, was a law passed by British Parliament that made significant reforms to the British parliamentary election process and electoral system. It was an outcome of changes brought by Industrial Revolution in the British socio-cultural, political, and economic sphere.

> "*It was not a good bill, but it was a great bill when it passed.*
> ***—John Bright***"

The passage of the Reform Act of 1832 marked the climax of a two-year era of intense political unrest brought on by a weakening of the British economy and poor harvest, which increased the cost of basic and essential goods, the unemployment rate, and the suffering of the working classes. The French Revolution of July

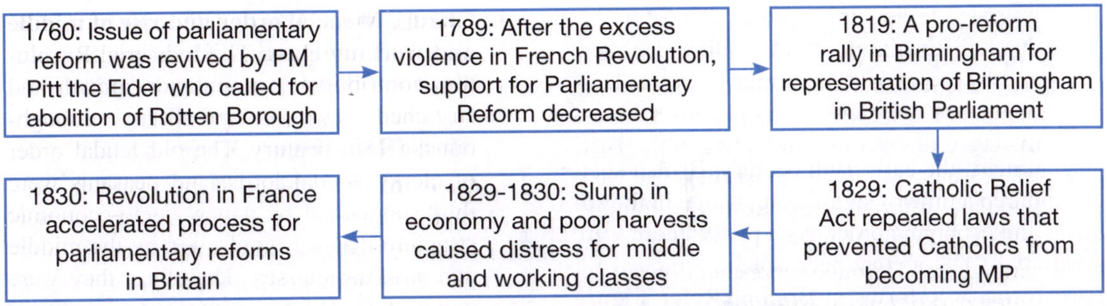

FIGURE 3.2: Background to Parliamentary Reforms in Britain

1830 made everything even more complicated. As a result, the movement for Parliamentary Reforms was reborn and led to passing of the Reform Act of 1832 **(Refer Figure 3.2).**

Reasons/Factors for Reform Act 1832

The Reform Act of 1832 was prompted by several factors and was made inevitable by several issues

> *"The Reform Act was a response to a perceived crisis of representation, in which the old system of parliamentary Boroughs had become corrupt, non-representative and ineffective in the face of social, economic and political change.*
>
> *—Eric J. Evans"*

with the contemporary British political system. These were:

1. **Consequences of the Industrial Revolution:** Industrial Revolution led to a significant influx of people from rural areas into industrial towns and cities. This led to depopulation among old constituencies which still enjoyed parliamentary representation. On the other hand, the newly established towns and cities lacked legislative representation.
2. **Problems and composition of unreformed House of Commons:** Two types of constituencies, counties, and Boroughs, were used to elect the 658 members to the unreformed British parliament. The county represented feudal lords and landowners, whereas Borough represented the mercantile and trading community **(Refer Figure 3.3).**

Points to Ponder

Boroughs

This term refers to a town or city that has its own elected representatives in parliament.

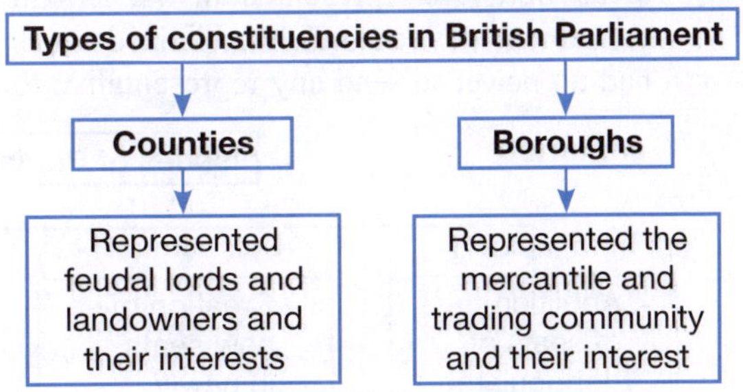

FIGURE 3.3: Types of Constituencies in British Parliament

At the time of the original enfranchisement, early Boroughs had sizable populations. However, these populations gradually migrated to new urban areas due to the Industrial Revolution and therefore declined, and by the early 19th century, several Boroughs had only few voters yet nevertheless managed to elect two members to the British Parliament. Such constituencies were popularly referred to as 'Rotten Boroughs,' as British Prime Minister 'Pitt the Elder' described such Borough representation as 'the rotten part of our Constitution.'

> **Points to Ponder**
>
> **Rotten Boroughs**
>
> These were electoral districts with very few voters, often controlled by wealthy landowners or aristocrats.

3. **Change in social order and rise of the middle and working class:** In place of the feudal society ruled by the clergy and landlords, Britain's rapid industrial growth contributed to urbanization and the rise of a new social order dominated by the middle and working classes. The emerging middle and working classes had very little political power as compared to feudal lords, therefore the change in social order did not mirror the change in the political order.

   Furthermore, certain depopulated rural areas were overrepresented in the British parliament while the newly urbanized towns had no power to send any representative to the parliament. Additionally, only the feudal class had voting rights. Therefore, the middle and working class demanded parliamentary change as a result of all these political issues **(Refer Figure 3.4).**

4. **Issue of franchise:** There were a very small number of voters due to the property qualification. Additionally, many middle-class industrialists and members of the working class were denied the right to vote; however, those who held property in various constituencies were permitted to cast multiple votes. The British parliament therefore only reflected the interests of the feudal class due to the drawbacks of the franchise system.

5. **Ills and issues of Electoral Corruption:** Political corruption was endemic in the British parliamentary system. Due to the absence of a secret ballot, landlords intimidated voters into supporting them, and in some Boroughs, voters were even bribed through money and other means.

Many constituencies with a small number of voters were indirectly under the control of feudal lords and were referred to as 'Pocket Boroughs'. This was because the members who represented them were merely puppets. They were expected to vote in the parliament in accordance with the wishes of their patrons or risk losing their seats in the subsequent election. Most patrons intimidated and influenced voters in favor of nominated candidates by using their local clout, prestige, and wealth.

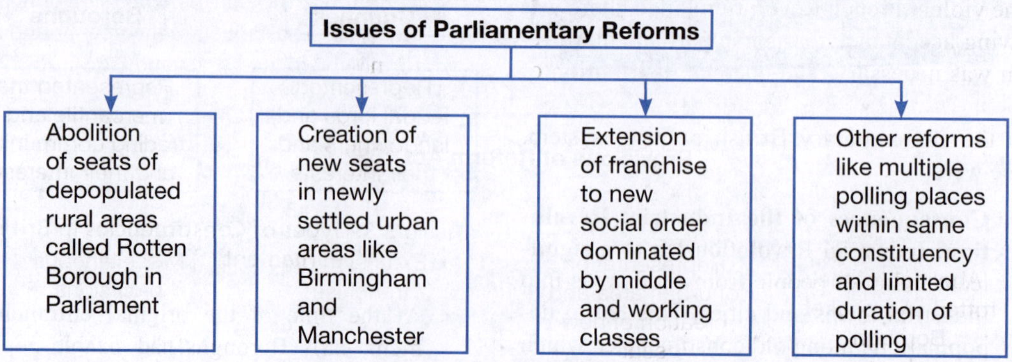

FIGURE 3.4: Issues of Parliamentary Reforms

Classes in Support of British Parliamentary Reforms

Many classes backed British parliamentary reforms for a particular reason. These were:

1. **Working and middle class:** The working and middle classes were excluded from the franchise, industrial town, and their interests were not adequately represented by the British parliament. Both classes, therefore, supported British parliamentary reform to improve social and economic conditions.
2. **Protestant class:** With 30% of the population, protestants were referred to as 'the life of the movement' for the Parliamentary Reform. They were not properly represented in parliament, deprived of civil rights, and subjected to taxes to fund the orthodox church. They backed parliamentary reform to improve their representation and get rid of the restrictions placed on them.
3. **Industrialists and businessmen:** Industrialists and businessmen preferred incremental parliamentary reform over a brutal uprising like the French Revolution, that resulted in a comprehensive political system change; for this reason, they too supported British parliamentary changes.

Provisions of Reform Act, 1832

As the 19th century progressed and the memory of the violent French Revolution faded, there was growing acceptance that some parliamentary reform was necessary. The unequal distribution of seats, the extension of the franchise, and 'Rotten Boroughs' were all the issues to be addressed. However, the Tory Prime Minister in 1830, Arthur Wellesley, First Duke of Wellington, was resolutely opposed to parliamentary reform. However, there was growing support for limited change within his party.

Points to Ponder

The Reform Act of 1832 extended franchise rights, abolished several 'Rotten Boroughs,' and provided seats to 'New Urbanized Town' in the British parliament.

The provisions were: **(Refer Figure 3.5)**

1. **Abolition of the Rotten and Pocket Borough:** The primary goal of the Parliamentary Reform Act was to abolish some of the Pocket and Rotten Boroughs that were ruled directly or indirectly by feudal lords. For the British parliament, 31 Boroughs with a population under 4000 could only send one representative instead of two, and 56 Boroughs with a population under 2000 lost the ability to send representatives. Thus 143 Borough seats were abolished in Britain by the Reform Act of 1832.
2. **Representation of urban area and creation of new seats:** Through the representation of newly urbanized towns and others, the Reform Act created 130 new seats for representation in the British Parliament. Therefore, the Parliamentary Boundaries Act of 1832 established the new boundaries for newly created seats and Boroughs.

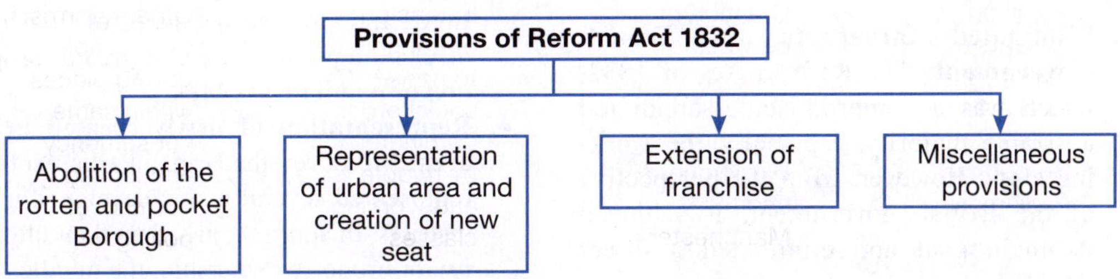

FIGURE 3.5: Provisions of Reform Act 1832

3. **Extension of Franchise:** The Reform Act broadened the franchise's property qualification in the counties, to include small landowners, tenant farmers, and shopkeepers. The Reform Act also established a standardized form of franchise in the Boroughs, granting the vote to all male householders who paid a yearly rental of £10 or more as well as some lodgers. Therefore, this was the first time that a standardized form of suffrage had been offered.

Points to Ponder

Approximately 400,000 English subjects were eligible to vote before the 1832 Reform Act was passed; after its enactment, that number rose to 650,000, an increase of more than 60%.

4. **Miscellaneous provisions**
   - **(a)** The Reform Act of 1832 authorized the use of several polling locations within the same constituency but limited the length of polling to two days instead of the previous 40 days.
   - **(b)** The Reform Act of 1832 established a voter registration system and a system of specialized courts to adjudicate cases involving voter qualifications.
   - **(c)** Members must reside in the Boroughs where they exercised their right to vote.

Consequences and Significance of Reform Act 1832

1. **Eliminated threat to the British Government:** The Reform Act of 1832, which was a compromise, disappointed a sizable majority, especially the working class. However, from the perspective of the British government, it achieved its main goal and eliminated a direct threat to national security, like the French Revolution in France.

> *"The Reform Act of 1832 was the first step towards the democratization of British politics, and marked the transition from an aristocratic oligarchy to a more broadly based system of representation, and set in motion a series of reforms which gradually extended political rights to more and more of the population.*
>
> ***—J.R. Green***
> ***(British Historian)"***

2. **Creation of a modern political system in Britain:** One of the most significant pieces of legislation in modern Britain's history, the Reform Act of 1832, played a key role in the country's transition to representative democracy and the creation of a modern political system in Britain. At the local level, voter registration lists were created for the first time. For the purpose of registering their supporters, political parties formed registration committees.
3. **Transferred sovereignty from the feudal class to the middle class:** It paved way for the entry of the middle class into British parliament. Additionally, it was the first effort to redefine the franchise right and redrew the political map. It was rightly referred to as the first parliamentary reform that effectively transferred sovereignty from the feudal class to the middle class because it reduced the influence of the House of Lords and elevated the status of the House of Commons, which had a greater proportion of middle-class MPs.
4. **Representation of newly created urban area:** Moreover, the British Parliament also represented several newly developed urban districts. In addition, based on their eligibility for property ownership, the middle class was given franchise rights.

5. **Opened a door to new reforms and political order in Britain:** The Reform Act of 1832 is rightly said to have 'opened a door to a new political world.' It was never going to be the final solution of a great constitutional question. It was the first in a string of events where the public protested for the expansion of voting rights and parliamentary reforms. Even though the Reform Act of 1832 extended the feudal class' hold on British Parliament by about 50 years, it paved the way for further parliamentary reforms in 1867, 1884, or 1918, which were crucial in establishing representative democracy in Britain. The Second Reform Act of 1867, gave adult male householders in an urban area the right to vote, resulting in working-class majorities in many urban constituencies. The Third Reform Act of 1884 marked the modest male franchise threshold in rural areas by granting miners and many agricultural laborers the right to vote. The Reforms Act of 1918 gave voting rights to all men with some women's franchise, while the Reforms Act of 1928 expanded complete female suffrage.

   In 1872, secret ballot voting replaced open voting because earlier feudal lords were able to intimidate people into voting for them. Furthermore, British parliamentary districts were divided into equal-sized ones from 1885 onwards. In addition, the feudal class' ability to cast several votes in several constituencies was abolished in 1948 when each voter was only allowed to vote once in a single constituency. Therefore, it is correctly stated by Eric Evans that the Reform Act of 1832 'opened a door to a new political world.'

Limitations and Criticism of Reform Act 1832

Although the Reform Act of 1832 brought about significant and far-reaching change, it still had several fundamental issues **(Refer Figure 3.6)**. These were:

> "*The Reform Act of 1832 was a step towards democracy, but it was a limited and cautious one. It extended the franchise to the middle classes, but it excluded the vast majority of the working population. It did not fundamentally alter the balance of power in British society, which remained firmly in the hands of the aristocracy and the landed gentry. In many ways, the Reform Act was a conservative measure, designed to defuse growing demands for radical change without fundamentally challenging the existing order.*
>
> ***—Asa Briggs***
> ***(British Historian)***"

1. **Unfranchised working class:** The property qualifications of £10 meant that the majority of working men still could not vote. This led to a breach in the working class's alliance with the middle class, which in turn gave rise to the Chartist Movement. Additionally,

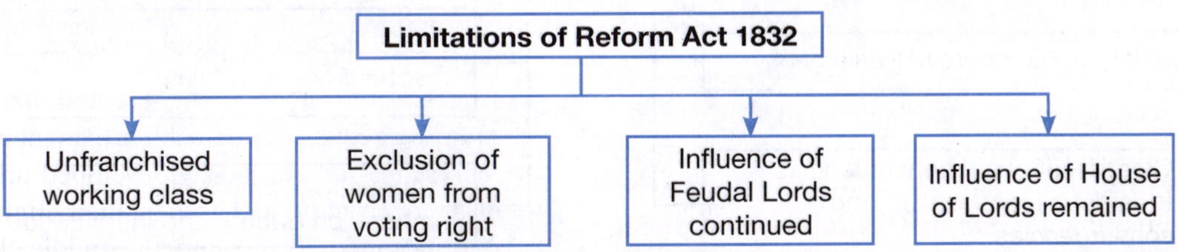

Figure 3.6: Limitations of Reform Act 1832

the number of voters went from approximately 400,000 to just 650,000, therefore the overall number of franchises was still quite low.

2. **Exclusion of women from voting right:** Since a voter was defined in the 1832 Reform Act to be a male individual, another change made by the Act was the explicit prohibition of women from voting in legislative elections. Instances of women voting existed before 1832, albeit rare and infrequently.
3. **Influence of Feudal Lords continued:** Voter bribery continued to be an important issue. Even though the Reform Act of 1832 eliminated the majority of Pocket Boroughs, tenants who paid a £50 annual rent were still granted the right to vote. Most tenants-at-will follow their landlords' instructions when casting their ballots. Additionally, even if the Act did disenfranchise Rotten Boroughs, a small number of them still existed.
4. **Influence of House of Lords remained:** By lowering the number of nomination Boroughs under feudal lord rule, the Reform Act strengthened the House of Commons. Nevertheless, the House of Lords and feudal lord's interests suffered very little from the Reform Act of 1832. The House of Lords maintained its power and even forced the House of Commons to approve a significant amendment to several bills. In contrast, the Second Reform Act of 1867 significantly reduced the legislative authority of the House of Lords.

CHARTIST MOVEMENT

Chartist Movement was first organized labor movement and a working-class movement in modern Britain between 1838 and 1848. Millions of working people signed petitions that were send to the British Parliament demanding political right for working class.

> *England was giving the world the first broad, truly mass, and politically clear-cut proletarian revolutionary movement.*
>
> ***—Vladimir Lenin***

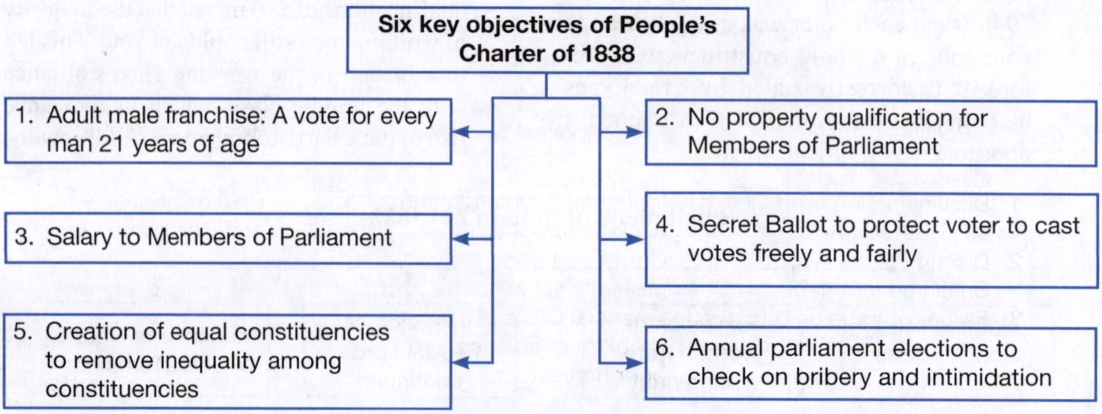

FIGURE 3.7: Six Key Objectives of People's Charter of 1838

Points to Ponder

People's Charter

This was a document created by the Chartists in 1838 that outlined their demands for political reform.

The Chartist Movement derived its name from the formal petition known as the People's Charter of 1838, drafted by Lovett with the help from Francis Place. It stated the six changes as its key objectives to make the British political system more representative and democratic **(Refer Figure 3.7).**

Although the People's Charter did not propose any novel ideas, it did provide a core doctrine for political system reform. Subsequently, support for the Charter spread rapidly and its proponent came to be known as the Chartists.

Causes of the Chartist Movement

> *The rise and fall of Chartism were a barometer of industrial and agricultural distress in England.*
>
> ***—David Thompson***

In contrast to the Reform Act of 1832, the aim of the Chartist Movement was to secure political rights mainly for working class. The Chartist Movement was primarily caused by political and economic causes, however social factors also played a part **(Refer Figure 3.8).**

Political Causes

1. **Dissatisfaction from the 1832 Reform Act:** The working class felt that parliamentary changes and political rights like the right to vote would solve all of their social and economic problems. However, the Reform Act of 1832 did not grant the working class the right to vote because the property requirement of £10 still prevented them from doing so. This led to the breach in the working class's alliance with the middle class as a result of the feeling of betrayal, which gave rise to the Chartist Movement.
2. **Several discriminatory acts of the British government:** British government's discriminatory and unpopular acts, such as the Factory Act of 1833 and new Poor Law in 1834, deprived the working class of a number of rights, sparked a major wave of protest in England and helped to catapult the Chartist Movement into the large-scale mass movement.

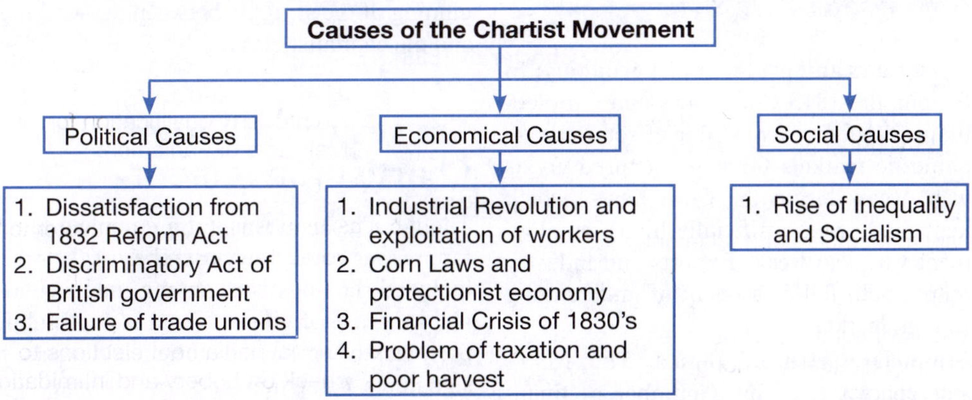

FIGURE 3.8: Causes of the Chartist Movement

3. **Failure of trade unions:** The Combination Acts of 1799 and 1800, which prohibited trade unions and strikes were abolished by legislation in 1825. As a result, trade unions were once more permitted, and numerous unions were formed after 1825, but none were successful in securing workers' interests or engaging in productive negotiations with employers.

Economic Causes

1. **Industrial Revolution and exploitation of worker:** Industrial Revolution led to migration of a large number of workers to industrial towns. However, working class were discontent due to the exploitation, poor working environment, long working hours, low wages, periodic unemployment and high prices of necessary goods. The working class started the Chartist Movement because they felt that political rights would resolve all of their social and economic issues.

> *Chartism was a knife and fork, a bread and cheese question.*
> ***—Joseph Stephens***

2. **Corn Laws and protectionist economy:** In Britain, the 1815 Corn Laws and a protectionist economy were still in effect. Because domestic markets for manufactured goods were weak due to the Corn Laws (which kept food prices artificially high), employment was also weak. Exports and industry output both fell as a result of undercutting foreign markets.
3. **Financial Crisis of 1830's:** The 1830's was characterised by a number of financial crises. Between 1830 until 1841, the Whigs held the reins of government and had a poor economic plan and left a huge deficit behind them. Moreover, about 63 English banks failed between 1836 and 1838. As a result of the lack of investment and the high cost of food, there was unemployment.
4. **Problem of taxation and poor harvest:** By 1941, fiscal, banking, and taxation reforms were also required. The working classes were mostly subject to indirect taxation which affected the poor more than rich. The tax burden accounted for at least 16% of actual wages. The circumstance was made worse by the repeal of income tax in 1816 which reduced the real value of wages. Additionally, several poor harvests worsened the situation.

Therefore, speaking in 1938 in favour of Chartist Movement, Joseph Stephens called Chartism a 'knife and fork, a bread and cheese question,' thereby highlighting the significance of economic factors in the inception of Chartist Movement.

Social Causes

The Industrial Revolution caused an increase in inequality, which caused ideas of socialism to spread quickly in Britain as the rich got richer and the poor get poorer. Thus, the social factor also caused the Chartist Movement and marked the beginning of the struggle between the working class and the capitalist class.

Causes of Failure of the Chartist Movement

Though Chartism was not a complete failure, its failure was caused by a number of factors which included factionalism among intellectuals and ideology, use of violence, and lack of public support, lack of able and experienced leaders, forged signatures campaign and revolutionary goal by constitutional means.

> *The Chartist Movement was ultimately unsuccessful because it failed to mobilize a broad enough base of support to challenge the existing power structures. It was too narrowly focused on political reform and did not address the wider social and economic issues that were affecting the working-class. The movement was also divided by internal factions and lacked effective leadership, making it vulnerable to repression by the authorities.*
>
> ***—Dorothy Thompson (British Historian)***

1. **Factionalism among intellectuals and Ideology:** The intellectual and ideological goals of Chartism were divided into various factions and ideology. The objective of the Chartist Movement ranged from the nationalization of land to currency reform, to the repeal of the poor Land Amendment Act, to social change. Chartism's demise was largely attributed to the factionalism-which led to the division of labor and resources. In fact, the Chartist Movement split in 1839 between those who supported constitutional tactics and those who insisted that an armed uprising was required for the revolution to succeed.
2. **Use of violence and lack of public support:** Due to violent protests and other socio-economic factors, middle-classes either ignored or rejected Chartism. Liberal British citizens found the demands of the Chartists to be too extreme and violent. Due to the use of violence and a lack of public support, the British Government was able to establish strict regulations and suppression of the Chartist Movement.
3. **Only political reforms included:** The Chartists misread the nature of anger since they only demanded political reforms and failed to address the economic and social issues that ordinary people faced.
4. **Lack of able and experienced leaders:** Factionalism and disagreements among leaders combined with the lack of experience and persuasive speakers who could convey the movement's goals to the general public contributed to the demise of Chartism.
5. **Forged signatures campaign:** Although dubious, the forged signatures Chartist employed in their signing campaign damaged their reputation, credibility and contributed to their disgrace and demise.
6. **Revolutionary goal by constitutional means:** The major issue facing the Chartist leader was whether to use constitutional means or through radical means to accomplish a revolutionary aim. Both methods failed to obtain support of middle class and parliamentary for Charter.

Significance of Chartism

Nevertheless, Chartism was not a complete failure, as most of the original Charter's six essential demands except the annual election was accepted by later parliamentary reforms.

> *By these channels [The Chartist Movement], a new and healthier wind blew through the community, a new national consciousness and social conscience about the ills of industrial England were begun....*
>
> ***—David Thompson***

1. The Chartist Movement had an effect on contemporary society. It was the first organized labor movement and it instilled a culture of cooperation and togetherness among the workforces.
2. Even though the movement declined by 1848, its aims were gradually implemented by subsequent reforms. Many of their demands were included in the Reform Acts of 1867 and 1884, such as franchise right to working class under the Act of 1867.
3. Infact, by 1918, all except the annual parliamentary elections of the Chartists' six demands had been met. These were:
   (a) Open voting was replaced by secret ballot by Ballot Act in 1872.
   (b) Property qualification for Members of Parliament Act 1858 repealed the requirement for a member to own property.
   (c) The Redistribution of Seats Act of 1885 created equal-sized constituencies.
   (d) The Parliament Act of 1911 created parliamentary salaries for MPs.
   (e) The Representation of the People Act of 1918 guaranteed the right to vote to all men over 21 and women over 30.
   (f) The Representation of the People Act of 1928 guaranteed the right to vote to all women over 21.
4. Women were given a political role by Chartism. Chartists were urged to act honorably and refrain from hitting their spouses. Chartists' spouses would only make purchases from store owners who supported their cause in the legislature.

LET'S REVISE

Reasons/Factors for the Rise of Parliamentary Reforms in Britain

1. Change in social order and rise of middle and working class.
2. Rise of newspapers and pressure groups and creation of public opinion.
3. Presence of philosophers in Britain.

Reasons/Factors for Reform Act 1832

1. Consequences of the Industrial Revolution.
2. Problems and composition of unreformed House of Commons.
3. Change in social order and rise of middle and working class.
4. Issue of Franchise
5. Ills and issues of Electoral Corruption.

Classes in Support of British Parliamentary Reform

1. Working and middle class
2. Protestant Class
3. Industrialists and businessmen

Provisions of Reform Act, 1832

1. Abolition of the 'Rotten and Pocket Borough'.
2. Representation of urban area and creation of new seats.
3. Extension of Franchises
4. Miscellaneous Provisions

Consequences and Significance of Reform Act, 1832

1. Eliminated threat to British Government.
2. Creation of a modern political system in Britain.
3. Transferred sovereignty from the feudal class to the middle class.
4. Representation of newly created urban area.
5. Opened a door to new reforms and political order in Britain.

Limitations and Criticism of Reform Act, 1832

1. Unfranchised working class
2. Exclusion of women from voting right
3. Influence of Feudal Lords continued
4. Influence of House of Lords remained

Six Key Objectives of People's Charter of 1838

1. Adult male franchise: A vote for every man 21 years of age.
2. No property qualification for Members of Parliament.
3. Salary to Members of Parliament
4. Secret Ballot to protect voter to cast votes freely and fairly.
5. Creation of equal constituencies to remove inequality among constituencies.
6. Annual parliament elections to check to bribery and intimidation.

Causes of the Chartist Movement

1. Political Causes
   - (a) Dissatisfaction from 1832 Reform Act .
   - (b) Discriminatory Act of British government.
   - (c) Failure of trade unions
2. Economical Causes
   - (a) Industrial Revolution and exploitation of worker.
   - (b) Corn Laws and protectionist economy.

(c) Financial Crisis of 1830s.
(d) Problem of Taxation and poor Harvest.

3. Social Causes
   (a) Rise of Inequality and Socialism.

Causes of Failure of the Chartist Movement

1. Factionalism among intellectual and Ideology.
2. Use of violence and lack of public support.
3. Only Political Reforms included
4. Lack of able and experienced leaders
5. Forged signatures campaign
6. Revolutionary goal by constitutional means

Significance of Chartism

1. Effect on contemporary society.
2. Chartist aims were gradually implemented by subsequent reforms.
3. Women were given a political role by Chartism.

PROBABLE QUESTIONS

1. The Chartist Movement failed to achieve its stated objective but succeeded in seeding the idea that a representative democracy should include all citizens. Comment.
2. The Reform Act of 1832 was criticized for a variety of reasons, yet it was nonetheless significant for what it was and what it started. Explain.
3. Though reform was inevitable, the Act (1832) by which it was accomplished was open to grave criticism. Comment.
4. The passage of the Reform Act' heralded the true start of modern party organization in England. Realistically speaking, England's current political structure dates to 1832. Comment.
5. The roots of Chartist Movement in Britain were partly political and partly economic. Comment.

TIMELINE (1215–1997)

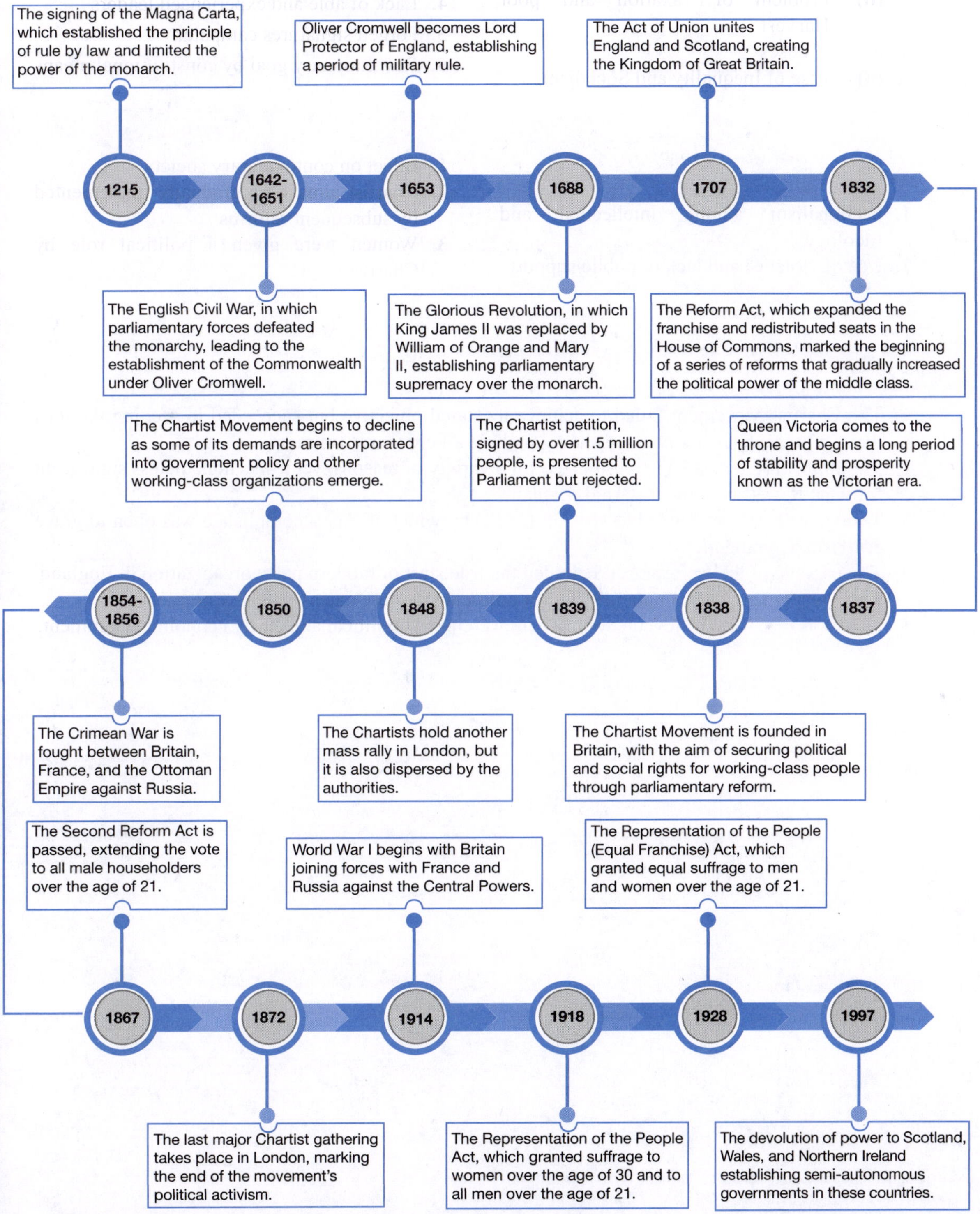

Europe's economy underwent a fundamental transformation [illegible] of the Commercial Revolution, that occurred between 1450 and 1750. These commercial revolutions increased European influence over other countries and helped the Europe to dominate rest of the world through trade and commerce. As a consequence, the governments' involvement in commercial enterprises was promoted in several European nations. This gave rise to the policy of Mercantilism, the economic policy that served as the economic equivalent of political absolutism (**Refer Figure 4.1**).

CHAPTER 4

Photo Credit: Ugis Riba / Shutterstock, Morphart Creation / Shutterstock

MERCANTILISM AND INDUSTRIAL REVOLUTION

> *Mercantilism is above all the economic system of the rising nation-state. It emerges when, and where, a single state is dominant enough to impose its own economic preoccupations on its neighbors.*
>
> ***—Fernand Braudel (Historian)***

INTRODUCTION

Europe's economy underwent a fundamental and revolutionary change as a result of the 'Commercial Revolution' that occurred between 1450 and 1750. The Commercial Revolution increased European influence on other countries and helped tie Europe to the rest of the world through trade and commerce. As a consequence, the government's involvement and intervention in commercial enterprises was promoted in several European nations. This gave rise to the policy of Mercantilism, the economic policy that served as the economic equivalent of political absolutism **(Refer Figure 4.1).**

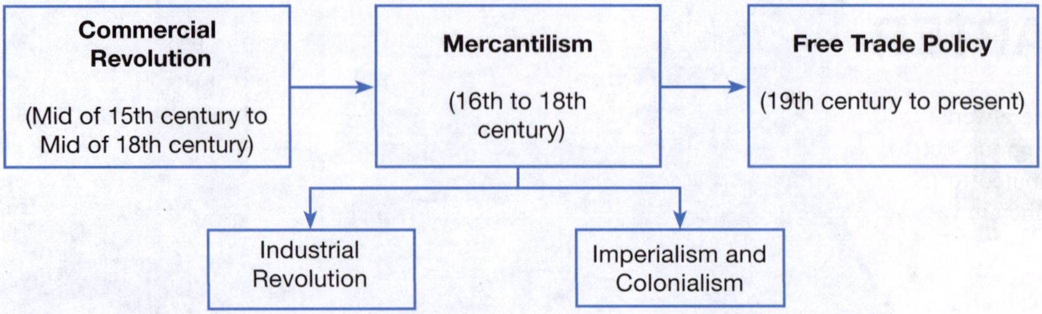

FIGURE 4.1: Chronology of Economic Policy in Europe

Points to Ponder

Mercantilism is an economic theory, based on the idea that a country's wealth and power depends on its ability to export more goods than it imports, thereby accumulating precious metals and maintaining a favorable balance of trade.

The Father of Economics, Adam Smith, used the term 'mercantilism' for the first time in his well-known book, *'Wealth of Nations.'* The term 'mercantilism' comes from the Latin word 'mercns,' which refers to the government's regulation and control over economic matters (particularly trade and industry), with the aim of enhancing state power at the expense of other national powers by accumulating financial reserves through a favourable trade balance.

The basic tenets of mercantilism included the notion that wealth in the world was relatively static; a nation's wealth could best be assessed by the number of precious metals or bullion it possessed; and the need to promote exports over imports in order to achieve a favourable trade balance. Thus, the Mercantile European state implemented numerous economic policies such as high tariffs and non-tariffs on manufactured goods, banning the export of gold and silver, forbidding colonies to trade with other nations, and support for exports to maintain favourable balance of trade **(Refer Figure 4.2).**

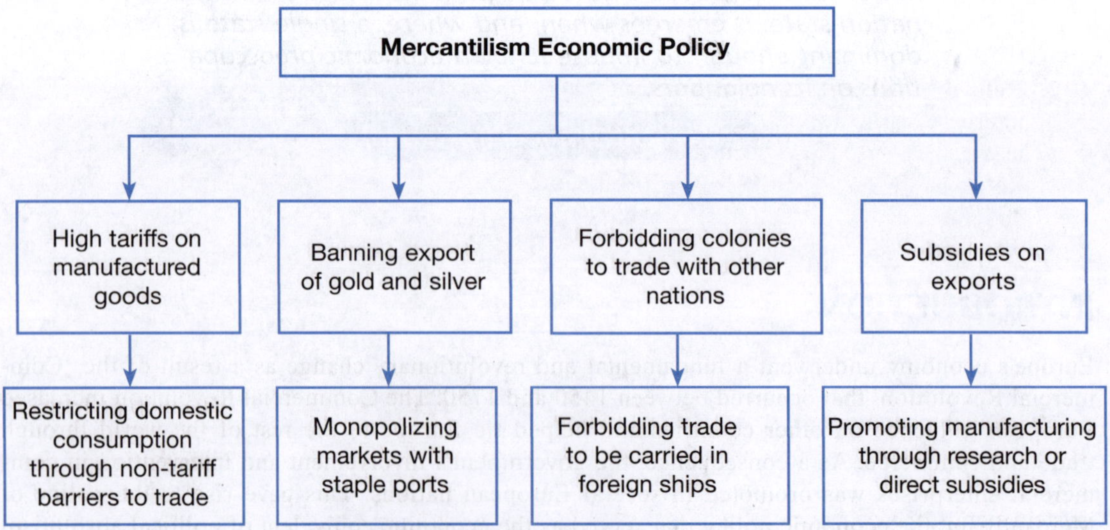

FIGURE 4.2: Mercantilism Economic Policy

CAUSES OF RISE OF MERCANTILISM

There were numerous factors, including political, religious, economic, and scientific ones, that contributed to the rise of the mercantilist economic policy in various European countries.

Political Causes

1. **Political patronage**: In order to lessen the influence of feudal lords, kings like Henry 'The Navigator' of Portugal and Queen Elizabeth of England encouraged traders to engage in commerce. Due to the political support, mercantilism was put on a firm foundation.
2. **Fall of feudalism**: Due to the collapse of agriculture brought about by the end of feudalism, factories developed. It produced export surpluses, which fuelled the emergence of mercantilism.

Religious Causes

1. **Renaissance**: The Renaissance promoted materialism as a means of achieving human happiness. As a result, everyone desired to live a happy and successful life, which gave rise to mercantilism.
2. **Reformation**: The churches' unnecessary intervention in the political and economic arena was condemned by the religious Reformation Movement led by Martin Luther and Henry VIII. Therefore, mercantilism was supported by the Reformation Movement, which pushed traders to carry out their businesses.

Economic Causes

By encouraging international trade and exporting excess to other countries, Guilds and the banking system significantly supported the growth of mercantilism.

Scientific Causes

Geographical and technological discoveries also promoted mercantilism. The development of mercantilism was aided by the sea voyages performed by Columbus, Vasco da Gama, and Magellan as well as scientific advancements like Galileo's telescope and the mariner's compass which greatly aided merchants in determining the direction inside the sea.

INDUSTRIAL REVOLUTION IN EUROPE

The term 'Industrial Revolution' refers to the changes brought in the mode of the production process from using hand tools to machine tools. The first country to experience the Industrial Revolution was Britain, where mechanized manufacturing began in the 1760s and continued to gather momentum with the passage of time. It then gradually spread to the rest of Europe and the US.

> "*The Industrial Revolution was the transformation in the methods of production and transformation through the general substitution of power-driven machinery for hand labour.*"
>
> ***—T.W. Ricker***

The shift in production processes included moving away from hand to machine mode of production, increasing the use of steam power, and switching from wood and other biofuels to coal. After 1840 the First Industrial Revolution transformed into the Second Industrial Revolution, which saw the innovation of transport (steam-powered railways, boats, and ships) and the use of technology in steam-powered enterprises **(Refer Figure 4.3).**

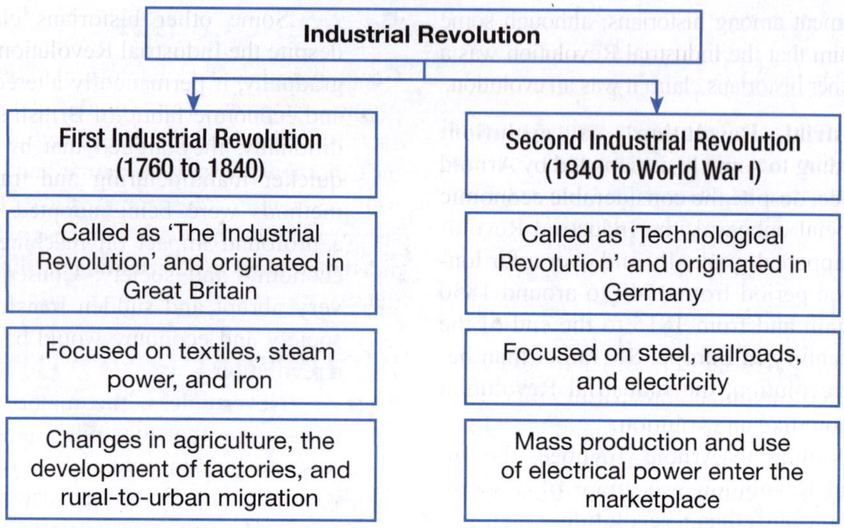

FIGURE 4.3: Difference between the First and Second Industrial Revolution

Features of the British Industrial Revolution

The characteristic features of the Industrial Revolution in Britain were are follows:

> *"The key to the Industrial Revolution was the creation of a new system of production that was more efficient than any that had come before. This was based on a combination of technological innovations and access to abundant and cheap energy sources. Together, these factors enabled British manufacturers to produce goods at a lower cost and a higher quality than their competitors, which in turn gave them a competitive advantage in the global marketplace.*
>
> ***—Robert Allen (Historian)"***

1. Gradual process of industrialization which took almost 150 years.
2. Role of the state was indirect as that of a facilitator.
3. Factory-based production on a mass scale.
4. Capitalist in nature because means of production were privately owned.
5. Exploitation of the working class.
6. Powered by innovation and dominated by market demands and forces.
7. Dominance of Laissez-faire principle.
8. Profit motive was dominant.
9. Initially textile based; later expanded to other goods.
10. Quality consciousness and prestige in products were high.

'Industrial Revolution' or 'Industrial Evolution'

According to Clive Trebilcock, the basic requirements of industrialization were new sources of power for production, increased organization in the manufacturing process, structural change within the economy, technical innovation, and investment.

Revolution means rapid and sudden change, as opposed to evolution, which suggests gradual changes that required a longer period of time. There is a disagreement among historians; although some historians claim that the Industrial Revolution was a revolution, other historians claim it was an evolution.

1. **'Industrial Revolution' as evolution:** According to some historians led by Arnold Toynbee, despite the considerable economic and social upheaval, the Industrial Revolution happened gradually and over a far longer time period from 1740 to around 1850 in Britain and from 1815 to the end of the 19th century in Europe. So, rather than being a revolution, the Industrial Revolution was more like an evolution.

   According to Arnold Toynbee, the Industrial Revolution was more of a socio-economic shift than a revolution.

2. **'Industrial Revolution' as revolution:** J.A. Blanqui, a French socialist thinker from the 19th century, coined the phrase 'Industrial Revolution,' claiming that the industrialization of the 18th and 19th centuries was undoubtedly revolutionary and signalled the beginning of a new civilization.

> *The Industrial Revolution was a true revolution in every sense of the word and transformed the way people lived and worked, the way societies were organized, and the way the world economy functioned. The Industrial Revolution marked the beginning of a new era, in which technological progress, economic growth, and social change would become the defining features of modern life.*
>
> ***—Jan de Vries (Historian)***

Some other historians claimed that despite the Industrial Revolution happening gradually, it permanently altered the social and economic fabric of British society. Additionally, they argued that by 1800, new quicker manufacturing and transportation methods were being adopted, which had a profound impact on machine efficiency, economy, and society. Consequently, this very abrupt and sudden transformation to society and economy would be considered a revolution.

Nevertheless, the majority of historians argue that the Industrial Revolution was revolutionary when it started and that it fundamentally altered social and economic structure, particularly in England. Nevertheless, as time passed, it became evolutionary.

Reason that England Witnessed the Industrial Revolution First

Britain was the first country to experience the Industrial Revolution and for more than half a century it was limited to it only. The mechanized production in Britain started in the 1760s and gained momentum over time as certain prerequisites for the Industrial Revolution were met **(Refer Figure 4.4).**

> *Whoever says Industrial Revolution, says cotton.*
>
> ***—Erik Hobson***

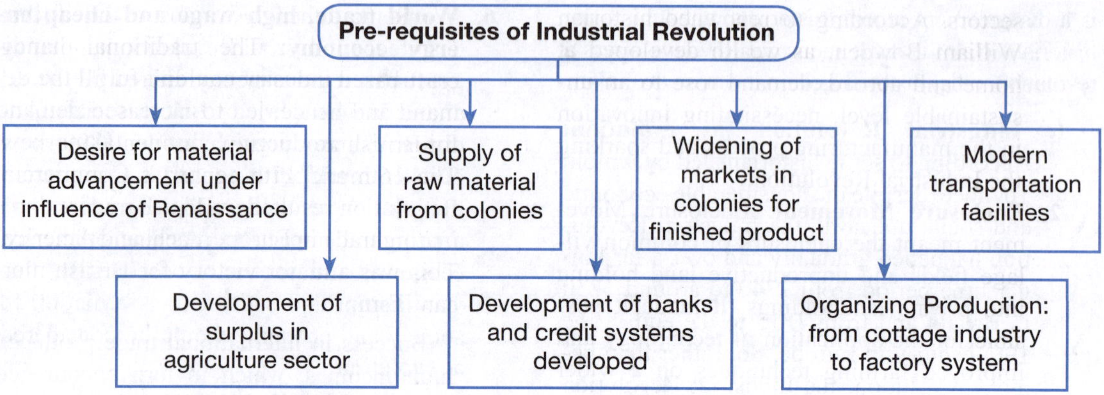

FIGURE 4.4: Pre-requisites of the Industrial Revolution

Reasons for Industrial Revolution in Britain and not in Other European Countries

> *Good roads, canals, and navigable rivers, by diminishing the expense of carriage, put the remote parts of the country more nearly upon a level with those in the neighbourhood of the town. They are upon that account the greatest of all improvements.*
>
> ***—Adam Smith***

Renowned historian Phyllis Deane in his book, '*The First Industrial Revolution*' mentions four factors for British industrialization. These were demographic, agricultural, commercial, and transport. Nevertheless, these factors could be divided into political, economic, cultural and geographical, factors.

Economic Factors

Renowned historian EJ Hobsbawm argued that industrialization in Britain was a result of the expansion of the local and export markets and increased government emphasis on industrialization.

Nevertheless, the Industrial Revolution was propelled in Britain due to a multitude of economic causes such as the agricultural revolution, the Enclosure Movement, better means of transport, availability of coal and iron mines, high wage and cheap energy economy.

1. **Agricultural Revolution**: Famous historians WJ Ashley and Robert Brenner highlighted the contribution of agricultural revolution to the British Industrial Revolution.

   Town industrial workers had access to surplus crops as a result of the agricultural revolution brought on by the increasing population, the use of advanced farm implements (narrow and better varieties of iron ploughshare), the management of insects, improved irrigation and farming techniques, the development of new crops, and the use of horsepower in fields to replace oxen as a source of power. Furthermore, it provided raw materials for the textile industry and other industries.

   Moreover, the agricultural surplus led to a rise in the accumulation of wealth which was further invested into other sectors such as industries, etc. Growth in wealth accumulation caused by agricultural excess was then invested in other businesses and sectors. According to renowned historian William Bowden, as wealth developed at home and abroad, demand rose to an unsustainable level, necessitating innovation in the manufacturing process and sparking the Industrial Revolution.

2. **Enclosure Movement**: Enclosure Movement meant the enclosure of common village fields and unproductive land holding into private landholdings. It made it possible for the application of technology and improved farming techniques on a wider scale and made a large number of peasants landless thereby forcing the migration of unemployed peasants into urban areas. Consequently, it provided both skilled and unskilled labour needed for the Industrial Revolution.
3. **Financial innovations and risk-taking private sector**: The Industrial Revolution occurred in Britain because of the presence of financial institutions including central banks, stock markets, and joint stock corporations. These institutions encouraged people to take chances with their investments, trade, and adoption of new technology.
4. **Better means of transport**: In Great Britain, modern means of transport like roads, navigable rivers, and canals reduced the cost of shipping raw materials and finished goods and interconnected far-flung regions.

   Further, inland navigation enabled progress of ship-building industries. These modes of communication were more advanced than the rest of Europe and Britain successfully industrialized without large-scale railway networks.

   Therefore, the first modern economist, Adam Smith, rightly argued that England's early Industrial Revolution was largely due to modern transportation.
5. **Availability of coal and iron mines**: Britain possessed the most abundant coal and iron reserves and the cheapest energy source in the world. It became vital to the growth of textile mills, locomotives, and other industries, driven by coal-fired machinery.
6. **World trade, high wage and cheap energy economy**: The traditional handicraft-based industry couldn't fulfill the demand and hence, led to increased demand for British products in continental markets. The 16th and 17th century's Commercial Revolution resulted in British traders dominating trade in Europe, Asia, and America. This was a major victory for British mercantilism.

   Success in international trade produced high incomes, which in turn encouraged higher education and a highly educated workforce, both of which contributed to the Industrial Revolution's many notable inventions like the steam engine **(Refer Figure 4.5)**.

Political Factors

1. **Stable political situation:** Liberal–progressive character of the British political system played an important role in the commencement of the Industrial Revolution.

   The Glorious Revolution of 1668 was a bloodless revolution in Britain that limited the king's power and changed Britain's political system from an absolute monarchy to a constitutional monarchy.

   After the Glorious Revolution of 1668, British society was more open to change and the governmental system was more stable than it was in other European nations fragmented political order, which later became the significant determinant of the Industrial Revolution.
2. **British government and policies**: The British government's policies promoted global trade by increasing the navy to safeguard trade, awarding monopolies or other financial incentives to firms so they would travel the world in search of resources.

   Moreover, the British government also encouraged innovation through the patent system which gave Britain an advantage over other European countries. These innovations were:

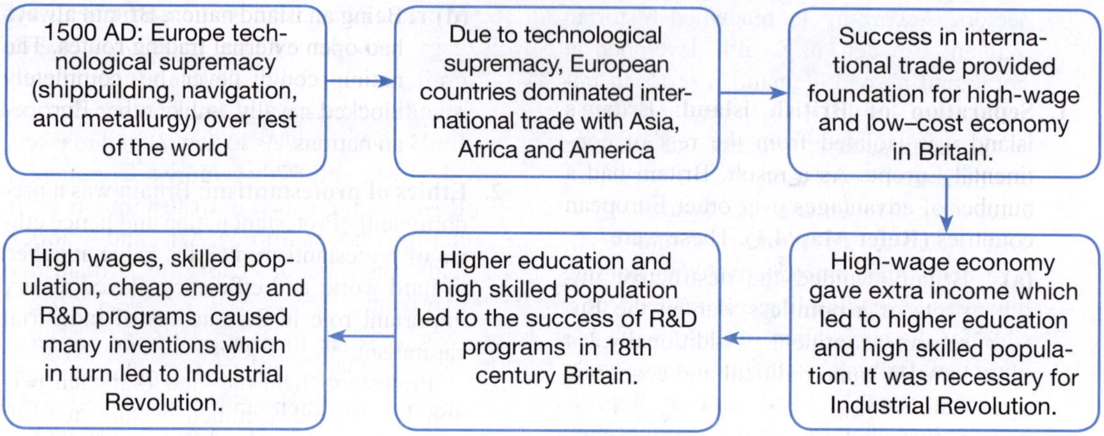

FIGURE 4.5: Consequences of High Wage and High Skilled Workers

- **(a)** Water frame in 1769
- **(b)** Boring mill in 1775
- **(c)** Seed drill in 1782
- **(d)** Printing machinery in 1783
- **(e)** John Kay Flying shuttle and weaving machine in 1733
- **(f)** James Hargreaves spinning jenny in 1764
- **(g)** James's Watt steam engine in 1769
- **(h)** Edward Cartwright power loom in 1785
- **(i)** Samuel Compton spinning mule in 1799

3. **Napoleonic wars**: The continental system of Napoleon was hostile to British trade and banned continental European trade for Britain. However, it encouraged Britain to innovate further and become independent.

   Additionally, Britain was the only country in Europe unaffected by the financial and economic catastrophe of the continental system. Therefore, it is rightly argued that 'Napoleon's career enabled Industrial Revolution to go forward in England and Industrial Revolution enabled England to overthrow Napoleon.'

4. **Imperialist policy and expansion of British empire**: Britain had an extensive colonial empire that provided it cheap raw materials, labour, and a monopolized market for finished goods. Expansion of the British empire stimulated the British economy as colonies provided raw materials as well as markets. Therefore, it is rightly argued that 'Britain's industrialization was at the cost of deindustrialization in colonies'.

Social Factors

1. **Population growth and British empire**: Britain's population grew vary rapidly from the 15th to 18th century. Moreover, Increased trade with British colonies like America and India caused Britain's population to rise further.

   Therefore, the demand for manufactured goods increased as a result of a rapidly growing population and colonial empire. Traditional handicraft-based industries were unable to meet this demand; necessitating mechanized production.

2. **High socio-cultural stability in Britain**: While social upheavals like the French Revolution were occurring in continental Europe for liberty, equality, and fraternity, there was high socio-cultural stability in Britain at the same time. It provided a stable environment for the growth of the economy.

   Moreover, British society was based on free thinking which encouraged research and innovation which in turn helped the evolution of the industrial revolution.

Geographical and Religious Factors

1. **Separation of British island**: Britain's island was isolated from the rest of continental Europe. As a result, Britain had a number of advantages over other European countries **(Refer Map 4.1).** These were:
   - (a) Britain avoided the destructive impacts of a pointless war on the European continent. Additionally, it brought some political and economic stability.
   - (b) British island separation and naval supremacy ensured the safety of Britain and no city in Britain witnessed any kind of destruction for the long time period until World War II.
   - (c) Since Britain had a long coastline, many ports were built to help with trade.
   - (d) Being an island nation, Britain always had open external trading routes. The nation could never be completely blocked navally, unlike other European nations.

2. **Ethics of protestantism**: Britain was a predominantly Protestant nation and hence ethics of protestantism, i.e., the value attached to hard work, and efficiency played a very important role in the success of industrial capitalism.

   Protestants held the view that each person has a predetermined destiny at birth that cannot be altered, but that a person's success in life indicates whether they are blessed or cursed. This is why every protestant worked hard to prove to others that he is blessed.

   Moreover, it encourages savings and capital accumulation. Thus, providing capital for investment.

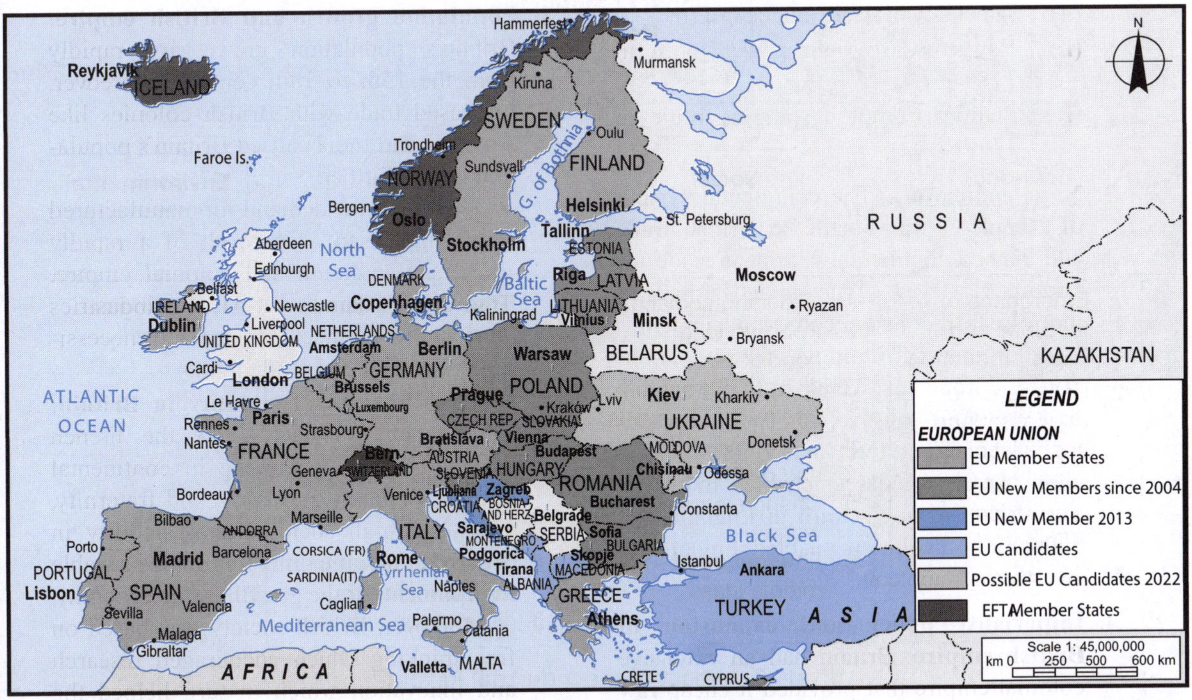

Map 4.1: Geographical Isolation of Britain

3. **Reformation**: Reformation was the term used to describe the 16th century religious reformation that resulted from corruption in the Western church. As a result, the English Protestant Church eventually split from the Roman Catholic Church. Additionally, land owned by the church was seized and a quarter of the nation's resources, which were formerly under its control, were put to productive use.

> *The Industrial Revolution transformed not only the way goods were produced, but also the way people lived and thought about the world. It created the conditions for the emergence of modern capitalism, modern industry, modern cities, modern politics, and modern culture. It also created new opportunities and laid the groundwork for the globalization of the economy and the spread of modern technology and ideas.*
>
> ***—Eric Hobsbawn (Historian)***

Impact of the Industrial Revolution

Industrial Revolution had significant and far-reaching economic, social, political, and environmental consequences. These were: **(Refer Figure 4.6)**

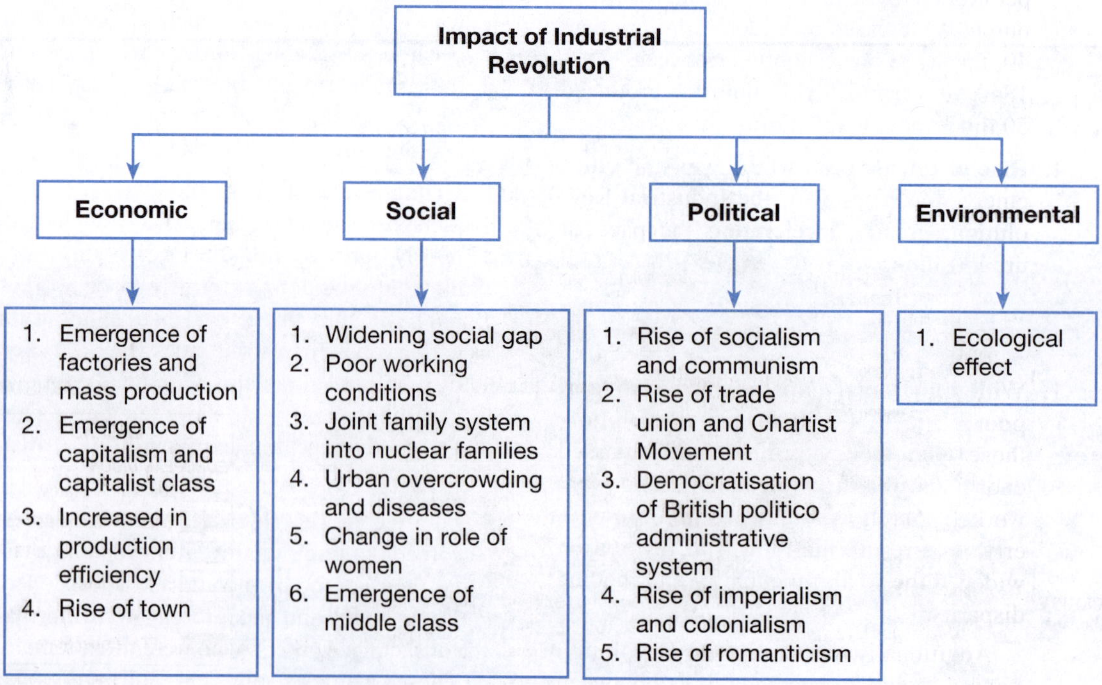

FIGURE 4.6: Impact of the Industrial Revolution

Impact on the Economy

1. **Emergence of factories and mass production**: Handicraft-based production gave way to factory-based mechanized production. This resulted in the emergence of factories, mass production, and industrial complexes across Britain. Moreover, Industrial products were much cheaper and better in quality than traditional handicraft-based products.
2. **Emergence of capitalism and capitalist class**: Industrial capitalism emerged as a result of the Industrial Revolution and British society got divided between capitalists and workers. Trade and commerce increased as a result of the availability of new products, wider markets, etc.
3. **Increased in production efficiency**: The use of machinery tripled a worker's productivity, which greatly enhanced production efficiency. Steam or water-powered machinery that spins cotton increases productivity per worker by a factor of 1,000. Workers' output is increased by a factor of more than 40, thanks to power looms. Between 1782-1840, the British textile industry produced 50 times more than before.
4. **Rise of towns**: Industrial towns and cities emerged as a result of the Industrial Revolution, greatly accelerating the pace of urbanization.

Impact on Society

1. **Widening social gap between rich and poor**: Due to the Industrial Revolution, those with money profited and amassed enormous wealth, while others who were workers merely continued to fall into poverty. As a result, the Industrial Revolution widened the wealth inequality and income disparity.

   Additionally, the Industrial Revolution caused society to become divided between the Proletariat and the Bourgeois which later led to the rise of socialism.
2. **Poor working conditions**: Feudal lords enclosed common village land as a result of the Enclosure Movement. People from villages moved to towns as a result. Because there were no regulations governing them in the early stages of the Industrial Revolution, it resulted in a high unemployment rate for workers and bad working conditions (from 1790 to 1840).

   In addition, the worker, who was in need of a job badly, lacked the ability to negotiate for better pay, more equitable working hours, or better working conditions with capitalists. Even worse, there was no democratic political system in place to advocate for rights and changes, as only wealthy people were allowed to vote.
3. **Joint family systems into nuclear families**: Large-scale migration of individuals from rural areas to industrial towns have a negative impact on the character and functioning of social institutions like the family. The traditional joint family system was transformed into nuclear families. It became challenging for these institutions of the families to function because most migrants were men, which resulted in tension and pressure within the family.
4. **Urban overcrowding and diseases**: Low diets, bad sanitation, and densely populated, poorly built working-class neighbourhoods all contributed to extremely poor worker public health. In the first half of the 19th century, new industrial cities were attacked by cholera, tuberculosis, typhus, typhoid, and influenza, which had a terrible impact on the average life expectancy of British people.
5. **Change in the role of women**: Factories forced out traditional weavers and eliminated their source of income and subsistence. Long hours and meagre pay were normal for factory workers, who were often female. These women's physical and emotional breakdown was brought on by hard workdays in factories combined with housework.

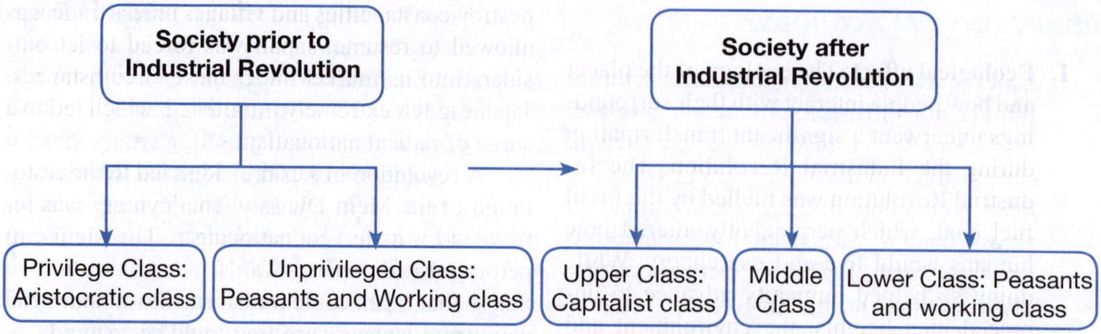

FIGURE 4.7: Emergence of Middle Class

6. **Emergence of middle class**: Towards the end of the 19th century, in particular, a middle class started to gradually emerge in industrial centres. Earlier aristocrats and low-income commoners had been the only two primary social classes up to the Industrial Revolution **(Refer Figure 4.7).**
7. **Rise of individualism and materialism:** Individualism and materialism gained popularity with the growth of industries.
8. **Reform in the education sector**: The British government progressively established a public school system at the same time that it began to control child labour in industry. The 1870 Education Act established school districts, and local boards had the authority to impose minimal fees and compel pupils to attend classes. The 1880 Education Act mandated that all children up to age 10 attend school.

Political Consequences

1. **Rise of socialism and communism**: Many intellectuals, such as Saint Simon and Louis Blanc, who felt greatly affected by the exploitation of the working class, advanced novel theories that led to the formation of socialism. When socialism failed to achieve much success, Karl Marx put forward his radical and scientific interpretation known as communism.
2. **Rise of trade union and Chartist Movement:** The Industrial Revolution caused society to become divided between the Proletariat and the Bourgeois. The Industrial Revolution and a critique of capitalism largely served as the catalyst for the rise of socialism, trade unions, and the Chartist Movement.
3. **Democratisation of the British politico administrative system**: People's political awakening grew as a result of the Industrial Revolution. Because of this, the political-administrative system was able to become more democratic. The British Parliament enacted the Reform Act of 1832, 1884, etc., which paved the way for the entry of the British middle class into the political system. Gradually, franchise was extended to working classes as well. The monopoly of feudal lords in political life was shattered.
4. **Rise of imperialism and colonialism**: The Industrial Revolution accelerated the colonization process because industrialized nations needed more raw materials and a larger market for finished products. The race for acquiring colonies intensified and resulted in a number of wars and battles.
5. **Rise of Romanticism**: An intellectual and artistic opposition to the new industrialization emerged during the Industrial Revolution and was called as Romantic Movement. In contrast to machines and factories, the movement emphasized the value of 'natural' in art and language.

Environmental Consequences

1. **Ecological effect**: The ecology of the planet and how people interact with their surroundings underwent a significant transformation during the Industrial Revolution. The Industrial Revolution was fuelled by the fossil fuel coal, which permanently altered how humans would live and use energy. While doing so helped humanity advance to unprecedented heights, the environment and ultimately the health of all living things suffered greatly as a result.

Industrialization in Japan

Between 1870 and 1980, modern industrialization began in Japan, the first nation in Asia. The policy of isolation was maintained until 1853 when

> *Japan was the first non-Western country to undergo industrialization, and the key to Japan's success was its ability to combine the benefits of Western technology and organization with its own traditional values and social structures. This allowed Japan to create a unique form of industrial capitalism that was both highly efficient and socially stable.*
>
> ***—Arthur Lewis (Historian)***

the Japanese government forbade the entry of European traders out of concern that it might come under colonial rule from Europe.

However, gunships under the leadership of American naval commander Matthew C. Perry arrived on the Japanese shore in 1853. He urged the government to let American and European traders inside its market. He threatened to bomb and destroy coastal cities and villages unless trade was allowed to resume. Japan was forced to let outsiders into its market under these circumstances. Japanese felt extremely humiliated, which led to a surge of radical nationalism.

A revolution in Japan in 1868 led to the restoration of the Meiji Dynasty. This dynasty was renowned for its fervent nationalism. The Meiji emperors pushed Japan towards industrialization so that so that Japan could transform into an industrial nation and Japanese prestige could be restored.

Features of Industrialization in Japan

Certain features of Japan's industrialization resembled and differed from those of Europe. These were:

1. **Similarity with West Industrialization**
   (a) Capitalist nature based on mass production.

> *The industrialization of Japan was characterized by a number of distinctive features, including a strong emphasis on state-led development, close cooperation between the government and private sector, and a focus on exporting manufactured goods to global markets. The Japanese government played a key role in promoting industrialization, providing financial and technical support to domestic firms and implementing policies aimed at protecting domestic industries from foreign competition.*
>
> ***—E. H. Norman (Historian)***

(b) Laissez-faire principal and profit emerged as dominant forces.

(c) Primacy to White goods.

2. **Dissimilarity with West Industrialization**

(a) **Role of State**: The role of the state was important as it provided the capital to entrepreneurs to set up factories. Since the Japanese rich class invested its capital in real estate and had no capital, so the state pushed for industrial growth.

(b) **Forced process**: When the Japanese markets were forced to open due to pressure, the local markets were swamped with foreign goods because there was no demand for Japanese goods in the global markets up until that point.

(c) **Fast pace of Industrialization**: Japan's industrialization progressed at an incredibly fast rate, reaching levels comparable to those attained by Europe in more than a century in just three decades. Japan had established itself as a great power at the start of the 20th century thanks to its win over Russia in 1905.

Points to Ponder

Japan was significantly more powerful than most of Europe by 1930.

(d) **Less emphasis on quality**: Initially, Japanese manufacturers lacked quality concern because their primary goal was to produce inexpensive products in large quantities so that domestic requirements could be met for less money, with the target market being common people.

(e) **Lack of Japanese invention**: Japanese invention played a minor role because they adopted a reverse engineering policy.

(f) **Less exploitation of the working class**: Because Japanese nationalism inspired people to work hard to gain national prestige, there was less working-class exploitation than in Europe.

LET'S REVISE

Mercantilism Economic Policy

1. High tariffs on manufactured goods.
2. Restricting domestic consumption through non-tariff barriers to trade.
3. Banning the export of gold and silver.
4. Monopolizing markets with staple ports.
5. Forbidding colonies to trade with other nations.
6. Forbidding trade to be carried in foreign ships.
7. Subsidies on exports.
8. Promoting manufacturing through research or direct subsidies.

Causes of the Rise of Mercantilism

1. Political Causes
    - (a) Political Patronage
    - (b) Fall of Feudalism
2. Religious Causes
    - (a) Renaissance
    - (b) Reformation
3. Economic Causes
4. Scientific Causes

Features of the British Industrial Revolution

1. Gradual process of industrialization which took almost 150 years.
2. Role of the state was indirect as that of a facilitator.
3. Factory-based production on a mass scale.
4. Capitalist in nature because means of production are privately owned.
5. Exploitation of the working class.
6. Powered by innovation and dominated by market demands and forces.
7. Dominance of Laissez-faire principle.
8. Profit motive was dominant.
9. Initially textile based later expanded to other goods.
10. Quality consciousness and prestige in products were high.

Reasons for Industrial Revolution in Britain and not in Other European Countries

1. Economic Factors
    - (a) Agricultural Revolution
    - (b) Enclosure Movement
    - (c) Financial Innovations and risk-taking private sector.
    - (d) Better means of transport
    - (e) Availability of coal and iron mines
    - (f) World trade, high wage and cheap energy economy.
2. Political Factors
    - (a) Stable political situation
    - (b) British government and policies
    - (c) Napoleonic wars
    - (d) Imperialist policy and expansion of the British empire.
3. Social Factors
    - (a) Population growth and British empire
    - (b) High socio-cultural stability in Britain
4. Geographical and Religious Factors
    - (a) Separation of British Island
    - (b) Ethics of protestantism
    - (c) Reformation

Impact of Industrial Revolution

1. Economic Impact
    - (a) Emergence of factories and mass production

(b) Emergence of capitalism and capitalist class
(c) Increased in production efficiency
(d) Rise of town

2. Social Impact
   (a) Widening social gap
   (b) Poor working conditions
   (c) Joint family system into nuclear families
   (d) Urban overcrowding and diseases
   (e) Change in the role of women

3. Political Impact
   (a) Rise of socialism and communism
   (b) Rise of the trade union and Chartist Movement
   (c) Democratisation of the British politico administrative system
   (d) Rise of imperialism and colonialism
   (e) Rise of romanticism

4. Environmental Consequences
   (a) Ecological effect

Features of Industrialization in Japan

1. Similarity with West Industrialization
   (a) Capitalist based on mass production
   (b) Laissez-faire principal
   (c) Profit emerged as the dominant forces
   (d) Primacy to white goods

2. Dissimilarity with West Industrialization
   (a) Role of state
   (b) Forced process
   (c) Fast pace of industrialization
   (d) Less emphasis on quality
   (e) Lack of Japanese invention
   (f) Less exploitation of the working class

UPSC PREVIOUS YEARS' QUESTIONS

1. Latecomer Industrial Revolution in Japan involved certain factors that were markedly different from what the west had experienced. Analyse. **[2013] (10 marks)**
2. Why did the Industrial Revolution first occur in England? Discuss the quality of life of the people during Industrialization. How does it compare with that in India at present? **[2015] (12.5 marks)**

PROBABLE QUESTIONS

1. With the introduction of assembly line factories, urbanization, and the emergence of the urban working class, the Industrial Revolution had significant social and political repercussions. Critically assess.
2. The Industrial Revolution brought about great changes in the social and economic life of Europe. Explain.
3. Why England became the harbinger of the Industrial Revolution? Explain. Also, throw light on its social consequences.

TIMELINE (1700–1890)

- **1700** – The invention of the flying shuttle by John Kay increased the speed of weaving by hand.
- **1712** – Thomas Newcomen patents the first practical steam engine.
- **1733** – James Kay invents the spinning frame, which mechanizes the spinning of yarn.
- **1760** – James Watt patents the modern steam engine.
- **1760s-1780** – The Industrial Revolution begins in Britain, characterized by the introduction of new machinery and technology in the textile industry.
- **1769** – James Hargreaves invents the spinning jenny, which allows for the production of multiple threads at once.
- **1784** – Edmund Cartwright invents the power loom, improving the efficiency of textile production.
- **1769-1843** – The steam engine is developed and improved by James Watt and others, leading to its widespread use in factories, mines, and transportation.
- **1793** – Henry Cort invents the puddling process for refining the iron, leading to an increase in iron production.
- **1800s** – The Industrial Revolution spreads to other industries, including coal mining, ceramics, and chemicals.
- **1806** – George Stephenson builds the first steam locomotive, revolutionizing transportation and leading to the development of the railway system.
- **1851** – The Great Exhibition is held in London's Crystal Palace, showcasing the achievements of British industry and technology.
- **1860-1870s** – The Second Industrial Revolution takes place, characterized by the introduction of new technologies such as the telegraph and telephone, as well as the growth of heavy industry.
- **1876** – Alexander Graham Bell patents the telephone, revolutionizing communication.
- **1870-1890s** – The steel industry experiences rapid growth, leading to the development of new construction techniques and the expansion of rail networks.

CHAPTER

5

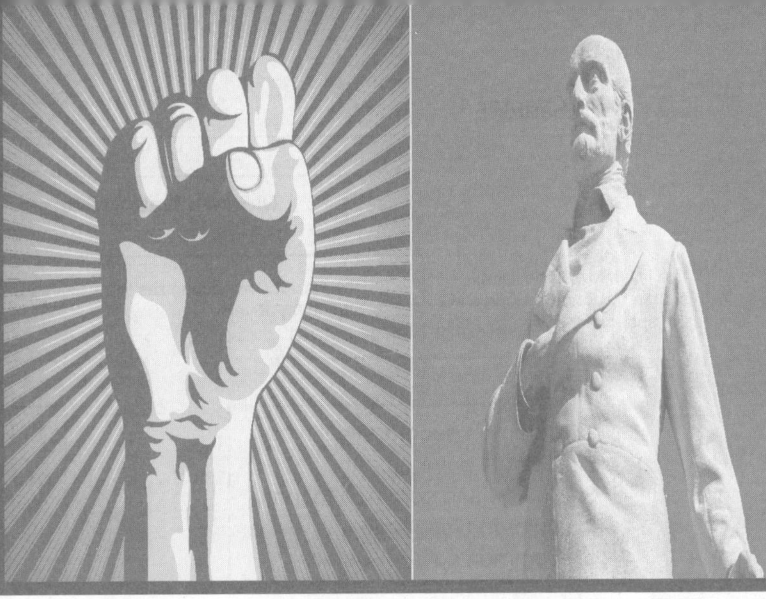

Photo Credit: Pixel Embargo / Shutterstock, milla74 / 123RF

RISE OF NATION STATES AND UNIFICATION OF ITALY

> *The Unification of Italy was an expression of the emerging nationalism that swept Europe in the 19th century. The movement for Italian Unification was driven by a sense of shared identity as well as by the influence of intellectuals and political activists who championed the cause of a united Italy. Ultimately, the Unification of Italy represented a triumph of nationalism over regionalism and paved the way for the creation of a modern Italian state.*
>
> ***—Eric Hobsbawm (Historian)***

INTRODUCTION

Nationalism became a powerful force in the 19th century and dramatically altered the political landscape of Europe. Instead of the multinational dynastic empires of Europe, it led to the creation of 'Nation-States.'

Although France, following the French Revolution (1787–99) is frequently mentioned by historians as the first nation-state, some historians believe that the English Commonwealth's founding in 1649 qualifies as the first instance of nation-state formation.

Nationalism not only changed Europe's political but also intellectual landscape drastically. These changes ultimately led to the demise of the multiple-nation dynastic empires of Europe and the rise of the nation-state.

The beginnings of the Concert of Europe, known as Vienna System after the Congress of Vienna (1814–15), was dominated by the five great powers of Europe: Austria, France, Prussia,

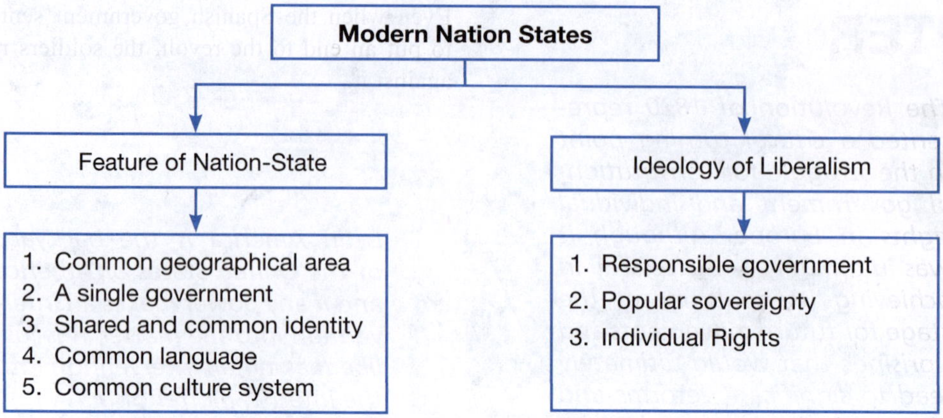

FIGURE 5.1: Rise of Nationalism and Unification of Italy and Germany

Russia, and the United Kingdom **(Refer Figure 5.1)**. The Congress of Vienna and Concert of Europe, which existed from 1815 to 1914, developed a set of principles, regulations, and procedures that assisted in maintaining the balance between the great powers after the Napoleonic wars, and prevented Europe from entering another major war.

Nevertheless, despite the best efforts of the Congress of Vienna and the Concert of Europe, the forces of modern ideas and nationalism as promoted by the French Revolution continued to represent a severe danger to the old order, and the old feudal system could not be maintained. As a result, there were several uprisings and revolutions across Europe between 1815 and 1848 **(Refer Figure 5.2)**.

THE REVOLT OF 1820'S

The Revolt of 1820 started in France when some revolutionaries, inspired by the romanticist approach, assassinated crown prince Duke De Berry. Later, this revolt spread from France to other regions of Europe. Consequently, uprisings also occurred in the Italian region, Spain, and Portugal.

Though the Concert of Europe succeeded in suppressing the Revolt of 1820, it also brought to light the Concert of Europe's incapacity to work together to uphold the *status quo*, particularly in Latin America and Greece.

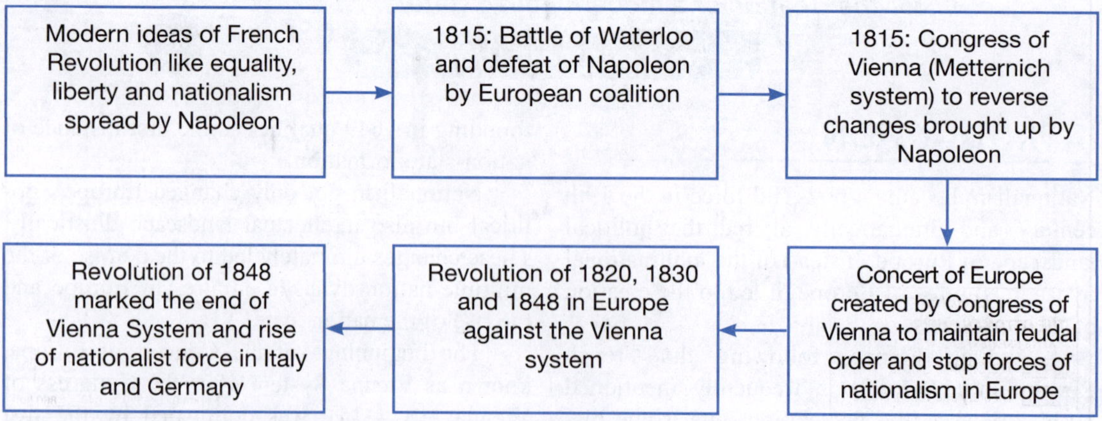

FIGURE 5.2: Chronology of Events from Napoleon's Defeat to the Revolution of 1848

> *The Revolution of 1820 represented a critical turning point in the struggle for constitutional government and individual rights in Europe. Although it was ultimately unsuccessful in achieving its goals, it set the stage for future movements and uprisings that would ultimately lead to significant reforms and changes in European society.*
>
> ***— Richard Evans (Historian)***

Failure of Concert of Europe in Latin America

Simon Bolivar led a revolt against Spain in the Spanish colony of Latin America during that time. Even when the Spanish government sent troops to put an end to the revolt, the soldiers rebelled against it.

> *Latin America is the backyard of the United States of America and if any power makes an intervention into the matter, it is just like making an intervention into the internal matter of U.S.A.*
>
> ***—Thomas Monroe***

However, members of Concert decided to intervene in the situation of Latin America and as a result, decided to send the army to Latin America to suppress the revolutionary movement. However, Britain rejected the proposal for the Concert of Europe. Although Britain wanted to keep Spain as an ally in post-Napoleonic Europe, it also wanted

Map 5.1: The Ottoman Empire

to put an end to Spanish colonialism in order to encourage more open trade and business in the Latin American continent.

Moreover, it was American President Thomas Munro who propounded his renowned 'Monroe Doctrine' where he argued 'American for Americans' and 'Latin America is the backyard of United States of America'. He, therefore, issued a dire consequence if European countries choose to interfere in American affairs in 1823.

Failure of Concert of Europe in Greece

The Greek uprising against the Ottoman Empire in 1821 was another significant development. Despite being a Muslim empire, the Ottoman Empire had a bigger Christian population in Eastern Europe. One of them was Greece.

According to the principle of legitimacy, the Concert of Europe might have supported the Ottoman Empire and put an end to the Greek rebellion against it. However, because Greece had a majority of the Christian population, Christians across Europe were sympathetic to Greece. As a result, even the Concert of Europe buckled under pressure and assisted Greece in achieving freedom. Hence, Greece got independence in 1832 **(Refer Map 5.1).**

REVOLUTION OF 1830

Similar to the 1820 revolt, a revolution against King Charles X started in France in 1830, which was successful in ousting both him and his ministers from office. It was replaced by a new French government under Louis Philip. Due to Charles X's government being recognized by the Concert of Europe under the principle of legitimacy, this change of government in France caused a rift among the members of Concert of Europe.

> *What did happen to Europe, whenever France sneezes, the whole of Europe catches cough.*
>
> ***—Austrian Chancellor Metternich***

Like 1820 revolt, the revolution of 1830 expanded to other parts of Europe from France. However, the impact of the revolution was felt more widely in western Europe than in eastern Europe.

1. **Revolution in Britain**: The introduction of a parliament reforms bill in 1832, which gave middle-class people the franchise right and gave representation for urban areas in the British parliament, prevented a revolution in Britain.
2. **Revolution in Belgium:** A revolution against Holland in Belgium eventually resulted in Belgium's independence and triggered a rift in the Concert of Europe.
3. **Revolution of 1830 in Italy**: A revolution in favour of unification in Italy began in 1830 under Mazzini, but it was later suppressed by the Concert of Europe, led by Metternich.
4. **Revolution of 1830 in Germany:** Similar to Italian unification, the German unification movement advanced in 1830, forcing the rulers of all German states (except states under Austria and Prussia), to adopt liberal constitutions. However, the Concert of Europe, led by Metternich, and with the help of Carlsbad Decrees ultimately suppressed it.

REVOLUTION OF 1848

Due to the effects of the Industrial Revolution, Europe underwent a period of profound transformation between 1830 and 1848. Middle-class position was bolstered by the Industrial Revolution and gave rise to an industrial working class **(Refer Figure 5.3).**

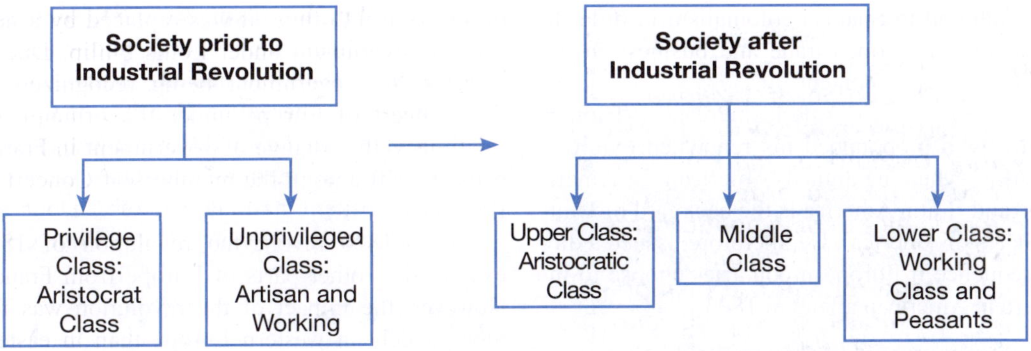

FIGURE 5.3: Emergence of Middle Class

> *The Revolution of 1848 was a defining moment in the history of Europe, marking the end of the old order and the emergence of new political, social, and cultural trends. Although the revolution failed to achieve all of its goals, it set the stage for the rise of modern democracy.*
>
> ***— Eric Hobsbawm***

As a result of the changes in the socio-economic composition, brought about by the Industrial Revolution, the revolution of 1848 began in France by Monarchists, Republicans, and Bonapartists against the administration of Louis Phillip, who had, surprisingly risen to power after the Revolution of 1830.

Charles Louis Napoléon (popularly known as Napoleon III) became the president of the French Republic in 1848 as a result of a decline of the government of Louis Phillip. Thus, four years later, history was repeated, as he like his uncle Napoleon Bonaparte, overthrew the republic and proclaimed himself emperor of France.

Despite starting in France, the revolution eventually expanded to other parts of Europe. The peaceful Chartist Movement began in Britain in 1848 as a result of widespread discontent of the working-class.

Revolution of 1848 in Central and Eastern Europe

1. **Revolution in Italy**: During the revolution of 1848, King Charles Albert of Piedmont started an initiative to unite Italy against Austria. However, Austria defeated him, which resulted in a significant setback for the unification of Italy.
2. **Revolution in Germany:** Similar to Italian unification initiatives, the liberals in the Frankfurt parliament attempted to unite Germany but were unsuccessful. The later Austrian victory over Frederick William IV was a significant severe blow and setback for the cause of German unification.
3. **Revolution in Austria:** People protested for constitutional rights even in Austria. Metternich, the Austrian chancellor fled to Britain for safety. As a result, the Austrian king yielded to pressure and approved a liberal constitution. However, the Russian army eventually arrived and backed the Austrian government, so the Austrian government suppressed the revolution and withdrew the liberal constitution.

Assessment of the Revolution of 1848

Although the 1848 revolution was suppressed, it wasn't a total failure because it set the groundwork for future change. The 1848 revolution was seen as an important turning point for future Europe and for the development of the ideology of nationalism and socialism.

> *"The Revolution of 1848 was a watershed moment in the history of Europe, marking the end of the old order and the emergence of new political and social forces. The revolution set the stage for the rise of modern democratic and socialist movements and paved the way for the development of modern European society.*
> ***— John Merriman (historian)"***

1. **Rise of scientific socialism:** As a result of the 1848 revolution's failure, socialism abandoned its former utopian and idealistic nature and significantly changed to a much more scientific methodology. Additionally, Karl Marx also released his renowned 'Communist Manifesto' in 1848.
2. **Rise of nationalism:** Similar to socialism, nationalism was liberal and idealistic prior to 1848, but became militaristic and pragmatic thereafter. Because of this, nationalists in Italy and Germany abandoned the liberal method and later embraced the militant nationalism of Cavour and Bismarck's leadership **(Refer Figure 5.4).**

UNIFICATION OF ITALY

The Italian Peninsula was divided into various islands and described as 'a mere geographic representation.' Following Napoleon's ascent to power, the Italian Peninsula was once more conquered, and Napoleon divided it into three parts. These were:

1. **Northern Italy:** Annexed to the French Empire
2. **Newly created kingdom of Italy:** Ruled by Napoleon himself.
3. **Kingdom of Naples:** Ruled by a relative of Napoleon

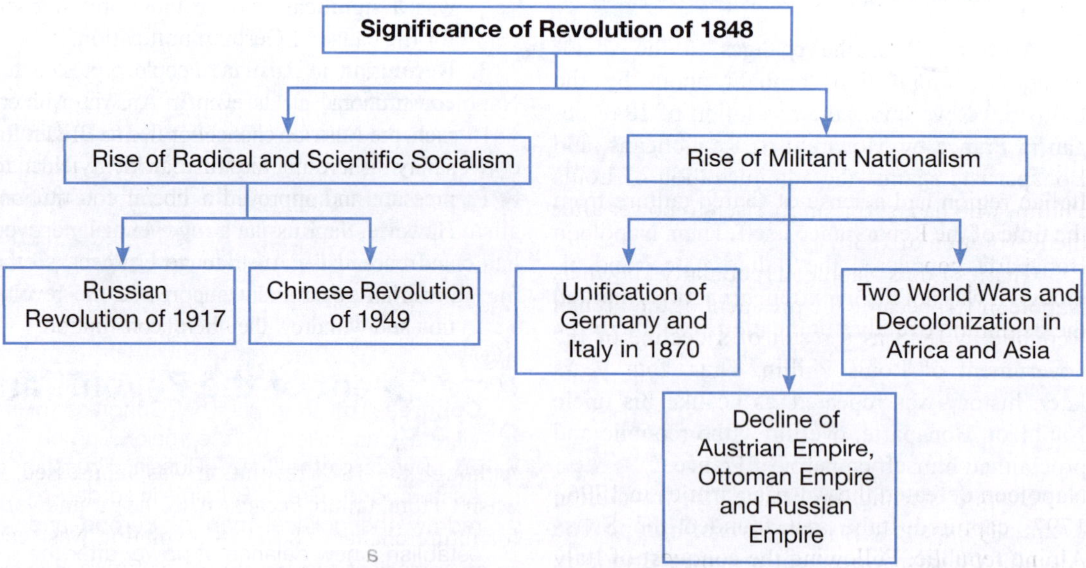

FIGURE 5.4: Significance of the Revolution of 1848

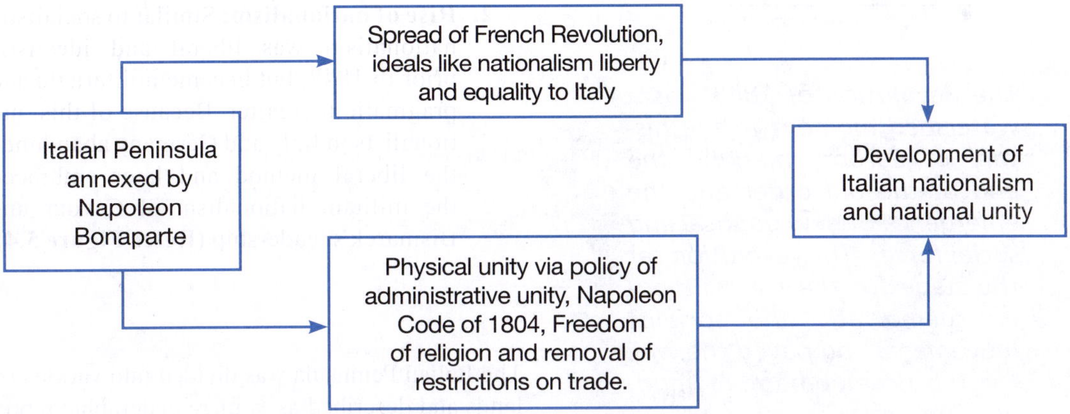

Figure 5.5: Unintended Role of Napoleon in Italian Unification

> *The Unification of Italy represented the triumph of nationalist aspirations and the emergence of a new, modern nation-state that challenged the traditional balance of power in Europe.*
>
> ***—Christopher Duggan (Historian)***

Rise of Nationalism in Italy

Italian region had a sense of shared culture from the time of the Renaissance itself. Then, Napoleon Bonaparte conquered the Italian states, and although it was not his intention, his actions marked the beginning of Italy's unification.

Unintended Role of Napoleon in Italian Unification

Napoleon defeated the Austrian armies in 1796–1797, captured Italy, and founded the Swiss Alpine republic. Following the conquest of Italy by the French, French soldiers entered into Italy along with ideals of the French Revolution like nationalism, liberty, and equality which led to the abolition of ancient feudal systems and feudalism. In addition, Napoleon brought forth administrative unity, the Napoleonic code, freedom of religion, and restrictions on trade were removed. As a result, Italy developed the seeds of Italian nationalism, growth of awakening, and a sense of national identity through contact with Napoleon and French ideals **(Refer Figure 5.5).**

Setback to Italian Unification under the Congress of Vienna

Napoleon's defeat at the Battle of Waterloo in 1815 prompted the Congress of Vienna (1815) to convene with the objective of redrawing the map of Europe and to suppress the concept of nationalism. The pre-Napoleonic geopolitical landscape had been recreated by the Vienna Congress, leaving Italy fragmented and weak.

Points to Ponder

Congress of Vienna: The Congress of Vienna was called by the major European powers of the time—Russia, Prussia, Austria, and Great Britain—in order to redraw the political map of Europe and establish a new balance of power after the Napoleonic Wars.

MAP 5.2: Italy as Represented Geographically in 1815

Under the principle of legitimacy, the Congress of Vienna (Metternich System) partitioned Italy into various parts and again reduced it to mere 'a geographical expression'. Austria and Metternich wanted Italy to be only 'a geographic expression' so that it would always be small and dependent on Austria for assistance. Thus, the Congress of Vienna caused a significant setback to the process of Italian unity and reversed the cycle of Italian unification **(Refer Map 5.2).**

1. Lombardi and Venetia were brought under the control of Austria to protect Italy against possible French aggression.
2. Parma, Modena, and Tuscany under the Austrian Habsburg dynasty.
3. Middle Italian region called Papal States under Pope and protected by French Empire.
4. Naples and Sicily under the Bourbon dynasty.
5. Only Piedmont-Sardinia had an Italian ruler and it was the most powerful state of Italy.

Nevertheless, the Congress of Vienna cleared the notion that the unification of Italy would be in opposition to the Austrian Hapsburg Empire because Austria ruled north Italy which was primarily Italian-speaking. Moreover, Italian was almost certain to reject the status quo for a long time because the idea of Italian nationalism had already been felt and spread among Italians.

Points to Ponder

The Carbonari were a secret revolutionary organization that originated in Italy in the early 19th century.
The Carbonari aimed to overthrow the ruling powers in Italy and establish a democratic republic based on the principles of liberty, equality, and fraternity.

The only thing that separated Italians was their differing views on the potential character of future unification and under whose leadership Italian unification would be carried out **(Refer Figure 5.6).**

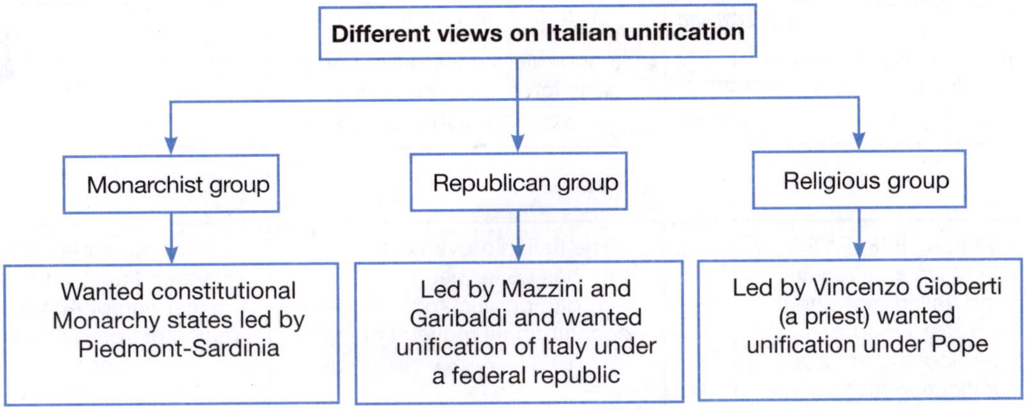

FIGURE 5.6: Different Views on Italian Unification

The Metternich system, which was established by the Vienna Congress, was opposed by Italians who had already felt a sense of nationalism. The reaction against the Metternich system was manifested in the form of several revolts in Italy.

Revolt of 1820 in Italian States

Although the 1820 revolt began in France, it also spread to Naples, Piedmont, and many other regions in Italy. Citizens in Piedmont revolted to drive out the Austrians and unify Italy under Piedmont Sardinia while people in Naples compelled King Ferdinand I to issue a constitution. As revolt and liberal ideas began to spread throughout Venice and Lombardy, Austria deployed an army to suppress the revolt and restored King Ferdinand, who abolished the constitution.

Revolution of 1830 in Italian States

Beginning in July 1830, the French Revolution of 1830 sparked a revolutionary mood for unification throughout Italy, sparking a series of revolts in the Papal, Parma, and Modena kingdoms, which Austria put down since Italy wasn't yet ready for revolution.

Points to Ponder

Italian nationalists formed the Carbonari organization in Naples in 1812 to discuss Italy's destiny.

The Italian revolt of 1820 and 1830 was greatly influenced by Carbonari, a secret revolutionary group. The main goal of Carbonari was to free all Italians and drive out all foreigners from Italy. The 'Risorgimento' movement for Italian unification was begun by Carbonari for unification and constitutional rule in Italy.

However, the lack of a unified strategy and inadequate leadership prevented the organization from having any meaningful impact. Both the unsuccessful revolutions in 1820 and 1830 were incited by Carbonari, highlighting Carbonari and revolutionary failure to lead the unification of Italy. Nevertheless, it was successful in causing Italians to become aware of Italian nationalism.

Revolution of 1848 in Italian States

Several economic problems like, poor harvests in 1846 and 1847, a famine, rising food prices, and the layoffs of industrial workers along with the downfall of Metternich

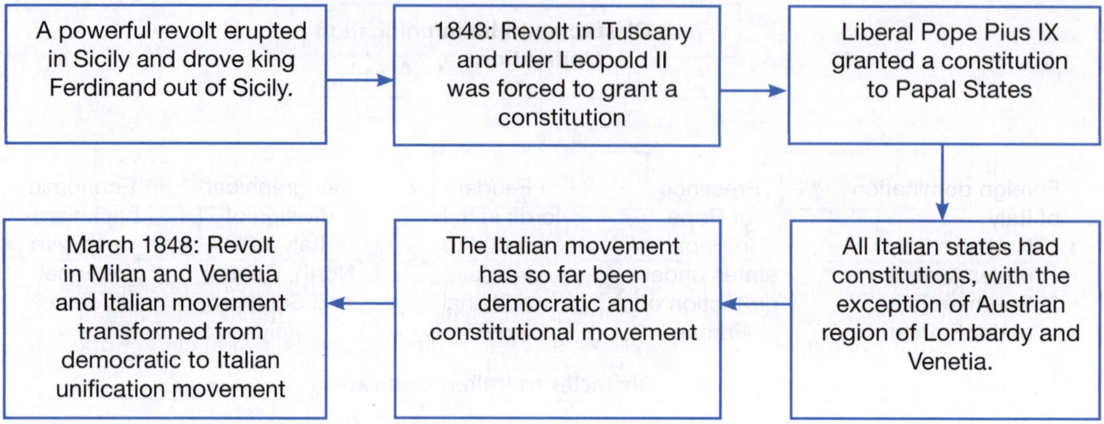

Figure 5.7: Chronology of the Italian Revolt in 1848

sparked a revolution of 1848 and protests in both rural and urban areas of Italy. Additionally, Pope Pius IX's reform initiatives in Papal States in June 1846, such as the establishment of a Council of State to share power, created great hopes for the unification of Italy. Due to the revolt in Italy, Metternich got nervous and occupied Ferrara with Austrian forces in 1847, which caused widespread anti-Austrian unrest throughout Italy for democratic right to Constitution **(Refer Figure 5.7).**

The Piedmont-Sardinia monarch, Charles Albert, was urged by the revolutionaries from Venetia and Milan to support the cause of the unification of Italy against Austria. As a result, Charles Albert with the help of King Ferdinand, Pope Pius IX, and other Italian kings tried to unite Italy under Piedmont-Sardinia by declaring war against Austria. However, Pope Pius IX and King Ferdinand withdrew their troops and Charles Albert of piedmont Sardinia was defeated by Austria at the Battle of Custoza in 1849, putting a serious jolt to the process of Italian unification.

Thus, Lombardy and Venetia were once again conquered and brought under Austrian control. All earlier kings were reinstated with the exception of Charles Albert of Piedmont, who abdicated the throne to Victor Emmanuel II.

Reason for Failure of 1848 Revolutions in Italy

1. **Different perspectives for Italian unification**: While Mazzini and Garibaldi wanted to create a republic, others wanted to create a constitutional monarchy under the leadership of piedmont Sardinia. As a result, the Italians were unable to agree on a single viewpoint for Italian unification other than Austria's expulsion.
2. **Lack of statesman**: Garibaldi and Mazzini both had inspiring prowess, but neither was a statesman. Additionally, Mazzini, Garibaldi, Charles Albert, and Pope Pius IX failed to unite all Italians because none of them were universally acceptable.
3. **Austrian and French intervention:** Austrian intervention led not only to the suppression of the 1848 uprisings but also to the restoration of earlier absolute monarchy in all Italian States, with the exception of Piedmont Sardinia. Likewise, France sent troops to the Papal States to re-establish Papal authority.
4. **Pope's refusal to support 1848 revolution:** Pope Pius IX initially supported the 1848 revolution and unification of Italy, but later he opposed both, and withdrew his forces against Austria. Thus, Pope opposed the war against Austria and also the idea of a united Italy.

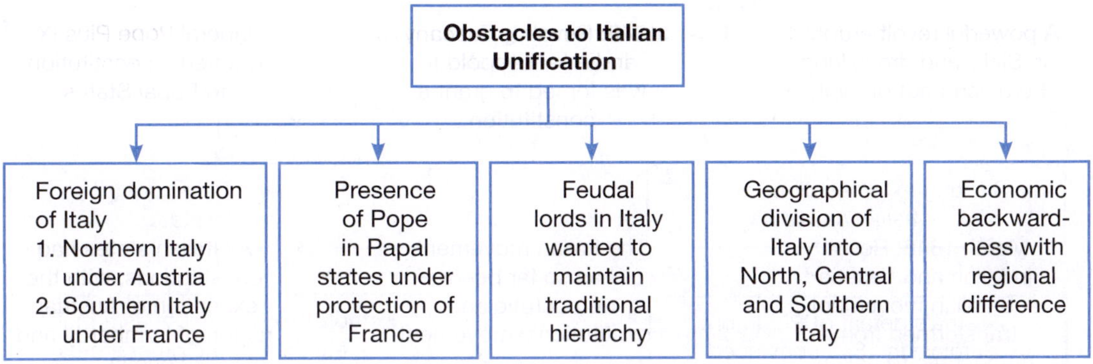

Figure 5.8: Obstacles to Italian Unification

5. **Lack of involvement from the masses:** Most peasants stayed out of the 1848 revolution which was mostly organized by radicals **(Refer Figure 5.8).**

Significance of the Revolution of 1848 in Italy

Although the Italian Revolution of 1848 was a failure, it was not a total failure because it had a considerable and far-reaching impact on Italy's unification.

1. **Succession of Victor Emmanuel II**: Victor Emmanuel II succeeded Charles Albert after latter abdicated the throne. Victor Immanuel II was a very competent ruler and his power of military organization and common sense in times of crisis proved crucial to the cause of Italian unification.
2. **Unification under Piedmont-Sardinia**: Due to the 1848 Italian Revolution's failure, which was primarily a liberal revolution, liberals and the idea of the Italian Republic were discredited. Now it was realized that a Constitutional monarchy led by Sardinia-Piedmont was the only solution to unify Italy because of:
   - **(a)** Charles Albert sacrificed his throne for an Italian cause.
   - **(b)** Only Piedmont Sardinia was engaged in a full-scale war with Austria.
   - **(c)** Piedmont-Sardinia was the only Italian state ruled by an Italian king and never subject to Austrian control.
   - **(d)** Piedmont-Sardinia was the only state with a liberal constitution.
   - **(e)** While Piedmont-Sardinia was witnessing rapid economic growth, other Italian states were experiencing economic and political stagnation.
3. **Search of Allies for Italian cause**: Failure of Piedmont-Sardinia to defeat Austria singlehandedly forced her to seek allies against Austria.

ERA OF VICTOR IMMANUEL II AND COUNT CAVOUR

(a) Victor Immanuel II: Victor Immanuel II was an extremely capable leader. He made the decision to make Piedmont-Sardinia a strong Italian state and appointed Count Cavour I as the finance minister for this reason. After that in 1852, Victor Immanuel II promoted Cavour to the post of prime minister.

> "*Piedmont must begin by raising herself by re-establishing in Europe as well as in Italy a position and a credit equal to her ambition.*
>
> *—Count Cavour*"

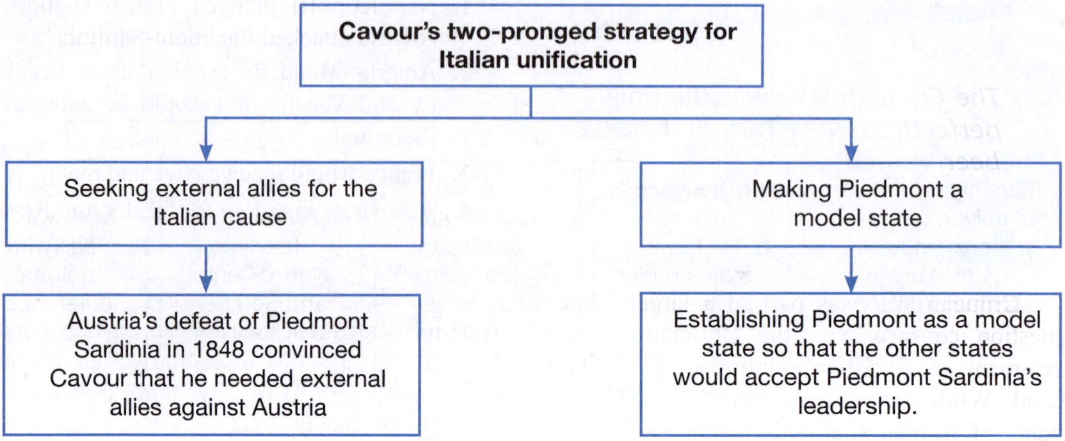

FIGURE 5.9: Cavour's two-pronged Strategy for Italian Unification

(b) **Count Cavour**: Cavour was the son of an Old Regime Piedmont's noble and a well-known monarchist who wanted to unite Italy under Piedmont-Sardinia. Although he was a liberal who supported free trade, freedom of speech, and secular government, he opposed the ideals of republicans and revolutionaries. Count Cavour's two-pronged strategy for Italian unification was making Piedmont a model state and seeking external allies for the Italian cause **(Refer Figure 5.9).**

1. **Cavour policy of making Piedmont-Sardinia as model state**: Cavour carried out a number of economic reforms, army reorganizations, and religious reforms to turn Piedmont-Sardinia into a model state. These were:
   (i) **Economic reform**: Cavour upheld the idea that economic development should come before the political change. In order to increase trade and business, Count Cavour built numerous railroads, established a national bank, sought to encourage industrialization, and carried out agricultural reforms. He also signed a free trade pact with a few European nations.
   (ii) **Reorganisation of Army**: Cavour believed that the unification of Italy would be achieved through war against Austria, thus he imposed higher taxes to bolster Piedmont's military organization and reorganisation of the army.
   (iii) **Reform in Church**: Cavour curtailed the privileges of the church and adhered to the 'A free church in a free state' principle and attempted to separate politics from religion.
2. **Seeking external allies for the Italian cause:** The biggest obstacle to Italian unification was Austria, but Cavour saw that a small state like Sardinia-Piedmont could not defeat Austria on its own and needed the assistance of powerful military allies.

   In addition, the problem of Papal States could not be resolved without international cooperation because the Congress of Vienna had already divided the Italian issue, so Cavour intended to internationalize the Italian issue and seek external allies for the cause of Italian unification.

Crimean War and Cavour's Diplomatic Achievements (1854–56)

After being prepared militarily and economically, Cavour entered international affairs and rejected King Charles Albert's Italia-fara-da-se (Italy shall go alone) ideology. Cavour began looking for an international ally, and the Crimean War provided a wonderful chance for him to take the Italian issue globally.

> *The Crimean War was the only perfectly useless war that has been waged.*
>
> *—H.R Anderson*

Crimean War was part of a larger Eastern question concern, i.e., the Ottoman Empire's treatment of Christian minorities in the Holy Land. While Britain and France defended the rights of Roman Catholics regarding access to Jerusalem and other locations under Turkish dominion that were regarded as holy by Christian sects, Russia supported the rights of Russian orthodox Christians.

Despite Italy's lack of direct engagement and lack of hostilities with Russia, Cavour participated in the Crimean War on behalf of Britain and France and sent a military contingent of 15,000 soldiers. Russia lost the Crimean War to an alliance of France, UK, Ottoman Empire, and Piedmont Sardinia. Piedmont-Sardinia was consequently invited to the Paris Peace Conference in 1856. Despite the Austrian representative's objections, Cavour internationalized the Italian issue and made the Italian issue a concern for all of Europe.

France and Britain were sympathetic to the Italian cause during the Paris Peace Conference, but Britain declined to assist out of strategic considerations. Cavour skillfully used Napoleon's sympathy and an unanticipated attempt on his life by an Italian named Orsini. Cavour criticized the crimes committed by Orsini as being misdirected acts, but he argued that Austria's oppressive reign was to blame as cause for such acts, which was also confirmed by Orsini's request for assistance from Emperor Napoleon III for Italian cause.

Treaty of Plombieres in 1858

A covert meeting between Napoleon III and Cavour led to the signing of the treaty of Plombieres. Provisions of Treaty included:

1. Napoleon III pledged French support, if Austria attacked Piedmont-Sardinia.
2. Austria would be expelled from Lombardy and Venetia and would be annexed to Piedmont.
3. France would receive Nice and Savoy.
4. A separate kingdom for Naples and Rome.

Austro-Sardinian War of 1859

As a result of French assurance, Cavour irritated Vienna with a series of military exercises near the border, with aggressive trade policies, and inciting discontent in Lombardy and Venetia.

> *The die is cast; we have made history.*
>
> *—Count Cavour*

Austria, however, did not revert. The 9th month had passed, and Cavour felt utterly hopeless. But Austria made the mistake of presenting an ultimatum, requiring Piedmont to disarm or risk war. Then France and Piedmont launched a united offensive against the Austrian empire, which resulted in the Austro-Sardinian War of 1859. As a result of the Franco-Piedmont soldiers' victory over Austria at the Battle of Magenta and Solferance, Lombardy was added to Piedmont Sardinia.

Louis Napoleon III, the French emperor, however, was unable to uphold the integrity of his statement in Plombieres. In actuality, Louis had joined the alliance in the hopes of Nice and Savoy from Piedmont, and Louis was expecting for support from the French people. But because France (a Roman Catholic country, was at war with Austria, another Roman Catholic country) this led to unrest and annoyance among the French populace. Thus, even though Austria was about to be expelled and Venice was within reach, Napoleon III signed the Treaty of Villafranca with Austria in July 1859.

Liberation and Unification of Italy (1850 – 1870)

- 1859: First unification: Annexation of Lombardy
- 1860: Second unification: Annexation of central duchies states
- 1861: Third unification: Annexation of Sicily and Naples
- 1866: Fourth unification: Annexation of Venetia
- 1870: Fifth unification: Annexation of Rome

FIGURE 5.10: : Liberation and Unification of Italy (1850 – 1870)

Treaty of Villafranca in 1859

The provisions of the Treaty of Villafranca included:

1. While retaining Venetia, Austria will give Sardinia Lombardy **(Refer Figure 5.10).**
2. Restoration of Central Italian rulers who had been driven out by revolt immediately after the start of the Austro-Sardinian War.

> *They have stopped me from making Italy by diplomacy from the North; I will make it by revolution from the South.*
>
> ***—Count Cavour***

Second Unification: Annexation of Central Duchies States in 1860

The news of the Austrians' evacuation of Lombardy fuelled nationalist emotions and sparked a public revolt in the Italian regions of Parma, Modena, and Tuscany. People expelled rulers set up a provisional government and unanimously voted for a merger with Piedmont. Austria and Prussia sought to intervene, but Britain countered that it was an Italian internal issue and that Italian should alone deal with it.

Moreover, Cavour wanted to hold a referendum to annex the central duchies states. But he required France's assistance for it. Louis Napoleon III of France received a diplomatic visit from Cavour and he assured him that after the referendum, France would once again receive the Nice and Savoy. As a result, with the help of France and Great Britain, the kingdom of Sardinia eventually acquired Parma, Modena, and Tuscany in central Italy through a referendum in 1860.

Third Unification: Annexation of Sicily and Naples in 1861

Garibaldi, a follower of Mazzini, played a crucial role in facilitating the integration of the southern states.

> *Italy is made. All are safe.*
>
> ***—Count Cavour***

Naples and Sicily, two Sicilian states, were ruled by the Bourbon dynasty. Sicily's revolution began in April 1860 as a result of dissatisfaction with the rule of a monarch. Garibaldi, therefore, gathered more than 1,000 volunteers in May 1860 for his mission to Sicily, which was known as the Expedition of thousand.

Since Cavour had a good relation with France, he employed Garibaldi as an independent invader to annex the Sicilian states. He retains his attitude of strict impartiality in the Sicilian states issue despite providing constant help to Garibaldi. The people in Naples welcomed Garibaldi, and as a result of the rising tide of nationalism, the Bourbon kings of Sicily and Naples fled from their respective capital cities. As a result, Garibaldi became dictator of Naples and Sicily in name of Victor Emmanuel.

Garibaldi intended to annex Rome because republicans encouraged him to do so. Due to France's protection of Papal States, however, it might start a war with France. Additionally, Cavour suspected that Garibaldi's republican views may lend the Italian movement a republican character. Therefore, Cavour held that Italy must be protected from foreigners (French intervention), evil principles (Garibaldi's republicanism), and madmen (Garibaldi).

As a result, Cavour advised Italian king Victor Immanuel II to travel to the south and to take charge of Naples and Sicily from Garibaldi. Victor Immanuel II proceeded southward, conquering Umbria and Marche, the Papal province, along the way. He then met with Garibaldi, and a civil war between him and Victor Immanuel II was a possibility. Garibaldi, however, opted not to engage in a civil war and handed power to Victor Immanuel II.

As a result, only Venetia (controlled by Austrians) and Rome, which the Pope had with the help of the French troops, remained outside Italian Union. Victor Emmanuel, therefore, met in Turin in February 1861 to assemble the first Italian Parliament's representatives. Finally, the Italian Parliament crowned Victor Emmanuel king of Italy in March 1861 **(Refer Map 5.3).**

Fourth Unification: Annexation of Venetia in 1866

The further development on the issues of Venetia and Rome was linked to the issue of the unification of Germany. In April 1866, Prussia and Italy forged a military alliance with the assistance of Emperor Napoleon III. Thus, Prussia and Italy waged war on Austria in June 1866. At

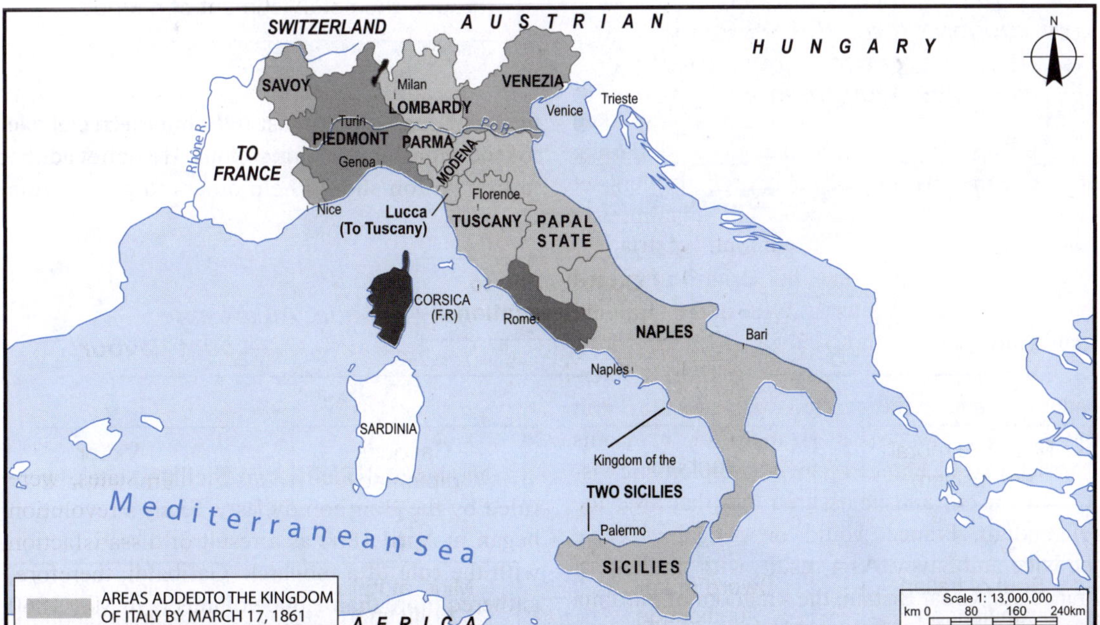

Map 5.3: Various phases of Unification of Italy

the Battle of Sadowa in 1866, Prussia defeated Austria, and as a result, Austria ceded Venetia to Italy under the terms of the Peace of Prague.

Fifth Unification: Annexation of Rome in 1870

The Franco-Prussian War broke out in July 1870, and Napoleon III called his garrison back from Rome. Napoleon and his army surrendered at the Battle of Sedan in 1870, and the newly formed French republican government was unable to retaliate against Italy. In order to defend the pope, King Victor Emmanuel II despatched his troops to Rome, but the pope declined the offer. Rome and Latium were consequently annexed to the kingdom of Italy following a referendum.

CONTRIBUTION OF MAZZINI, COUNT CAVOUR, GARIBALDI AND VICTOR IMMANUEL II

> "*Where France had failed in not supporting the Italians in 1830, Italy showed men how to use their new-won freedom right.*
> ***—Mazzini***"

Role of Mazzini

Mazzini was a great visionary and soul of Italian unification who ignited the concept of a united Italy and turned a united Italy into a popular movement. Mazzini's speeches and writings sparked an intellectual revolution in Italy.

Giuseppe Mazzini founded the nationalist association known as 'Young Italy' in 1831. It was successful in promoting a sense of brotherhood among people and instilling nationalism in young Italians. Its goals included organizing public uprisings and bringing about a political awakening among the populace.

Mazzini believed that popular revolution might successfully bring about a republic in Italy, but uprisings, such as the one in Piedmont in 1834 that was organized in conjunction with Garibaldi, were unsuccessful, leading to Mazzini's arrest and his forced exile to London.

Points to Ponder

In Mazzini's view, the three pillars of Italian national identity—independence, unity, and liberty—would be attained through the establishment of a republic.

Mazzini's conception of Italian nationality was not exclusive to just Italy but the recreation of the moral unity of mankind. He believed that a free nation should help others to get freedom

Figure 5.11: Contribution to Italian Unification

and to create moral 'unity of mankind'. In fact, Mazzini was one of the early proponents of European unification and the idea of a 'United States of Europe.' He asserted that Italian unification was a logical step toward the European Union.

Mazzini also gave the concept of three-fold unity-

(a) **Unity of man**: Unity of all man to overcome the isolation of modern man in an industrialized mass civilization.

(b) **Unity of nation:** Unity of nation to bind all free individuals and community of liberty and equality.

(c) **Unity of mankind**: Unity of mankind for peace and collaboration of all nations.

However, Mazzini's strategy was overly idealistic. Republicanism was his first priority and unification was the second one **(Refer Figure 5.11).**

> *Cavour was the man who made it possible for Italy to emerge as a united country. His vision, his political skill and his relentless determination were the driving forces behind the unification movement. He was a pragmatist who understood the realities of power politics, and he was a master of diplomacy who knew how to win allies and influence people. Without Cavour, Italy might never have emerged as a united country, and his legacy remains a vital part of Italian history.*
>
> ***—Denis Mack Smith (Historian)***

Role of Count Cavour

He was a shrewd politician and the prime minister of Piedmont. His judgement was clear when, in 1861, when he sent Victor Immanuel II to curb Garibaldi's zeal in order to avert a conflict between France and the Italian revolutionary. Moreover, Cavour's internal reforms and establishment of Piedmont Sardinia as a model state aided in the unification of Italy.

Being a monarchist and mind of Italian unification, Count Cavour's initial goal was to create a constitutional monarchy under the leadership of Piedmont-Sardinia. He had previously not favoured the union of all of Italy, and his primary goal was to enlarge Piedmont-Sardinia by annexing the regions of Lombardy and Venetia.

Cavour's vision of Italian unification was limited to northern Italy therefore he did not favour annexing southern Italy following the unification of northern Italy. However, when Garibaldi opted for an independent course of action, Cavour interfered and sent Victor Immanuel II to acquire southern states out of concern that they would turn republican. Therefore, Count Cavour did not envision the Italy that eventually came to exist in 1870.

Role of Garibaldi

Garibaldi was a student of Mazzini and the sword of Italian unification. A skilled soldier, Garibaldi organized revolutions with the Red Shirt (guerrilla group).

Points to Ponder

Giuseppe Garibaldi: An Italian military leader and nationalist who played a crucial role in the Italian Unification, leading successful campaigns in the south of Italy and Sicily.

Even though he was a Republican, he prioritized unification over republican ideas, always choosing the path of unification wherever there was a conflict between the two. Thus, he loved his country more than he loved his Republican principles. He had a heart of a lion but the mind of a fox.

Cavour once said in anguish 'Aah, what have you done, we have expelled Bourbon from Naples and Sicily but brought another dynasty of Immanuel II, we have removed a corpse from the throne but restored on that his sick brother'.

Scholars have therefore correctly argued that the unification of Italy was neither entirely in the vision of Cavour nor in the vision of Garibaldi and that both had to make a great deal of compromises.

Role of Victor Immanuel II

After Charles Albert, his predecessor, failed, Victor Immanuel II assumed control of the Piedmont Sardinia. He made significant contributions to modernizing Piedmont-Sardinia and strengthening its military. In addition, he not only appointed Count Cavour as Italy's prime minister but also provided him the authority he needed to handle the Italian's affairs.

While Mazzini spiritually attempted to unite the nation and disseminate nationalism throughout the country, Garibaldi militarily defended Rome and occupied Naples and Sicily in the South, while Cavour logically planned each step of Italian unification.

Comparison between Count Cavour and Garibaldi

1. Cavour was a wise politician who carefully evaluated all choices before acting, in contrast to Garibaldi, who was more extreme and a proponent of revolutionary ideas.
2. Cavour was a politician and a proponent of constitutional monarchy, whereas Garibaldi was a republican, a warrior, and an opponent of Catholicism.
3. When it was essential, Cavour partnered with France because he exploited international influence to further his domestic objectives. In contrast, Garibaldi relied on the grassroots strength, helped by young Italian republicans.
4. While Garibaldi used his military prowess to protect Rome and capture southern Italy, Cavour used his political acumen to organize every move Piedmont would make.
5. Though Garibaldi and Cavour disagreed, both made significant contributions to the movement for Italian unification.

> "*Cavour, as the architect of Italian Unification, was a master of realpolitik, using diplomacy and cunning to achieve his aims. Garibaldi, on the other hand, was a man of action, whose daring military exploits captured the imagination of the Italian people. Cavour was a strategist who saw the value of alliances and international support, while Garibaldi was a guerrilla fighter who relied on the support of the people. Together, they were the two sides of the Risorgimento coin: one the visionary, the other the pragmatist.*
>
> ***—R. J. B. Bosworth (Historian)***"

LET'S REVISE

Assessment of the Revolution of 1848

1. Rise of Scientific Socialism
2. Rise of Nationalism

Reasons for Failure of 1848 Revolutions in Italy

1. Different perspectives for Italian unification
2. Lack of statesman
3. Austrian and French intervention
4. Pope's refusal to support the 1848 revolution
5. Lack of involvement from the masses

Significance of the Revolution of 1848 in Italy

1. Succession of Victor Emmanuel II
2. Unification Under Piedmont Sardinia
3. Search of Allies for Italian Cause

Obstacles to Italian Unification

1. Foreign domination of Italy
2. Presence of the Pope in the Papal States under the protection of France
3. Feudal lords in Italy wanted to maintain a traditional hierarchy
4. Geographical division of Italy into North, Central, and Southern Italy
5. Economic backwardness with a regional difference

Cavour's two-pronged Strategy for Italian Unification

1. Seeking external allies for the Italian cause
2. Making Piedmont a model state

Cavour Policy of Making Piedmont Sardinia as Model State

1. Economic Reform
2. Reorganisation of the Army
3. Reform in Church

Liberation and Unification of Italy (1850 – 1870)

1. **First unification:** Annexation of Lombardy in 1859.
2. **Second unification:** Annexation of central duchies states in 1860.
3. **Third unification:** Annexation of Sicily and Naples in 1861.
4. **Fourth unification:** Annexation of Venetia in 1866.
5. **Fifth unification:** Annexation of Rome in 1870.

PROBABLE QUESTIONS

1. How was Italy transformed from 'a geographical expression' to a nation-state?
2. The unification was made possible by Count Cavour. Comment.
3. Highlight the importance of Mazzini, Count Cavour, and Garibaldi to the cause of Italian Unification?
4. Though Garibaldi and Cavour disagreed, yet both made significant contributions to the movement for Italian unification. Explain the statements.
5. 'Mazzini's conception of Italian nationality was not exclusive, and his dominant ideal was the recreation of the moral unity of mankind.' Critically examine.
6. 'They have stopped me from making Italy by diplomacy from the North; I will make it by revolution from the South.' Comment.

TIMELINE (1797–1866)

- **1796-1797**: Napoleon's forces conquer Northern Italy.
- **1805**: Napoleon creates the Kingdom of Italy.
- **1815**: The Congress of Vienna creates the Kingdom of Sardinia, which becomes the main force for Italian unification.
- **1815-1848**: The Italian states are ruled by Austria.
- **1820**: Carbonari secret society is formed to promote Italian unification.
- **1831**: Giuseppe Mazzini finds Young Italy, a secret society to promote Italian unification.
- **1848-1849**: Revolutions break out across Europe, including in Italy, but are quickly suppressed. The First War of Italian Independence is fought, but Piedmont Sardinia was defeated.
- **1852**: Count Camillo di Cavour becomes the Prime Minister of Sardinia and begins implementing reforms to modernize the economy and strengthen the state.
- **1859**: Sardinia and France defeat Austria in the Second Italian War of Independence, leading to the creation of the Kingdom of Lombardy-Venetia.
- **1860**: Garibaldi leads the Expedition of the Thousand, unifying the Kingdom of the Two Sicilies with Sardinia.
- **1861**: Victor Emmanuel II is proclaimed King of Italy, and the country is officially unified as the Kingdom of Italy.
- **1866**: Italy defeats Austria in the Third Italian War of Independence, leading to the acquisition of Venetia.
- **1870**: Rome is captured by Italian forces, and the city becomes the capital of the newly unified kingdom.

CHAPTER

6

Source: AD.BRAUN & Cie Dornach, Public domain, via Wikimedia Commons, , accessed on 5th June 2023 and internet, Public domain, via Wikimedia Commons, accessed on 5th June 2023

UNIFICATION OF GERMANY

> *The great questions of the day will not be settled by means of speeches and majority decisions but by iron and blood.*
>
> *—Otto Von Bismarck*

INTRODUCTION

German and Italian unification both proceeded concurrently, even though their natures, characters, and methods of leadership differed from each other. The protestant Reformation Movement led by Martin Luther gave Germany a common cultural identity because of his translation of the Bible into the German language. The enlightenment philosophers from Germany highlighted, strengthened, and deepened the cultural unity among Germans. Thus, Immanuel Kant and the German thinkers who came after him, including Hegel and Marx, helped to lay the groundwork for the cultural unification of German identity.

ROLE OF NAPOLEON IN GERMAN UNIFICATION

> *Napoleon kindled German national sentiment and Bismarck carried out political unification.*

Until 1806, Germany was divided into more than 300 sovereign city states that spoke German, making it 'merely a geographical expression.' Most of them were governed differently and were part of the Holy Roman Empire under the Habsburg family.

> **Points to Ponder**
>
> Battle of Austerlitz, also known as the Battle of the Three Emperors, was fought on December 2, 1805, between the French army, commanded by Napoleon Bonaparte, and the combined forces of the Russian and Austrian armies.

Similar to the Italian unification, Napoleon Bonaparte proved to be an unintentional stimulator for German unification. After defeating Austria in the Battle of Austerlitz in December 1805, Napoleon imposed Peace of Pressburg on Austria. With the intention of establishing a French satellite in Germany, Napoleon reorganized, and simplified the German state system following the Battle of Austerlitz; nonetheless, this ultimately led to German unification. Napoleon proved an unconscious stimulator for German unification in the following manner:

1. Abolition and dissolution of the Holy Roman Empire.
2. Napoleon created administrative unification among the German states by reorganizing more than 300 small German states into 39 states Rhine Confederation, followed by 16 larger states and made them dependent on France.
3. Napoleon was proclaimed as saviour of the Rhine Confederation.
4. Napoleon, like in Italy, implemented the Napoleonic Code, destroyed feudalism and freedom of the press, removed restrictions on trade, and promoted the modern ideals of the French Revolution throughout the German states.
5. Napoleon's catastrophic Moscow campaign in 1812 resulted in the death of over a lakh German soldiers, which in turn disenchanted many Germans. Furthermore, numerous Germans became disillusioned as a result of Napoleon's Continental System, which destroyed the German economy. Therefore, Germans desired to get rid of Napoleon's influence in Germany.
6. Napoleon's defeat in the Moscow expedition allowed him to lose his hold on German princes. Therefore, most of the German states led by Prussia took part in a war against Napoleon Bonaparte in the battle of Leipzig and Waterloo. Thus, the German states unintentionally began to experience a sense of feeling.

The unification of Germany was influenced by several factors, including cultural-ideological factors, economic-industrial factors, and political-diplomatic factors, along with the unconscious stimulator provided by Napoleon Bonaparte **(Refer Figure 6.1).**

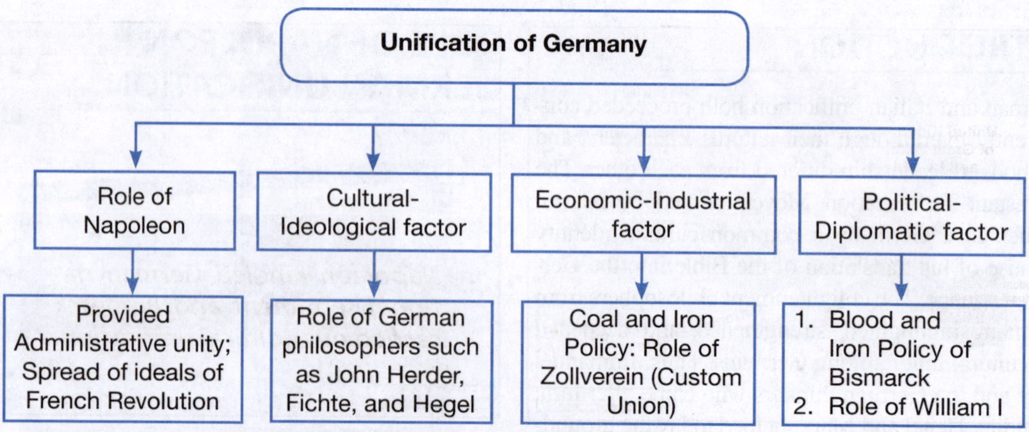

FIGURE 6.1: Various Factors for the Unification of Germany

THE CULTURAL-IDEOLOGICAL FACTOR FOR THE UNIFICATION OF GERMANY

From the middle of the 18th century, German states witnessed cultural nationalism in arts, literature, and philosophy. This movement started out as cultural, moved into politics, and inspired German nationalism.

German intellectuals like Immanuel Kant, Johann Herder, Fichte, Hegel, and others greatly aided in the development of a sense of national consciousness among the German states.

> **Points to Ponder**
>
> German thinkers opposed enlightenment and universalism and instead laid focus on the unification of Germany.

German nationalism was articulated by Immanuel Kant. Hegel's ideas reinforced his feelings of nationalism. Hegel referred to the German spirit as the spirit of the new world. He simply refers to 'Germanic people' as anyone who speaks 'German,' and in particular, Germans. Hegel may have had certain nationalistic beliefs, but he was never a staunch nationalist. He actually backed Napoleon's victory over Prussia because he believed that the French Revolution's principles were a step towards Germany.

J.G Fichte proclaimed the German language as a fountain head of language and called Germans as 'oldest and most ethical of nations'. Johann Herder is known as 'the intellectual father of the national movement' not only in Germany but also in the Slavic nations of Central, Eastern, and South-Eastern Europe because of his writings and contributions to nationalism.

All of these philosophers emphasized factors that promote unification and promoted cultural unity among German.

Congress of Vienna 1815 (Metternich System)

The Vienna Congress, which decided against the unification of Germany and instead reduced it to a mere geographic expression, caused the setback to the unification of Germany. It undoes the unintentional unification process that Napoleon Bonaparte began.

The Congress of Vienna transformed Europe into spheres of influence of four 'great powers,' namely Great Britain, France, Russia, and Austria, and established a new political order based on the 'balance of power,' which stifled German and Italian aspirations **(Refer Map 6.1)**.

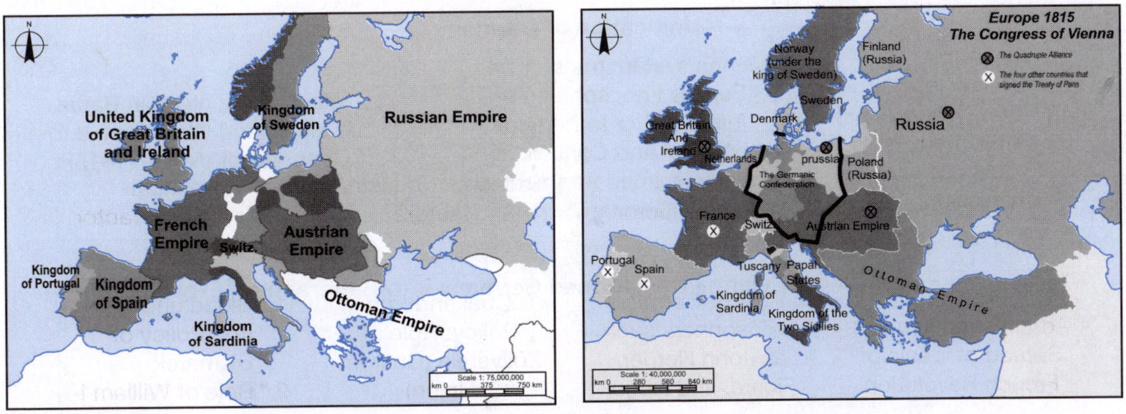

Map 6.1: Europe before and after the Congress of Vienna

Moreover, Vienna Congress was unable to return to more than 300 states, therefore, Germany was split once more into 39 states by the Metternich system. The German Confederation (1815–1866), which Austria presided over as president of the 'Federal Diet' and Prussia as vice president, was born out of the Vienna System and the Austrian–Prussian dualism was established in Germany **(Refer Figure 6.2).**

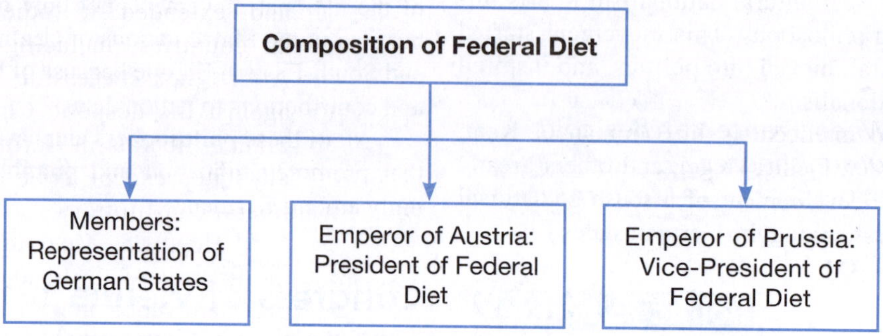

FIGURE 6.2: Austrian–Prussian Dualism and Composition of Federal Diet

Furthermore, Metternich's division of Europe into the geographical sphere of influence of four 'great powers,' namely Great Britain, France, Russia, and Austria, dependent on fragmented rather than unified German states **(Refer Figure 6.3).**

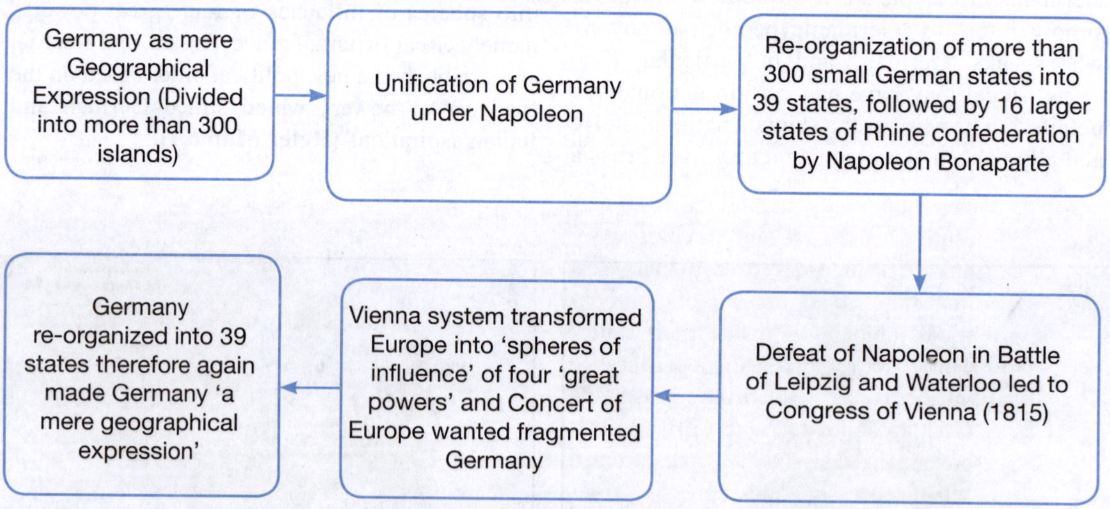

FIGURE 6.3: Congress of Vienna transformed Germany into Geographical Expression

POLITICAL-DIPLOMATIC FACTORS

1. **Rise of revolutions as a reaction to Congress of Vienna**

> *When France catches cold, all Europe sneezes.*
>
> ***—Metternich***

(a) **Revolution of 1820**: The revolutions of 1820 were the first challenge to the conservative order of Europe established by the Congress of Vienna. The 1820 Revolution began in France, but it quickly extended to other European nations, including Germany. It sparked the revolutionary atrocities by Burschenschaften (student clubs in universities) for German Unity, most notably the assassination of conservative August Kotzebue by a member of a radical student organization Karl Sand.

Carlsbad Decrees: Metternich, who saw the threat posed by the 1820 revolution, used recent revolutionary atrocities in order to convince German states to suppress liberal and patriotic tendencies inside their states. Thus, Metternich during a conference in Carlsbad, Bohemia, persuaded German states to issue Carlsbad Decrees. The Carlsbad Decrees were a set of regressive and repressive rules that included censorship and the dissolution of student organizations. Consequently, Metternich temporarily succeeded in suppressing the 1820 Revolution and liberal political activity with the aid of the repressive Carlsbad Decree.

(b) **Revolution of 1830 in Germany:** Similar to the 1820 revolution, the 1830 revolution started in France and extended to other European countries, including Germany. After the successful revolution against the despotic Charles X in France, liberals in Germans forced all states except Prussia to adopt liberal constitutions.

However, Metternich revived the oppressive Carlsbad Decrees in 1832 and once more succeeded in putting down the revolution of 1830.

(c) **Revolution of 1848 (March Revolution)**:

> *I want liberty, I want unity for Germany.*
>
> ***—Fredrick William IV during the 1848 rebellion***

Similar to the 1820 and 1830 revolutions, the revolution of 1848 started in France with the abdication by King Louis Philippe and spread to other European countries, including Germany. Metternich remarked, because of his frustration, that 'when France catches cold, all Europe sneezes.' He made this statement because he believed that what happened in France had an impact and influence on events elsewhere in Europe.

The Liberal-led revolution of 1848 was largely a democratic movement that compelled the European absolute monarchies to grant the Constitution. Many monarchs of German states were shocked and surprised by the might of the 1848 revolution, which scared them into issuing a constitution such as Frederick William IV of Prussia, who was followed by rulers of Saxony, Hanover, and Bavaria.

As the 1848 Revolution expanded to Austria, Metternich resigned from his position as chief minister to Emperor Ferdinand I of Austria and fled to Britain. Austria was mired in domestic problems, which gave liberals the chance to liberate Austrian influence over the German Federation. As a consequence, German liberals called a Frankfurt National Assembly (May 1848–June 1849) to draft a constitution for a unified Germany. In March 1849, the Frankfurt National Assembly suggested an Austria-free constitutional monarchy.

The Frankfurt National Assembly then offered Frederick William of Prussia the throne of the German Federation, but he rejected the proposed constitution for the reason that it was being offered by a revolutionary assembly dominated by liberals. As a result, the majority of German states also refused to accept the constitution.

After the Frankfurt Parliament was dissolved, Frederick William IV of Prussia proposed the creation of the Erfurt Union, a federation of German states excluding Austria and headed by the Emperor of Prussia. But by that point, Austria had recovered from the 1848 Revolution, and in 1850, Austrian forces compelled the Prussian King to sign the Olmutz Convention after defeating Frederick William IV at the battle of Olmutz. William IV renounced the idea of the Erfurt Union through the Olmutz Convention, which resulted in the restoration of the German Confederation under Austrian control **(Refer Figure 6.4).**

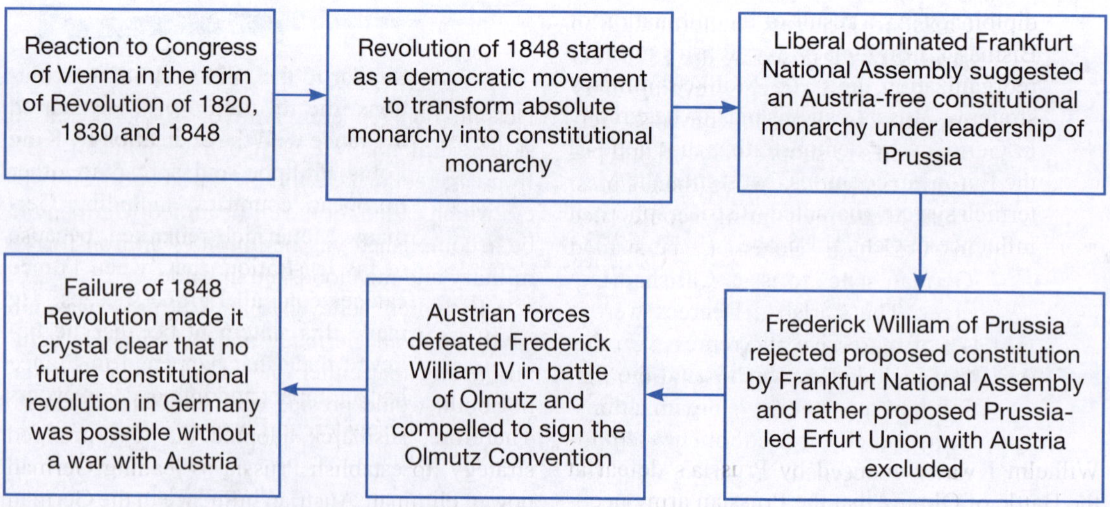

FIGURE 6.4: Chronology of Events During the Revolution of 1848

2. **Era of Otto Von Bismarck and Wilhelm I:** Similar to how Victor Emmanuel II replaced Charles Albert in the Italian Revolution of 1848, William IV was succeeded by Wilhelm I. After suffering a stroke in 1857, King Frederick William IV was unable to continue to reign of Prussia; as a result, Prince Wilhelm I became king in 1861. He was a competent and capable ruler who gave the Prussian Policy fresh life.

> *Prussians we are, and Prussians we will remain.*
> ***—Otto Von Bismarck***

In contrast to William IV, Wilhelm I had the foresight to choose wisely and the insight to have full faith in them.

To accomplish the ultimate aim of unifying Germany, Wilhelm I appointed von Roon for military modernization, von Moltke for military strategy, and Otto von Bismarck for diplomacy. As a result of a combination of Bismarck's diplomacy, von Roon's military reorganization, and von Moltke's military strategy, Prussia established its hegemony in Germany by demonstrating that none of the European countries that signed the Metternich system guarantee Austria's sphere of influence in Central Europe.

Struggle Over Army Reforms with Prussian Diet (Parliament)

Wilhelm I was convinced by Prussia's defeat at the Battle of Olmutz that the Prussian army needed to be reorganized and modernized and that Prussia's existence relied on the might of her army. To accomplish this, Wilhelm I appointed Von Moltke, the best strategist of his period, as the head of the Prussian General Staff.

The Prussian state had to impose new taxes to fund the modernization of the Prussian army, and the Prussian Diet would have to approve them. In the Prussian Diet, which was under liberal control, required funds were not granted. Further, when liberals wanted constitutional reforms prior to military reforms, which Wilhelm I refused to implement, the army modernization issue became even more problematic and caused a constitutional crisis in 1860. The deadlock between Wilhelm I and Prussian Diet persisted until 1862, and in this context, Wilhelm I met Otto von Bismarck, who supported Wilhelm's cause.

Otto von Bismarck

> *What we learn from History is that no one learns from History.*
> ***—Otto von Bismarck***

Despite being a conservative, Bismarck was a skilled diplomat. He earned the epithet of 'The Iron Chancellor' due to his 'Blood and Iron Policy,' which called for the unification of Germany to be accomplished via the might of an iron-forged military and the bloodshed in battle.

Bismarck believed that 'Germany was too small for both Germany and Austria'. He actually meant that either one of Austria or Prussia, not both, would preside over the German states. Therefore, Bismarck adopted the 'two-pronged strategy' to establish Prussia as leading German power, eliminate Austrian influence in the German states, and unite them **(Refer Figure 6.5).**

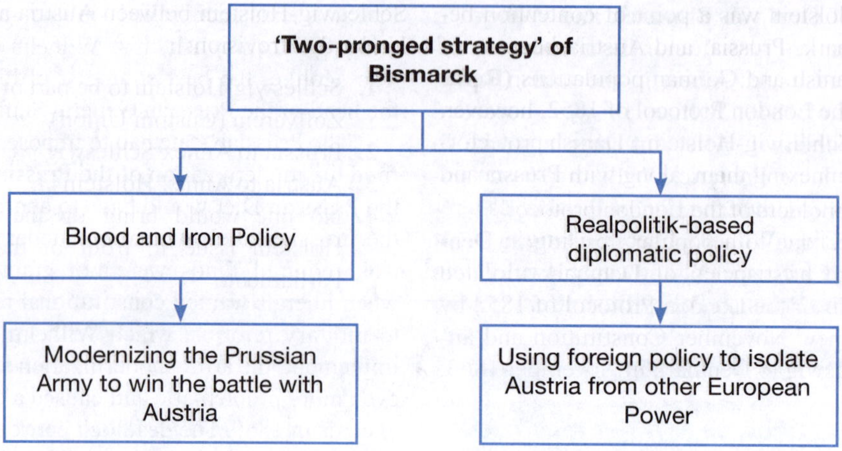

FIGURE 6.5: Two-Pronged Strategy of Otto von Bismarck

> *The great questions of the day will not be settled by means of speeches and majority decisions but by iron and blood.*
>
> ***—Otto von Bismarck***

Bismarck's Policy of Blood and Iron

Because Bismarck believed that Germany was relying on Prussia's military might rather than Prussian Diet or liberals, He declared that 'the main concerns of the day would not be settled by words and majority decisions but by 'iron and blood.'

Unlike the 1848 revolution in Germany, Bismarck believed that Blood and Iron (War), not speeches or the majority of the Prussian Diet, could decide the great questions of the day (German unification). In essence, Bismarck argued that if Germany were to be united completely under Prussian rule, Austria would have to go and Austria would not voluntarily do so; consequently, the war would be inevitable to unite Germany under Prussia.

Hence, Bismarck made the decision to implement army modernization not with standing the Constitution and Prussian Diet. He continued to levy and collect new taxes without the consent of the Prussian Diet to implement military reforms.

Schleswig-Holstein Question

> *The Schleswig-Holstein question is so complicated, only three men in Europe have ever understood it. One was Prince Albert, who is dead. The second was a German professor who became mad. I am the third and I have forgotten all about it.*
>
> ***—Lord Palmerston (British PM)***

Schleswig-Holstein was a point of contention between Denmark, Prussia, and Austria because of its mixed Danish and German populations **(Refer Map 6.2)**. The London Protocol of 1852, however, established Schleswig-Holstein a Danish protectorate without annexing them, along with Prussia and Austria as upholders of the London protocol.

However, due to a popular uprising in Denmark, King Christian IX of Denmark violated the provisions of the London Protocol of 1852 by signing the new November Constitution and annexing Schleswig to Denmark in November 1863.

Bismarck Exploited the Schleswig-Holstein Issue

Bismarck's first strategy was to use Austria as an ally in a battle against Denmark to defend the London Protocol. It culminated in the German-Danish War in 1864, and Prussian-Austrian soldiers jointly defeated Denmark. Consequently, Christian IX ceded Schleswig and Holstein to Austria and Prussia by the provisions of the Treaty of Vienna.

Convention of Gastein (1865)

The convention of Gastein was signed between Austria and Prussian. The provisions of the Convention of Gastein provided for the division of Schleswig-Holstein between Austria and Prussia. Under the Provision:

1. Schleswig-Holstein to be part of Prussia led Zollverein (Custom Union)
2. Prussia to Annex Schleswig
3. Austria to Annex Holstein
4. No one would bring up the Schleswig-Holstein issue in front of the Frankfurt Parliament.

> "*Gastein Convention papered over the cracks.*
> ***— Otto von Bismarck***"

The Gastein Convention was a significant diplomatic accomplishment for Bismarck because:

(a) He included Schleswig-Holstein into Prussia led Zollverein with no Austria.

(b) Holstein was ceded to Austria, but because it was surrounded by Prussian territory to the south and Schleswig (Prussian region) to the north, Austria found it impossible to rule there **(Refer Map 6.2)**.

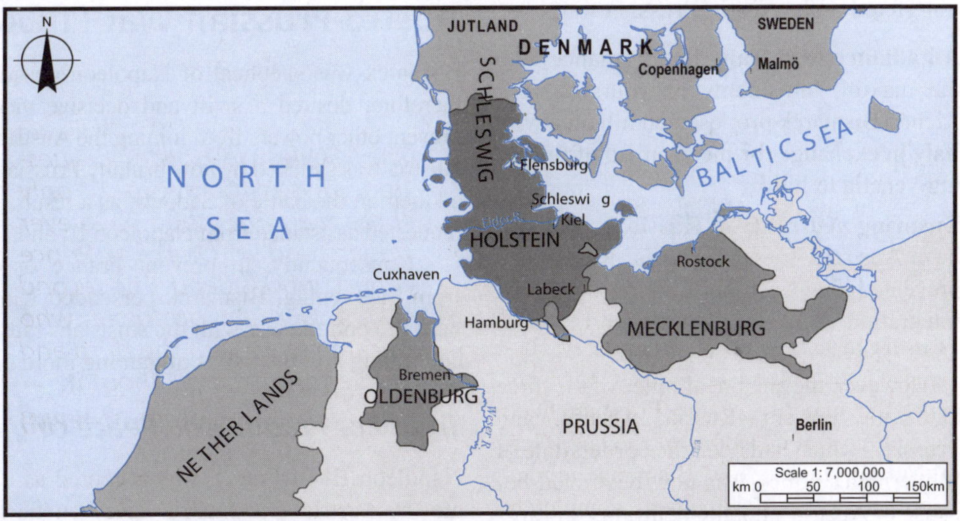

Map 6.2: Geographical Location of Schleswig-Holstein

(c) Schleswig-Holstein issue to be settled by Frankfurt Parliament.

The Gastein Convention was Bismarck's invention, and he was aware that it would be detrimental to Austria and not likely to continue for very long. It was invented by Bismarck because a war with Austria was required to unify Germany under Prussian leadership.

Bismarck's Provocation for War

Austria petitioned the Frankfurt Parliament for a resolution since it had no desire to retain Holstein. Consequently, Prussia invaded and occupied Holstein for the breach of the Gastein Convention.

Bismarck further inflamed Austria, by proposing a German Confederation with Austria excluded. Obviously, Austria rejected Prussia's proposed reforms and forced the Frankfurt Diet to send federal troops to fight Prussia. Consequently, Prussia left the German Confederation. Bismarck saw Austria's actions as hostile to Prussia's interests and declared war against Austria.

Bismarck Diplomacy: Bismarck Isolated Austria

Bismarck wanted to isolate Austria diplomatically before the war by making sure that no European power interfered in the Austro-Prussian war.

1. **An alliance with Italy**: In accordance with the maxim, 'an enemy of yours is your friend.' Bismarck proposed an alliance with Italy in exchange for the promise of returning Venetia to Italy.
2. **Ensuring neutrality of Russia**: Russia had been Austria's friend for ages. Russia had prevented the Austrian Empire from disintegrating during the Hungarian revolt of 1848–1849.

   However, the ancient alliance of the three autocratic powers—Russia, Austria, and Prussia—which had been the cornerstone of Metternich's policy was now destroyed because of Austria's hostile neutrality towards Russia during the Crimean War (1856). Russia, on the other hand, appreciated Prussia's friendly neutrality.

   Furthermore, the Polish rebelled against Russian rule in Poland to gain independence in 1863, and powerful nations like Britain, France, and Austria showed their support for the Polish people. However, Bismarck promised the Tsar assistance in suppressing the Polish uprising, which proved to be one of his greatest decisions. On the other hand, Austria lost the Tsar's friendship because of her support for Poland. Therefore, Bismarck believed that it was improbable that Russia would support Austria in the Austro-Prussian War.
3. **Ensuring the neutrality of France**: A powerful Prussia/Germany was not in France's strategic interest; hence, it was most likely that France would enter the Austro-Prussian War. Napoleon III, however, who presided over France, lacked Bismarck's diplomatic aptitude and statesmanship.

   By presenting Napoleon III with a profitable trade agreement, Bismarck secured his friendship. Many historians believe that Bismarck was given a guarantee of French neutrality in the Austro-Prussian War when he met Napoleon III in Biarritz.

Austro-Prussian War (1866)

Bismarck was skeptical of Napoleon's assurances, therefore, desired a swift and decisive victory to prevent other powers from joining the Austrian side. Austria was shocked by how brutally Prussia defeated them in the battle of Sadowa; as a result, Austria requested assistance from Napoleon III and Tsar.

Consequently, to prevent France or Russia from intervening, Bismarck persuaded King William I to end the war with the Austrians rather than continuing it in the hopes of gaining more ground.

Treaty of Prague and Peace of Vienna

Napoleon III of France was accepted as a mediator by Austria, and Austria gave Venetia to Italy because of the Peace of Vienna.

Consequently, the Peace of Prague was signed between Austria and Prussian and had a provision for:

1. Dissolution of the German Federation
2. Creation of North German Confederation under Prussian leadership
3. Permanent exclusion of Austria from German affairs.
4. Annexation of Schleswig-Holstein to Prussia

The Rivalry between France and Prussia

After the Austro-Prussian war (1866), Bismarck was conscious that a war with France was necessary to inspire German nationalism and establish a powerful German empire. Thus, he used German Nationalism for bringing southern German states into his hold and consciously created tension with France. Furthermore, Prussia formed the North German Confederation and annexed several provinces, which also terrified France.

> *It was France that was defeated in Sadowa.*

Franco-Prussian War (1870-71)

Prince Leopold's candidacy for the Spanish crown, who was related to the Prussian royal family, served as the immediate cause for the war. Bismarck who wanted war with France to unify southern German states persuaded Leopold to accept the Spanish throne. It severely frightened France as Prussia could completely encircle it from the west and east **(Refer Map 6.3).**

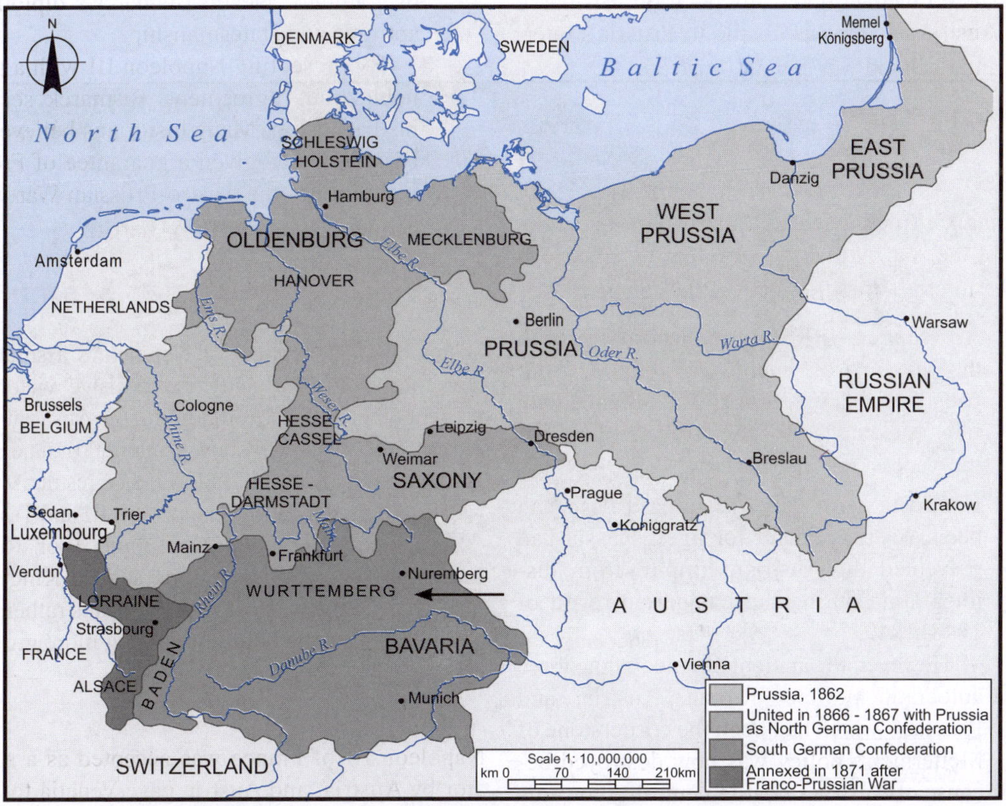

Map 6.3: Northern German States joined German Federation but not Southern State

> *I knew that a Franco-Prussian War must take place before a united Germany was formed.*
> **—Otto von Bismarck**

Therefore, the possibility of a two-front war led France to exert pressure on Prussia to abandon its claim to the Spanish throne. Wilhelm I agreed to withdraw Leopold's candidacy because he did not want to go to war with France. However, Wilhelm I politely refused the demands of the French ambassador to never again allow a candidacy for the Spanish crown **(Refer Map 6.4)**.

EMS Telegram

The EMS telegram's contents outlined the details of a disagreement between Wilhelm and the French ambassador concerning the succession to the Spanish throne. Nevertheless, Bismarck wanted war with France and therefore edited William's EMS telegram to make it more provocative, and published it in the German newspapers as the 'EMS Dispatch'. It ultimately caused the Franco-Prussian war of 1870-71.

Points to Ponder

The EMS telegram was sent by the Prussian Chancellor, Otto von Bismarck, to King Wilhelm I of Prussia, informing him of a dispute between the French Ambassador to Prussia and the King's cousin, Prince Leopold of Hohenzollern, over the possible candidacy of the latter for the Spanish throne.

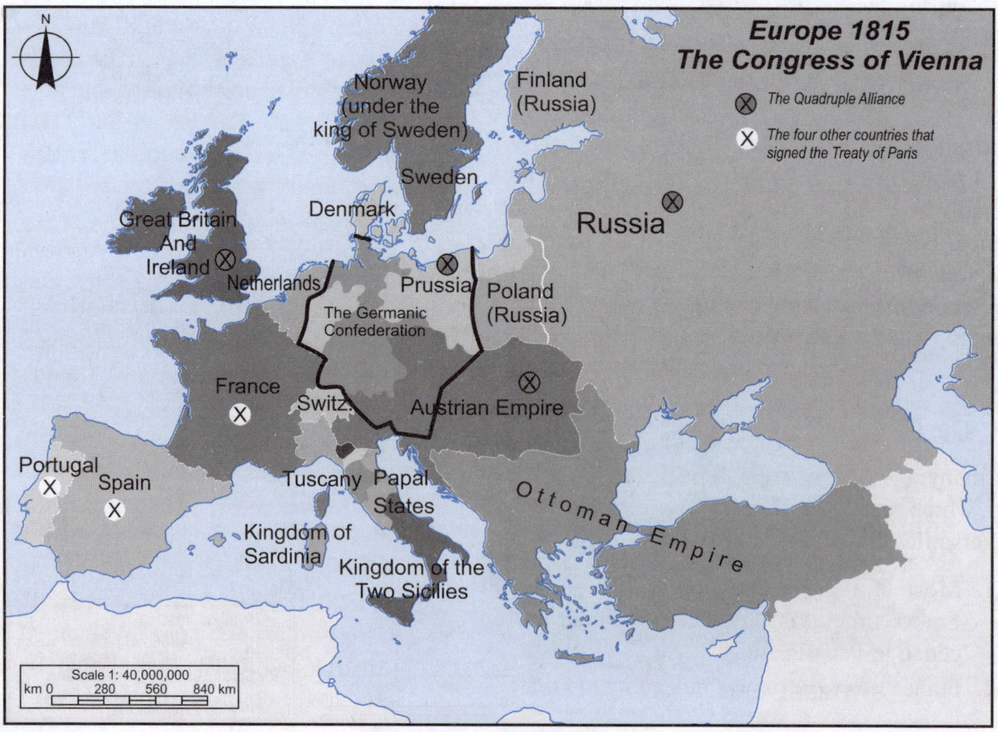

Map 6.4: Geographical Location of France vis - a - vis Spain and France

Bismarck's Diplomacy Isolates France

Bismarck used diplomacy to isolate France because he desired a war with France without the involvement of any other European nations.

1. **Neutrality of Russia**: Throughout the Crimean War and the Polish Revolt, Bismarck had already secured the Tsar of Russia's neutrality. Additionally, Bismarck agreed with the Russian strategy to conquer Turkey and seize the Black Sea.
2. **Neutrality of Austria**: After the Austro-Prussian War, Bismarck presented Austria with a modest peace; he avoided Austria any territorial losses and spared Austria the humiliation of having troops stationed in Vienna.
3. **Neutrality of Italy:** Italy was offered an alliance by Bismarck in exchange for taking over the French-held city of Rome. But Victor Emmanuel pledged to remain neutral during the Franco-Prussian War.

Franco-German War 1870-71

A misunderstanding with EMS telegram triggered the Franco-Prussian War, which Prussia unexpectedly won on practically all fronts, shocking France. Following several battles, a decisive war was fought at Sedan that resulted in the fall of the Second French Empire under Napoleon III in France.

Treaty of Frankfurt

Germany and France signed the Treaty of Frankfurt, which served as the foundation for the Treaty of Versailles. Under the treaty:

1. Most of the German-speaking regions of France, including Alsace Lorraine, were ceded to Prussia and,
2. France was to pay a war indemnity to Prussia.

Consequences of Franco-Prussian War and Battle of Sedan

The Franco-German War had profound and lasting repercussions as follows:

1. **Completion of the Unification of Germany:** The Franco-Prussian War resulted in the formation of the German Empire and the merger of the southern states into the German Confederation, which survived until the Second World War. Therefore, King William of Prussia was declared German Emperor in 1871 at the Royal Palace of Versailles.
2. **Completion of the Unification of Germany**: Following the withdrawal of French forces from the Papal States, Italy annexed the Papal States, completing the unification of the country.
3. **Third Republic in France**: Napoleon III's monarchy was overthrown by the Franco-Prussian War, and the Third Republic of France was established. This republic was successful in providing a stable government.
4. **Rivalry between France and Germany:** It marks the era of French- Germany rivalry. The Frankfurt Treaty humiliated France and led to Germany's annexation of Alsace-Lorraine, which hurt French national pride. From 1871 until 1914, there was a very fragile era of peace because of France's desire to recapture Alsace-Lorraine and Germany's growing imperialist ambitions. This put both countries constantly on the brink of war, which eventually led to World War I.
5. **Indirect cause of World War I:** German and Italian unification disturbed the balance of power in Europe. Bismarck made Germany the most powerful military force and established the alliance of the three Emperors, a covert alliance system involving Germany, Austria, and Russia that ultimately contributed to the outbreak of World War I.

6. **Russia violated the Treaty of Paris:** Russia used the conflict to violate provisions of the Treaty of Paris, which it had signed following its defeat in the Crimean War, and occupied the Black Sea.

ECONOMIC–INDUSTRIAL FACTORS FOR THE UNIFICATION OF GERMANY

The Industrial Revolution began in Prussia at the beginning of the 19th century and quickly expanded to the other German states. All other German states looked to Prussia for leadership because Prussia was the region that led to industrialization. Additionally, the expansion of railways in Germany throughout the 1830s and 1840s led to a stronger integration of the German market.

> *"It was not blood and iron rather iron and coal which made the unification of Germany possible.*
> *—Maynard Keynes"*

Role of Zollverein in the unification of Germany

The Zollverein was a Prussian customs union that Prussian FM Bulow started in 1818 and eventually fully operationalized in 1833-34. As all German states, except for Austria, joined the Customs Union, therefore, Zollverein connected Prussian and other German states. Therefore, the economic -industrial component was very important in the unification of Germany.

Impact of the Zollverein on German Unification

There is debate and disagreement among historians over the impact of the Zollverein (Customs Union) on the unification of Germany. Traditional historians argued that the Zollverein had an adverse effect on German unification, while modern historians were of the opinion that it played a greater part in the unification of Germany.

Traditional View: Adverse Impact on German Unification

The Zollverein (Customs Union), according to traditional historians, had a negative impact on the unification of Germany as:

1. Only monetary considerations led the German states to join the customs union; there was no desire for unification.
2. Some of the German states remained anti-Prussian and largely pro-Austrian.
3. The greater revenue brought about by Zollverein allowed many German states to strengthen their independence.
4. Austria was defeated in the 1866 Prussia-Austria war. Even then, the southern German states decided against joining the Prussia-led German Federation. Thus, traditional historians contend that participation in Zollverein did not result in any kind of political commitment.

However, modern historians believed that the Zollverein (Customs Union) contributed more to the unity of Germany. Zollverein contributed to the unification of German states in the following ways:

> **Points to Ponder**
>
> British economist John Maynard Keynes said, 'It was not blood and iron but iron and coal which made the unification of Germany possible.'

1. A sense of nationalism was established in Germany because of the increase in communication due to industrial growth. Additionally, economic development resulted in the rise of the capitalist elite, who desired

a strong German empire and pushed for political unification among the German states due to competition from Britain and France.

2. Zollverein (Customs Union) lowered protectionist barriers, which sparked a sense of economic unification among German States.
3. The Zollverein (Customs Union) lessens agriculture's sway over the German economy.

Prussia's economic dominance in Germany can be attributed in large part to Zollverein. Germany's political unification in 1871 was made possible by Prussia's industrial prowess.

How was German Unification Achieved?

John Maynard Keynes, a notable British economist of the 20th century, believed that the German Empire was not built on 'blood and iron,' but rather on 'coal and iron.' Blood and iron refer to the unification of Germany through war, while 'coal and iron' refer to unification through economic linkages and economic power.

Unification of Germany by Coal and Iron

According to John Maynard Keynes, Prussia became strong economically because of fast industrialization. It laid the foundation for unification, which was subsequently expanded by Bismarck's skilful diplomacy. The policy of coal and iron created the foundation by:

1. **Weaken regionalism among the German States**: Members of the Prussian-led Zollverein (Customs Union) enacted uniform economic policies and tariffs towards non-members, which promoted collaboration and dependence among the German States. Consequently, regional barriers and rivalry between German states were broken down by economic unification, which eventually resulted in political unification among German states.
2. **Established leadership of Prussia**: With the help of Zollverein, Prussia became the country's economic leader. Many German states, therefore, saw Prussia as the obvious choice to lead a united Germany. By 1851, all the German states had joined the Zollverein, with Austria being the only exception. This demonstrates that Prussian dominance was established in the economic arena even before the appointment of Bismarck in the 1860s.
3. **Coal and iron created the foundation for blood and iron policy:** Without Prussia's economic dominance, which supplied the resources and technology for the military, Bismarck's Blood and Iron policy would not have been feasible.

Unification of Germany by Blood and Iron

Other scholars, however, suggest that 'blood and iron' rather than 'coal and iron' was responsible for the unification of Germany. They argue that:

1. Bismarck's contribution to the unification of Germany was the most important factor. Before Germany was united, Bismarck followed a policy of 'blood and iron' and fought three wars against Denmark, Austria, and France for the unification of Germany.
2. Although Zollverein (Customs Union) was established in 1834, attempts to unify Germany in the revolution of 1848 were unsuccessful, highlighting the fact that coal and iron were not the primary factors in unification.
3. The majority of German states still looked to Austria for political affairs, despite the economic unification of Germany brought about by Zollverein.

It is true that Austria was economically isolated from the rest of Germany while Prussia was integrated due to Zollverein. But, it is also true, however, that political integration was not conceivable until Austria's decline as a major political force, notwithstanding the economic integration. Therefore, according to modern scholars, the 'coal and iron' foundation for German unification was laid, upon which Bismarck's 'blood and iron' policy was built. As a result, both had an impact on unification, albeit to varying degrees and at different times.

COMPARISON BETWEEN THE UNIFICATION OF ITALY AND THAT OF GERMANY

> *The difference between the German and the Italian unification is the difference between the longbow and the revolver. The Italian unification was a slow and difficult process that relied on traditional political and military methods, while the German unification was a more rapid and decisive process that made use of modern military technology and strategy.*
>
> ***—Eric Hobsbawm (Historian)***

Similarity

1. **Role of Napoleon**: Napoleon was responsible for the initial attempt to unite both Germany and Italy. Efforts of Napoleon in the form of the Rhine federation and the propagation of ideals of the French Revolution laid the basis for the rise of German nationalism. Similarly, Napoleonic measures of establishing the Swiss alpine republic and reforms in accordance with the ideals of the French Revolution triggered the growth of awakening in Italy.
2. **Vienna Congress**: The Vienna Congress of 1815 attempted to reverse the changes made by Napoleon in both Germany and Italy, but they were only partially successful.
3. **Revolution of 1848**: The 1848 revolution failed to bring liberty or unity to Germany, as it had failed in Italy. However, the 1848 Revolution made it obvious that under Prussian leadership, German unification would be realized, whereas Italian unification would be under Piedmont Sardinia.

Dissimilarity

1. **Role of leader**: Unlike Italy, where Garibaldi and Mazzini aided Cavour in his efforts to unify Italy, Bismarck single-handedly brought German unification.
2. **Foreign assistance**: Cavour was successful in gaining the support of France and Great Britain for the cause of Italian unification through diplomatic tactics, such as offering support in the Crimean War. Unlike Cavour, Bismarck was able to unite Germany using military force rather than foreign assistance.
3. **Zollverein**: No customs union equivalent to Prussia's Zollverein helped Italy move towards unification, which played a role in making Prussia the most economically advanced German state.
4. **Parliamentary politics**: The deliberate combination of military diplomacy, parliamentary politics, and a popular movement led to the unification of Italy. However, there was less scope for popular agitation and parliamentary politics during the unification of Germany. In his speech, Bismarck expressed his contempt for parliamentary politics by saying, 'Germany is not looking to your liberalism, but to your strength.'
5. **Nature of merger of states**: The unification of Italy was influenced by several factors. The Piedmont-Sardinian monarchy had to accept the liberal constitution's limitations on its power since it had made a compromise to liberal ideology. However, Prussia proceeded on with its own terms for German unification. That is why some scholars have remarked that whereas the Piedmont-Sardinia state merged with Italian states, German states just vanished into Prussia.

LET'S REVISE

The Factors for Unification of Germany

1. Role of Napoleon
   (a) Provided Administrative Unity
   (b) Spread of Ideals of the French Revolution
2. Cultural-Ideological factor
   (a) Role of German philosophers like John Herder, Fichte, and Hegel
3. Economic-Industrial factor
   (a) Coal and Iron Policy: Role of Zollverein (Custom union)
4. Political-Diplomatic Factor
   (a) Blood and Iron Policy of Bismarck
   (b) Role of William I

'Two-pronged Strategy' of Bismarck

1. Blood and Iron Policy
2. Realpolitik-based diplomatic policy

Consequences of Franco-Prussian War and Battle of Sedan

1. Completion of the unification of Germany
2. Completion of the unification of Germany
3. Third Republic in France
4. Rivalry between France and Germany
5. Indirect cause of World War I
6. Russia violated the Treaty of Paris

Comparison between the Unification of Italy and that of Germany

1. Similarity
   (a) Role of Napoleon
   (b) Vienna Congress
   (c) Revolution of 1848
2. Dissimilarity
   (a) Role of Leader
   (b) Foreign Assistance
   (c) Zollverein
   (d) Parliamentary politics
   (e) Nature of Merger of State

PROBABLE QUESTIONS

1. What determinant factors, along with diplomatic, shaped the process of German unification?
2. 'Napoleon kindled the national sentiment, but German unity was achieved by Bismarck.' Discuss.
3. 'From Bismarck's 'Blood and Iron' speech and his forceful actions to achieve German unification, Bismarck came to be known as the Iron Chancellor.' Critically examine.
4. Was German unification achieved more by 'coal and iron' than by 'blood and iron'?
5. At the end of the Battle of Sedan (1870), 'Europe lost a mistress and gained a master'. Critically examine.
6. Compare and contrast the history of the unification of Germany and that of Italy.

TIMELINE (1815–1914)

- **1815**: The Congress of Vienna redraws the map of Europe and creates the German Confederation, a loose union of 39 states.
- **1848**: The Revolutions of 1848 break out in Germany, leading to a failed attempt to establish a constitutional monarchy and a strong, centralized government.
- **1850**: Austrian forces compelled the Prussian King to sign the Olmutz Convention after defeating Frederick William IV at the battle of Olmutz.
- **1857-1861**: After suffering a stroke, King Frederick William IV was unable to continue to reign of Prussia; as a result, Prince Wilhelm I became king.
- **1860-1862**: Deadlock between Wilhelm I and Prussian Diet over Army Reforms.
- **1864**: Prussian-Austrian soldiers jointly defeated Denmark in German-Danish War.
- **1866**: Austria was shocked by how brutally Prussia defeated them in the battle of Sadowa during the Austro-Prussian War.
- **1870-1871**: France was defeated in Franco-Prussian War and Germany and France signed the Treaty of Frankfurt.
- **1871**: The German Empire is established, with Wilhelm I as its first emperor and Otto von Bismarck as its chancellor.
- **1871-1890**: Bismarck implements a series of domestic and foreign policies that would strengthen the empire and make Germany a major European power.
- **1888**: Wilhelm II becomes German Emperor, Bismarck is dismissed and the era of 'New Course' begins, marked by a shift away from Bismarck's policies.
- **1890**: The German Empire begins a period of rapid industrialization.
- **1890-1914s**: Germany becomes increasingly assertive in foreign affairs, leading to tensions with other European powers and contributing to the outbreak of World War I in 1914.

CHAPTER

7

Photo Credit: Everett Historical / Shutterstock, Everett Collection / Shutterstock

RISE OF NATIONALISM AND WORLD WAR I

> *Nationalism is a very powerful force and it can be very positive or very negative. In the late 19th century, it became a negative force as countries competed with one another for resources, territories, and prestige. These rivalries and tensions eventually exploded into the First World War.*
>
> *—Margaret MacMillan (Historian)*

INTRODUCTION

The emergence of nationalism during the French Revolution and the subsequent Revolution of 1848 had far-reaching consequences on Europe in the 19th century, both unifying and dividing the continent. The rise of nationalism in the backdrop of Italy and Germany resulted in their unification. However, in the case of old, multiracial, multiregional, and multilingual European empires, like the Ottoman Empire, Habsburg Empire, and Russian Empire, it resulted in their collapse and disintegration into new nations **(Refer Map 7.1)**.

The advent of modern nationalism had different effects in the western Europe and the eastern Europe. The nations of the western Europe over the time transformed into modern nation-states, but the multiracial and multilingual empires of the eastern Europe remained medieval in character and never attempted to unify different races under a unified nationality.

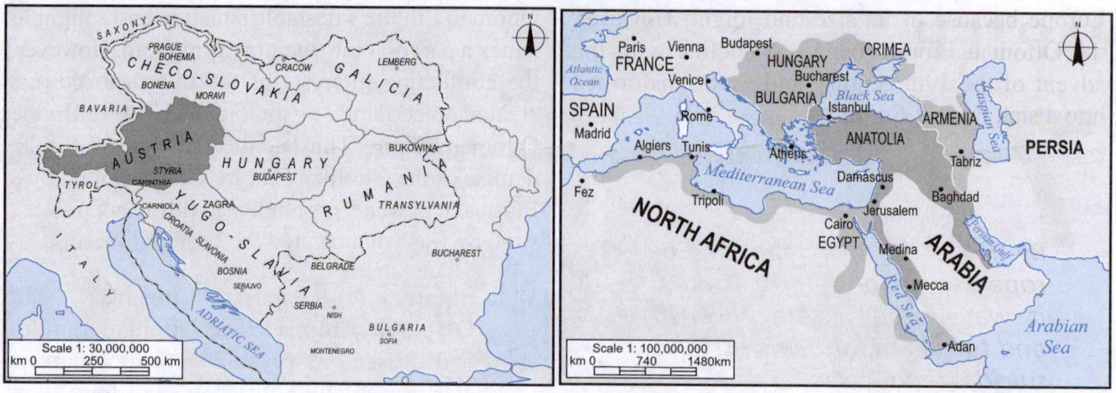

MAP 7.1: The Ottoman Empire

As a consequence, various linguistic and racial communities considering themselves as distinct nationalities, and old empires, particularly the Ottoman and the Austrian Empires, continued to resist pressure from such social groups. This trend put intense pressure on Europe, which ultimately led to the First World War **(Refer Figure 7.1).**

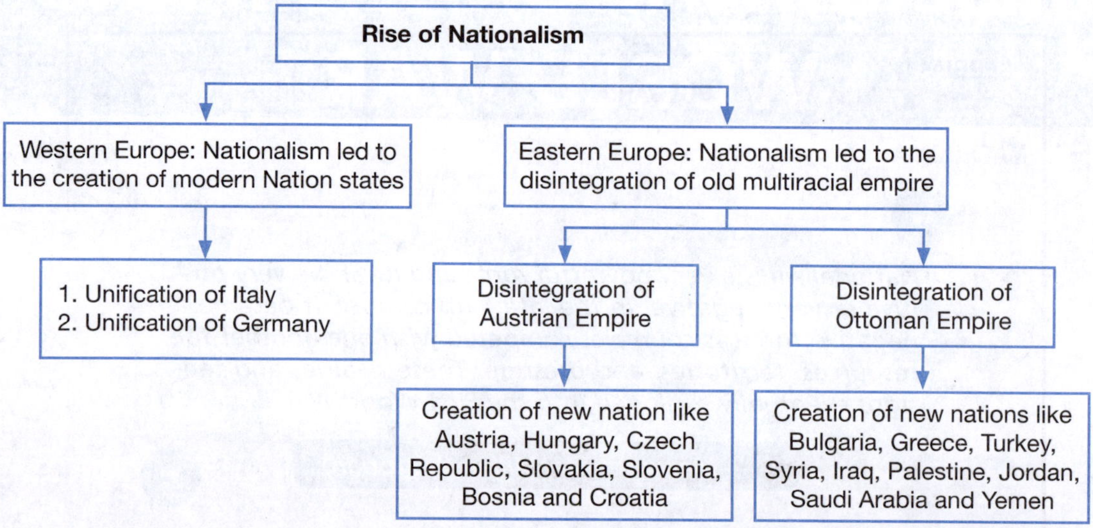

FIGURE 7.1: Consequences of the Rise of Nationalism

EASTERN QUESTION/BALKAN QUESTION

The Ottoman Empire's situations were significantly different from those of other contemporary empires, such as the Austrian Empire. As a Muslim kingdom with a substantial Christian population, the Ottoman Empire was more susceptible to intervention from Christian powers in Europe at the times of racial unrest.

> **Points to Ponder**
>
> The Eastern Question refers to the complex geopolitical and diplomatic issues surrounding the decline of the Ottoman Empire in the late 19th and early 20th centuries, and the subsequent struggle for control over the Balkans.

The Ottoman Empire was initially considered to be a serious threat to the Christian nations of

Europe because of its size and might. However, the Ottoman Empire began to decline with the advent of the 19th century and was transformed into a sick man of Europe.

> "*By 1914, the sick man of Europe was no longer just Turkey, it was Europe itself, feverish and turbulent, and with strong suicidal tendencies.*
> —***David Thomson***"

As a consequence, various European countries were inclined to take benefit from the Ottoman Empire's unstable situation and sought to annex a part of it into their own kingdom. However, the conflicting interests of the European powers created uncertainty in their policies towards the Ottoman Empire. Thus, neither the survival nor the demise of the Ottoman Empire was permitted by a European power. This duality in European power's strategy was what created the Eastern Question.

1. **Strategy of Russia towards sick Ottoman Empire:** The Ottoman Empire had Russia as a neighbouring country, and Russia had both short- and long-term goals in the Ottoman Empire. The short-term goal was to capture the Dardanelles and Bosporus straits, which would provide access from the Black Sea directly to the Mediterranean Sea **(Refer Map 7.2).**

MAP 7.2: Russian Foreign Policy always aimed at capturing Bosporus and Dardanelles strait

Furthermore, Russia's long-term goal was to completely dismantle the Ottoman Empire and seize a bigger territory as a result of the Ottoman Empire's disintegration.

2. **Strategy of Austria towards sick Ottoman Empire:** Similar to Russia, Austria and the Ottoman Empire were both neighbouring regions and had shared some common races (Slavs). Austria was concerned about the formation of new states based on racial movement within the Ottoman Empire, as the dissolution of the Ottoman Empire meant the collapse of the Austrian Empire as well. However, the Austrian Empire also aspired to seize and annex territory from the Ottoman Empire's disintegration.

3. **Strategy of Britain towards sick Ottoman Empire:** Britain adopted a different strategy than Austria and Russia since Britain was anxious that the disintegration of the Ottoman Empire might significantly alter the balance of power in the Europe and was also apprehensive of the Russian approach to the Ottoman Empire. Moreover, Russian influence in the Ottoman Empire may have hindered the British route to eastern colonies like India. Due to this, Britain never endorsed the disintegration of the Ottoman Empire. Nevertheless, Britain was more than willing to annex some of the territories from the Ottoman Empire.
4. **Strategy of France towards sick Ottoman Empire**: In the Ottoman Empire, the French had a different issue and strategy than Austria, Russia, and Britain. French had made large investments in Egypt (a part of the Ottoman Empire) and were worried about their investments after the fall of the Ottoman Empire.

Due to the conflicting and diverse strategies adopted by the major European powers in regard to the disintegration of the Ottoman Empire, the Eastern Question was transformed into an international question. It is rightly regarded that 'By 1914 the sick man of the Europe was no longer just Turkey, it was the Europe itself, feverish and turbulent, and with strong suicidal tendencies.'

Transformation of Eastern Question into International Question

The Ottoman Empire's disintegration process accelerated as a result of the European nations' interference in its affairs.

1. **Independence of Greece from the Ottoman Empire**: In the 1820s, Greece witnessed the emergence of a nationalist movement aiming to separate itself from the Ottoman Empire. The Concert of Europe (Austria, France, Prussia, Russia, and the United Kingdom) was expected to intervene on the behalf of the Ottoman Empire under the principle of legitimacy. Since a significant proportion of Greece's population was Christian, Christian nations in Europe intervened to assist Greece rather than the Ottoman Empire. As a result, Greece eventually won its freedom and separated from the Ottoman Empire in 1832.

> “*Young Turks started the wind of nationalism, and in return, they had to face the whirlpool of nationalism.*”

2. **Independence of Romania from the Ottoman Empire**: Britain and France allied with the Ottoman Empire in the Crimean War (1856) against Russia, and in the Paris Peace Treaty that followed the Crimean War, the integration of the Ottoman Empire was emphasized. However, the Rum ethnic minority revolted in an independence struggle against the Ottoman Empire just three years after the Paris Peace Treaty. Once more, the European powers' differing strategies led to Romania's declaration of independence and secession from the Ottoman Empire, in 1859.

Points to Ponder

The Pan-Slavic movement in Serbia emerged in the 19th century and aimed to unite all Slavic peoples into a single political entity. In Serbia, the Pan-Slavic movement was closely linked to the struggle for independence from the Ottoman Empire, which had ruled the Balkans for centuries.

3. **Independence of Serbia, Montenegro, and Bosnia Herzegovina from the Ottoman Empire:** Austria was against the Pan-Slavic movement of Serbia under which Serbia tried to unite the whole of the Slav region of the Ottoman Empire. Revolts for independence against the Otto-

man Empire by the people of Serbia, Montenegro, and Bosnia-Herzegovina led to a conference in Berlin.

The Berlin Congress (1878) was presided over by Bismarck, who did not take a neutral stance, but rather endorsed the Austrian Empire's claim on a region of the Ottoman Empire that had disintegrated. The Berlin Congress recognized independence of Serbia and Montenegro but also ceded control of Bosnia and Herzegovina from the Ottoman Empire to the Austrian Empire.

Points to Ponder

Serbia's Pan-Slavic movement suffered a huge setback at the Berlin Congress in (1878).

> *The settlement reached at the Congress of Berlin had the remarkable outcome that it left each power dissatisfied and more anxious than ever.*
>
> ***—David Thomson***

4. **Independence of Bulgaria from the Ottoman Empire**: Although the Berlin Congress had opposed the liberation of the Bulgarian people, a nationalist movement against the Ottoman Empire began among the Bulgarian people with assistance from the Russian Empire. Consequently, a separate Bulgaria was established as an independent nation, in 1885.
5. **Failure of the Young Turk Movement (1908):** The Young Turk Movement was founded in 1908 by a group of Young Turks to attempt and save the Ottoman Empire from its declining state and the secessionist movement that followed from it. Thus, the Young Turk was a political reform movement that supported the overthrow of the Ottoman Empire's absolute monarchy in favour of a constitutional monarchy, liberalising the state, and restoring imperial authority within historical boundaries. In 1908, they were the organizers of a rebellion against Sultan Abdulhamid II oppressive rule. Young Turk sought to modernize the government, liberalize the state, and restore imperial authority within historical boundaries.

   However, Young Turks nationalistic attempts were unproductive since they actually accelerated the rise of nationalism among the multiracial Ottoman Empire's population and the consequent disintegration of the Ottoman Empire. In 1912, Balkan nations including Greece, Romania, Serbia, Bulgaria, and others attacked the Ottoman Empire in reaction to young Turks. Additionally, the First Balkan war, which lasted from 1912 to 1913, was also brought caused by various acts of the Young Turk. Thus, the majority of historians have rightly argued that 'Young Turks started the wind of nationalism and in return, they had to face the whirlpool of nationalism.'

   European countries intervened when the Balkan War started, and it was through their intervention that the London Conference was held in 1912–1913. Because of the London Conference, which also led to Albania gaining its independence, this war came to an end.

EVENTS LEADING TO THE OUTBREAK OF WAR

The concept of the balance of power based on geographical spheres of influence which was created by the Congress of Vienna and Concert of Europe was

> *The Franco-German war made Germany mistress of Europe and Bismarck master of Germany.*
>
> ***—C.D.M. Ketelbey***

completely disrupted by the unification of Germany and Italy and the consequent rise of nationalism. Thus, the early decade (1900–1914) saw a series of events between 1906–1914 that culminated into World War I because of the disturbance in the balance of power concept, the rise of Germany, and the rise of nationalism in Europe **(Refer Figure 7.2).**

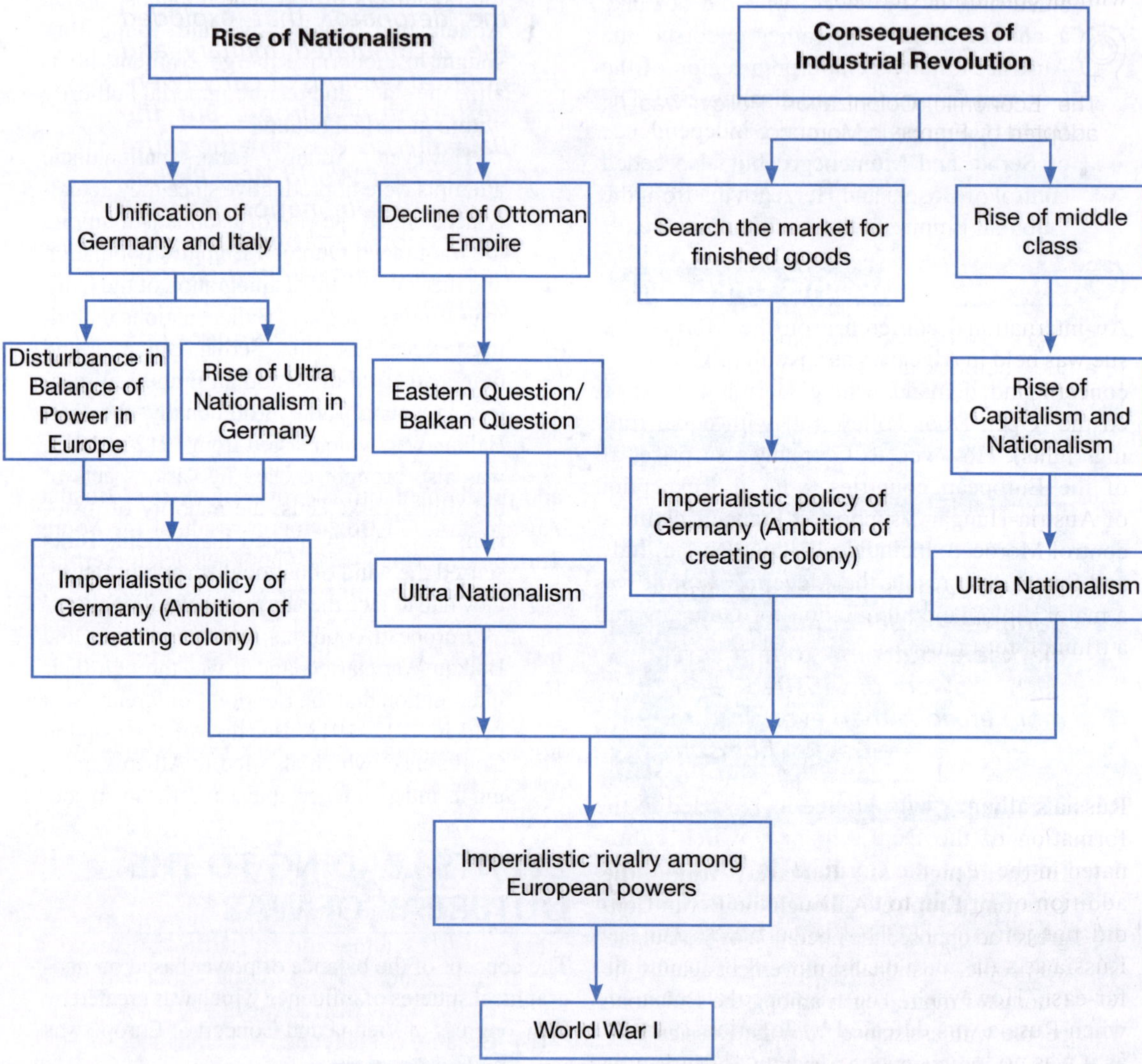

FIGURE 7.2: Factors for Series of Events in 1906–1914

First Moroccan Crisis (1905–06)

The First Moroccan Crisis, which was also the first test of the Anglo-French 'Entente Cordiale' established in 1904, was caused by German ambitions to expand her empire in Africa under the policy of Weltpolitik (World Politics). The German Empire's imperialist foreign policy, known as Weltpolitik, was enacted by Emperor Wilhelm II with the intention of making Germany a major colonial power.

By signing the Entente Cordial, France agreed to accept Britain's dominant position in

Egypt while the British pledged to accept France's dominant position in Morocco. Germany was equally interested in Morocco and felt dissatisfied that France's dominant position had been decided without consulting Germany.

Points to Ponder

The Economic Colonization Policy was adopted by France in Morocco.

Algeciras Conference (Spain, Jan 1906)

An international conference on the Morocco issue was held in Algeciras as a result of Germany's concern and demand, where Germany promoted the 'Open Door Policy' (all with equal trading rights). However, to Germany's surprise, all of the European countries, with the exception of Austria-Hungary, supported France's claim to control Morocco, including Britain, Russia, Italy, and Spain. As a result, the Algeciras summit was a major diplomatic humiliation for Germany and a triumph for France.

British Agreement with Russia (1907) and Triple Entente

Russia's alliance with France in 1894 led to the formation of the Dual Alliance, which culminated in the 'Entente Cordiale' in 1907 with the addition of Britain to the Dual Alliance. Britain did not join the Dual Alliance because it saw Russia as a threat to its colonies in India and the far-east. However, Britain's approach changed when Russia was defeated by Japan in 1904-05, as it was no longer a threat to her colonies in the far-east.

First Balkan Crisis: Bosnian Crisis (1908)

Bosnia had a mixed Serbian, and Muslim populations. It was part of the Ottoman Empire but was governed by Austria. The Young Turk Movement objected to Austrian presence in Bosnia

> *The Balkan crisis of 1914 was the detonator that exploded the accumulated military and political tensions of early-twentieth-century Europe. But the Balkan crisis was not the cause of the First World War. Rather, it was the culmination of a long process of destabilization that had been underway in Europe for years.*
>
> ***—Christopher Clark***

and proclaimed Turkish sovereignty over Bosnia. Austria annexed Bosnia as a result of the Young Turk policy, which was a major setback to Serbia's pan-Slavic nation plan.

Russia, a Slavic nation, supported Serbia, hence Serbia appealed to Russians for help in Bosnia Crisis. Consequently, a European conference was held but Britain and France preferred not to engage in the Bosnia Crisis, which was a victory for the Austro-German alliance.

Consequences of the Bosnia Crisis

(a) Austria's annexation of Bosnia sparked a long-standing rivalry with Serbia that eventually led to World War I.

(b) Because of the feeling of helplessness during the Bosnian Crisis, the Russians began modernizing their military in order to assist Serbia, if Serbia once again request help.

Second Balkan Crisis: First Balkan War (1912-1913)

The Berlin Agreement of 1878 restored Macedonia to Ottoman administration, but the settlement was unable to stop Turkish misrule in Macedonia, which sparked the First Balkan War in 1912. In order to acquire more territory from Ottoman empire, Serbia, Greece, Montenegro, and Bulgaria formed the Balkan League and attacked the Ottoman (Sick Man of Europe).

European nations did not intend war, so they called a peace conference in London, which resulted in the 1913 Treaty of London. Balkan states acquired a part of the former Ottoman Empire's territory as part of the settlement. The fact that Austria declared Albania an independent state to prevent Serbia from becoming more powerful, however, did not make Serbs happy, and this further increased hostility between Austria and Serbia.

Second Balkan War (1913)

The London peace agreement left Bulgarians upset since Macedonia was ceded to Serbia rather than to them. As a result, Bulgaria attacked Serbia in the Second Balkan War, but it failed because Greece, Romania, and Turkey took a side of Serbia. Bulgaria was defeated and lost the majority of its gains from the First Balkan War under the terms of the Treaty of Bucharest (1913).

Consequences of Balkan War

1. Disintegration of the Ottoman Empire and rise of Christian kingdoms on the Balkan peninsula.
2. Balkan state rivalries were fiercer as a result of the Second Balkan War.
3. Bulgaria joined the German and Austrian coalition out of intense anger.
4. The victory of Serbia and Greece in the second Balkan war prevented Austria from expanding into the Aegean, which intensified Austria and Serbia's hostility.
5. Due to Serbia's advocacy of Pan-Slavic nationalism, Austria, which had millions of Slavic subjects, feared secession from the Austrian Empire.
6. Germans interpreted Britain's cooperation in the Second Balkan War as a sign that it was getting prepared to break away from France and Russia as a member of the Triple Entente.

Third Balkan Crisis (1914)

The assassination of Austrian Prince Ferdinand in Sarajevo, the capital of Bosnia, by Serbian Gavrilo Princip in June 1914 ignited the Third Balkan crisis, which was the immediate cause of World War I against the background of Austria and Serbia's bitter rivalry.

Austrian government blamed the Serbian government for the assassination of Austrian Prince Ferdinand and issued a strict ultimatum with an unqualified acceptance within 48 hours. The majority of the demands were accepted by Serbia, but Austria rejected those that went against her sovereignty and instead promised to refer the matter to the Hague Tribunal or the Conference of Great Powers.

The majority of Europe, including Germany, thought the Serbian response was legitimate and that 'every pretext for war' had been eliminated. However, because of Germany's unconditional support, Austria did not satisfy, and it used assassination as justification for war against Serbia. As a result, several series of events followed, and these were as follows **(Refer Figure 7.3)**:

1. **July 28, 1914**: Austria-Hungary declares war on Serbia
2. **July 29, 1914**: Russia orders general mobilization of troops
3. **August 1, 1914**: Germany declares war on Russia
4. **August 3, 1914**: Germany declares war on France
5. **August 4, 1914**: Britain enters; declares war on Germany
6. **August 6, 1914**: Austria-Hungary declares war on Russia.

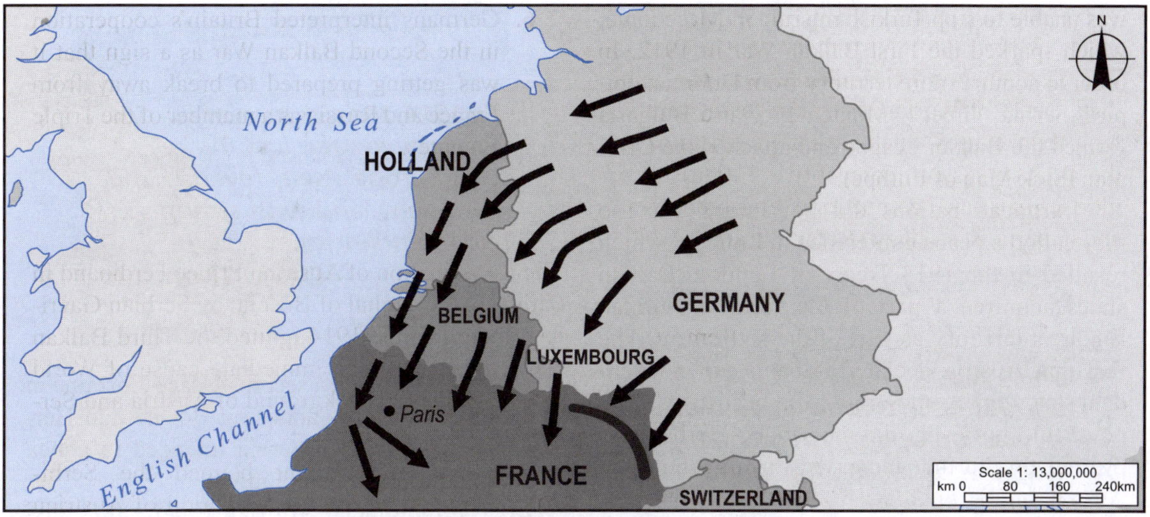

Map 7.3: Schlieffen Plan and attack on Belgium

REASONS FOR BRITAIN JOINING WORLD WAR I

Germany was fighting two front wars that is against France and Russia. According to the Schlieffen Plan, Germany would launch a swift and decisive attack on France before moving on to Russia.

However, France concentrated all of its forces around the eastern border, making it hard to strike back against France swiftly and effectively. Germans thus wanted unrestricted access to Belgian territory in order to attack France. However, Belgium rejected the deployment of German forces. As a result, Germany invaded Belgium, violating the neutrality Belgium had been guaranteed by Britain **(Refer Map 7.3).**

Participants of World War I

Allies or Entente Powers

1. Britain and her empire (Australia, Canada, India and New Zealand)
2. France
3. Russia (left December 1917)
4. Italy (entered May 1915)
5. Serbia
6. Belgium
7. Romania (entered August 1916)
8. USA (entered April 1917)
9. Japan

Central Powers

1. Germany
2. Austria-Hungary
3. Ottoman Empire (entered November 1914)
4. Bulgaria (entered October 1915)

Figure 7.3: Participants of World War I

CAUSES OF FIRST WORLD WAR

The assassination of Ferdinand was the immediate cause of World War I, but there were also long-term causes, such as extreme nationalism, the alliance system, competitive militarism, Anglo-German naval competition, economic rivalry, and imperialist strategy **(Refer Figure 7.4).**

> *The most important thing about the first world war is that it was unsought, unintended, and the product of a long sequence of events which began in 1871.*
>
> ***—David Thomson***

Immediate Causes of War

The Ottoman Empire's disintegration and the subsequent rivalry between Austria and Serbia in the Balkans, known as the 'Eastern Question', were the immediate causes of World War I. The sick man of Europe (disintegration of the Ottoman Empire) led to rivalry between Austria and Serbia due to the fact that-

> *By 1914, the sick man of Europe was no longer just Turkey, it was Europe itself, feverish and turbulent, and with strong suicidal tendencies.*
>
> ***—David Thomson***

(a) Austria created a second Alsace-Lorraine in the Balkans by annexing Bosnia and Herzegovina, which Serbia intended to annex into the Pan-Slavic Empire.

(b) The multiracial Austrian Empire may disintegrate as a result of the Serbian Pan-Slavic Movement's aspirations for a state of Yugoslavia.

(c) The creation of the state of Albania during the First Balkan Wars in 1912–1913 prevented Serbia from gaining access to the sea.

Under these circumstances, the visit of Archduke Francis and the subsequent murder of Archduke Francis at Sarajevo by a Bosnian named Gavrilo Princip sparked a sequence of events that culminated in the outbreak of World War I.

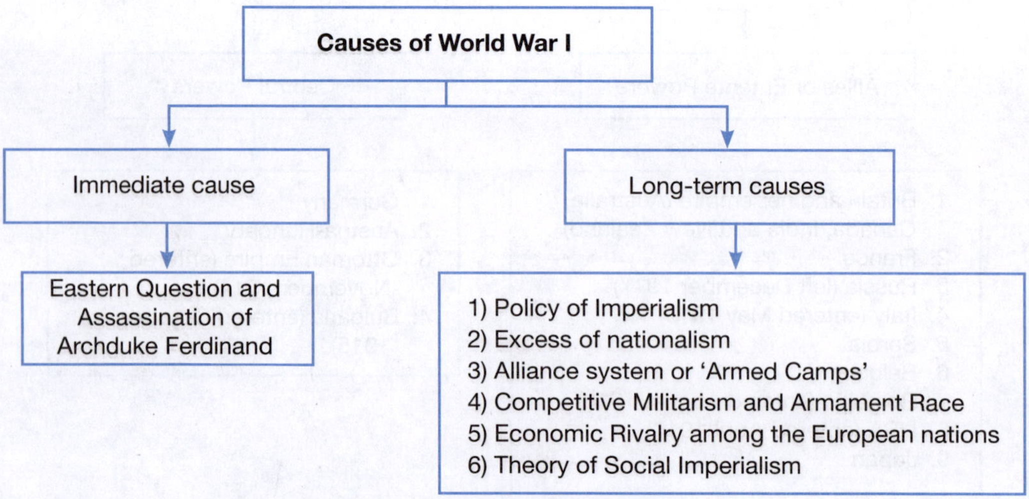

FIGURE 7.4: Causes of World War I

Long-term Causes of World War I

Although the assassination of Archduke Ferdinand is commonly quoted as having started the World War I, its outbreak was actually the outcome of a prolonged sequence of circumstances brought on by economic, political, and social factors that began in 1871.

The assassination of a king and a prince was actually not such a significant moment that it should have triggered a war. Before this incident, in 1900 and 1909, respectively, the kings of Italy and Portugal were assassinated. However, these events failed to spark a war. The fundamental reasons for the ignition of war were:

Policy of Imperialism by the European Nation

The Industrial Revolution played an important economic role during World War I. Multipolar centres were developed in Europe during the Industrial Revolution. In other words, after the Industrial Revolution, the search for a market and imperialistic rivalry commenced **(Refer Figure 7.5).**

> *We do not want to put anyone into the shade, but we demand a place for ourselves in the sun.*
>
> ***—German Chancellor Bernhard von Bulow***

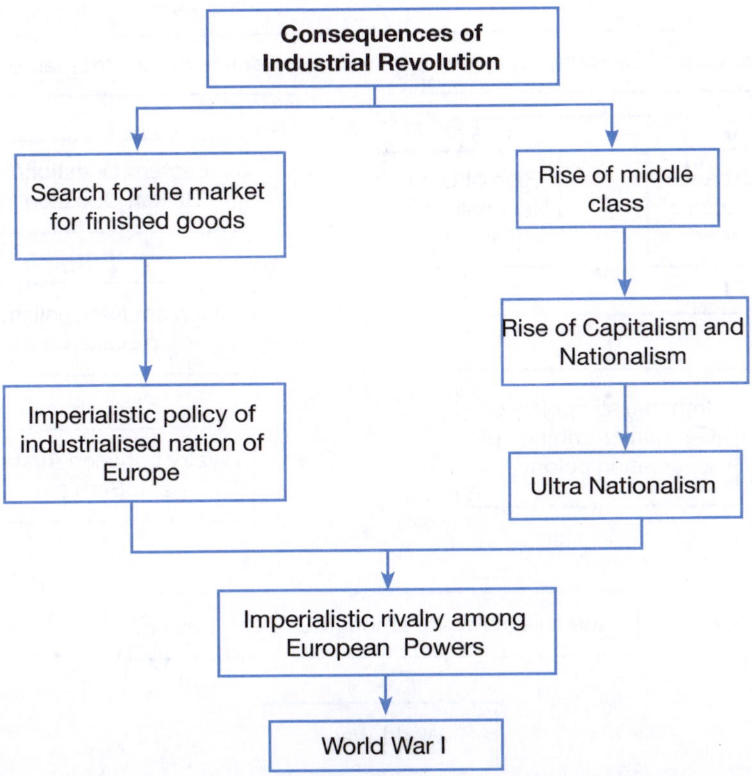

FIGURE 7.5: Industrial Revolution and World War I

Moreover, the greatness of the European nations were dependent on their power position in Europe as well as non-European possessions in Asia and Africa. Large colonial empires and non-European possessions were held by Russia, France, and England. Germany, however, possessed very few colonies inside and outside of Europe. Hence, Wilhelm II and Germany desired 'Weltpolitik', or 'The Place in The Sun.' Moreover, Bernhard von Bulow, the chancellor of Germany, stated in 1897, 'We do not want to put anyone into the shade, but we demand a position for ourselves in the sun.' Therefore, the unfulfilled imperialist ambitions of Germany and other European nations were the major cause of the international tensions and crisis that culminated in the outbreak of the World War I.

Ultra-Nationalism in Europe and Incipient Nationalism in Balkan

Ultra-nationalism in Italy, France, Serbia, and Germany inflamed cultural and national pride among Europeans and ignited World War I. Ultra-nationalism supported by the imperialism policy, various European nations created imperialist rivalries, such as those between Austria and Serbia in the Balkans and Germany and Great Britain in naval and military competition **(Refer Figure 7.6).**

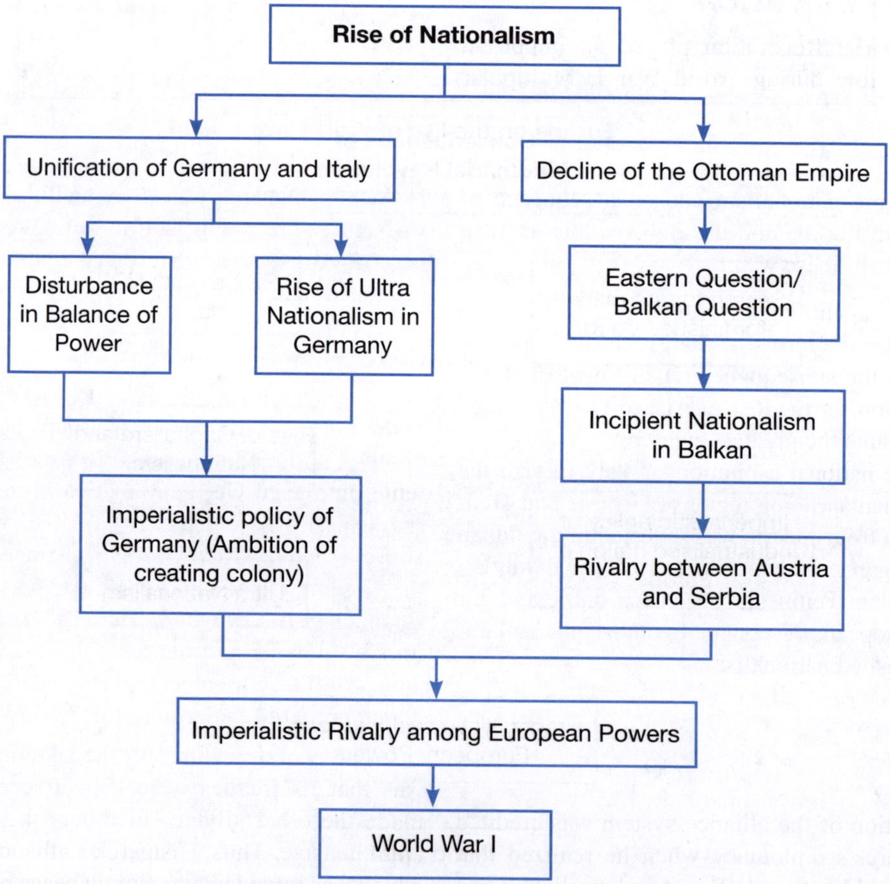

FIGURE 7.6: Nationalism and World War I

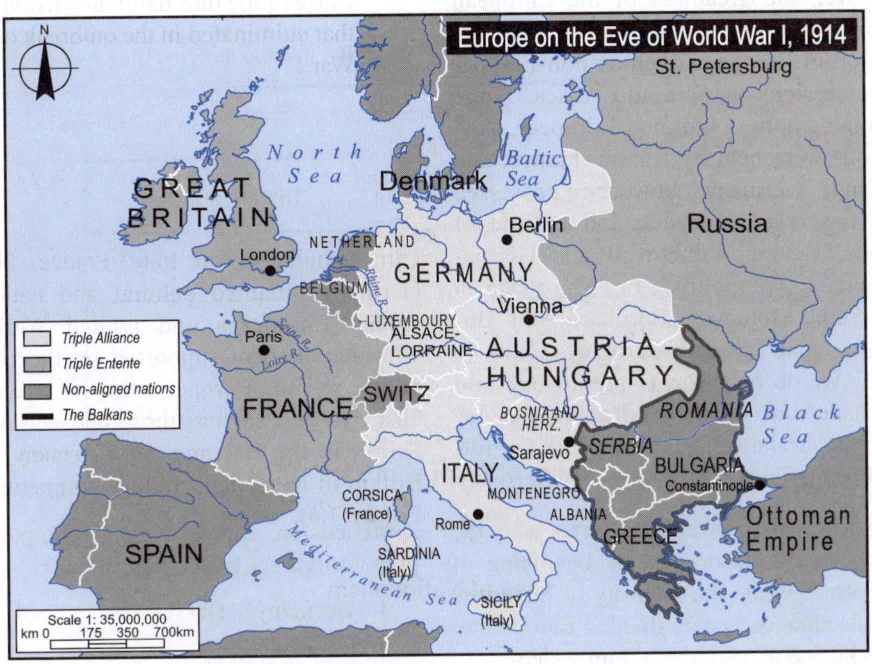

Map 7.4: Europe on the Eve of World War I, 1914

Extreme nationalism caused a sequence of conflicts in Europe and the Balkans that sparked World War I. These were:

1. Due to the annexation of Alsace Lorraine under the terms of the Treaty of Frankfurt and the subsequent French Spirit of Retribution for the loss of Alsace Lorraine, they became the greatest enemies.
2. The national aspiration of Italy to take the Italian-speaking regions of Trieste and Trentino from Austria was reflected in the Italian Slogan Italia Irredenta (unredeemed Italy).
3. Balkan Peninsula became a battlefield for European powers due to embryonic and unsatisfied nationalism.

Alliance system or 'Armed Camps'

The creation of the alliance system was credited to Bismarck's diplomacy when he realized that France would not easily forget its humiliation and loss of Alsace-Lorraine and to maintain Peace. However, Bismarck was also mindful that France was not a threat if it had no allies. As a result, he created a system of military alliances, which prompted counter-alliances and caused Europe to become divided into two hostile armed camps **(Refer Figure 7.7 and Map 7.4).**

The several events that took place between 1906 and 1914 divided rival groups against one another, and made it a prestige issue. Triple Entente outplayed Germany in two Moroccan crises, which was seen as Triple Alliance's defeat. However, the Austro-German alliance defeated the Triple Entente and humiliated Russia in the Bosnian Crisis of 1908. These alternating diplomatic defeats and successes created hostility among alliance members and intensified rivalry, which prepared the ground for World War I.

The worst feature of the alliance system was that its treaties were kept a secret, which made the other alliance members skeptical and apprehensive. Thus, Bismarck's alliance system, which was intended to maintain peace but instead led to war.

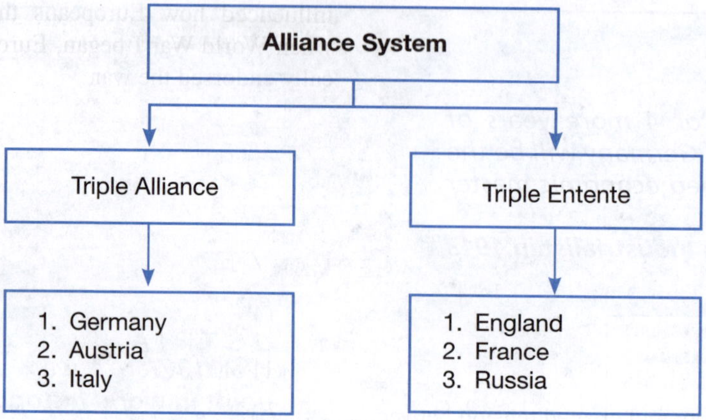

FIGURE 7.7: Division of Europe into the Alliance System

Some historians, however, differed with the Alliance system's influence at the beginning of the World War I. While the majority of historians argue that the alliance system divided Europe into army units and was a major contributing element to World War I, some historians disagree and believe that the alliance system was not a major factor in the war. In addition, they argue that due to alliance treaties, no European nation officially declared war. They cite several incidents that have occurred since 1904 to support their argument, none of which have resulted in a major conflict. These were:

1. Despite being a member of the dual alliance, France sent no assistance to Russia during its war with Japan from 1904–05.
2. When Russia objected to the Austrian annexing Bosnia, France and Britain did not support her.
3. Austria took no interest in Germany's unsuccessful attempts in the Morocco crisis.
4. Despite being a part of the Triple Alliance, Italy enjoyed good relations with France and Britain and went to war against Germany in 1915.

Competitive Militarism and Armament Race

Rising ultra nationalism and the establishment of alliance structures developed a feeling of apprehension and fear that prompted military preparations for a potential invasion.

1. Germany's standing army and navy were both expanded.
2. France increased the length of the compulsory two-year military service requirement to three years.
3. Russia began a new initiative for modernizing its military.
4. Great Britain further increased its already high naval expenditures.

All nations became fearful and hostile as a result of this competitive arms race. Each declaration by the European nations to increase their spending on arms and armaments was allegedly considered as a threat by rivals, who in turn increased their own spending on guns.

Economic Rivalry Among the European Nation

Marxist historians argue that during the late 19th and early 20th centuries, the economic competition brought on by the Industrial Revolution provided as the major cause of the global crisis and was marked by a struggle for markets, sources of raw materials, and investment of surplus capital.

Germany's rapid industrialization and her desire to rule the global economy brought Great

> *Give us 3 or 4 more years of peace, and Germany will be the unchallenged economic master of Europe.*
>
> ***—German Industrialist in 1913***

Britain great anxiety and created tension between the two countries. Marxist historians argue further that, to a lesser extent, comparable economic rivalries exist between other European countries. Therefore, German businesses and capitalists were driven to go to war with Britain due to their vision of Economic mastery of the world because Britain controlled the majority of international trade.

However, modern historians have criticized the Marxist theory because Germany was on its way to business prosperity. In fact, a prominent German businessman predicted in 1913 that Germany would be the undisputed economic leader of Europe if there were three or four more years of peace. Therefore, they argue that a prolonged war was the last thing Germany needed.

Theory of Social Imperialism

Hegel claimed that the state is the development of divine ideas on earth and projected it as a divine phenomenon. People became very proud of their nation as a result, which contributed to the emergence of ultranationalism.

Similarly, Charles Darwin, a scientist of the 19th century, developed his well-known theory 'Origin of Species' and established that conflict makes strong people stronger. The ideology of Social Darwinism, which idealized violence and struggle, was born out of this perception. In reality, the idea of the war as a progressive process influenced how Europeans thought. Therefore, when World War I began, Europeans enthusiastically endorsed the war.

IMPACT OF WORLD WAR I

> *World War I was a turning point in world history, marking the end of the long nineteenth century and the beginning of the turbulent twentieth. It shattered the old political, social, and cultural order of Europe, and paved the way for the rise of new ideologies and movements, such as fascism and communism. Furthermore, the war transformed the nature of warfare itself, leading to the development of new technologies and tactics that would shape the course of future conflicts.*
>
> ***—Eric Hobsbawm***

World War I had significant and lasting political, economic, and socio-cultural impacts on both Europe and the rest of the world.

Political Impact of World War I

The World War I had several significant political effects, from the overthrow of traditional monarchy to the creation of new nations to the revolutions in Turkey and Russia **(Refer Figure 7.8).**

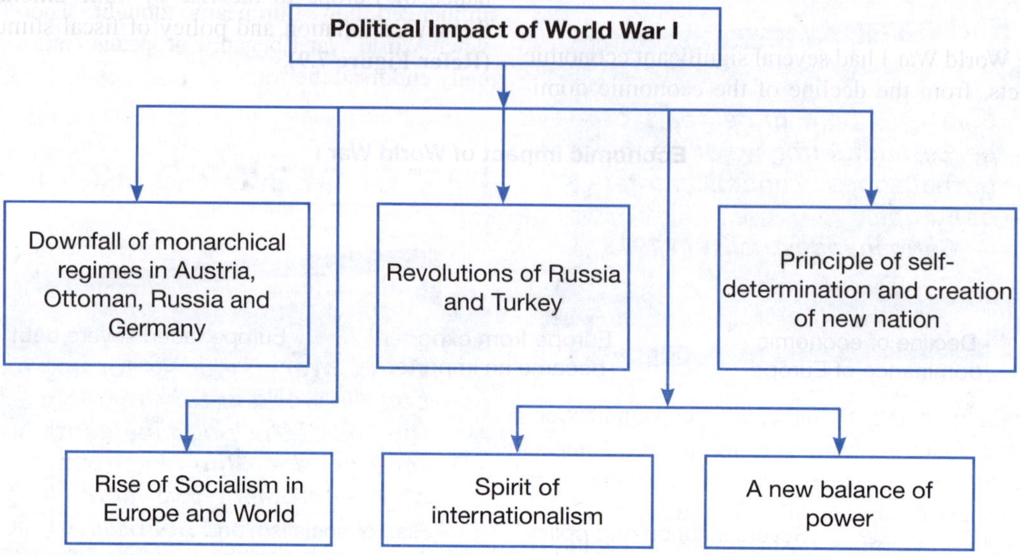

FIGURE 7.8: Political Impact of World War I

1. **Downfall of monarchical regimes**: Four great empires—Germany, Austria, Russia, and the Ottoman Empire fell as a result of World War I, and democratic governments came into existence.
2. **Revolutions of Russia and Turkey**: Tsar's (Russian King) participation in World War I started the Russian Revolution in 1917. The foundation of the first communist state in history as a result of the Russian Revolution of 1917 is recognized as one of the key watershed moments in world history.

   Similarly, the Ottoman Empire's participation in World War I caused the Turkish Revolution of 1921, which was led by Mustafa Kemal Pasha and resulted in the abolition of the post of Khalifa (religious and spiritual king of Muslims) and the formation of secular Turkey.
3. **Creation of new nations**: The self-determination principle was supported by World War I victors and peacemakers at the Paris Peace Conference in the Austrian and German Empires. A nation or group of people with identical political aspirations can attempt to establish its own independent government or state under the principle of 'self-determination'. Due to this, new nations such as Austria, Hungary, Poland, Czechoslovakia, Latvia, Lithuania, and Estonia were created.
4. **Emergence of a new Balance of Power**: After World War I, Central European powers like Germany, Austria, Hungary, and Russia lost their hegemony, and Britain, France, and America rose to prominence as the most powerful countries.
5. **Rise of socialism:** Marxist historians usually argue that the imperialist war among the European nations that ultimately led to World War I was triggered by greed for profit and the search for markets. Therefore, the cause of World War I was attributed to capitalism.

   As a result, after the war, socialism became a significant ideology. After World War I, a new state role characterized as the welfare state gained popularity.
6. **Spirit of internationalism**: The massive devastation caused by World War I prompted world leaders to work together for better global cooperation. The League of Nations was established in the spirit of internationalism in order to maintain peace in Europe.

Economic Impact of World War I

The World War I had several significant economic effects, from the decline of the economic dominance of Europe to the rise of trade unions to the severe inflation and policy of fiscal stimulus **(Refer Figure 7.9).**

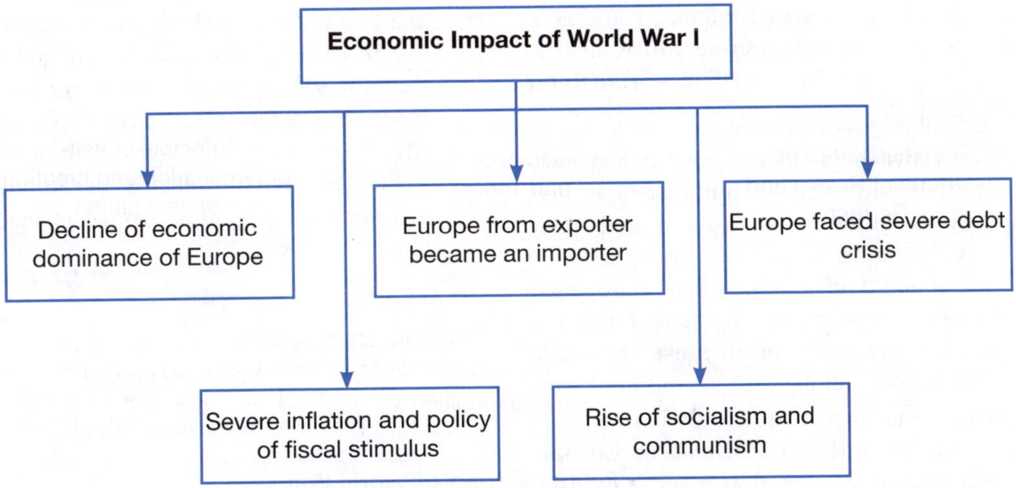

FIGURE 7.9: Economic Impact of World War I

1. **Decline of the economic dominance of Europe**: The economic dominance of Europe over the rest of the world intensified as a consequence of the industrial revolution. The bombing of industrial cities during World War I destroyed Europe's economic dominance and caused enormous economic destruction. Europe's business sector experienced severe losses and declined to 25% of its pre-World War I level.

2. **Change the direction of international trade**: After the Industrial Revolution, a powerful European nation established an empire and utilized the colony's resources for its own purposes. As a result, Europe transformed from being an importer to a major exporter of goods. However, following World War I, Europe again transformed from being an exporter to an importer **(Refer Figure 7.10).**

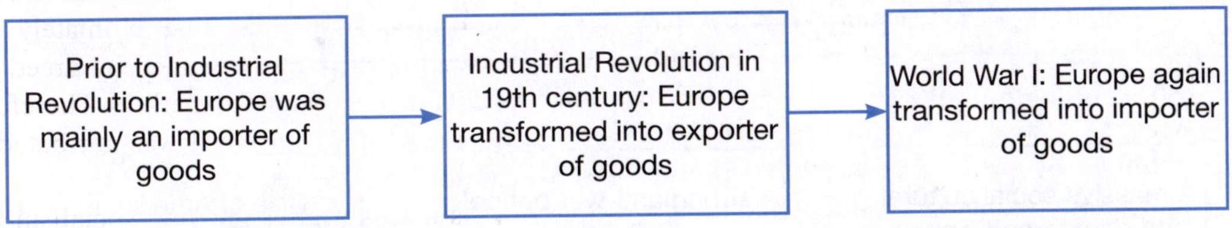

FIGURE 7.10: Transformation of European Economy after World War I

3. **Severe debt crisis in Europe**: The cost of World War I to Europe was approximately $400 billion. Moreover, European countries borrowed a lot of money from America during World War I, but when the US requested repayment, they were unable to do so because of the cost of the war.

4. **Rise of socialism and communism:** Due to high inflation and a period of the severe economic crisis in the capitalist world, the ideology of socialism and communism became more prominent as economic ideas in Europe and the outside world.

Socio-cultural Impact of World War I

The World War I had several significant socio-cultural effects, from social cultural and demographic crisis to the empowerment of women to the rise of the concept of welfare states **(Refer Figure 7.11).**

1. **A massive socio-cultural and demographic crisis**: More than 8.5 million people died, over 21 million were injured, and many more were lost in the war, causing a severe social and demographic crisis. Europe experienced a severe demographic crisis as a result of the social death caused by World War I since the majority of the dead were young and single male breadwinners.
2. **A strong anti-war outlook in Europe**: After World War I and its massive devastation, there was a strong anti-war sentiment in most of Europe, especially in democratic countries, like Britain and France. Due to anti-war sentiments, Britain and France pursued an appeasement policy toward Germany.
3. **Rise of atheism in Europe:** Due to the increasing amount of casualties, atheism has become more popular in Europe. People began to doubt God's very existence as they contended that if God would have been there, such destruction would never have occurred.
4. **Empowerment of women**: World War I also brought about some positive social and cultural transformations. Women were not permitted to participate in public life in Catholic society prior to 1914, but the war led to their involvement in economic activities. Consequently, the World War I assisted in the liberation of women as the attitude of European society toward women changed.

Points to Ponder

The feminist movement developed as a result of the World War I, and women were granted the right to vote in Britain and the USA, in 1918 and 1920, respectively.

5. **Rise of the concept of the welfare state**: After World War I, the state's function significantly transformed to become a welfare state. The majority of European nations paid attention to educational advancement. Because of the labour shortage that followed the war, Europeans also established a variety of social policies, which considerably enhanced the social position of the working class.

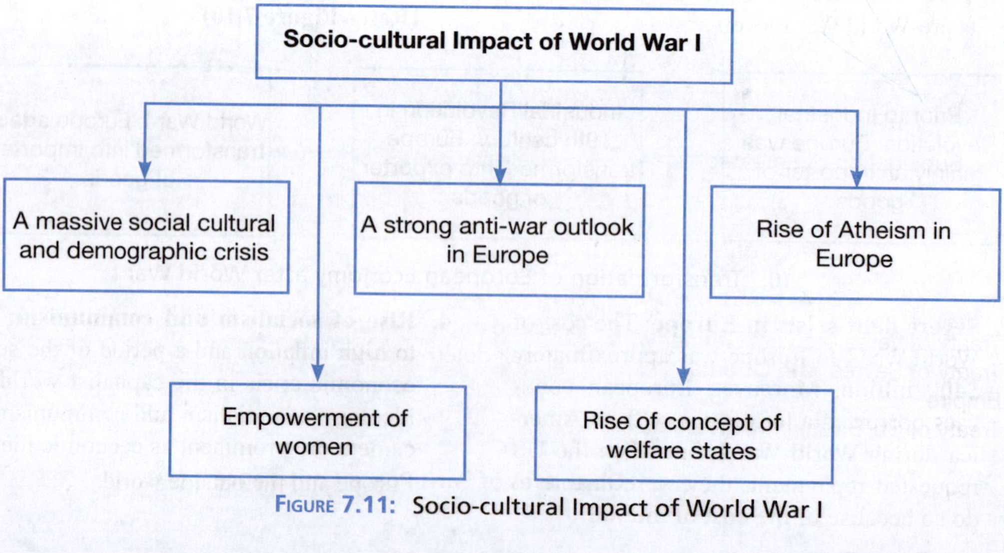

FIGURE 7.11: Socio-cultural Impact of World War I

PARIS PEACE CONFERENCE AND TREATY OF VERSAILLES

The World War I came to an end on November 11, 1918, and on January 18, 1919, a conference was held in Paris named as Paris Peace Conference. The Council of four, sometimes referred to as the Big Four—Prime Ministers Lloyd George of Great Britain, Georges Clemenceau of France, Vittorio Orlando of Italy, and U.S. President Woodrow Wilson—acted as the major decision-makers throughout the peace-making process.

However, the victors of the Paris Peace Conference had different objectives. While France sought to protect its empire and punish Germany, Britain wanted to defend its financial interests, and the United States intended to establish a new international order based on Woodrow Wilson's 14 Points.

Woodrow Wilson 14 Points

1. Open diplomacy without secret treaties
2. Economic free trade on the seas during war and peace
3. Equal trade conditions
4. Decrease armaments among all nations
5. Adjust colonial claims
6. Evacuation of all central powers from Russia and allow it to define its own independence
7. Belgium to be evacuated and restored
8. Return of the Alsace-Lorraine region and all French territories
9. Re-adjust Italian borders
10. Austria-Hungary to be provided an opportunity for self-determination
11. Redraw the borders of the Balkan region creating Romania, Serbia and Montenegro
12. Creation of a Turkish state with guaranteed free trade in the Dardanelles
13. Creation of an independent Polish state
14. Creation of the League of Nations

The Objective of the Paris Peace Conference

The fundamental goals of the Paris Peace Conference were to maintain collective peace, subjugate the defeated party, and impose limited forms of self-determination. Thus, the Big Four met to sign the Treaties of Versailles with Germany, Sevres with the Ottoman Empire, and St. Germain with Austria **(Refer Figure 7.12).**

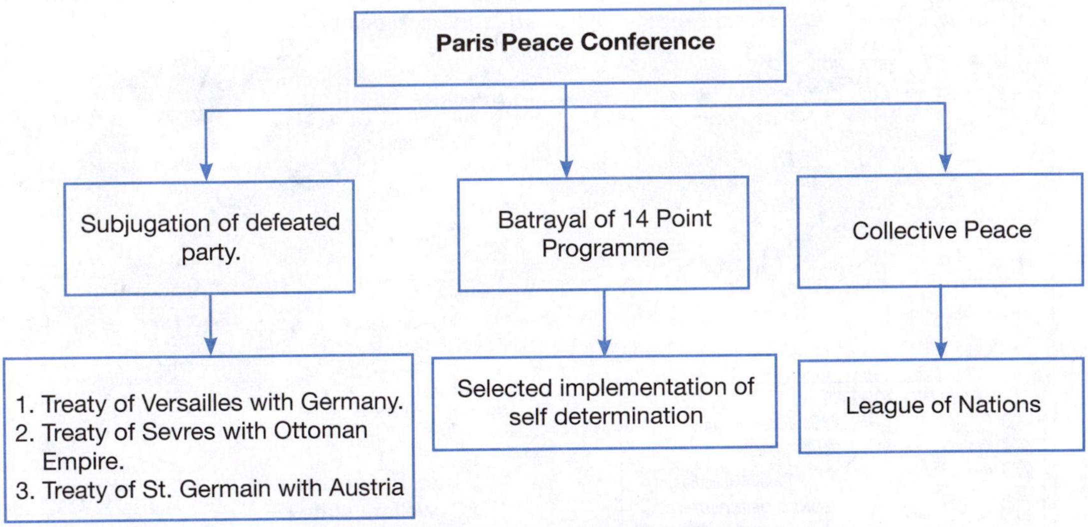

FIGURE 7.12: Objectives of Paris Peace Conference

Consequences of the Paris Peace Conference

The Paris Peace Conference had a significant and far-reaching impact on Europe and the world.

1. **Betrayal of Arab nationalism:** Paris Peace Conference betrayed Arab Nationalism in the following manner **(Refer Map 7.5):**
   - **(a)** Principle of self-determination was applied to Arab nations. However, instead of a single Arab nation, several Arab nations would be created, including Yemen, Iraq, Transjordan, Palestine, Syria, and Lebanon.
   - **(b)** Under the mandate system, victors awarded territories in Asia and Africa that were formerly under the control of Germany and the Ottoman Empire among each other. Similarly, under the pretext of the mandate system, Britain and France colonized some Arab countries.
   - **(c)** **Arab-Israel Issue:** A perpetual conflict is caused in the Palestine region by British efforts to establish Jews as a homeland there **(Refer Map 7.6)**.

2. **Harsh Treaty of Versailles with Germany:**

> *If I were the Germans, I shouldn't sign for a moment.*
>
> ***— Harold Nicolson, a British diplomat***

A harsh treaty was imposed on Germany during the Paris Peace Conference. The Treaty of Versailles was harsh due to the following reasons:

   - **(a)** It was a peace treaty without peace and an imposed peace treaty because all of its terms were determined by the victors. Even German representatives were prohibited from speaking or participating in conferences. There would have been two beneficial outcomes if the German representatives had been allowed to express their opinions:

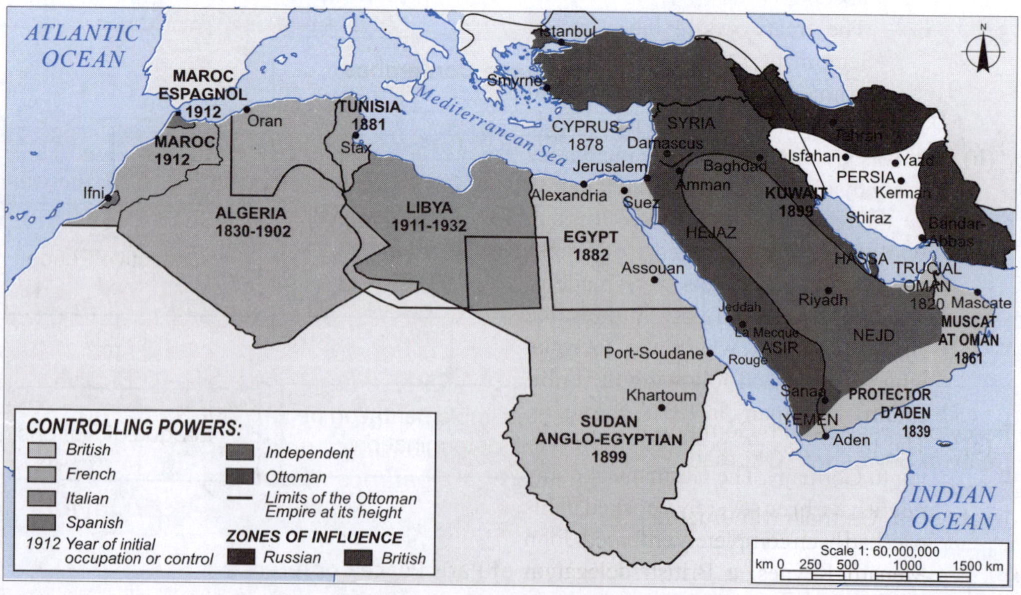

MAP 7.5: Setback to Arabian Nationalism

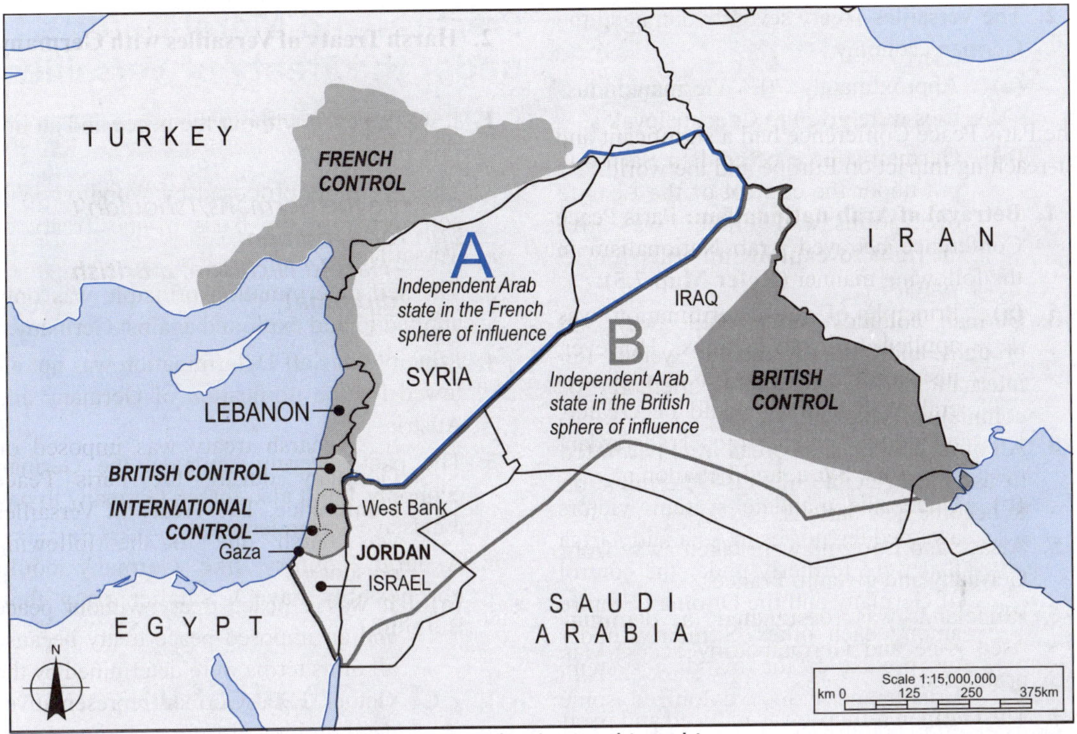

MAP 7.6: Palestine and Israel Issue

i. The Treaty of Versailles could have been more lenient and acceptable.

ii. The treaty would have gained legitimacy, and the German government might have worked to get its provisions put into effect.

(b) It was a humiliating and retaliatory treaty that France enacted in retaliation for the revenge of the Franco-Prussian War of 1871 and the Treaty of Frankfurt. In fact, Germans were made to sign the Versailles Treaty in the same Hall of Mirrors where the German king was crowned following the unification of Germany in 1870–1871.

(c) The treaty was economically devastating to Germany. The German economy might have been severely wrecked if this pact had been completely enforced. John Menard Keynes, a British delegation member, and economist resigned from his position on account of this.

(d) Only Germany alone was blamed for the creation of World War I.

Provisions of Treaty of Versailles

1. Germany is solely to blame for the war and was forced to pay a massive 6,600 million pounds as war indemnity.

> *Versailles Treaty was vindictive, crushing which lacked moral validity and failed to create a balance of powers.*
>
> *—A.P.J. Taylor*

2. The Versailles Treaty severely damaged the German economy.
   (a) Approximately 70% German industries were given to Czechoslovakia.
   (b) German source of coal in Sarr was put under the control of the League of Nations and France was given right to exploit minerals for 15 years.
3. German colonies were taken away and brought under the Mandate System (an internationally sanctioned method of colonialism).
4. All of its non-German areas were permitted to use the Principle of Self-Determination to become new nations.
5. Alsace and Lorraine were taken away from Germany and given to France.
6. Rhineland was designated a demilitarised zone and German army access was prohibited.
7. The German military was reduced and fixed at one lakh men, which was even less than Belgium. Even maintaining law and order was not enough **(Refer Map 7.7)**.

Practical and Moral Defects under the Treaty of Versailles

1. It was a peace without the peace and an imposed Treaty.
2. The 14 points proposed by Woodrow Wilson were not the basis of the Treaty of Versailles.
3. The self-determination principle was only applied to and exploited against Germany.
4. Principle of Self Determination was not allowed for the unification of Germany and Austria.
5. The pact severely damaged the German economy, but it also forced Germany to pay a massive war indemnity.
6. A large country like Germany could not possibly have a smaller army than Belgium.

Impact of Treaty of Versailles

The Treaty of Versailles, according to E.H. Carr and A.P.J. Taylor, was the primary cause of the World War II as:

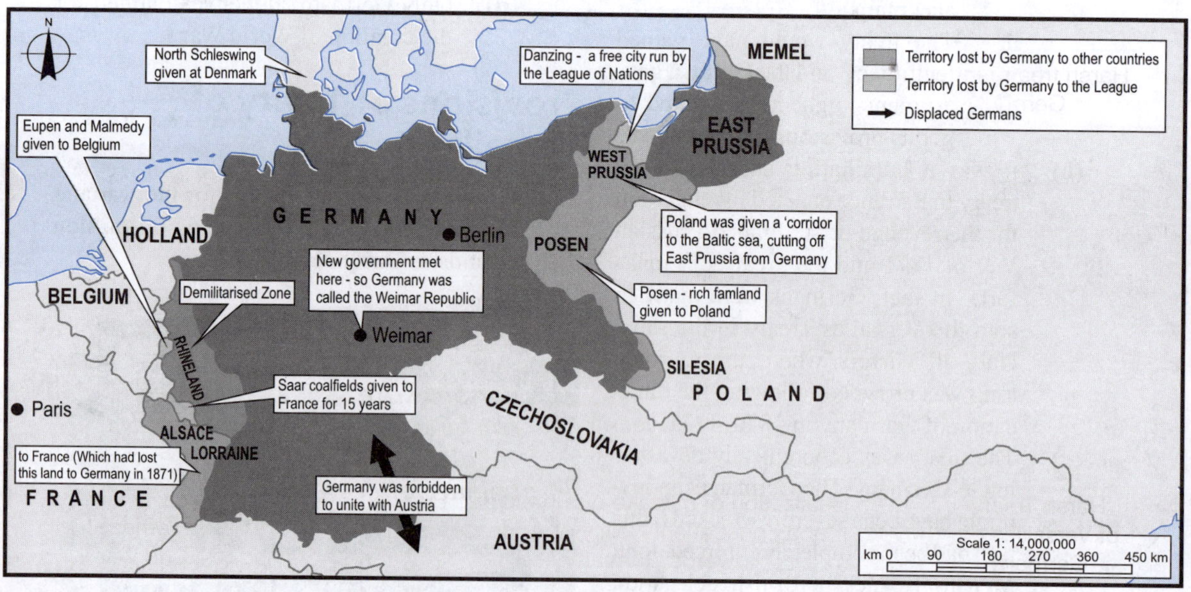

Map 7.7: Treaty of Versailles

1. **No lasting peace:** The Treaty of Versailles did not bring forth permanent peace. Even though it was a peace conference, the peacemakers in Paris were at war with Germany. As a result, the treaty did not bring about permanent peace in Europe and only offered an armistice for 20 years.
2. **Rise of Fascism and Nazism**: Hitler and Mussolini used the Treaty of Versailles as a political tool to grab power. Thus, the pact triggered a rise of extreme nationalism in Germany that eventually led to the emergence of Nazism and Hitler **(Refer Figure 7.13).**
3. **Policy of Appeasement:** The Policy of Appeasement came after the blunder at the Treaty of Versailles. The use of an appeasement policy against the aggressive actions of Germany, Italy, and Japan serves as an additional proof that the victors of the Paris Peace Conference were responsible for drafting a flawed treaty **(Refer Figure 7.14).**

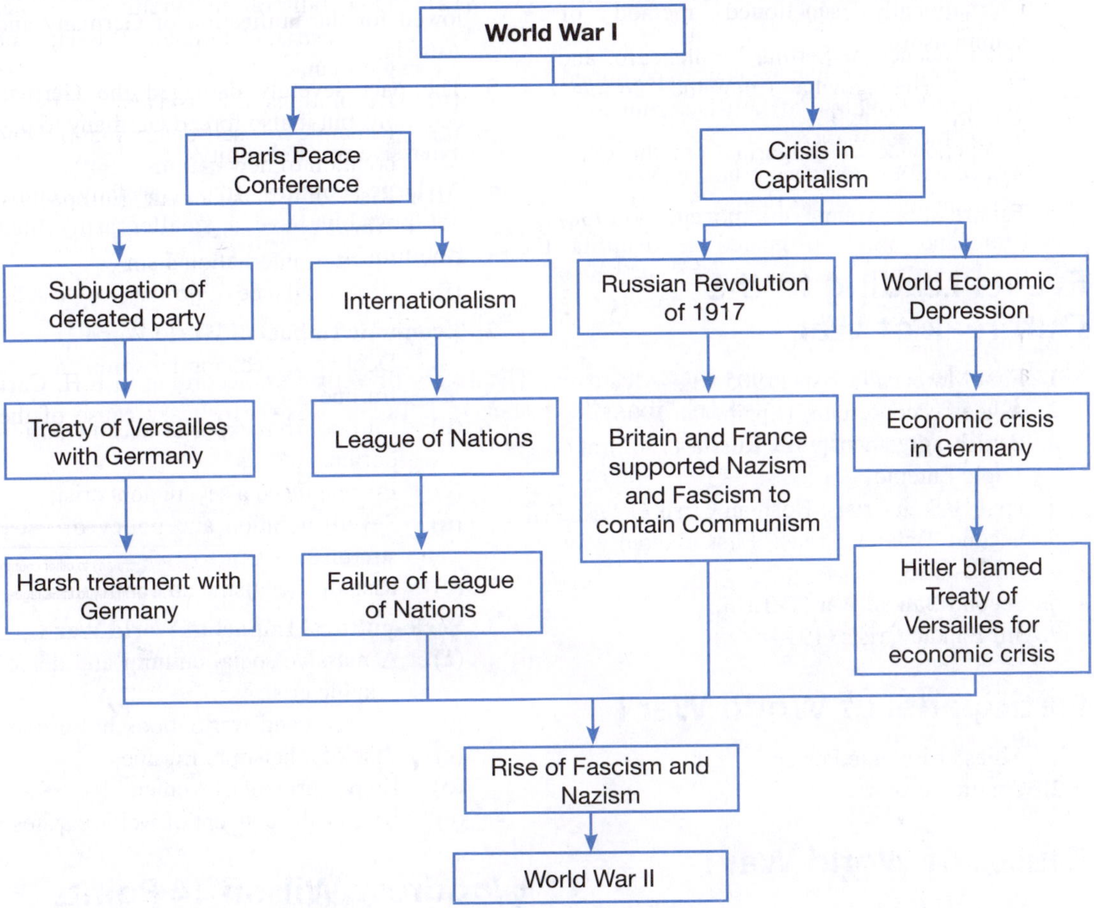

FIGURE 7.13: Linkage between World War I and World War II

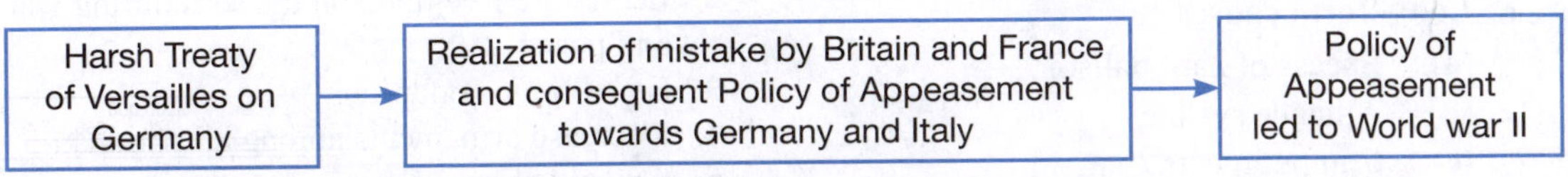

FIGURE 7.14: Treaty of Versailles to World War II

LET'S REVISE

Transformation of Eastern Question into International Question

1. Independence of Greece from the Ottoman Empire
2. Independence of Romania from the Ottoman Empire
3. Independence of Serbia, Montenegro, and Bosnia Herzegovina from the Ottoman Empire
4. Independence of Bulgaria from the Ottoman Empire
5. Failure of the Young Turk movement (1908)

Events Leading to the Outbreak of War

1. First Moroccan Crisis (1905-6)
2. Algeciras conference (Spain, Jan 1906)
3. British agreement with Russia (1907) and Triple Entente
4. First Balkan Crisis: Bosnian Crisis (1908)
5. Second Balkan Crisis: First Balkan War (1912-1913)
6. Second Balkan War (1913)
7. 3rd Balkan Crisis (1914)

Participants of World War I

1. Allies or Entente Powers
2. Central Powers

Causes of World War I

1. **Immediate cause**
   (a) Assassination of Archduke Ferdinand
2. **Long-Term causes**
   (a) Excess of nationalism
   (b) Alliance system
   (c) Competitive militarism
   (d) Theory of Social Imperialism
   (e) Economic rivalry
   (f) Policy of Imperialism

Impact of World War I

1. **Political Impact of World War I**
   (a) Downfall of monarchical regimes in Austria, Ottoman, Russia, and Germany
   (b) Revolutions of Russia and Turkey
   (c) Principle of self-determination and creation of new nations
   (d) Rise of socialism in Europe and World
   (e) Spirit of internationalism
   (f) A new balance of power
2. **Economic Impact of World War I**
   (a) Decline of economic dominance of Europe
   (b) Europe from exporter became an importer
   (c) Europe faced a severe debt crisis
   (d) Severe inflation and policy of fiscal stimulus
   (e) Rise of socialism and communism
3. **Socio-cultural Impact of World War I**
   (a) A massive social cultural and demographic crisis
   (b) A strong anti-war outlook in Europe
   (c) Rise of atheism in Europe
   (d) Empowerment of women
   (e) Rise of the concept of welfare states

Woodrow Wilson 14 Points

1. Open diplomacy without secret treaties
2. Economic free trade on the seas during war and peace
3. Equal trade conditions
4. Decrease armaments among all nations
5. Adjust colonial claims

6. Evacuation of all central powers from Russia
7. Belgium to be evacuated and restored
8. Return of the Alsace-Lorraine region and all French territories
9. Readjust Italian borders
10. Austria-Hungary to be provided an opportunity for self-determination
11. Redraw the borders of the Balkan region
12. Creation of a Turkish state
13. Creation of an independent Polish state
14. Creation of the League of Nations

Consequences of the Paris Peace Conference

1. Betrayal of Arab Nationalism
2. Harsh Treaty of Versailles with Germany
   - **(a)** No Lasting Peace
   - **(b)** Rise of Fascism and Nazism
   - **(c)** Policy of Appeasement

PROBABLE QUESTIONS

1. 'By 1914, the sick man of Europe was no longer just Turkey: it was Europe itself.' Explain.
2. 'Any single explanation for the outbreak of the World War I likely to be too simple. An amalgam of factors intellectual, social, economic as well as political and diplomatic contributed to this horrifying conflict of monumental propositions.' Explain.
3. How far is it correct to say that the World War I was fought essentially for the preservation of the balance of power?
4. Do you agree with the view that the Treaty of Versailles was a bad compromise between a treaty based upon force and a treaty based on ideas?
5. The disintegration of the Ottoman Empire was largely the product of European intervention than the product of nationalist pressure. Examine.
6. 'Treaty of Versailles contained the seeds of future conflicts.' Comment.
7. While the Ottoman Empire and Habsburg Empire disintegrated Russian Empire could save itself. Do you agree?
8. Balkan question always remained to be an all-European question. Comment.

TIMELINE (1882–1914)

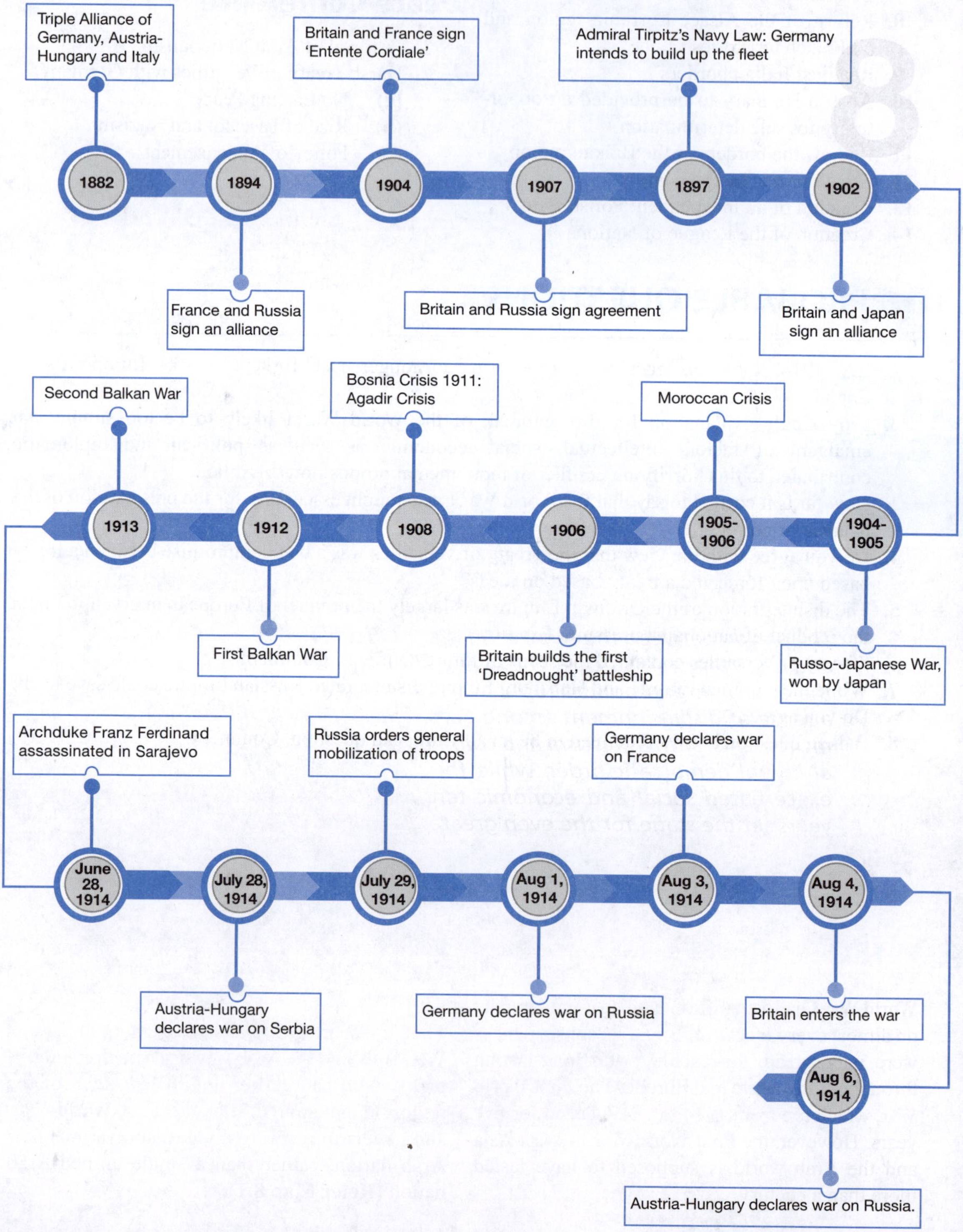

CHAPTER

8

Photo Credit: svetlanka / 123RF, HelloSSTK / Shutterstock

EUROPE BETWEEN TWO WORLD WARS (1919–39)

> *The period between the two World Wars was a time of great instability and uncertainty in Europe. The trauma of World War I, combined with the economic and political upheavals of the inter-war period, created a sense of disillusionment among Europeans. The rise of new political movements, such as fascism and communism, challenged the traditional liberal democratic order, while the Great Depression of the 1930s exacerbated social and economic tensions. Ultimately, the inter-war years set the stage for the even greater cataclysm of World War II.*
>
> *—Tony Judt*

INTRODUCTION

World War I had a significant and profound impact on almost every facet of life, and its consequences were widespread, far-reaching, and long-lasting throughout the world and Europe. The First World War, which ran from 1914 to 1919, lasted for five years. However, the First World War in West Asia and the Arab world is supposed to have lasted more than a century.

FIRST WORLD WAR ON WEST ASIA AND THE ARAB WORLD

The First World War had a devastating impact on West Asia and the Arab world. The Ottoman Empire, which had earlier dominated much of the region, disintegrated after the First World War, and its territories were divided into various new Arab nations rather than a single unified Arab nation **(Refer Map 8.1)**.

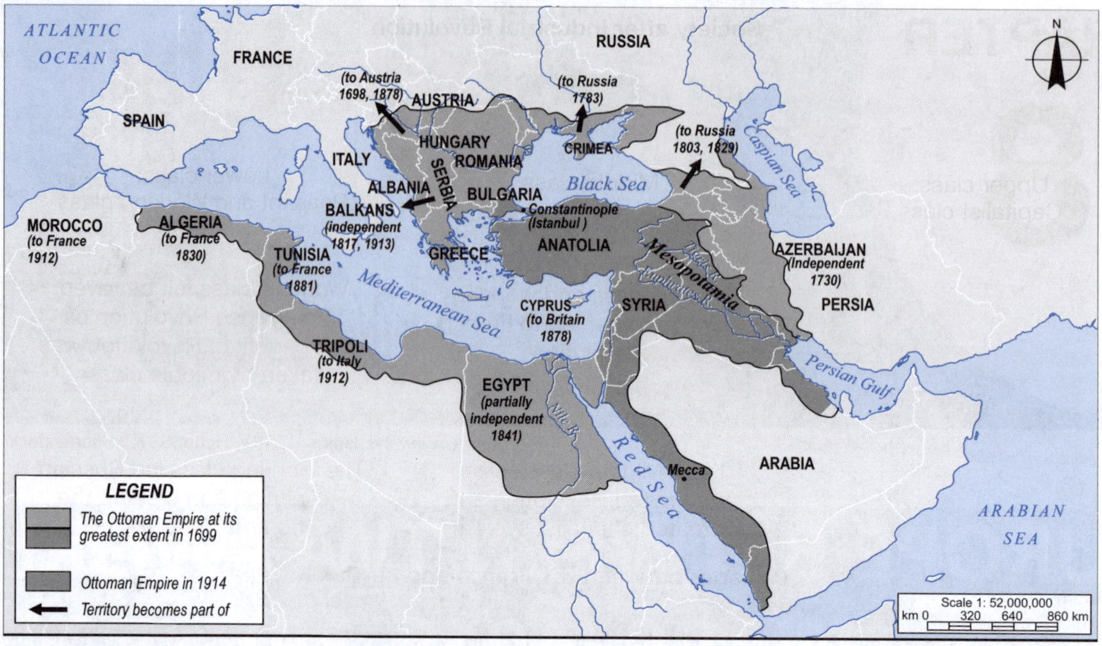

Map 8.1: Ottoman Empire (1699–1914)

The First World War also brought European nation's control over the Arab world, which caused intense political unrest and instability. The war also caused famine and had a huge economic impact on the region, leading to increased poverty and economic hardship. Finally, it caused the displacement of millions of people, creating large refugee populations throughout the region.

Impact of the First World War on West Asia and the Arab World

1. **Hussain-Mac Mahon Agreement:** The Hussain-Mac Mahon Agreement was a treaty signed in 1915 between the British and the Ottoman Empire (Turkey) during World War I. British concluded a secret treaty with Arabian leaders like Hussain, the Grand Sheriff of Mecca, and his son Faisal. They had to organize a revolt against Ottoman Empire. As a reward after the war, they had to be offered a unified Arab nation.

   Hussain-Mac Mahon Agreement also allowed the British to occupy Iraq and provided for the establishment of an international commission to oversee the transition to an independent Iraq, under the rule of the Hashemite family.

2. **Sykes-Picot Agreement:** The Sykes-Picot Agreement (formally the Asia Minor Agreement) was a 1916 secret agreement between the governments of Britain and France, with the assent of imperial Russia, defining their proposed spheres of influence and control in the Middle East should the Triple Entente (Britain, France, and Russia) succeed in defeating the Ottoman Empire during World War I.

   The Sykes-Picot Agreement is interpreted by many historians as a turning point in the relationship between the West and Arab Nations. It divided the Middle East into French and British spheres of influence and is widely seen as a precursor to the colonization of the region by the two powers.

3. **Balfour Declaration:** The Balfour Declaration was a statement issued by the British government in 1917 during World War I which expressed support for the establishment of a 'national home for the Jewish people' in Palestine, then an Ottoman region with a minority Jewish population.

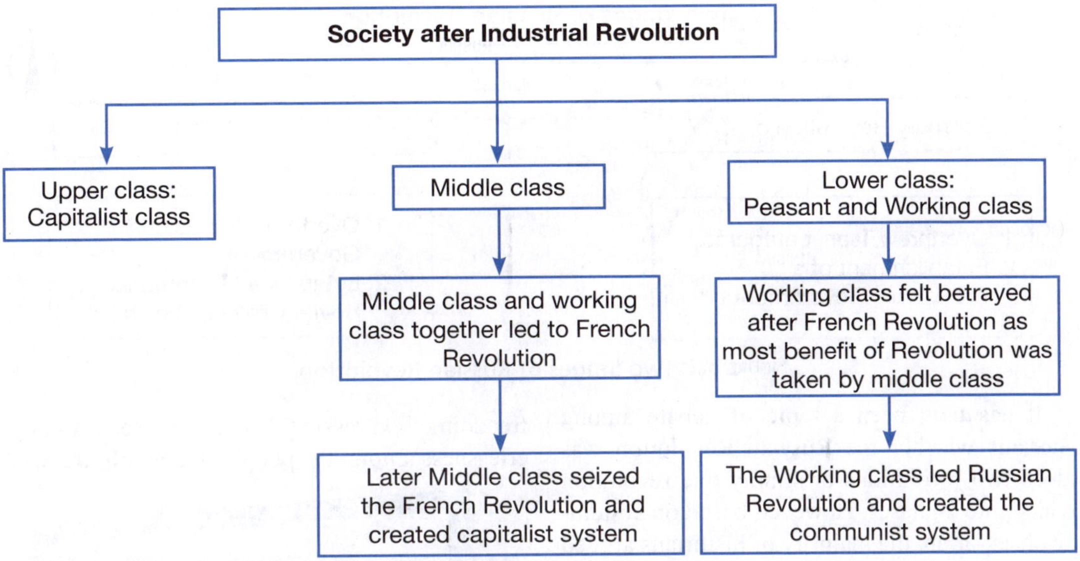

Figure 8.1: Linkages between the French and Russian Revolution

The statement was written by British Foreign Secretary Arthur Balfour and addressed to Lord Rothschild, a leader of the British Jewish community. The Balfour Declaration was later incorporated into both the Sevres peace treaty with the Ottoman Empire and the Mandate system for Palestine. It has been seen by many historians as a key moment in the history of the Israel-Palestine conflict.

RUSSIAN REVOLUTION OF 1917

The Russian Revolution of 1917 was a period of political and social upheaval in Russia, in which the Tsarist autocratic rule was overthrown and replaced by the Bolshevik-led communist Soviet Union. The revolution began in February 1917 with strikes and mass demonstrations in St. Petersburg, then spread to other parts of the country and led to the abdication of Tsar Nicholas II. Russian Revolution ended with the Bolshevik victory in the October Revolution of 1917, in which the Bolsheviks led by Vladimir Lenin overthrew the Provisional Government and established a single-party socialist state. The events of the revolution had a significant and far-reaching impact on world history, leading to the eventual rise of Communism, the Soviet Union, and the Cold War. This revolution had such a significant impact on world history; some historians regarded it as the most significant event that occurred in the 20th century.

> *"The Russian Revolution was the most momentous occurrence of the 20th century, not only for its consequences for Russia, but for its consequences for the world.*
> ***—Richard Pipes (American Historian)"***

The Russian Revolution (1917) was unique in that it was led by long-standing discontent. Nearly all of the earlier revolutions occurred suddenly and were not properly organized. However, a concrete plan and programme were used to organize the Bolshevik revolution in Russia. Thus, it was also referred to as a 'Textbook Revolution.'

Russian Revolution tried to answer some of those questions that had remained unanswered during the French Revolution, i.e., the relationship between the bourgeois class and the proletariat class **(Refer Figure 8.1).**

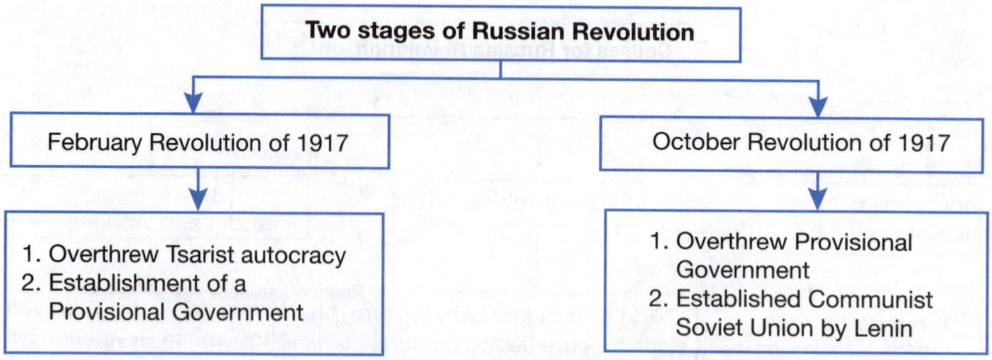

FIGURE 8.2: Two Stages of Russian Revolution

It has long been a topic of debate among historians whether the Russian Revolution was indeed two revolutions or simply one revolution divided into 2 phases. However, based on systematic observation, the majority of historians argued that it was the two stages of a single revolution (the bourgeoisie stage and the proletariat stage).

The first phase was the February Revolution of 1917, which overthrew the Tsarist autocracy and led to the establishment of a Provisional Government. The second phase was the October Revolution of 1917, also known as the Bolshevik Revolution, which overthrew the Provisional Government and established the Soviet Union, led by the Bolshevik Party. In fact, the significance of the Russian revolution lay in the second stage. If it would have stopped at the first stage, hardly it could go beyond the French Revolution **(Refer Figure 8.2).**

Causes of the Russian Revolution

The Russian Revolution of 1917 was a major event in world history and had a profound impact on the course of modern history. The revolution was the result of many factors, both long-term and short-term causes including economic hardship, government corruption, and a long-standing sense of frustration among the working class. Economic hardship was caused by World War I, which left the country in a state of economic crisis. The government was plagued by corruption and inefficiency, leading to poor decision-making and a lack of trust in the government by the people. This sense of frustration was further compounded by the Tsar's refusal to grant basic civil liberties and freedom of expression, leading to a sense of powerlessness among the people **(Refer Figure 8.3).**

> *"The Russian Revolution of 1917 was a complex and multifaceted event, a convulsion of political, social, and economic forces that shook the foundations of the old regime and transformed the Russian Empire into the Soviet Union.*
>
> ***—Sheila Fitzpatrick (American Historian)"***

Fundamental Causes of the Russian Revolution

The Russian Revolution resulted due to certain fundamental factors which included the political causes, the economic decline, economic and social inequality and the influence of Russian philosophers.

Political Causes

1. **The Tsar's incompetence:** The Tsar, or the ruling monarch, had absolute power over the people and the government. The Tsarist rule was autocratic and oppressive, with no real representation of the people or their interests.

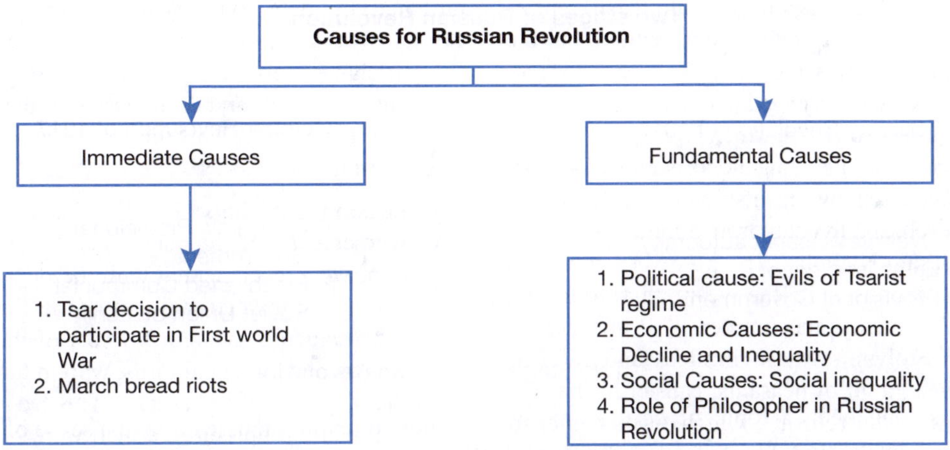

FIGURE 8.3: Causes for the Russian Revolution

Tsar Nicholas II was a weak and ineffective leader who was unable to respond effectively to the problems facing Russia, such as poverty and social unrest.

Moreover, the ideas of Tsar Nicholas II, which included royal absolutism, semi-divine monarchy, aristocratic privileges, exploitative feudal institutions, and an arbitrary legal system, resulted in a great deal of suffering and dissatisfaction among the Russian people. In fact, the situation of the Russian monarchy in 1917 was worse than that of the French monarchy in 1789. Additionally, the policy of Russification (the policy to promote the Russian language and culture across the empire) pursued by the Russian Emperor Czar Nicholas II sparked outrage among the various racial groups living in Russia.

> *"The fundamental cause of the Russian Revolution was the failure of the Tsarist autocracy to respond to the needs and aspirations of the people.*
>
> ***—E.H. Carr"***

2. **Russia defeated by the Japanese in 1905:** In 1904, Russia went to war with Japan. The war was a disaster for Russia, and it cost them both lives and money. It was a big blow to Tsarist power and prestige which further led to the weakening of the Tsar's rule.

3. **The Russian Revolution of 1905:** The Russian Revolution of 1905 was caused by Japan's defeat of Russia in 1905. It was a major uprising in the Russian Empire against the autocratic rule of Tsar Nicholas II. It began with a peaceful protest of workers in St. Petersburg on January 9, 1905, and soon escalated into a series of massive strikes, demonstrations, and riots that would spread throughout the empire.

> *"The seeds of the Russian Revolution were sown in the nineteenth century with the oppressive policies of the Tsars and their refusal to share power with the people.*
>
> ***—Richard Pipes"***

The Tsar responded with harsh repression, including military intervention, but the movement was too powerful to be stopped. The Revolution ended with the Tsar's October Manifesto of 1906, which promised a number of reforms, including the formation of a legislative assembly, universal suffrage, freedom of speech, and freedom from arbitrary arrest.

Tsar Nicholas II, however, breached his promises in the years that followed. Additionally, the murder of Prime Minister Stolypin, whose limited land reforms helped a lot of peasants, caused further delays in the reforms, which further intensified mistrust and dissatisfaction against the Tsarist authority. Therefore, it is rightly regarded by historian Richard Pipes that 'the seeds of the Russian Revolution were sown in the nineteenth century with the oppressive policies of the Tsars and their refusal to share power with the people.' Thus, the Revolution of 1905 was a watershed moment in Russian history and laid the groundwork for the subsequent revolutions of 1917 **(Refer Figure 8.4).**

4. **Rasputin affair:** The alleged story of the affair between Tsarina (wife of Nicholas II) and her spiritual teacher Grigori Rasputin gave a further blow to the prestige of the royal house.

Economic Causes

Russia had experienced a number of economic problems leading up to the revolution. Russia's economy was in a state of turmoil, heavily burdened by debt, with sharply rising prices, shortages of food, and growing unemployment. The Russian government was unable to address the economic issues, and the suffering of the lower classes only increased. This further fuelled the fire of revolution.

1. **Peasant uprisings:** The Russian peasants, who constituted the majority of the population, were discontented with the oppressive and unjust taxation policies of the Tsar and the aristocrats. Moreover, most of the land was owned by feudal lords, who in turn further exploited the peasantry. This led to several peasant uprisings, which were brutally suppressed by the Tsarist government.
2. **An excessive reliance on agriculture:** Russia's economy was largely dependent on agriculture, much like France before the French Revolution. While some modern industries did emerge in Russia, the Industrial Revolution had not yet started in Russia, while other European countries reaped immense prosperity as a consequence of the Industrial Revolution. In the words of some critics, industries in Russia were an island in the vast sea.

   Moreover, most of the industries were concentrated in a particular region which led to the concentration of workers in a specific region. This phenomenon led to growing proletarianization among Russian workers and the formation of some workers' parties, like the Social Democratic Party which later divided between the Bolshevik Party and the Menshevik Party.

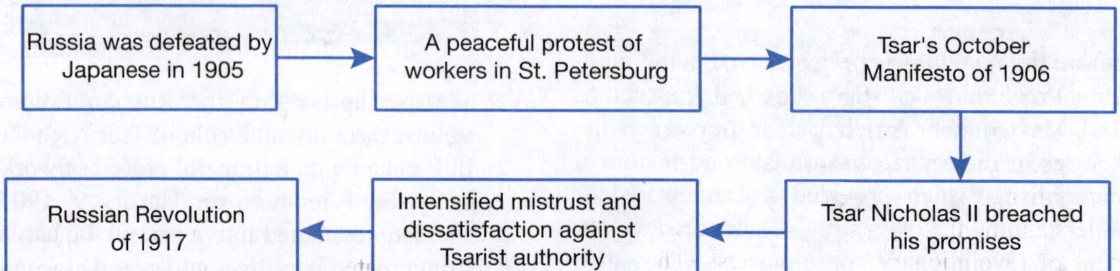

FIGURE 8.4: Linkage between the Russian Revolution of 1905 and 1917

3. **Poor working conditions:** Poor working conditions, low wages and long hours of work were common in Russia prior to the Revolution. Factory workers and peasants lived in poverty and were deprived of the basic necessities of life.
4. **Abolition of slavery:** Tsar Alexander II abolished the slavery system but the condition of slaves did not improve as there was no redistribution of land.

Social Causes

1. **Social inequality:** Russian society was divided into two distinct classes—the privileged upper class and the oppressed lower class. This social inequality was one of the major causes of the revolution.
2. **Poverty:** The majority of the population was living in poverty and lacked the basic necessities of life. The workers were paid very low wages, while the few feudal lords enjoyed the luxuries of life.
3. **Non-implementation of reforms:** The Tsar had refused to implement any meaningful reforms like land reforms to help improve the lives of the people. This caused further unrest and resentment among the people, which eventually led to revolution.
4. **Discrimination against non-Russian:** The Tsarist government was extremely oppressive and discriminated against certain groups, such as Jews and non-Russians. This further fuelled the flames of revolution.

Role of Philosophers in the Russian Revolution

Before the revolution, there occurred some intellectual revolutions as well. Philosophers, such as Karl Marx and Friedrich Engels developed the theories of dialectical materialism and historical materialism, which provided a framework for understanding the class struggle and the development of revolutionary consciousness. They also provided a critique of capitalism and a vision of a socialist society.

Other philosophers, including Vladimir Lenin, Leon Trotsky, and Nikolai Bukharin, developed these theories further and applied them to the Russian context, and encouraged newer ideas in Russia. Philosophers played a crucial role in developing the ideology of the Revolution and in helping to shape the political and social movements that ultimately led to its success.

Immediate Causes of the Russian Revolution

First World War's outbreak contributed to the downfall of the Tsar. Despite the economic and social crises that Russia was going through, Tsar Nicholas II decided to enter Russia into the First World War without preparation. The aim of Tsar Nicholas II's strategy was to divert people's attention from the domestic problem towards the First World War, believing that victory in the war would enhance the Tsar's prestige.

> “*The immediate cause of the Revolution was the economic breakdown of the country, which had been brought about by the long war with Germany.*
>
> ***—Robert Service*** ”

However contrary to Tsar Nicholas II's intentions, the First World War actually prepared the ground for the revolution in the following manner:

1. War created a further gulf between the executive and the legislative body.
2. Internal administration collapsed as a result of the Tsar's focus on the war.
3. Massive casualties and failure on the battlefront created huge discontentment.
4. As the Russian government followed the 'Scorched Earth Policy' (a military strategy

that involves destroying anything that might be useful to the enemy while withdrawing from an area) so it created discontentment among Russian people as it led to inflation and scarcity of goods.

March Bread Riots and March Revolution

The March Bread Riots in Russia were a series of protests and riots in March 1917 that occurred in Petrograd (capital of the Russian Empire) in the wake of food shortages and rising prices. The riots began in the Vyborg district and quickly spread to other areas of the city, resulting in violence and looting by hungry and desperate citizens.

The lack of essential goods deeply hurt the workforce, and at least 4 lakh workers came onto Petrograd's streets. The government passed an order to soldiers to open fire on the mob but the soldiers refused to follow the command. Thus, the mob established control over Petrograd (capital of the Russian Empire). Tsar also ordered that Duma (a Russian parliament established in 1906) to be dissolved, but it was refused. Therefore, the government was powerless, and on March 15, Tsar Nicholas II's government resigned. Thus, the March Revolution had begun in Russia.

March Revolution in Russia

The March Revolution of 1917, also known as the February Revolution of Russia, was the first of two revolutions that took place in Russia during 1917. It began on March 8 (February 23, Old Style) and lasted until March 16, 1917 (March 3 Old Style).

It was sparked by mass demonstrations and labour strikes in Petrograd, which culminated in the replacement of the monarchy with the Provisional Government, an interim governing body initially dominated by members of the Duma (a Russian parliament established in 1906). The revolution was led by a variety of socialist and liberal organizations and political parties, including the Socialist Revolutionary Party, the Mensheviks, and the Bolsheviks.

Formation of the Provisional Government

The Tsar's abdication led to the formation of the Provisional Government, which was initially led by Prince George but soon replaced by Alexander Kerensky, a reformist socialist **(Refer Figure 8.2)**.

The Provisional Government attempted to establish a liberal democracy and implemented a number of important reforms including granting political freedoms and civil liberties, establishing universal suffrage, and creating a democratic constituent assembly but, it could not function for long due to the following reasons:

1. Apart from political freedom, the Russian people aspired for socio-economic freedom as well. The Kerensky government did not carry out land reforms or take any steps to improve the condition of workers.
2. The Russian government got divided between the Duma (a Russian parliament) and the Petrograd Soviet (political organization of workers) as both had contrary objectives.
3. The Provisional Government inherited a number of problems from the Tsar's government such as a lack of resources, military defeat, and a weakened economy. This made it difficult for the government to meet the demands of the people and caused widespread discontent.
4. One major challenge before the government was regarding the role of Russia in the First World War. While the majority supported to end the war, the Provisional Government supported continuing the First World War.

Points to Ponder

The Kerensky government launched a major offensive against Germany in June 1917, but it was a miserable failure and the arrival of dead soldiers fuelled greater dissatisfaction.

October Revolution of 1917

The February Revolution was followed by the October Revolution in October 1917. It was the second phase of the Russian Revolution and was led by the Bolshevik Party. The Bolshevik Revolution was a successful *coup d'état* against the provisional government of Alexander Kerensky and replaced it with the Soviet Union, a socialist state. The October Revolution was the beginning of the Soviet Union and the communism that would come to define it. The October Revolution also saw the end of capitalism in Russia and the beginning of a new era of collective ownership of the means of production.

> *"The Bolshevik Revolution of 1917 was one of the most important events of the twentieth century. It overturned the existing order, destroyed the old system of government, and established a new political and economic system in Russia."*
> ***—Geoffrey Hosking, (British Historian)***

Role of the Bolshevik Party and Vladimir Lenin

Lenin came back to Russia in April 1917 from Germany where he had been deported by Tsar Nicholas II due to his revolutionary acts. Then Vladimir Lenin released his popular '*April Thesis*'.

The '*April Thesis*' is the document that served as the foundation for the Bolshevik Revolution of 1917. It was created in the midst of the February Revolution and the provisional government was in power. It outlines Lenin's view of the need for the overthrow of the Provisional Government and the establishment of a new type of state—a Soviet Republic. It also explains the importance of creating a new type of economy and society, based on the principles of Marxism and the emergence of the working class as the ruling class.

Lenin 1st Attempt

A Russian offensive against Germany was launched by Kerensky Government in Galicia in the middle of July 1917, but the Bolsheviks attempted an uprising and failed, thus all of their leaders were imprisoned. The action of the Bolsheviks was also criticized by the Mensheviks. Some Mensheviks and Socialist Republic then walked out of the All Russian Executive Committee of Soviets to protest against the Bolshevik insurrection.

Lenin 2nd Attempt

Lenin used his position as leader of the Bolsheviks to garner support from the Bolsheviks party and Red Guard by appealing to their sense of national pride and by promising to deliver a better future.

> *"Lenin was the founder of the world's first communist state, and his political theories and practices have had an enduring impact on the post-Soviet world."*
> ***—A. James Gregor, (Historian)***

Lenin created the Red Guard in 1917 to help protect the newly established Bolshevik Government. The Red Guard was a paramilitary organization composed of workers and peasants, and they were given the task of defending the revolution against any counter-revolutionary threats. Lenin used Red Guard support to launch a military coup against the Provisional Government, which was in power at the time and captured power in November 1917 and Russia was now declared a communist state.

Difference between Menshevik and Bolsheviks

The Mensheviks (which means minority) and Bolsheviks (which means majority) were two factions of the Russian Social Democratic Labour Party, which was a political party in Russia in the late 19th and early 20th centuries.

The major difference between the two was in their views on how the working class should achieve its goals of establishing a socialist society. The Mensheviks believed in a more gradual, democratic, and liberal approach to developing a socialist society, while the Bolsheviks advocated for a more radical, violent, and revolutionary approach. The Bolsheviks eventually emerged victorious, leading to the October Revolution of 1917 and the establishment of the Soviet Union.

Contributions of Lenin in the Bolshevik Revolution

1. Lenin redefined the philosophy of Marxism according to the specific condition and needs of Russia.
2. Lenin presented pragmatic tactics for the revolution in Russia. He mentioned it in his famous pamphlet '*Two Tactics of Social-Democrats*'. The main theme of '*Two Tactics of Social-Democrats*' is the importance of organizing a revolutionary socialist movement in order to achieve political and economic justice.
3. When necessary, he was willing to pursue an opportunistic policy and sometimes even collaborated with his opponent. For example, he once cooperated with Kerensky's government.
4. Lenin created the Red Guard in 1917 with the task of defending the revolution against any counter-revolutionary threats. Lenin used Red Guard support to launch a military coup against the Provisional Government.

Steps Taken by Lenin to Consolidate the Revolution

1. **Establish a one-party state:** Lenin created a single-party Totalitarian state, the Communist Party of the Soviet Union, as the ruling political force in the newly formed USSR.
2. **Accept the Treaty of Brest-Litovsk:** The priority of Lenin was to consolidate the revolution in Russia, so he decided to end the war with Germany. Lenin accepted the harsh terms of the Brest-Litovsk Treaty, which ended Russia's involvement in World War I. Germany was unwilling to offer moderate terms, so Lenin agreed to surrender one-fourth of its European territory. However, making peace with Germany provoked the allied forces, who then invaded Russia. But Lenin repelled the invading army with the assistance of the Red Army led by Trotsky.
3. **Establish the Soviet Union:** Lenin established the Union of Soviet Socialist Republics (USSR), a federation of 15 republics that served as the new Russian state.
4. **Nationalize all industries:** Under the socialist concept, Lenin nationalized all industry and put it under the control of the state.
5. **Create the Cheka:** Lenin created the secret police organization known as the Cheka, which was responsible for rooting out enemies of the revolution but rather it unleashed coercive machinery against his rivals.
6. **Create the Comin tern:** Lenin established the Comin tern, an organization dedicated to the spread of communism internationally.
7. **Land reforms:** He permitted the peasants, who had already seized land from the landlords at the time of the March revolution, to retain the land.
8. **Establish a state-controlled media:** Lenin established a state-controlled media apparatus to ensure the spread of communist propaganda.

9. **Promote atheism:** Lenin promoted atheism and a secular state in order to break the power of the Russian Orthodox Church.
10. **Distinct identity of minority groups in the USSR:** Marxism or communism didn't recognize racial or cultural division but Lenin accepted the distinct identity of minority groups in the USSR. In the new constitution of the USSR, the special position of minority groups was accepted under the Russian Federation.

New Economic Policy by Lenin

After coming to power Lenin initially followed a very strict approach towards economic policy. This system was known as 'War Communism' and it was established in 1918. But by 1921, Lenin realized that the production in USSR was continuously decreasing as industrial production was just 13% of what it was in 1914. So, he brought a major modification into his system in 1921 and introduced the New Economic Policy (NEP).

> *The New Economic Policy is in essence a step towards socialism and the most direct road to the complete victory of socialism.* —*V.I. Lenin*

Points to Ponder

The New Economic Policy was a set of economic policies introduced by Vladimir Lenin in 1921, following the end of the Russian Civil War to rebuild the Soviet economy.

The NEP was an economic policy introduced in 1921 in the wake of the Russian Civil War (between Bolsheviks against various anti-Bolshevik groups, and foreign forces such as the British and French Empires). The policy was intended to revive the Russian economy, which had been severely damaged by the war, by allowing some private ownership of businesses and by allowing some private trade. It was seen by Lenin as a temporary measure, to be replaced by a more socialist system once the economy had recovered.

The NEP was a major departure from traditional Marxist-Leninist economic policy, which had advocated for the complete nationalization of all private businesses and the complete abolition of private ownership. Under the NEP,

1. Businesses were allowed to be owned and operated by private individuals, and a limited amount of private trade was allowed.
2. Nearly 90% of the Russian economy was placed under private capital.
3. Lenin abolished the policy of storage of grains from farmers and now they were permitted to sell the min the open markets.
4. Foreign capitalists were allowed to run industries in Russia on the condition that their products would only be sold to the government.

However, certain industries and resources were still in the hands of the government, and the government also imposed taxes on businesses and income. The NEP was largely successful in helping to revive the Soviet economy. In fact, the USSR was the only country to escape the Great Depression and was among the most industrialized nations because of the NEP 1921. However, NEP 1921 was eventually replaced by Stalin's Five-Year Plans in 1928.

Comparison between Marx and Lenin

Karl Marx and Vladimir Lenin are two of the most influential political theorists of the 19th and 20th centuries. Marx was a philosopher, economist, and a revolutionary. He is best known for his analysis

> *Marx and Lenin were both revolutionary socialists who sought to overthrow the existing order and establish a new, more just society. However, they differed in their approach. Marx believed that socialism would emerge naturally from the contradictions of capitalism, while Lenin believed that socialism could only be achieved through the vanguard action of a revolutionary party. Marx was an internationalist who believed in the universal nature of the proletarian struggle, while Lenin was a nationalist who believed that socialism could only be achieved within the context of a particular country. Finally, Marx was a theorist who wrote extensively about the future of socialism, while Lenin was a practical politician who focused on the immediate tasks of revolution and the construction of a socialist state. Despite these differences, both Marx and Lenin were important figures in the development of socialist thought.*
>
> ***—Eric Hobsbawm***

of capitalism and his writings on class struggle. He believed that the working class should overthrow the capitalist system in order to create a socialist society. He also believed that the state should be abolished in order to create a more equitable society.

Both Marx and Lenin were instrumental in the development of modern socialism and communism. While the two had many similarities, there were also a few key differences between their philosophies. Marx was just a theorist whereas Lenin was a political worker. This was the reason that Lenin, at times, deviated from the course of Marxism to adjust the revolution to the prevailing situation.

1. Although both Marx and Lenin shared an interest in socialism and communism, their views on how to achieve it differed. Marx advocated for a gradual transformation from capitalism to socialism, while Lenin advocated for a more rapid and violent overthrow of the capitalist system.
2. Marx declared that the proletarian revolution (revolution led by the working class) would take place in the most industrialized nation but Lenin organized a socialist revolution in Russia which was lagging behind many European countries in terms of industrialization.
3. Marx believed that the working class should be in the leadership of the socialist revolution. However, in the Russian Revolution, a few Bolshevik party members seized power instead of the working class.
4. Marx believed that the state should be abolished, while Lenin believed that a strong centralized government was necessary to protect the new socialist state.

Limitations of Lenin

1. Lenin made compromises to the certain principle of Marxism to meet his objectives.
2. Leninism emphasizes a centralized form of government, which can lead to a lack of independent decision-making and initiative from below. This can also lead to a lack of accountability and can breed corruption and abuse of power.
3. Lenin established the dominance of a party in Soviet Russia, which was converted into the dominance of a single man under Stalin.
4. According to Lenin's vision, a small group of dedicated and highly trained revolutionaries should lead the working class in its struggle for emancipation. This resulted in a lack of diversity and participation in the revolutionary process, and lead to a lack of accountability to the masses.
5. In order to achieve his goals, Lenin often relied heavily on the use of violence and coercion. This can lead to further alienation of the masses and can result in a lack of legitimacy and support for the revolutionary cause.

6. Lenin carried out a series of experiments and due to the experiments, the Russian people had to suffer.

Advent of Stalin and the Phase of One-man Dictatorship in Russia

Joseph Stalin rose to power in the Soviet Union following the death of Lenin, the first leader of the Soviet Union. Trotsky was Lenin's chosen successor, but an ambitious leader, Stalin, overthrew him and seized power. Stalin was the General Secretary of the Communist Party of the Soviet Union from 1922 and rose to become the de facto leader of the Soviet Union in the late 1920s.

> "*Joseph Stalin was a ruthless dictator who imposed a reign of terror over the Soviet Union from 1929 to 1953, a period of history characterized by mass repression, violence, and terror that scarred the country and cost millions of lives.*
>
> ***—Michael J. Haynes (British Historian)***"

Stalin was the primary force behind the industrialization of the Soviet Union and the collectivization of its agriculture. He also oversaw the Great Purge of the 1930s, which saw millions of people deported, imprisoned, and executed. During World War II, Stalin was a key ally of the Allies, helping to defeat Nazi Germany. His rule lasted until his death in 1953.

Changes Introduced by Stalin

1. **Change in ideology:** Lenin emphasized on establishing a socialist revolution in Russia, while Stalin wanted to make it as a worldwide revolution.
2. **Policy of collectivization:** A strong agricultural base was required for industrialization. Therefore, Stalin abolished private property on land and enforced collectivization of agriculture (co-operative farming). The policy of collectivization was intended to increase farm output and help the Soviet Union become a major industrial power.
3. **Five-Year Plans:** Lenin emphasized rapid industrialization and with this purpose, he introduced economic planning in 1928. Stalin implemented the Five-Year Plans, which focused on heavy industry and the development of a centrally planned economy. The plans allowed for the rapid industrialization of the Soviet Union and the creation of a powerful military force. The Russian economy was completely transformed under Stalin.
4. **Dictatorship of the one man:** During his reign, the dictatorship of a party was transformed into the dictatorship of a single man. All dissents were silenced with an iron hand.
5. **Purges and show trials:** To maintain his grip on power, Stalin used a system of purges and show trials to eliminate anyone who opposed his rule. This included former political allies, military officers, and members of the Communist Party.
6. **Gulags:** Stalin created a system of gulags, or forced labour camps, to punish political opponents and criminals. The prisoners were forced to work in harsh conditions, leading to thousands of deaths.
7. **Censorship:** Stalin implemented strict censorship of the press, books, films, and other forms of media. This was intended to control what the public could see and hear.

Significance of the Russian Revolution

1. **First successful Communist Revolution:** With the first serious attempt at a communist revolution, the 1917 Bolshevik

Revolution transformed Marx's theory of communism into reality.

2. **Impact on the political landscape:** The Revolution had a huge impact on the political landscape of the world. For the first time, a communist government had come to power. This was a major challenge to the capitalist world order and it sparked a wave of revolutions in other countries, such as Germany, Hungary, and China. The Revolution also inspired other movements, such as the Civil Rights Movement in the United States.
3. **Civil War in Russia:** The success of the Bolshevik revolution in 1917 led to the civil war in Russia in the 1920s. The Russian Civil War (1917-1923) was a conflict between the Bolshevik Red Army and the forces of the White Army, which were made up of monarchists, conservatives, liberals, and non-Bolshevik socialists. The war ended with the victory of the Red Army, which led to the establishment of the Soviet Union.
4. **Impact on the economy:** The Soviet Union established a centrally planned economy, with the goal of achieving economic equality. This system of economic planning was adopted by many other countries, including China and Cuba.
5. **Policy of appeasement:** The rise of communism in Russia forced western democracies like Britain and France to follow the policy of appeasement which led to the rise of Fascism and Nazism. The policy of appeasement was the idea of giving in to the demands of a potentially aggressive nation in order to avoid war. This policy was most famously employed by British Prime Minister Neville Chamberlain in 1938 when he allowed Nazi Germany to annex the Sudetenland, a region of Czechoslovakia, in order to avoid conflict. The policy of appeasement ultimately failed to prevent World War II and has since been widely criticized.
6. **Great depression and rise of Socialism:** The success of the Russian Revolution and the Great Depression of 1929 introduced a period of conflict for capitalist nations, enhancing the influence and prestige of Communist Russia. Socialism gained favour as a feasible alternative to capitalism's problems.
7. **Profound effect on international relations:** The Soviet Union and the United States became adversaries in the Cold War, a struggle that lasted nearly fifty years. The Revolution also led to the formation of the United Nations; an organization dedicated to maintaining world peace.

In conclusion, the Russian Revolution of 1917 was a major event in world history. It had a profound effect on politics, economics, culture, and international relations. It helped to shape the world we live in today and it is a reminder of the power of collective action.

LEAGUE OF NATIONS

The League of Nations was an international organization founded in 1919 after the First World War in order to promote collective peace and interna-

> "*The League of Nations was a noble experiment, but it failed. Its failure was due not only to the short-sighted policies of certain of its members but to the fact that it was an experiment before its time.*
>
> ***— Sir Winston Churchill***"

tional cooperation. It was created under the Treaty of Versailles and was in operation from 1920 until its dissolution in 1946. Its primary goals included preventing wars through collective security and disarmament, and settling international disputes through negotiation and arbitration. The League is widely regarded as a failure for a number of reasons. The main reasons for the failure of the League of Nations are as follows:

1. **League was Anglo-French in nature:** There was a difference of opinion between Britain and the U.S. on the one hand and France on the other regarding the nature of the League. The USA didn't become a member of the League of Nations. Germany was not allowed to join until 1926, and the USSR until 1933. Moreover, in 1934, Germany and Japan left the League.
2. **No power to enforce its decisions:** The League had no power to enforce its decisions. It was dependent on its members to implement any decisions it made, and many countries were unwilling to do so. This meant that the League was unable to effectively address conflicts or disputes between countries, and was unable to prevent wars.
3. **No army of its own:** League had no army, navy, or air force of its own, and it could not compel member states to abide by its rulings. This meant that if a nation chose to ignore the League, there was nothing to stop them from doing so. When Japan captured Manchuria in 1931, the League adopted a resolution that was in opposition to Japanese aspirations. As a result, Japan refused and left the league. The Manchurian issue was frequently argued to have determined the League of Nations' fate.
4. **Structural problem:** Two important organs of the League of Nations were the assembly and council. But both were having equal powers.
5. **Dominated by the major powers:** The League was dominated by the major powers of the time, such as Britain, France, and the United States. This meant that smaller countries were unable to influence the League's decisions, which led to a lack of trust in the League among some countries.
6. **Financial dependence:** The League was largely dependent on the major powers for funding. This meant that it was unable to respond quickly and effectively to crises, as it was often unable to secure the necessary funds. Moreover, big powers like Britain, France, and others were severely impacted by the Great Depression of 1929 and had little time or resources for the League.
7. **Policy of appeasement:** The western democracies' appeasement policy in response to Germany, Japan, and Italy's aggressive behaviour also contributed to League's inefficiency.
8. **Rising threat of Fascism and Militarism:** The League was unable to effectively address the rising threat of fascism and militarism in Europe. This proved to be a major factor in the onset of the Second World War, as the League was unable to prevent or stop the aggressive actions of countries such as Germany, Italy, and Japan.

In conclusion, the League of Nations was a failure for a number of reasons, including its lack of power, its domination by the major powers, its dependence on those powers for funding, and its inability to effectively address the rising threat of fascism.

RISE OF NAZISM

Nazism, also known as National Socialism, is a far-right, authoritarian, nationalist ideology and political movement that rose in Germany in the

> *"The rise of Nazism was a complex phenomenon, involving a combination of economic, social, cultural and political factors that allowed Hitler and the Nazi party to seize power in Germany and transform it into a totalitarian state.*
> ***—Richard Evans"***

early 1920s. It sought to establish a totalitarian regime based on racial purity and extreme nationalism. The Nazi Party was founded in 1919 by Adolf Hitler and was initially a small fringe group with limited success. It rose to prominence in the aftermath of World War I when Germany was suffering from economic and political turmoil. By 1930, the Nazi Party had become the largest political party in Germany, and Hitler was appointed Chancellor in 1933 **(Refer Figure 8.5)**.

Factors behind the Rise of Nazism

Political thinkers, like Hannah Arendt and Carl Friedrich call Nazism as a totalitarian movement. The rise of Adolf Hitler in German politics and his appointment as the German chancellor in January 1933 was far-reaching in significance not only for Germany but for the entire Europe. His rise marked the beginning of a new phase in European history and was a result of not one but many factors and forces. These were:

1. **Weak Weimar Republic and political instability:** In the years leading up to the rise of Nazism, Germany was in a state of political turmoil. The Weimar Republic was weak and unable to address the country's issues. The Weimar Republic was the German government from 1919 to 1933, the period of Germany's history between the end of World War I and the rise of Nazi Germany. It was named after the city of Weimar, where a national assembly convened to produce a new democratic constitution.

> "*Nazism, like Communism, was a movement of reaction against the liberalism and materialism of the 19th century, and both sought to restore a more 'natural' order based on race and blood.*
>
> ***—Richard J. Evans***"

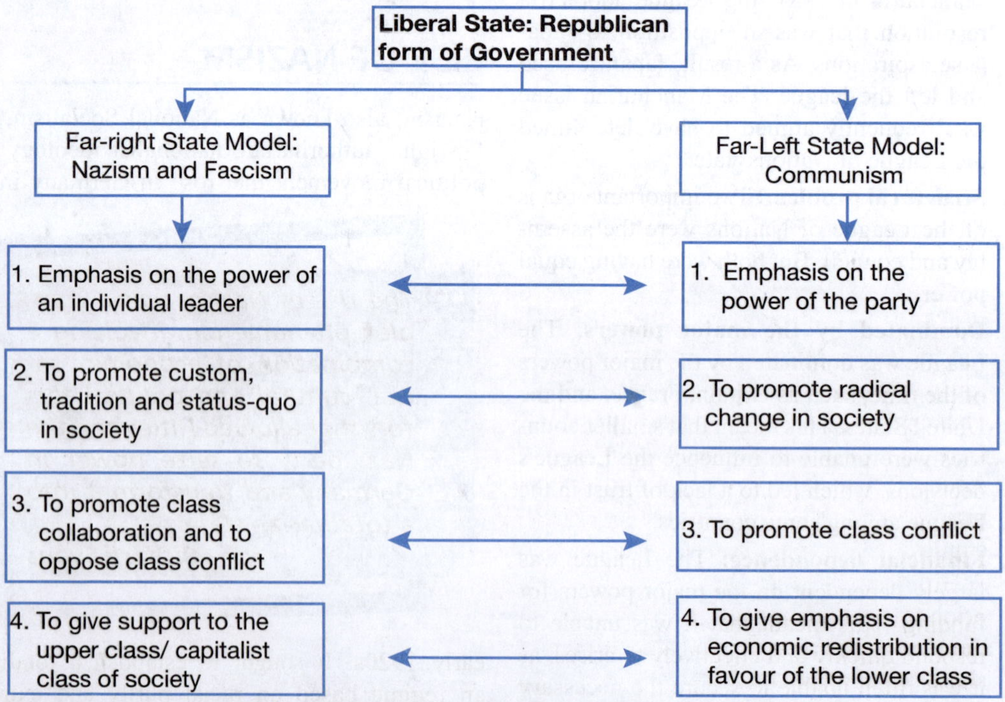

Figure 8.5: Differences between the Rightist and Leftist Model of State

Points to Ponder

The Weimar Republic was the democratic government of Germany that existed from 1919 to 1933 and established after the end of World War I and the abdication of the German Emperor, Wilhelm II.

The Weimar Republic faced numerous problems, including hyperinflation, and political extremism (from both left and right). Its collapse in 1933 ushered in the Nazi era. Political turmoil created an opportunity for the Nazis to gain a foothold in politics.

2. **Treaty of Versailles:** The Treaty of Versailles, in which Germany was humiliated, created a favourable situation for the rise of Nazism. Hitler's political propaganda to undo the treaty brought him mass political support.

3. **The economic crisis:** World War I led to economic devastation all over the Europe. But the German economy was badly shattered. The economic crisis created an extremely volatile environment in Germany and Hitler was a product of the same. Economic recovery after 1924 was based on short-term loans from America, which were used to build up infrastructure and heavy industry. These were however withdrawn after the start of the Great Depression.

   The Great Depression of 1929 was a major factor in the rise of Nazism. Germany was hit hard by the Great Depression which caused massive unemployment and poverty. This created a feeling of despair among the German people and they were desperate for solutions. The Nazis promised to solve Germany's economic problems and create full employment.

   Hitler was not a very popular leader prior to the Great Depression of 1929. In the elections of 1928, Hitler was running short of the expected number of seats. In fact, it was the world economic recession of 1929-30 which proved a game-changer as Hitler's popularity shot up during the time of this economic crisis. That's why in the elections of 1932, the Nazi party got the majority votes and German president Hindenburg invited him to take charge of Chancellor (or P.M.). Thus, Hitler came to power.

   In the Weimar constitution, there was a provision for a national emergency, which had been mentioned in Article-48. Through misusing this article, Hitler destroyed the republic after coming to power in 1933.

4. **Fear of communism:** The fear of a Communist Revolution (Far left) in Germany was also a major factor in the rise of Nazism. The economic crisis prevailing in Germany provided a fertile ground for communism to gain popularity and the Communist Party was increasing in its size rapidly.

   The Liberal ruling classes saw the Nazi Party as a bulwark against communism and were willing to support it financially and politically to prevent a communist takeover of Germany. Moreover, having been scared about the growing influence of communism both the German Junker Class (Zamindar) and the German capitalist class strengthened the hand of Hitler or the Nazi party.

5. **Blame and resentment:** The Nazi party proved to be extremely effective in discrediting others and spreading their message among people. The Nazis were able to blame the country's problems on certain scapegoats such as Jews, Communists, and other minority groups.

   Moreover, slogans of the kind like a 'stab in the back' etc., were used to discredit the Republicans. Jews were held responsible for the German defeat. Such messages widely appealed to the German masses and enabled them to gain support from the German people.

6. **Propaganda:** The Nazi party was highly effective at using propaganda to spread its message and attract supporters. They used powerful images, slogans, and speeches to promote their cause.

7. **Hitler's charismatic leadership:** Hitler was a charismatic leader who was able to stir up emotions and draw large crowds with his speeches. He was also able to tap into the nationalistic sentiments of the German people and use them to his advantage.

As a nationalist Hitler promised to undo the Treaty of Versailles and provide jobs to youth from military conscription. While German peasants were promised markets for their goods, the capitalists were promised safety from communism. These promises convinced the German population that Hitler was the only solution to all of their economic problems.

Reasons Behind the Decline of the Weimar Republic

1. **Economic crisis:** The Weimar Republic was plagued by an economic crisis that it was unable to solve. Hyperinflation, the collapse of the German currency, and a massive national debt crippled the economy and caused widespread unemployment.

> *"The Weimar Republic was a failed experiment in democracy. It was plagued by hyperinflation, economic despair, and a lack of strong leadership. Ultimately, its failure to address the country's problems led to the rise of the Nazi party and the collapse of the Republic.*
>
> ***—Richard Evans"***

This economic crisis resulted in a lack of public confidence in the Weimar Republic and led to the rise of extremist political parties.

2. **Treaty of Versailles:** Right from the very beginning, this Weimar Republic was associated with the humiliating Treaty of Versailles. The Weimar Republic signed the Versailles treaty which brought humiliation to Germany. Germans strongly resented the War Guilt Clause which held them solely responsible for the war. Hitler's political propaganda to undo the treaty brought him mass political support.

3. **System of proportional representation:** There was a provision for proportional representation in the Weimar Constitution. This provision prevented the formation of a powerful Central Government.

4. **Poor leadership:** The Weimar Republic was led by a succession of weak and ineffective leaders who were unable to provide the stability and leadership needed to overcome the economic crisis.

5. **Political and social divisions:** The Weimar Republic was a democracy that was divided along political, social, and ideological lines. Moreover, As the Weimar republic represented a centrist party government, so, right from the very beginning, it faced the situation of attack from rightist and leftist parties both. This division resulted in a lack of consensus on how to deal with the economic crisis and allowed extremist groups to gain influence.

6. **Lack of support from the military and conservative elites:** The military and conservative elites did not support the Weimar Republic and actively sought to undermine it. This lack of support made it difficult for the Weimar Republic to establish a stable government.

7. **Rise of extremist political parties:** The economic crisis and political divisions allowed extremist political parties, such as the Nazis, to gain influence and power. The Nazis were able to exploit the divisions in the Weimar Republic and ultimately take control of the government.

Historian Debate on the Rise of Nazism

The historians' debate over the rise of Nazism centres around several key questions.

1. Firstly, why did the German populace accept the Nazi Party and its policies, despite the violence and aggressive rhetoric that accompanied them?
2. Secondly, what role did economic and social factors, such as the Great Depression, play in the rise of Nazism?
3. Thirdly, how successful were Nazi propaganda and indoctrination in swaying public opinion?
4. Fourthly, what can be done to prevent the emergence of similar totalitarian regimes in the future?

The rise of Nazism in Germany is a complex issue and there is no single answer to any of these questions and has been debated by historians for decades.

First Debate: Role of the Great Depression vs Success of Nazi Propaganda

Some historians point to the role of the Great Depression, arguing that the economic crisis created a climate of fear and desperation in which Nazi ideology, with its promise of a return to national greatness and prosperity, resonated strongly. Other historians point to the success of Nazi propaganda in appealing to grievances and fears, as well as its use of powerful images and rhetoric to sway public opinion.

Nevertheless, there is also agreement among historians that the rise of Nazism was ultimately enabled by a combination of factors, including political and economic conditions, the failure of democracy, the complicity of the German population, and the appeal of Nazi ideology. In other words, while no single factor can explain the rise of Nazism, it was a complex mix of factors that ultimately enabled the Nazi Party to come to power.

Second Debate: Unique Circumstances in Germany vs Part of a Broader Trend in Europe

Some other historians argue that Nazism was a unique movement that was enabled by unique circumstances in Germany in the 1930s. These historians point to the economic instability, political divisions, and the rising tide of nationalism in Germany as key factors in the success of the Nazi Party. They also point to the charisma of Adolf Hitler and the appeal of his vision of a strong, unified Germany as major factors in the Nazi's rise to power.

Other historians take a different view and argue that the rise of Nazism was part of a broader trend in Europe in the 1930s. These historians point to the rise of authoritarian regimes across the continent, from Mussolini's Italy to Franco's Spain, as evidence that the rise of Nazism was part of a broader trend. They also point to the weakening of democracy in many countries and the appeal of strong, unified leadership as key factors in the success of the Nazis.

The debate over the rise of Nazism is an ongoing one, and there is no consensus among historians as to the exact causes of the Nazi Party's success. However, it is clear that a combination of factors, both unique to Germany and part of a broader trend, enabled the Nazis to come to power.

Hitler's Consolidation of Power

Adolf Hitler and the Nazi Party rose to power in Germany following the Great Depression and a series of political manoeuvrings in the early 1930s. After taking office in 1933, Hitler began consolidating power for himself and the Nazi Party in several key areas.

1. After coming to power Hitler invoked Article-48 of the Weimar Republic and declared a national emergency.
2. In 1933, the Nazis abolished the free press, allowing them to control what information was released to the public.
3. Hitler used a series of laws to limit the political power of other political parties and organizations. In March 1933, the Enabling Act granted Hitler and the Nazi Party the power to pass laws without the approval of the Reichstag, the German parliament. Later that same year, the Law for the reconstruction of the Reich abolished the offices of Germany's individual states, centralizing power with the Nazi Party.
4. In 1934, President Hindenburg passed away. So, Hitler, on the basis of a referendum, combined both, the post of Chancellor and President, into a single one and occupied the post.
5. In June 1934, Hitler carried out a purge within the party and eliminated his enemies within the party. This incident is known as 'Night of the Long Knives'. After that, he also carried the purge within the army and provided some important posts to his supporters.
6. Hitler and the Nazi Party used the police and paramilitary organizations to suppress political opposition. The Sturmabteilung (SA), or Storm Detachment, was a Nazi militia that terrorized political opponents and helped keep them in line. The Gestapo, or Secret State Police, was a secret police force used to root out political dissidents.
7. Hitler created a working-class front in order to put control over the strikes and through this front, he brought the working class under his control.
8. Hitler brought changes in the educational curriculum and encouraged scholars and artists to glorify the Nazi party and Hitler.
9. On the front of employment, Hitler achieved unparallel success, as he unconsciously adopted the same Keynesian method for promoting employment by the state through increasing state spending.
10. Hitler and the Nazi party adopted conservative and harsh methods for women. They prescribed only Kinder (kids), Kirch (Church), Kuch (kitchen) to women.
11. Hitler adopted a very harsh approach to Jews on the basis of Nuremberg law. Jews were deprived of their citizenship and from 1938 onwards, riots started against them.

Foreign Policy of Adolf Hitler

The rise of Adolf Hitler and his appointment as German chancellor in January 1933 marked the start of a new era in the history of Europe since his foreign policy brought about a number of changes worldwide. He destroyed the Paris Peace agreement, which ultimately led to the outbreak of the Second World War.

> "*The foreign policy of Hitler was a radical departure from the traditional foreign policy of Germany, seeking to break away from the restrictions of the Treaty of Versailles and pursuing an aggressive, expansionist agenda in Europe and beyond.*
>
> ***—Norman Naimark***"

Nature of Hitler's Foreign Policy

1. Hitler's foreign policy was driven by his desire to achieve power and glory for Germany and himself. He sought to expand German borders, claiming more 'Lebensraum' (living space) for the German people. This involved invading and occupying neighbouring countries, and forcing them to accept German rule.
2. Most of Hitler's policies were aimed at undermining the Treaty of Versailles and his foreign policy was opposed to the system established by the Paris Peace Conference.

3. It was guided by German national interest and Hitler also sought to restore Germany as a powerful world power, and to gain international recognition of this status.
4. Militarism and expansionism were dominant features in Hitler's foreign policy.
5. Idea of the third Reichstag also inspired Hitler's foreign policy. He wanted to create the third German Empire on the lines of the empire created by Frederick the Great and Bismarck.
6. Hitler built a large army using conscription as desired by the Germans. His industrial policy resulted in the large-scale production of weapons. This powerful German army persuaded him to pursue an aggressive foreign policy. His foreign policy had a systematic step-by-step approach.

   Hitler's systematic step-by-step approach to achieve his goals was the so-called 'Führerprinzip,' or the 'Leader Principle.' This system was based on a top-down hierarchy, where Hitler was the supreme leader and all decisions were made by him. Under the Führerprinzip, Hitler and his inner circle had absolute control over the Nazi Party and its policies. Hitler's goal was to create a totalitarian state where he could rule by decree, and the Führerprinzip allowed him to do this.
7. Idea of pan-Germanism was also dominant in Hitler's foreign policy. He wanted to bring all Germans together as part of one unit.
8. His foreign policy was guided even by racism. For example, in his text,'*The secret book*', he mentioned that Germans were pure Aryans so they deserve to possess a larger chunk of the region. However, although being of a lesser race, Slabs (Russia) had more land than they were supposed to. Therefore, it was necessary to remove the Slab people from the additional area.

Different Stages of Hitler's Foreign Policy

The First Stage (1933-36)

After Hitler became Chancellor in 1933, he began to re-arm Germany and restore national pride. In this stage, he had consistently broken the clauses of the Treaty of Versailles but simultaneously, tried to convince the allied powers that he was not opposed to the European order.

1. After becoming the German Chancellor Hitler withdrew from the disarmament conflict claiming that the disarmament regime that had been created was discriminatory.
2. In October 1933, he left the League of Nations.
3. In January 1934, a 10-year non-aggression pact was signed with Poland to convince other European countries that his intentions were peaceful.
4. In January 1935, SARR region was reintegrated with Germany through a plebiscite as the period of 15 years decided by the Treaty of Versailles had lapsed.
5. In 1935, Hitler reintroduced compulsory military service and expanded the German army and navy.
6. In June 1935, Anglo-German naval pact was signed through which Hitler promised to limit German Navy to 35% of British naval strength.

The Second Stage (1936-38)

Hitler then pursued an aggressive policy of expansion in Europe.

1. In March 1936, Rhineland was remilitarized by Hitler.
2. In October 1936, Rome Berlin axis was created.
3. In October 1937, Anti-Comintern Pact was signed with Japan and the Rome Berlin Tokyo axis came into existence.

4. Hitler participated in the Spanish Civil War in 1937. His victory in this war further emboldened him and his foreign policy. Afterwards, Hitler became more aggressive.
5. In March 1938, Austria was annexed.
6. Hitler received Sudetenland (comprised of a 3 million German Population) from Czechoslovakia in September 1938 through the Munich pact.

Third Stage (After 1938)

1. In March 1939, Hitler annexed Czechoslovakia.
2. In April 1939, Hitler demanded rail and road links across the Polish corridor.
3. On August 24, 1939, Hitler entered into a 10 years non-aggression pact with the Soviet Union. The Nonaggression Pact of Germany and Russia, also known as the Molotov-Ribbentrop Pact, was a non-aggression pact between Nazi Germany and the Soviet Union signed in Moscow on August 23, 1939. The pact was an agreement between the two powers that they would not attack one another and also included secret protocols that divided eastern Europe including Poland, into German and Soviet spheres of influence. The pact allowed Germany to launch its invasion of Poland without fear of Soviet intervention. The pact remained in effect until June 22, 1941, when Nazi Germany invaded the Soviet Union.

RISE OF FASCISM IN ITALY

Fascism, which drew its inspiration from both Social Darwinism and Freudian psychology, originated in Italy in the early 20th century. It was an authoritarian, nationalist, and anti-communist ideology led by Benito Mussolini. It was initially a nationalist and populist movement that sought to bring together the various social classes of Italy.

> “*Fascism is a form of authoritarianism that seeks to increase its power and control of the population by any means necessary, often through manipulation, coercion, and violence.*
>
> ***–David Thompson***”

The political ideology of fascism is characterized by extreme nationalism, militarism, totalitarianism, and one-party rule. The main goals of the fascist movement were to create a unified Italian state, suppress class conflicts, and establish a totalitarian dictatorship. Nevertheless, fascism was not any consistent philosophy rather it was a mixture of Hegelian idealism, Social Darwinism, anti-intellectualism, etc.

In 1922, Mussolini and the National Fascist Party (PNF) came to power in Italy. They were able to establish a one-party state and enact several policies in order to create a unified Italian nation-state. These policies included the suppression of all political opposition, the establishment of a corporate state, the promotion of a cult of personality around Mussolini, and the promotion of extreme nationalism.

The fascist regime was known for its repression of civil liberties, censorship of the press, promotion of racism and anti-Semitism, and the use of violence to achieve political and economic objectives. During Mussolini's rule, Italy became involved in a number of international conflicts, including the Italo-Ethiopian War (1935-1936) and World War II (1939-1945).

Factors behind the Rise of Fascism in Europe

1. **Development of radical ideologies:** The growth of new ideologies like Social Darwinism and Freud's psychology, which pleaded for the primacy of individuals in society.

2. **Paris Peace Conference:** Disenchantment of Italy and Germany in the Paris Peace Conference.
3. **Economic instability:** Economic instability caused by the Great Depression and the subsequent rise in unemployment and poverty provided fertile ground for the spread of fascism. The World Economic Depression in 1929-30 appeared to be a crisis in the capitalist system so capitalism tried to save itself from communism even through the fascist method.
4. **Political unrest:** Political unrest caused by the rise of radical ideologies and the weakening of traditional political structures created an environment in which fascist ideologies could gain widespread support.
5. **Nationalism:** The aftermath of World War I left many Europeans feeling disenchanted with the international system and in search of a stronger national identity, which fascism promised.
6. **Fear of communism:** The spread of communism in the Soviet Union and elsewhere in Europe was seen as a direct threat to the existing order and prompted many to turn to fascism as a bulwark against it.
7. **Authoritarianism:** Fascist leaders promised to restore order and stability to a chaotic and divided Europe and to protect it from external threats. This appeal to a desire for strong leadership and order resonated with many Europeans.

Factors for the Rise of Mussolini in Italy

1. One major factor for the rise of Benito Mussolini in Italy was the country's dissatisfaction with the results of the Paris Peace Conference. Italy had entered the war expecting to gain territory. The regions of Dalmatia that Italy wanted were never given to it and that of Fiume was given much later. Italian Prime Minister Orlando had left the Paris Conference midway when the big three leaders did not take him seriously. This led to a sense of betrayal and frustration among many Italians, who were eager for a leader who could restore the country's pride and standing in the world.
2. Mussolini was able to capitalize on this dissatisfaction by presenting himself as a strong, authoritarian leader who could restore Italy's greatness. He promised to take decisive action to defeat political opponents, end the economic crisis, and reclaim the country's lost territories. He also promised to restore Italy's honour and pride and to make it a powerful and respected world leader.
3. Political instability prevailing in Italy was also responsible for the rise of a Fascist system. Within a short span of three years, the number of governments has changed in Italy. Stephen J. Lee remarked that Italy witnessed 22 governments between Cavour and 1900, 9 governments between 1900 and 14, and 7 governments between 1914 and 1922. Consequently, Democratic regimes failed in satisfying the aspirations of people in the circumstances that created the mass appeal of Mussolini.
4. Fear of communism played an important role in the rise of Mussolini. Italian capitalist threw their weight behind Mussolini as he was their only hope against communism
5. He consciously encouraged the ultra-nationalist emotions among the people and he tried to win over different social groups in his favour by giving them some promise. He removed the historical norms which were done to Italy in Paris Peace Conference.
6. But still in the elections of 1921, the Fascist party bagged only 35 seats. Now Mussolini decided to use its power to achieve his objective. So, he consciously promoted his volunteers to fight against communists in the streets and on the roads. Then in 1922, he organized 50 thousand volunteers and carried a march to Rome to King Victor Immanuel III, to succumb to his pressure and provided him with the post of Prime Minister.

Common Features of Fascism

The inter-war period witnessed the emergence of radical nationalist regimes in many parts of the world these are termed as fascist regimes because of their similarities to the fascist regime in Italy. Some of them are General Togo in Japan, Metaxas in Mexico, Dolphus in Austria and Francisco Franco in Spain.

Fascism was having different manifestations in different parts of the world but still, they were having some common points or certain points of similarity.

1. **Authoritarian leadership:** Fascist regimes were totalitarian in character. Fascism is a form of government led by an authoritarian leader who exercises absolute control over all aspects of society. The glorification of leadership and the promotion of the cult of hero-worship.
2. **Extreme nationalism:** Belief in the supremacy of the state was the most fundamental feature of Fascist regimes. These regimes practiced the idea of state worship. Fascism glorifies the nation above everything else and calls for the subordination of individual rights and freedom to the power and interests of the state.
3. **Anti-communism:** Fascism is typically highly critical of communism and other forms of socialism, perceiving them as threats to national identity and interests.
4. **Militarism:** Fascism glorifies military power, often advocating for a strong military presence both domestically and abroad. They had no faith in the efficacy of peaceful methods to resolve conflicts in international scenarios.
5. **Control of the media and education:** Fascism seeks to control the media and education in order to influence public opinion and shape the values and beliefs of its citizens.
6. **Self-sufficiency of the state:** Emphasis on the self-sufficiency of the state was another important feature of Fascist regimes for the state to be powerful. Fascism promotes a corporatist economic system, in which economic power is concentrated in the hands of the state and large corporations.
7. **Conservative in nature:** Fascist forces emphasised on traditionalism to promote status-quo in society and thus gave emphasis on customs and traditions.
8. **Against liberalism:** These regimes were against liberalism. They were opportunistic and behaved as per the needs of the situation.
9. **Cynical approach:** Fascist regimes were also identified by their cynical approach. They drew strength by criticizing others.

Foreign Policy of Benito Mussolini

The foreign policy of Mussolini was inspired by the following ideas that the unification of Italy was still an unfinished agenda, so, Italy should make a fresh extension in the Balkan region.

> “*Mussolini's foreign policy was based on the principles of self-determination, irredentism, and the establishment of a 'New Roman Empire.' It was a policy of expansion, aimed at increasing Italy's prestige and power on the international stage, by gaining control of strategic territories in the Mediterranean basin and beyond.*
> ***—Professor Elizabeth B. White***”

1. Mussolini's foreign policy was based on the principles of self-determination, irredentism, and the establishment of a New Roman Empire.

2. The foreign policy of Benito Mussolini was shaped by his ambition to make Italy a major world power. Mussolini visioned Italy as a strong, unified nation that was capable of dominating its neighbours and achieving great power status. He sought to build an Italian empire, increase Italy's influence in Europe, and promote Italian culture and language abroad. Apart from that, his objective was to make an expansion in the region of Africa as well.
3. Benito Mussolini was against the treaty of St. Germain, so, one of his objectives was to break the clauses of the treaty of St. Germain.
4. Mussolini sought to increase Italy's influence in Europe by engaging in a number of diplomatic activities. He formed an alliance with Nazi Germany, which helped to gain Italy a larger say in European affairs.
5. Mussolini also pursued an expansionist foreign policy, seeking to expand Italy's territorial control in Europe, Africa, and the Mediterranean. He became an ally of Japan, which allowed Italy to gain access to East Asian markets and resources.

Overall, Mussolini's foreign policy was aggressive and expansionist. He sought to increase Italy's power and influence in Europe and the world and to promote Italian culture and language abroad.

Mussolini's Foreign Policy Initiatives

1. **1924:** Possession of Fume port after a treaty with Yugoslavia (1924).
2. **1925:** Mussolini signs a treaty of friendship with France.
3. **1926:** Italy becomes a member of the Locarno Pact, a mutual guarantee of the territorial integrity of Belgium, France, Germany, Italy, and Luxembourg.
4. **1927:** He came to develop patronage over Albania after concluding a treaty of Tirana.
5. He invaded the Korfu region in Greece. Although he had to evacuate this region, he got 5 Crore Lira as compensation.
6. **1929:** Italy joins the Little Entente, a mutual defense agreement between Czechoslovakia, Romania, and Yugoslavia.
7. **1931:** Italy invades Ethiopia, launching the Second Italo-Ethiopian War.
8. **1933:** Earlier there was a rivalry between Italy and France but after the rise of Hitler, France, and Italy came near to each other with the conclusion of the Lobal-Mussolini Pact.
9. **1934:** Italy joins the Stresa Front, a diplomatic agreement between Britain, France, and Italy, in opposition to German rearmament.
10. **1935:** But after the invasion of Ethiopia in October 1935, Mussolini was isolated and then he decided to come near to Hitler.
11. **1935:** Italy signs the Rome-Berlin Axis, forming an alliance with Nazi Germany.
12. **1936:** Italy sends an expeditionary force to Spain to support General Francisco Franco in the Spanish Civil War.
13. **1939:** Italy signs the Pact of Steel with Nazi Germany, further strengthening the Rome-Berlin Axis.
14. **1940:** Italy enters World War II, joining the Axis powers.

Italian Corporate State

When Mussolini became the Italian Prime Minister in October 1922 Italy was passing through a serious crisis. The corporate state of Mussolini was an answer to the social economic and political changes faced by Italy during the interwar period. Even though Italy was on the winning side in World War I financial burden of the war ruined it, more than seven lakh Italians lost their lives in the war.

The Italian Corporate State was a fascist state that was established in Italy in the 1920s. This state was characterized by absolute control of the government over the economy and a strong emphasis on national identity and traditions. The state was characterized by its heavy regulation of the economy, its promotion of national unity and loyalty to the state, and its disregard for civil

> *The Italian Corporate State was a sort of 'revolution from above' that sought to modernize Italy and foster a spirit of national unity, but it also entailed the suppression of civil liberties, a cult of the personality of Mussolini, and the subordination of all economic and social interests to the fascist government.*
> ***—Mark Mazower, (Historian)***

Points to Ponder

Under the Italian Corporate State, the economy was organized into various corporations (guild) and each corporation was responsible for setting wages, working conditions, and production targets, and was overseen by a government-appointed official.

rights and liberties. Economic policy was focused on public works, infrastructure projects, and state-run industries. The labour force was strictly regulated and labour unions were banned. The Corporate State also sought to promote a strong sense of national identity, through the celebration of Italian culture, history, and traditions. The goal of the Corporate State was to promote a unified and powerful Italy, and it ultimately failed in its mission.

Reason for the Rise of the Italian Corporate State

The rise of the Italian Corporate State can be attributed to several factors, including the economic and political turmoil of the 1920s and 1930s, the rise of fascism, and the need to create a stronger, more unified Italian nation. The economic and political turmoil of the 1920s led to a period of instability and unrest, which the fascist government sought to address by creating a powerful and unified state. This new Italian Corporate State was designed to provide a sense of stability and direction by centralizing economic and political power in the hands of the government.

Factors for the Rise of the Italian Corporate State

1. Corporate State of Mussolini was an answer to the social economic and political changes faced by Italy during the interwar period.
2. The protectionist policy adopted by European nations after 1919 worsened the economic crisis because of the stagnation of international trade and commerce.
3. Due to inadequate of market demand, various industries were closing down. Workers' salaries were being decreased, and many workers were being laid off. The rate of unemployment was dramatically rising. These workers are struggling to meet their basic demands.
4. Workers were gradually embracing communist ideology. Lockouts and strikes were occurring more frequently. Class conflicts between capitalists and workers led to a major social crisis.
5. In order to pull Italy out of this deep trouble Mussolini adopted the idea of the Corporate State. The entire social-economic life of Italy was restructured to pave the way for economic prosperity.

The Consequences of the Policy of the Italian Corporate State

The policy of the Italian Corporate State had far-reaching consequences for the country.

1. It led to a period of tremendous economic growth, increased employment, and a high standard of living for many Italians.
2. The Corporate State created a centralized economy in which the state was the sole owner of all economic activity, and it

favoured large corporations and denied the rights of labour unions.

3. It resulted in the growth of large industrial conglomerates, known as 'cartels', which had a virtual monopoly on the production of goods and services. This led to decreased competition, increased prices for goods, and decreased wages for the working classes.
4. Establishment of a corporate state reduced the prevailing social and economic crisis and normalize relations between workers and industries.
5. Revival of the economy enhanced the popularity of the fascist regime and Mussolini could rule effectively.
6. Threat of communism was successfully prevented in Italy. Workers were no longer resorting to strikes. The Corporate State of Mussolini was an answer to his social political and economic problems.

COMPARISON BETWEEN GERMAN NAZISM AND ITALIAN FASCISM

According to a historian Richard J. Evans, 'Nazi Germany and Fascist Italy were two different dictatorships, each with its own distinct ideologies and structure. While both regimes were oppressive and militaristic, the Nazi regime was far more extreme, both in its aims and in its methods of achieving them.'

Similarities between Nazism and Fascism

1. Both Nazism and Fascism are totalitarian regimes that seek to control all aspects of life, including the economy and government.
2. Both ideologies emphasize nationalism, militarism, and authoritarianism.
3. Both stressed the supremacy of the state, glorification of war, and the cult of the hero/leader who would guide the rebirth of the nation from its troubles.
4. Both ideologies believe in the supremacy of their own nation and seek to expand their influence and power through aggressive foreign policies.
5. Both regimes were inspired by extreme racism and anti-Semitism.
6. Both regimes sought to create a unified, homogeneous society by suppressing differences. They emphasized the close unity of all classes working together to achieve these ends.
7. Both opposed the ideology of Communism, Socialism and Liberalism. Both were intensely anti-communist and, because of this, drew a solid basis of support from all classes.
8. Both ideologies reject egalitarianism and embrace a hierarchical social structure with a privileged few at the top and a large mass of people at the bottom.
9. Both ideologies use propaganda to indoctrinate the masses and promote their respective ideologies.

Dissimilarities between Nazism and Fascism

1. **Difference in ideology:** The primary ideological difference between Nazism and Fascism is that Nazism was rooted in racial nationalism, while Fascism was rooted in cultural nationalism. Nazism was based on the belief that the Aryan race was superior and should be the ruling force in society, while Fascism was based on the belief that the Italian nation was superior and should be the ruling force in society.
2. **Antisemitism:** While Nazism was deeply associated with racialism and antisemitism (discrimination against Jews), Mussolini's fascism had less scope for antisemitism. In Germany, more than 6 million Jews were killed in concentration camps and gas chambers. Italian fascism was not particularly anti-Jewish or racist until 1938 when Mussolini adopted the policy to emulate Hitler.

3. **Radical and violent:** German Nazism was far more radical than Italian fascism. Hitler followed a violent policy on both internal and external fronts.

Points to Ponder

Fascism never seemed to take root in Italy as deeply as the Nazi system did in Germany.

4. **Leadership:** The leadership of Nazi Germany was centralized around Adolf Hitler, while the leadership of fascist Italy was more decentralized and based around the principles of collective leadership and the Corporate State.
5. **Different forms of government:** Nazi Germany was an authoritarian government, while Fascist Italy was a totalitarian government. Nazi Germany was ruled by a single party, while Fascist Italy was ruled by a coalition of parties. Mussolini strengthened his position but not equally the position of his party.
6. **Different constitutional positions:** The monarchy still remained in Italy, and though Mussolini normally ignored monarch Victor Emmanuel, the monarch played a vital role in 1943 when he announced Mussolini's dismissal and order his arrest. Unfortunately, no such constitutional position or authority existed in Germany who could dismiss Hitler.
7. **Economic system:** Nazi Germany adopted a policy of a centrally planned economy and autarky, or self-sufficiency while Fascist Italy adopted a state-controlled economy and a policy of corporatism. The corporate economy was organized along socialist lines. Such an economic reorganization was absent in Germany. Nazis rejected corporatism although they supported state intervention in the economy.
8. **Foreign policy:** Nazi Germany was aggressive and expansionist, while Fascist Italy was more nationalist, moderate, and non-interventionist. Nazi Germany sought to dominate Europe, while Fascist Italy sought to maintain a balance of power within Europe.
9. **Economic achievement:** Italian system was not as efficient as that in Germany. The Italians never came anywhere near achieving self-sufficiency and never eliminated unemployment; in fact, unemployment rose. The Nazis succeeded in eliminating unemployment, though they never achieved complete autarky.
10. **Religious policy:** Mussolini was more successful than Hitler with his religious policy after his agreement with the Pope in 1929.

THE SECOND CRISIS OF CAPITALISM: GREAT ECONOMIC DEPRESSION(1929–30)

The Great Economic Depression was a severe and prolonged economic depression that began in 1929 and lasted until the late 1930s. Its causes and effects were complex and far-reaching, and it was the longest and deepest economic depression of the 20th century.

The Great Depression began with the stock market crash of 1929 and was marked by a severe decline in investment, production, employment, and prices. It led to a dramatic rise in unemployment, poverty, and homelessness. It also had a major impact on the banking and financial system, causing a collapse of the banking system and a severe contraction of credit. It finally ended in the late 1930s, with the onset of World War II.

In one sense the phenomenon of recession and depression is inherent in the capitalist economy itself. In its over-enthusiasm for profit, the capitalist class destroys its own market.

Causes of The Great Economic Depression

According to Historian Craig L. Lamay,'The Great Depression was caused by a combination of factors, including the stock market crash of 1929, a lack of consumer confidence, and the failure of policymakers to act quickly enough to stem the crisis.'

1. **Stock market crash of 1929:** The most significant cause of the Great Depression was the dramatic fall in stock prices that began in October of 1929 and lasted through most of the 1930s. This stock market crash, known as the Wall Street Crash of 1929, marked the start of the Great Depression. Prior to this, people put their money into the stock market in the hope of making a quick profit. Unfortunately, the stock market crashed in October 1929, wiping out millions of investors.

   The crash was followed by a severe economic depression that lasted for more than a decade. The causes of the crash are still debated, but it is generally agreed that a combination of excessive speculation, economic inequality, and weak government regulation led to the collapse of the market.
2. **Excessive speculation:** American economy profited during the First World War because it supplied everything to Europe. By end of the war, Europe became a big American market. Americans were extremely optimistic as a result of rapid economic growth, which led to massive capacity expansion. Consequently, banks forwarded unsecured loans for capacity expansion in the hope of making big profits.
3. **Failures of banking institutions:** The stock market crash led to a chain reaction of bank failures throughout the United States. Banks had invested heavily in the stock market, and when the prices dropped, they had no assets to cover their losses. This caused a massive financial crisis, as people could no longer access their bank accounts or withdraw money. This led to a collapse of the banking system, which in turn caused a further decline in spending and investment.
4. **Weak banking system:** The banking system in the United States was not well regulated or prepared to handle such a large economic collapse. Many banks were undercapitalized and did not have enough money to cover the losses incurred in the stock market crash. This led to a massive wave of bank failures throughout the country.
5. **Protectionism and international trade:** The Great Depression was also worsened by a collapse in the international trade. In the 1920s, the U.S. government implemented high tariffs on goods imported from other countries. This policy, known as protectionism, was meant to encourage people to buy American-made goods. However, it had the opposite effect, as it caused other countries to impose their own tariffs, which led to a decrease in global trade.
6. **Income inequality:** The 1920s saw a rapid increase in income inequality, as the wealthy enjoyed a large increase in their incomes while the poor were stuck in poverty. This led to a decrease in consumer spending, which further exacerbated the economic crisis.
7. **Overproduction and underconsumption:** Prior to the Great Depression, businesses had been producing goods faster than people could buy them. This caused overproduction, which led to a decrease in demand. In addition, many people were unable to purchase goods due to their limited incomes. This combination of overproduction and underconsumption led to a decrease in economic activity.
8. **Drought:** The Great Plains were hit with a severe drought in 1930, which led to a decrease in agricultural production. This had a devastating impact on the economy, as the agricultural sector was one of the largest employers in the United States.
9. **Government policies:** Government policies were also to blame for the depression. The Smoot-Hawley Tariff of 1930 raised tariffs on a wide range of imported goods, which further reduced international trade. The Federal Reserve also made a series of mistakes during this period, such as not tightening the money supply when the stock market crashed, which caused a further decline in economic activity.

Consequences of the Great Economic Depression

1. **Increased unemployment:** The most devastating consequence of the Great Depression was the high unemployment rate. The unemployment rate rose to its peak of 25%, in 1933. This meant that over one-fourth of the working population was out of work.
2. **Increase in poverty increase:** The Great Depression had a severe impact on the living standards of people. The poverty rate rose to a high of 32.1% in 1933. This meant that one out of every three people was living below the poverty line.
3. **Reduced income and wages:** As businesses closed and unemployment rose, wages and income decreased significantly.
4. **Bank failures:** The economic crisis of the Great Depression led to a wave of bank failures across the United States. Over 9,000 banks failed during the 1930s, wiping out people's life savings.
5. **Increased homelessness:** The lack of jobs, income and housing options caused many people to become homeless.
6. **Reduced economic activity:** As businesses closed and people had less money to spend, economic activity decreased substantially. In America, the trade collapsed by 50%.
7. **Increased crime:** With scarce resources, people resorted to criminal activities to survive.
8. **Reduced confidence in the economy:** The Great Economic Depression led to a loss of confidence in the economy, as people feared that a similar crisis could happen again in the future.

Methods Adopted to Tackle Economic Depression

Upon taking office in 1933, President Franklin D. Roosevelt took a number of bold steps to address the Economic Depression of 1929 and promulgated the New Deal Policy.

New Deal Policy of Franklin D Roosevelt

Franklin D Roosevelt implemented the New Deal; a series of economic policies, designed to stimulate the economy and provide relief to those who were hit the hardest by the depression. These included the establishment of relief programs such as the Civilian Conservation Corps, the Works Progress Administration, and the Social Security Act.

He also sought to increase consumer spending by launching major public works projects like the Hoover Dam and the Tennessee Valley Authority. In addition, Roosevelt pushed for bank reforms, implemented the Glass-Steagall Act, and created the Federal Deposit Insurance Corporation.

All policy instruments and initiatives undertaken by the administration of President Roosevelt were guided by three main principles that are '3 Rs': Relief, Recovery, and Reform.

1. **Relief:** To provide relief to those who were suffering.
2. **Recovery:** To immediately set the way for recovery.
3. **Reform:** To initiate reforms wiping out limitations.

Various Policies Adopted Under New Deal

1. **National Recovery Administration (NRA):** The NRA was established in 1933 to promote fair competition and help businesses to get out of the Great Depression.
2. **Federal Emergency Relief Administration:** It was created with a $500 billion corpus to be distributed among state governments in order to help citizens in need.
3. **Agricultural Adjustment Act (AAA):** The AAA was enacted in 1933 to help farmers by reducing the amount of agricultural production. The government paid farmers to reduce their production, which was meant to raise the prices of agricultural goods by reducing the supply.

4. **Works Progress Administration (WPA):** The WPA was created in 1935 to provide jobs for the unemployed. It was the largest and most ambitious of the New Deal programs and employed millions of people in public works projects, such as building roads and bridges.
5. **Fair Labour Standards Act (FLSA):** The FLSA was enacted in 1938 to set minimum wages and maximum hours for workers in the private sector. It also outlawed child labour and established a federal minimum wage.
6. **Banking and stock market reforms:** Established the Federal Deposit Insurance Corporation (FDIC) to insure deposits up to $5000 to restore public faith and revive the banking system. Similarly, the Securities and Exchange Commission (SEC) regulates the stock market.
7. **Rural Electrification Administration (REA):** The REA was created in 1935 to bring electricity to rural areas. This program was instrumental in modernizing rural America and providing much-needed jobs in the process.

Keynesian Economics

In 1936, John Maynard Keynes published his famous text, 'The theory of employment interest and money' and in this text, he attacked the gold standard and free market. Keynes prescribed demand management in the economy. For demand management, John Keynes talked about two rules:

1. Taxation
2. Expenditure

These steps were highly successful and by 1939 American economy as well as the capitalist world had revived.

LET'S REVISE

Impact of the First World War on West Asia and the Arab world

1. Hussain-Mac Mahon Agreement
2. Sykes Picot Agreement
3. Balfour Declaration

Two Stages of the Russian Revolution

1. **February Revolution of 1917:** Establishment of a Provisional Government
2. **October Revolution of 1917:** established Communist Soviet Union

Causes for the Russian Revolution

1. Immediate Causes
   - (a) Tsar decision to participate in First World War
   - (b) March bread riots
2. Fundamental Causes
   - (a) **Political Causes:** Evils of Tsarist regime
     - (i) The Tsar's incompetence
     - (ii) Russia defeats by Japanese in 1905
     - (iii) The Russian Revolution of 1905
   - (b) **Economic Causes:** Economic Decline and Inequality
     - (i) Peasant Uprisings
     - (ii) An excessive reliance on agriculture
     - (iii) Poor working conditions
   - (c) **Social Causes:** Social inequality
     - (i) Social Inequality
     - (ii) Poverty
     - (iii) Non-Implementation of Reforms
     - (iv) Discrimination against Non-Russian
   - (d) Role of Philosopher in Russian Revolution

Steps Taken by Lenin to Consolidate the Revolution

1. Establish a one-party state
2. Accept the Treaty of Brest-Litovsk
3. Establish the Soviet Union
4. Nationalize all industry
5. Create the Cheka
6. Create the Comintern
7. Land Reforms
8. Establish a state-controlled media

Changes Introduced by Stalin

1. Change in Ideology
2. Policy of collectivization
3. Five-Year Plans
4. Dictatorship of the one man
5. Purges and Show Trials
6. Gulags
7. Censorship

Significance of Russia Revolution

1. First successful communist revolution
2. Impact on the political landscape
3. Civil war in Russia
4. Impact on the economy
5. Policy of appeasement
6. Great Depression and Rise of Socialism
7. Profound effect on international relations

Reason for the Failure of the League of Nations

1. League was Anglo-French in nature
2. No power to enforce its decisions
3. No Army of Its own
4. Structural problem
5. Dominated by the major powers
6. Financial dependence
7. Policy of appeasement
8. Rising threat of fascism and militarism

Factors Behind the Rise of Nazism

1. Weak Weimar Republic and Political Instability
2. Treaty of Versailles
3. The Economic Crisis
4. Fear of Communism
5. Blame and Resentment
6. Propaganda
7. Hitler's Charismatic Leadership

Factors Behind the Rise of Fascism in Europe

1. Development of radical ideologies
2. Paris Peace Conference
3. Economic instability
4. Political unrest
5. Nationalism
6. Fear of Communism
7. Authoritarianism

Common Features of Fascism

1. Authoritarian leadership
2. Extreme nationalism
3. Anti-communism
4. Militarism
5. Control of the media and education
6. Self-sufficiency of the state
7. Conservative in Nature
8. Against liberalism
9. Cynical approach

Causes for Great Economic Depression

1. Stock Market Crash of 1929
2. Excessive speculation
3. Failures of banking institution
4. Weak banking system
5. Protectionism and international trade
6. Income inequality
7. Overproduction and underconsumption
8. Drought
9. Government policies

Methods Adopted to Tackle Economic Depression

1. New Deal Policy of Franklin D Roosevelt
2. Keynesian Economics

UPSC PREVIOUS YEARS' QUESTIONS

1. What policy instruments were deployed to contain the Great Economic Depression? **[2013] (10 marks)**
2. The New Economic Policy 1921 of Lenin influenced the policies adopted by India soon after independence. Evaluate. **[2014] (10 marks)**
3. 'There arose a serious challenge to the Democratic State system between the Two World Wars.' Evaluate the statement. **[2019] (15 marks)**

PROBABLE QUESTIONS

1. Examine the causes of the Russian Revolution of 1917 and indicate its significance in world history.
2. 'The Russian Revolution (1917) was an economic explosion hastened by the stupidities of the autocratic government.' Comment.
3. Russia transformed in to cruel and authoritarian despot under Stalin. Critically examine.
4. How did Stalin build on Lenin's legacy of Bolshevik Revolution and introduce new elements of totalitarianism to transform USSR as a superpower?
5. Discuss the main characteristics of fascism?
6. Examine the circumstances which led to the overthrow of democracy and the establishment of Fascist dictatorship in Italy.
7. 'Corporate State' was Mussolini's answer to socio-political problems of his country. Elucidate.
8. Critically examine the main features of the foreign policy of Nazi Germany.

TIMELINE OF THE RUSSIAN REVOLUTION (1703–1991)

- **1703** – Peter the Great finds the city of Saint Petersburg, which becomes the capital of Russia.
- **1721** – Peter the Great declares himself Emperor of Russia.
- **1762** – Catherine II seizes power from her husband, Peter III.
- **1773** – Catherine II creates the first state-sponsored educational system in Russia.
- **1812** – Napoleon's invasion of Russia leads to the retreat of his army.
- **1861** – Tsar Alexander II abolishes serfdom in Russia.
- **1881** – Tsar Alexander II is assassinated by a group of revolutionaries.
- **1905** – The Bloody Sunday Massacre sets off a series of protests and strikes across Russia, prompting the creation of the first Russian Parliament.
- **1917** – The February Revolution overthrows Tsar Nicholas II and establishes a provisional government.
- **1918** – The Bolsheviks, led by Vladimir Lenin, seize power in the October Revolution by overthrowing the provisional government and establishing the Soviet Union.
- **1918** – The Russian Civil War begins between the Red Army and White Russian forces.
- **1921** – The Soviet Union is established and the New Economic Policy is introduced.
- **1922** – The Union of Soviet Socialist Republics (USSR) is formed.
- **1924** – Lenin dies and Joseph Stalin succeeds him as leader of the USSR.
- **1939** – The Soviet Union invades Poland, beginning World War II.
- **1941** – World War II begins; the Soviet Union is invaded by Nazi Germany.
- **1945** – The Soviet Union defeats Nazi Germany and Japan in World War II and emerges as one of the two major powers of the post war world
- **1953** – Stalin dies and Nikita Khrushchev becomes the leader of the USSR.
- **1991** – The Soviet Union is dissolved and the Commonwealth of Independent States is created.

TIMELINE OF NAZISM (1918–1934)

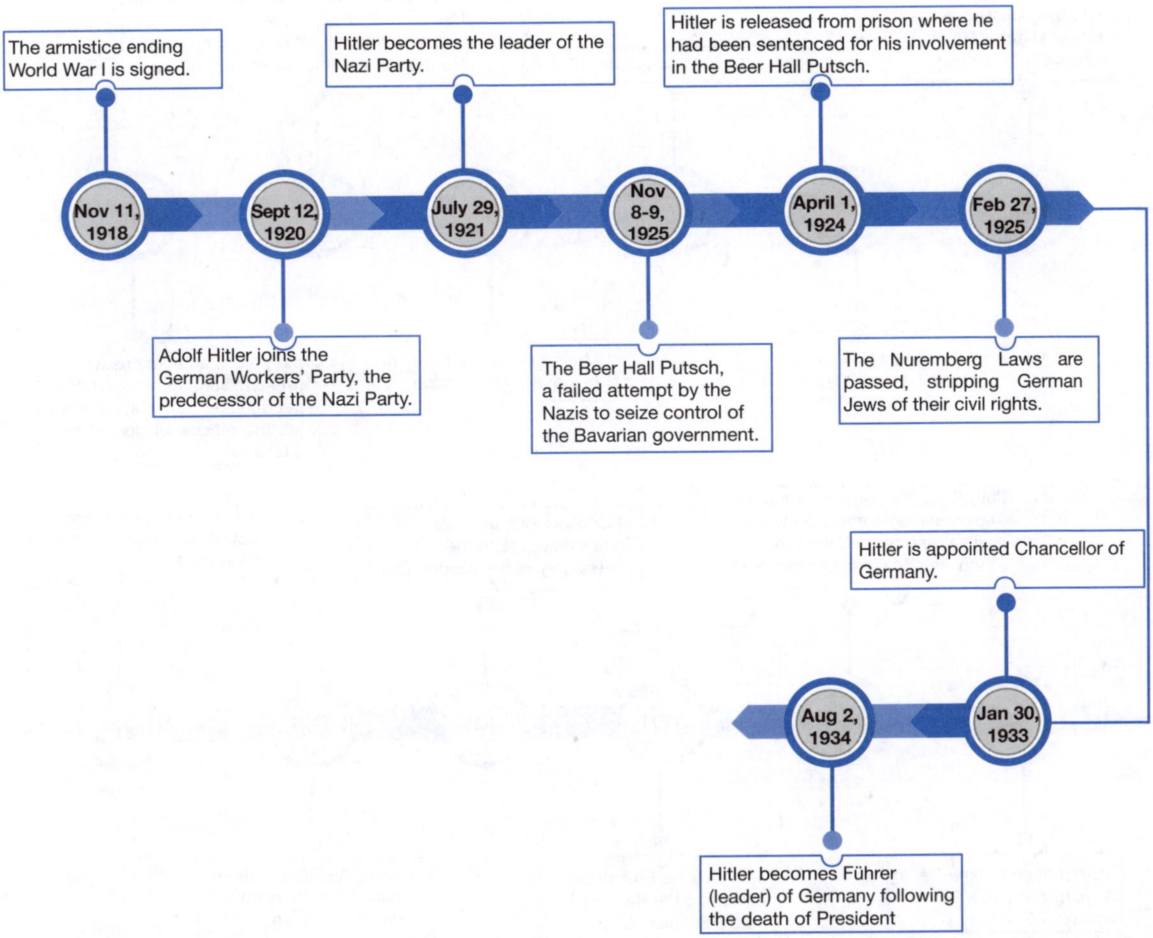

TIMELINE OF ITALY (1922–1945)

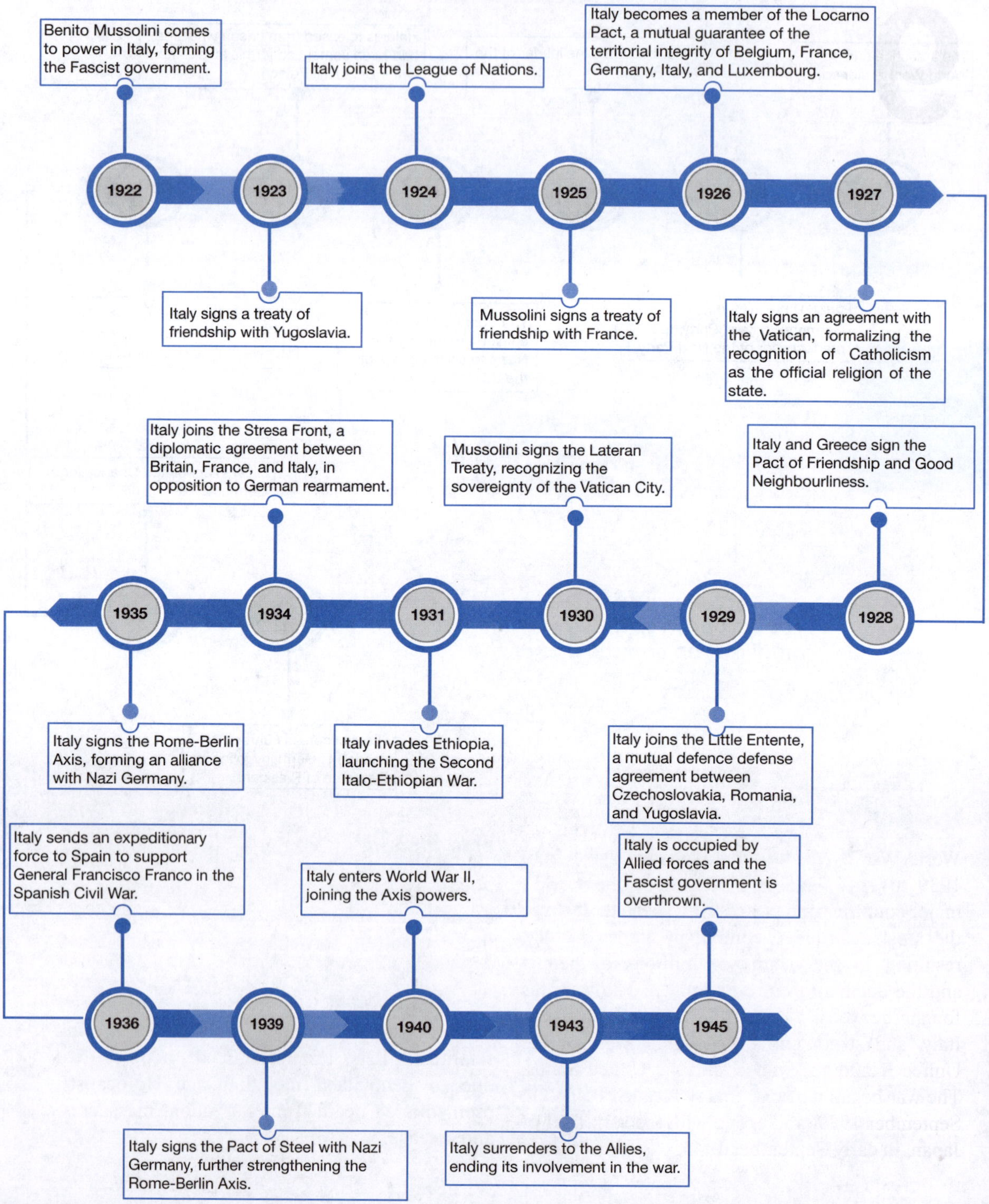

CHAPTER

9

Photo Credit: Ivan Cholakov / Shutterstock, maradon 333 / Shutterstock

SECOND WORLD WAR (1939–1945)

> *The Second World War was the last of the wars of mass mobilization and the first of the wars of technology.*
>
> *—A.J.P. Taylor*

INTRODUCTION

World War II was a global war that lasted from 1939 to 1945, and involved all of the world's major countries and powers. It was the largest and the most destructive conflict in human history, resulting in the deaths of millions of people and the decimation of entire cities. The war was fought between the Axis Powers of Germany, Italy, and Japan and the Allied Powers of the United Kingdom, France, and the United States. The war began when Germany invaded Poland in September 1939, and ended with the surrender of Japan, in early September 1945.

In a state of total war, directly involving more than 100 million people from more than 30 countries, the major participants threw their entire economic, industrial, and scientific capabilities behind the war effort, blurring the distinction between civilian and military resources.

World War II was the deadliest conflict in human history, resulting in 70 to 85 million fatalities. Tens of millions of people died due to genocides (including the Holocaust), premeditated death from starvation, massacres, and disease.

CAUSES OF THE SECOND WORLD WAR

According to historian Erick Hobsbawm, the Second World War was a war of 31 years which ended on August 15, 1945. A number of fundamental and immediate factors caused the Second World War including the Treaty of Versailles, the Great Depression of 1929, the development of fascism, the establishment of the Rome–Berlin–Tokyo axis, and the failure of the League of Nations **(Refer Figure 9.1).**

> “*The Second World War was the inevitable consequence of the unresolved problems of the First World War, of Hitler’s ambition and the weakness of the European democracies.*
>
> —***A.J.P. Taylor***”

Immediate Causes

Following the signing of the German-Soviet Non-aggression Pact (a non-aggression pact signed between Nazi Germany and the Soviet Union), Germany’s invasion of Poland, in 1939 was the final straw for Britain and France and led to the outbreak of World War II. This was the result of a series of diplomatic manoeuvres between Germany, Britain, France and other countries in Europe in the 1930s, as Hitler sought to expand German territories.

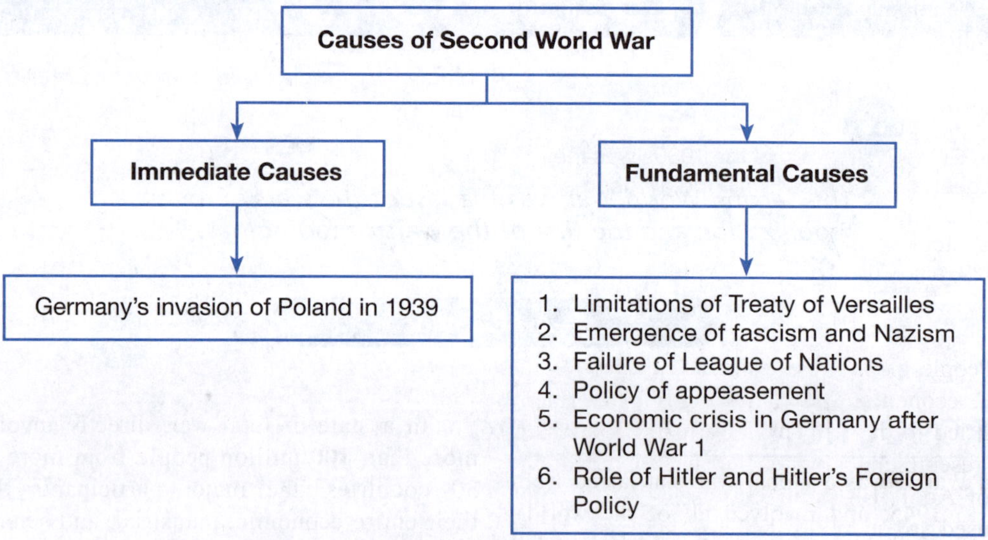

FIGURE 9.1: Causes of the Second World War

Fundamental Causes

Even though the Second World War began with Hitler’s invasion of Poland, according to Professor Alan Bullock (British Historian), ‘it was caused by the political and economic disorders of the inter-war years, the failure of collective security, and the rise of militarism and totalitarianism in Europe and Asia.’

Limitations of The Treaty of Versailles

The Treaty of Versailles is widely regarded by historians as one of the primary causes of the

> *The Treaty of Versailles, with its demand for German disarmament and its heavy reparations, was a major cause of World War II. It poisoned international relations and helped Adolf Hitler to come to power in Germany.*
>
> ***—A.J.P. Taylor***

Second World War. After World War I, the Allies imposed a harsh Treaty of Versailles on Germany which required it to pay heavy reparations and accept full responsibility for the war. This caused a great deal of resentment in Germany, which was further compounded by the Great Depression of the 1930s.

Points to Ponder

The Great Depression of the 1930s was the longest and the most widespread depression of the 20th century, that started with the stock market crash on October 29, 1929, also known as Black Tuesday.

People blamed the Versailles Treaty for the social, economic and political ills of Germany which led to the revival of German nationalism. This resentment provided fertile ground for the rise of Adolf Hitler and his Nazi Party, which promised to undo the harsh conditions of the Treaty of Versailles and restore Germany's former glory. Hitler's aggressive expansionism and refusal to abide by the terms of the treaty led to the outbreak of the Second World War in 1939.

Emergence of Ideology of Fascism and Nazism

The rise of Fascism (an extreme version of nationalism) in Europe in the 1930s was a major

> *The rise of Fascism in Europe, especially in Germany and Italy, was a major factor in the outbreak of the Second World War. The combination of authoritarianism, militarism, and racism, along with a rejection of democratic values, created a powerful and dangerous force that threatened the stability of Europe and the world.*
>
> ***—Professor Robert O. Paxton***

factor in the outbreak of the Second World War. The rise of Hitler's Nazi party in Germany and Mussolini's Fascist Party in Italy created two powerful regimes that sought to expand their territories and influence. The aggressive expansionist policies of the Fascists (for example Hitler's lebensraum: Living Space Policy), were combined with their militaristic rhetoric and propaganda. When the Allies did not resist these moves (for example Munich Agreement), it encouraged the Axis Powers (Germany, Japan, and Italy) to continue their aggression. But later, as a consequence of Fascist policies that combined authoritarianism, militarism, and racism, diplomatic tension and conflicts in Europe escalated. This, in turn, led to a series of diplomatic crises after the Munich Agreement. Moreover, by 1939, the two Fascist powers had formed an alliance, the Axis Powers, which would ultimately lead to the outbreak of the Second World War.

Moreover, the oppressive and totalitarian nature of the Fascist regimes, their disregard for human rights and for international law were seen as a direct threat to the peace and stability in Europe. As a result, their ambitions were opposed by the other major powers, leading to a cycle of increased militarization, diplomatic crises, and ultimately the outbreak of the war.

Failure of the League of Nations

The failure of the League of Nations to prevent the Second World War was a direct result of its inability to enforce its decisions in the face of aggressive, expansionist nations. The League was established in 1919 with the aim of preventing war, but it failed to stop the aggression of the Axis Powers (Germany, Japan, and Italy) as they undermined league by the refusing to accept its authority. Moreover, even major power like the United States, which refused to join, and the Soviet Union, which left in 1939 contributed to its failure.

> *The League of Nations did nothing to prevent the Second World War. In fact, its failure to take decisive action in the face of aggression by the Axis Powers was one of the main causes of the conflict.*
>
> ***—Professor David Stevenson (Historian)***

The League's powers were also limited by its lack of an army of its own, and its failure to respond effectively to the aggressive actions of Japan, Italy, and Germany, such as:

1. Japanese attack on Manchuria and Italian Abyssinian attack tarnished the image of the league of Nations.
2. Failure of the League to act against the aggressive foreign policy of Hitler aimed at creating a living space for Germany.
3. No action was taken by the League in the Spanish Civil War to restrict Franco's rise as a dictator against the elected government in Spain which practically marked the end of the League of Nations.

This led to a build-up of tensions which was not resolved by the League, culminating in the outbreak of the Second World War in 1939.

The Appeasement Policy

Appeasement is a policy of making concessions to an aggressive power to avoid conflict. It is usually pursued through diplomatic negotiations and is designed to satisfy the demands of the aggressive power in order to prevent war. Appeasement is generally viewed as a failed foreign policy due to its inability to prevent war and its encouragement of further aggression.

> *The Policy of Appeasement, by which Britain and France sacrificed Czechoslovakia on the altar of peace in 1938, was the main cause of the Second World War. It encouraged Hitler to believe that he could act with impunity and aggression.*
>
> ***—Alan Bullock (Historian)***

The appeasement policy, adopted by British Prime Minister Neville Chamberlain and France in the 1930s, was an attempt to avoid war by allowing Adolf Hitler to annex parts of Czechoslovakia and other territories without offering any resistance. Chamberlain's policy of appeasement was rooted in his belief that it was possible to negotiate with Hitler and the Nazi regime, in order to preserve peace in Europe.

The policy of appeasement was a major contributing factor to the outbreak of the Second World War. It was an attempt to satisfy Adolf Hitler's expansionist ambitions by giving him the territories he desired in Europe. This policy was pursued by Britain and France and was in effect from 1936 to 1939. It was designed to try and avert a war with Germany by allowing Fascist forces to gain certain territories without a fight such as:

1. **Italy's attack on Abyssinia**: Despite the fact that Britain and France condemned Italy's attack on Abyssinia in October

1935, no effective actions were taken in response.

2. **Hitler's invasion of Austria and Czechoslovakia**: Hitler's invasion of Austria and Czechoslovakia was also ignored by Britain and France. In fact, British PM Neville Chamberlain followed the policy of appeasement as he agreed that the failure of the Versailles Treaty along with the failure of the League of Nations, appeasement was the only right option to prevent the war **(Refer Map 9.1)**.

Map 9.1: Expansion of Hitler in Eastern Europe

However, this appeasement policy ultimately failed, as Hitler took advantage of it and continued to make further territorial demands. This ultimately led to the outbreak of the Second World War in 1939, when Hitler invaded Poland in 1939 under his desire to gain 'living space' as Britain and France declared war on Germany in 1939. Therefore, it can be argued that the policy of appeasement was a major factor in the outbreak of the Second World War **(Refer Map 9.1)**.

Renowned historian A.J.P. Taylor strongly opposed the policy of appeasement. He believed that it was a cowardly way to deal with the aggression of dictators and that it only encouraged them to become more aggressive. He believed that Britain should have taken a firm stance against German aggression earlier on and that it was a mistake to allow Hitler to have so much power. He argued that appeasement only delayed the inevitable and that it would ultimately lead to World War II.

Economic Crisis and Economic Depression of 1929

The economic depression of the 1930s played a major role in creating the conditions for the outbreak of the Second World War. The Great Depression, sparked by the stock market crash of 1929, caused widespread economic hardship throughout the world. The economic collapse of the 1920s and 1930s had a devastating impact on the global economy, leading to rampant unemployment, poverty, and economic instability. This economic instability, combined with the rise of authoritarian regimes and the spread of militaristic ideologies, created a volatile global situation.

Moreover, the rising levels of unemployment and a collapse in the international trade, caused countries to pursue increasingly protectionist policies. This in turn caused a further decline in global trade, further exacerbating the economic crisis **(Refer Figure 9.2)**.

FIGURE 9.2: Linkage between Economic Crisis and the Second World War

The economic crisis also had a major political impact. The Dawes Plan (an initiative proposed by the United States in 1924 to restructure Germany's World War I reparations payments and stabilize its economy) proved successful in stabilizing the German economy. However, after the Great Depression of 1929, no more loans were granted to Germany from America which further increased economic hardship. Moreover, the Great Depression meant that nations were unable to pay the reparations from the First World War, leading to political instability and the rise of extremist leaders, such as Adolf Hitler in Germany.

In Germany, the rise of the Nazi Party was partly fuelled by the economic hardship caused by the Great Depression. All economic hardships such as unemployment, poverty, etc., caused by the economic depression was blamed on allied demand for war indemnity, Treaty of Versailles and the Weimar Republic by Hitler and Nazi Party.

Similarly, in Japan, the military government was able to seize power partly because of the economic crisis, and their aggressive expansionist policies were an attempt to alleviate economic distress.

The economic crisis of the 1930s also had a major impact on international relations. Countries became increasingly hostile towards each other and the failure of the League of Nations to address the economic crisis further eroded international trust. This, combined with the aggressive expansionist policies of certain countries, helped to create an atmosphere of mutual distrust that eventually led to the outbreak of the Second World War.

Role of Hitler and Hitler's Foreign Policy

Adolf Hitler was the dictator of Nazi Germany and was the main driving force behind World War II. Hitler was an Austrian-born German politician who was the leader of the Nazi Party. He rose to power in Germany during the 1930s and became Chancellor in 1933. He quickly established an authoritarian regime, under which he pursued an aggressive foreign policy with the aim of expanding German Lebensraum ('living space') at the expense of other European nations. This included:

> *Adolf Hitler was the driving force behind the Second World War. His ambition to dominate Europe and gain 'living space' for the German people led to his aggressive foreign policy, which ultimately resulted in the invasion of Poland and the outbreak of the war in 1939.*
>
> ***—Sir Ian Kershaw (Historian)***

1. Hitler withdrew Germany from the World Disarmament Conference and the League of Nations.
2. Hitler started the rearmament of the German army in 1935 causing international tensions.
3. Hitler signed a non-aggression pact with Russia to bring Poland under German influence.
4. March 1936: Hitler recaptured Rhineland against the provision of the Treaty of Versailles.
5. Hitler's support to Fascist leaders like Mussolini and Francisco Franco.
6. In 1938, after seizing control of Austria's foreign policy, Hitler threatened the Chancellor of Austria. Finally, on March 12, 1938, Hitler annexed Austria with German forces.
7. The invasion of Czechoslovakia and Poland in 1939, marked the beginning of World War II.

THE COURSE OF THE SECOND WORLD WAR

The Second World War was a global war that lasted from 1939 to 1945 and involved the majority of the world's countries. It was fought between the Axis Powers (Germany, Italy, and Japan) and the Allied Powers (Britain, France, Russia, the United States, and others).

1. **Czechoslovakia and Munich Agreement:** Czechoslovakia comprised a variety of mixed ethnicities that were artificially combined to form a nation by the Versailles peacemakers. The Sudetenland was an area of western Czechoslovakia that was mainly inhabited by ethnic Germans. The Sudeten German Party protested the government of Czechoslovakia in 1938. In 1938, Adolf Hitler used the issue of the Sudetenland to pressure the Czech government.

Points to Ponder

> The problem of the Sudetenland was a major source of tension between Germany, Czechoslovakia, and other European powers.

The Munich Agreement was an agreement signed between Nazi Germany, the United Kingdom, France, and Italy in September 1938. It allowed Nazi Germany to annex the Sudetenland region of Czechoslovakia. In exchange for allowing Nazi Germany to annex the Sudetenland, the other signatories to the agreement promised that the German government would not make any further territorial claims in Europe.

Munich Agreement ended a significant German grievance in Europe without starting a war, but it was an act of betrayal towards Czechoslovakia. The Czechoslovak government was not a party to the agreement and was not consulted beforehand. They were forced to accept the agreement or face the possibility of a German invasion. This led to a widespread outrage in Czechoslovakia and other countries, as the agreement was seen as a betrayal of Czechoslovakia's sovereignty. The agreement was seen as a major failure of the policy of appeasement which had been adopted by the British and French governments.

2. **Invasion of Czechoslovakia**: Hitler violated the Munich Agreement by invading and annexing Czechoslovakia, in March 1939.

Points to Ponder

The primary intention of Adolf Hitler behind the issue of Sudetenland was to expand Nazi Germany's borders and gain access to the strategically important area of Czechoslovakia.

3. Britain and France signed an agreement to prevent German aggression. Moreover, Britain and France agreed to protect Poland, Romania, Greece and Turkey from German aggression.
4. **Non-aggression Pact between Germany and Russia**: On August 24, 1939 Hitler entered into a 10 years non-aggression pact with the Soviet Union. The pact was an agreement between the two powers that they would not attack one another and also included secret protocols that divided eastern Europe including Poland, into German and Soviet spheres of influence. Moreover, when Hitler signed the Nazi-Soviet alliance, the USSR, which had not previously participated in any European negotiations, became the central focus of European diplomacy.
5. **Invasion of Poland (1939)**: Hitler assumed that Britain and France would not go to war to save Poland. Therefore, on September 01, 1939 Hitler attacked Poland, following which Britain and France declared war on Germany.
6. **Phoney War**: The Phoney War was the name given to the period of time between September 3, 1939 (the day Britain and France declared war on Germany) and May 10, 1940 (the day Germany invaded France).

   The period was characterized by a lack of military action on both sides, with a few minor incidents occurring. Winston Churchill referred to the same period as the 'Twilight War', while Germans referred to it as 'Sitzkrieg' – 'Sitting War'.

   The most notable incident during the Phoney War was the sinking of the German battleship - the Graf Spee, off the coast of Uruguay in December 1939, and the German air raid on the British town of Scapa Flow in March 1940.
7. **Battle of Britain (1940)**: The Battle of Britain was a prolonged air battle that took place between the German Luftwaffe and the Royal Air Force (RAF) of the United Kingdom from July to October 1940. By the end of the 1940s, Hitler had taken over France and most of Europe, and Britain was the only country fighting Germany.
8. **Hitler invasion of USSR**: On June 22, 1941, Adolf Hitler launched Operation Barbarossa, a massive invasion of the Soviet Union. The invasion force included more than three million German soldiers, hundreds of tanks, thousands of aircraft, and other military forces. The invasion was a surprise attack that caught the Soviet Union off guard. By the end of 1941, the Germans had advanced deep into Soviet territory and inflicted massive casualties on the Red Army. The Nazi forces captured much of western Russia, but they were eventually pushed back by the Soviet counter offensive in the winter of 1941–1942.
9. **Attack on Pearl Harbour (1941)**: The attack on Pearl Harbour was a surprise military strike conducted by the Imperial Japanese Navy against the United States naval base at Pearl Harbour, Hawaii, on the morning of December 7, 1941. The attack, also known as the Battle of Pearl Harbour, led to the United States' entry into World War II. The Japanese attack crippled the U.S. Pacific Fleet, destroyed 188 planes, damaged another 159, and killed 2,403 people, including 2,335 military personnel, 68 civilians, and one Japanese pilot.
10. **Battle of Midway (1942)**: The Battle of Midway was a key naval battle in the Pacific theatre of World War II. It took place between June 04 and 07, 1942, six months

after Japan's attack on Pearl Harbour. The United States Navy decisively defeated an attacking fleet of the Imperial Japanese Navy near Midway Atoll, inflicting devastating damage on the Japanese fleet that proved irreparable.

The Japanese operation, like the earlier attack on Pearl Harbour, sought to eliminate the United States as a strategic power in the Pacific, thereby giving Japan a free hand in establishing its Greater East Asia Co-Prosperity Sphere. The Japanese hoped another demoralizing defeat would force the U.S. to capitulate in the Pacific War and thus ensure Japanese dominance in the Pacific.

The battle was the first major victory for the United States and its allies in the Pacific. It marked a turning point in the war, as it was the first major defeat of the Japanese navy, and it marked the end of Japan's string of victories. Historians have hailed the battle as an important victory for the United States and its allies, noting the importance of America's decisive victory and Japan's failure to achieve its goals.

11. **Battle of Stalingrad (1942–1943)**: The Battle of Stalingrad (August 23, 1942 – February 2, 1943) was a major battle of World War II in which Nazi Germany and its allies fought the Soviet Union for control of the city of Stalingrad (now Volgograd) in Southern Russia. It was one of the bloodiest battles in history and marked a turning point in the war as the German advance into the Soviet Union was halted.

    The battle resulted in a decisive victory for the Soviets, who were able to encircle and capture the German 6th Army, leading to Hitler's eventual defeat in the war. The battle lasted for five months and resulted in over two million casualties, making it one of the bloodiest battles in the human history.

12. **D-Day (1944)**: The D-Day invasion, also known as Operation Overlord, was the Allied forces' successful invasion of German-occupied France in 1944. D-Day was the code name for the Allied invasion of Normandy, France, on June 6, 1944, during World War II. It was the largest seaborne invasion in history, involving over 156,000 troops from the United States, United Kingdom, Canada, and other Allied forces landing on five beaches along a 50-mile stretch of the Normandy coast. The operation was a success and was a major turning point in the war, allowing Allied forces to push back the German army and liberate Western Europe from Nazi control.

13. **Battle of the Bulge (1944-1945)**: The Battle of the Bulge was a major German offensive that took place in December 1944 and January 1945. The Battle was a major battle in World War II, fought in the Ardennes region of France and Belgium. It was the last major German offensive of the war and was launched with the goal of splitting the Allied forces in half and capturing Antwerp, a major port city in Belgium. The Germans were successful in the initial stages of the battle, but the Allies eventually rallied and drove the Germans back. The battle resulted in over 100,000 casualties and is considered as one of the most important battles of the war.

14. **Atomic bombs dropped on Hiroshima and Nagasaki (1945)**: On August 6, 1945, the United States dropped an atomic bomb on Hiroshima, Japan. Three days later, on August 09, 1945, the United States dropped a second atomic bomb on Nagasaki, Japan. The bombings killed an estimated 140,000 people in Hiroshima and 80,000 in Nagasaki, leading to Japan's surrender and the end of World War II.

15. **Germany signs the unconditional surrender**: On May 8, 1945, Germany signed an unconditional surrender, officially ending the Second World War in Europe.

CONSEQUENCES OF SECOND WORLD WAR

The consequences of the Second World War were far-reaching, and permanent. It affected almost every country in the world and permanently altered the international balance of power.

> *The Second World War was, in many ways, the most destructive conflict in human history. It reshaped the world politically, economically, culturally, and socially, leaving deep and lasting scars in its wake. It ushered in a new era of global politics, one that would be dominated by the Cold War and its consequences for the next four decades.*
>
> ***—Martin Folly (Historian)***

1. **Massive death and destruction**: The Second World War was the deadliest conflict in human history. The total number of casualties is estimated at around 60 million people (about 3% of the world population), with civilian deaths making up the majority of the total. The war also caused immense damage to infrastructure and the environment, with cities being destroyed and large areas of land rendered uninhabitable.
2. **Displacement of people**: Millions of people were displaced during and after the war, either by force or by choice. Refugees fled from war zones in Europe and Asia, while others sought a better life in different parts of the world.
3. **Economic devastation and economic hardship**: The Second World War caused massive economic devastation, with the destruction of billions of dollars' worth of property and resources. The Second World War also caused widespread economic hardships in Europe and Asia. Many countries had to borrow heavily to pay for the war, and they were left with huge debts along with many countries experiencing a severe economic depression as the aftermath of the war.

    The United States and the Soviet Union were the main beneficiaries of the war, as the two superpowers were able to rebuild their economies with the help of the Marshall Plan and the Soviet Union's five-year plans. The war also saw the end of the gold standard, which had been used to stabilize currency values, and ushered in an era of inflation and economic instability.
4. **Political realignments**: The war led to the disintegration of many old empires, such as the Austro-Hungarian and Ottoman Empires, and the emergence of new political entities. The defeat of Nazi Germany and Japan in 1945 saw the rise of new democracies in Europe and Asia. It also changed the balance of power in Europe and Asia, with the United States and the Soviet Union emerging as the two dominant super powers.
5. **The Cold War**: The Cold War was a geopolitical, ideological, and an economic struggle between the two superpowers of the world, the United States and the Soviet Union. It lasted from the end of the Second World War in 1945 to the dissolution of the Soviet Union in 1991 **(Refer Figure 9.3).**
6. **Social changes**: The war also had a profound effect on social structures. Millions of people were killed or displaced, and many countries experienced a large-scale demographic crisis. Women, in particular, benefited from the war, as they were able to take up jobs that had previously been reserved for men.

7. **Lasting trauma**: The Second World War also left an indelible psychological scar on those who survived it. Many veterans of the conflict suffered from post-traumatic stress disorder, and the legacy of the war is still felt in many parts of the world today.

RESPONSIBILITY OF THE SECOND WORLD WAR

Historians have debated who was responsible for the outbreak of World War II, since the conflict ended in 1945.

1. **Traditional historians: Hitler and Germany responsible:** Traditional historians hold Hitler and Germany solely responsible for the war. They point to the rise of fascism and the policies of Adolf Hitler as the key factors in the outbreak of the Second World War. Hitler's aggressive expansionism, particularly through the annexation of Austria and Czechoslovakia, violated the territorial integrity of Europe and set off a chain of events that eventually led to war. Hitler's invasion of Poland in 1939 is seen as the immediate cause of the conflict.

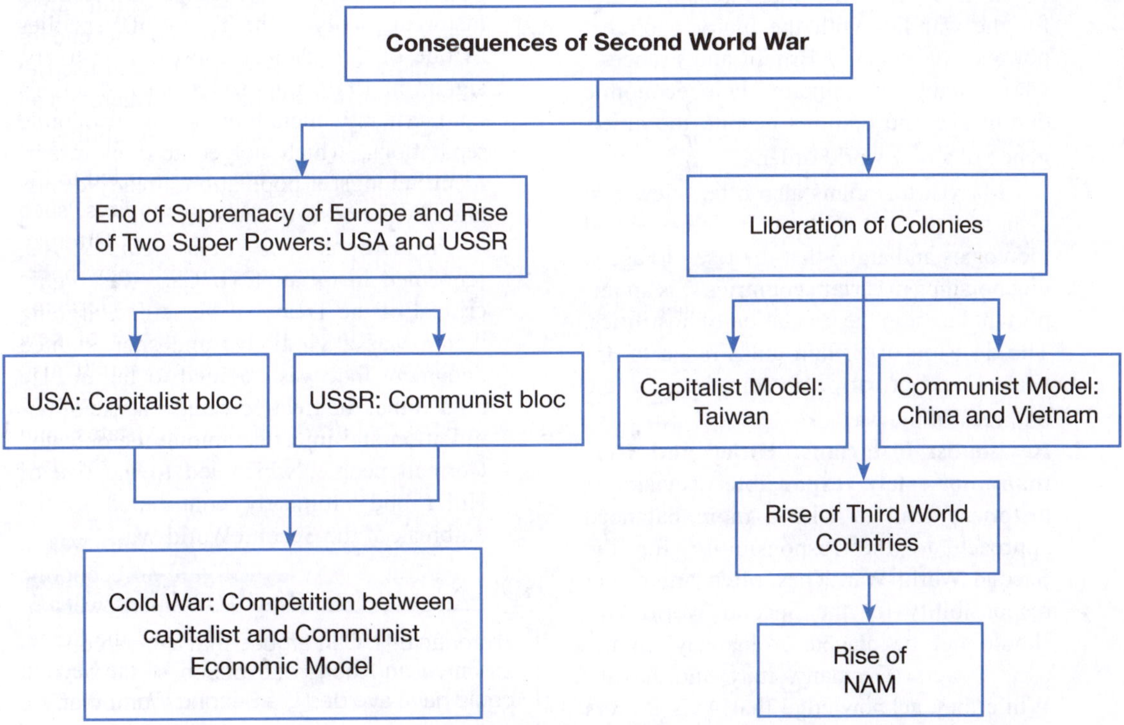

FIGURE 9.3: Consequences of Second World War

Traditional historian Hugh Trevor Roper was one of the first historians to examine Adolf Hitler and the Second World War in depth. He argued that Hitler was a very complex, multifaceted character. Roper believed that Hitler had the master plan which was laid out in his book '*Mein Kamp*' and his desire for Lebensraum (living space in Eastern Europe) ultimately led to the Second World War. Therefore, he believed that Hitler was ultimately responsible for the war, but argued that he was only one of a number of factors that led to its outbreak. He also argued that the war was caused by a combination of military, economic and political factors, as well as by the ambition of Hitler and his Axis partners.

2. **Marxist historians: unresolved economic crisis:** Marxist historians tend to view World War II as a result of the underlying structural tensions of capitalist world order and as a continuation of the inter-imperialist rivalry which had been escalating since the end of World War I. They argue that the underlying cause of the war was the struggle for the control of markets, colonies, and resources.

   In this view, the main responsibility for the war lies with the major capitalist powers—particularly Britain and France—who sought to maintain their economic dominance and empires despite the emergence of a new world order.

   Marxist historians also often view fascism as a product of capitalist interests and ideologies and argue that the rise of Fascist dictatorships in certain countries was an important factor in the escalation of hostilities. The decision of Britain and France to appease Nazi Germany also contributed to the outbreak of the war.

3. **Revisionist historians: Hitler and Germany not solely responsible**: Revisionist historians tend to take a more balanced approach to the responsibility for the Second World War. They often argue that responsibility for the Second World War should not be placed exclusively on the Axis Powers (Germany, Italy and Japan). While they acknowledge that Axis Powers (Germany, Italy and Japan) bear significant responsibility, the Allies (Britain, France and USA) also share some responsibilities, either through their own aggressive actions or by failing to prevent war.

   Revisionist historians point to a number of factors that contributed to the outbreak of the war, including the appeasement policies of the Western democracies, the failure of the League of Nations to prevent conflict, and the aggressive behaviour of the Soviet Union in Eastern Europe. As such, revisionist historians argue that the responsibility for the war cannot be attributed solely to Nazi Germany but must also be shared by a variety of other actors. For example, revisionists argue that the Allies' refusal to compromise or negotiate with the Axis Powers before the war, as well as their desire to expand their own influence, use of economic sanctions and military threats against the Axis Powers, were some of the factors that contributed to the outbreak of war.

4. **Role of Treaty of Versailles**: Some other historian points to the Treaty of Versailles as one of the primary causes. This treaty, signed in 1919, imposed strict restrictions on Germany, including severe economic reparations, which helped to fuel resentment amongst a population already devastated by the costs of the war.

   In his book '*The Twenty Years*' *Crisis*, renowned historian E.H. Carr was highly critical of the Treaty of Versailles, arguing that it was a vindictive and short-sighted document that was doomed to failure. He argued that the treaty created a sense of humiliation and injustice among the defeated German people, which led to the rise of Hitler and ultimately contributed to the outbreak of the Second World War.

Points to Ponder

Historian E.H. Carr argued that a more constructive and generous peace settlement could have avoided the Second World War.

5. **Policy of Appeasement**: Some historians have argued that the Allied Powers, such as Britain and France, shared responsibility for the war due to their appeasement policies in the late 1930s. Britain and France, in particular, are criticized for not taking stronger action to stop the aggression of Nazi Germany, including the failure of the British government to negotiate a

peaceful settlement with Hitler in 1938. These policies emboldened the Nazi regime and allowed Nazi Germany to expand its power unchecked, thus creating the conditions for war.

6. **Unresolved issue of First World War**: Some historians argue that the outbreak of the Second World War was an inevitable result of the geopolitical tensions created by the First World War. This argument suggests that the post-war settlement of 1919 was inadequate, creating a situation in which the major European powers were unable to contain the rising power of Nazi Germany.
7. **Recent historiography**: Recent historiography on the responsibility of the Second World War has largely focused on the role of the major powers in the conflict. Historians have argued whether the war was the result of conscious decisions made by leaders, or if it was the result of more complex factors.

According to renowned historian A.P.J. Taylor, Hitler did not desire the World War but rather a limited war in Poland. A.P.J. Taylor believed that Allied Powers followed an inconsistent policy towards Hitler which led to the Second World War. Whereas on the one hand, on the issue of Czechoslovakia, they remained to be much soft with Hitler but on the issue of Poland they quickly launched the war so Hitler was caught unaware.

The majority of recent historians also agree with A.P.J. Taylor's view that it is true that Hitler did not seek out world war because he understood the risk and devastation involved. On August 22, 1939, just 9 days before the attack on Poland, Hitler in his conversation with his military Generals, made this point clear that Allied Powers could not take any risk of war with us. Nevertheless, it is also true that Hitler's relentless desire for territory made the Second World War inevitable even though he did not want it. Hitler was having his ambition to move further east of Poland and this desire has been proved by Hitler's invasion of Soviet Russia.

Finally, it is difficult to say with certainty who is responsible for the Second World War. The war was a complex international event with many contributing factors, and the history of the war is still being debated by scholars today. It is difficult to definitively assign responsibility for the outbreak of World War II. Historians have debated the issue for decades, and no single answer has yet emerged.

LET'S REVISE

Causes of The Second World War

1. **Immediate Causes**: Germany's invasion of Poland in 1939
2. **Fundamental Causes**:
   (a) Limitation of Treaty of Versailles
   (b) Emergence of Fascism and Nazism
   (c) Failure of the League of Nations
   (d) Policy of appeasement
   (e) Economic crisis in Germany after World War I.
   (f) Role of Hitler and Hitler's foreign policy

The Course of The Second World War

1. Czechoslovakia and Munich Agreement
2. Invasion of Czechoslovakia
3. Non-aggression Pact between Germany and Russia
4. Invasion of Poland (1939)
5. Phoney War
6. Battle of Britain (1940)
7. Hitler's Invasion of the USSR
8. Attack on Pearl Harbour (1941)
9. Battle of Midway (1942)
10. Battle of Stalingrad (1942–1943)
11. D-Day (1944)
12. Battle of the Bulge (1944-1945)
13. Atomic bombs dropped on Hiroshima and Nagasaki (1945)
14. Germany signs the unconditional surrender

Consequences of The Second World War

1. Massive death and destruction
2. Displacement of People
3. Economic Devastation and Economic hardship
4. Political Realignments
5. The Cold War
6. Social Changes
7. Lasting trauma

Responsibility of The Second World War

1. **Traditional Historian:** Hitler and Germany responsible
2. **Marxist Historian:** Unresolved Economic Crisis
3. **Revisionist Historians:** Hitler and Germany not solely responsible
4. Role of the Treaty of Versailles
5. Policy of Appeasement
6. Unresolved issue of First World War
7. Recent Historiography

PROBABLE QUESTIONS

1. Explain the causes of the Second World War.
2. Was Czechoslovakia served on a dish to Hitler at Munich? What were its implications?
3. Hitler did not want the world war but rather a limited war in Poland. Critically examine.
4. One of the most important consequences of the Second World War was 'Division of Europe', eastern and western. Comment.

TIMELINE (1939–1945)

- **Sep-Dec, 1939**: Germany and Soviet Union invades Poland, beginning World War II in Europe; and Japanese attack on Pearl Harbour marks the US entry into World War II
- **May 10, 1940**: Germany invades France, Belgium, Netherlands and Luxembourg.
- **June 22, 1940**: France signs an armistice with Germany, effectively ending the war in Western Europe.
- **Sep-Dec 1940**: Germany, Italy and Japan sign the Tripartite Pact, forming the Axis Powers and Japan invades British-controlled Hong Kong.
- **June-Dec 1941**: Germany invades the Soviet Union. Japan declares war on the US and the British Empire and attacks the US naval base at Pearl Harbour, Hawaii
- **Dec 1941- Feb 1942**: Japan captures the British colony of Singapore along with Dutch East Indies.
- **June-Aug 1942**: US and its allies, along with US Marines launch their first major offensive in the Pacific, the Battle of Midway and Guadalcanal, respectively.; Soviet forces launch a counteroffensive against the Germans at Stalingrad
- **Feb 2, 1943**: The Germans surrender at the Battle of Stalingrad, ending the German advance into the Soviet Union.
- **July 7, 1943**: US and British forces launch their invasion of Sicily, beginning the liberation of Europe.
- **Sep-Oct 1943**: Italy surrenders to the Allies and Soviet forces launch a massive counteroffensive against the Germans at the Battle of Kursk.
- **June 6, 1944**: The Allies launch their invasion of Normandy, beginning the liberation of Western Europe.
- **June 22, 1944**: The Soviet Union launches a massive summer offensive against the Germans, pushing them out of the Soviet Union.
- **Sep 17, 1944**: The Allies launch their invasion of the Netherlands, beginning the liberation of the Netherlands.
- **Dec 17, 1944**: US forces launch their invasion of the Philippines, beginning the liberation of the Philippines.
- **Mar 6, 1945**: US forces launch their invasion of Iwo Jima, beginning the liberation of Japan.
- **April 25, 1945**: The Allies launch their invasion of Italy, beginning the liberation of Italy and accept Germany's unconditional surrender, ending the war in Europe.
- **Aug 6 and 9, 1945**: The US drops an atomic bomb on Hiroshima and Nagasaki, Japan.
- **Aug 15, 1945**: Japan officially surrendered, ending World War II.

CHAPTER

10

Photo Credit: Faberr Ink / Shutterstock, tkunited / Shutterstock

COLD WAR

> *The Cold War was a state of political and military tension between powers in the Western Bloc, dominated by the United States with NATO among its allies, and powers in the Eastern Bloc, dominated by the Soviet Union along with the Warsaw Pact.*
>
> *—John Lewis Gaddis (Historian)*

INTRODUCTION

The Cold War was a period of sustained political, diplomatic, and military tension between the powers of the Western world (led by the United States and its NATO allies) and the Communist world (led by the Soviet Union, its satellite states and allies). This began after World War II and lasted until the collapse of the Soviet Union in 1991.

The term Cold War was coined by the British historian George Orwell to highlight the difference and conflicts between capitalists' and communists' ideological blocs. The Cold War was characterized by a constant state of political and military competition, economic competition, ideological competition, as well as diplomatic, technological, and cultural battles between the two sides.

During this time, both sides were also engaged in a nuclear arms race and spread their respective ideologies while attempting to limit each other's global influence. It is called the Cold War and not a hot war because it was a period of relative peace and low-level aggression between the two sides without any direct military confrontation. The Cold War was not an open military conflict. Rather it was a psychological or diplomatic war whose objective was to put a check over the area of influence of one block by the other. According to the renowned historian Eric Hobsbawm, Second World War just ended, and in the meantime a new war started. It should be better known as the Third World War.

Points to Ponder

The Cold War was a geopolitical conflict between the United States and the Soviet Union. It was called a 'cold' war because there was no direct military conflict between the two superpowers.

THE BACKGROUND OF THE COLD WAR

It is said that friends during the Second World War didn't remain together at the end of the war as fresh issues of conflict appeared among them.

> "*The Cold War was caused by the Soviet Union's determination to spread communism around the world, and the United States determination to prevent the spread of communism.*
>
> ***—Paul Johnson (British Historian)***"

Opening of the Second Military Front

The issue of opening of the second military front during the Second World War led to differences between Russia and Western power. Although Britain and USA fought together along with USSR, USSR was converted into the worst battlefield, facing the situation of unparallel devastation. Therefore, Russia suggested Allied Powers to open a second front in France against Germany.

The primary argument for opening a second front was to relieve pressure on the Soviet Union, which was bearing the brunt of the Nazi forces in Europe. By opening a second front, the Allies (Britain, France, the U.S., the Soviet Union, and China) could divert some of the Nazi forces away from the Eastern Front. Additionally, a second front would be a sign of solidarity with the Soviets.

On the other hand, it is argued that the Allies were simply not ready to open a second front. Britain argued that the Allies lacked the manpower, resources, and technology to launch a large-scale operation. Britain replied that as she had already been involved in a war against Italy, it was not advisable to open a new front in Greece. Additionally, the consequences of failure would have been catastrophic and could have resulted in the collapse of the entire Allied effort. As such, it is argued that the Allies had no choice but to wait until they were ready before opening a second front.

Issue of the Surrender of Italy

The issue of the surrender of Italy in 1943 also created distrust between Britain and Russia. With the Italian government having already declared its intention to surrender, the Allies sent a delegation to Rome to negotiate the terms of the surrender. The delegation was led by the British General Harold Alexander, who was accompanied by US General Dwight Eisenhower and French General Henri Giraud. Britain and the USA chose to negotiate with Italy separately, but USSR was not invited to negotiate.

Percentage Agreement

The 'Percentage Agreement' was signed in October 1944, between British PM Churchill, and the head of the USSR Stalin. It was part of the broader negotiations of the Yalta Conference, which ultimately led to the end of World War

II. The agreement stated that the Soviet Union would receive a percentage of all reparations that Germany was to pay to the Allied countries after the Second World War. This Soviet percentage was fixed at 90%, with the remaining 10% to be divided among the other Allied countries.

However, having been suspicious of the Russian move, British Prime Minister Churchill decided to divide Russian-occupied region in Europe between capitalist and communist spheres of influence, under the Percentage Agreement. While Western Europe agreed to be the capitalist sphere of influence, Eastern Europe was recognized as the Russian sphere (Communist) of influence. However, Stalin later broke the agreement and attempted to establish communist governments across Western Europe as well.

Nuclear Bombardment of Hiroshima and Nagasaki

The two Allies, the United States and the United Kingdom, had a major role in the decision to drop the atomic bombs on Hiroshima and Nagasaki. The United States and its allies believed that the bombings would bring a swift end to the war, while Russia was not consulted and was not part of the decision-making process.

USSR under Stalin raised the issue that being a coalition partner, the USSR was having every right to be consulted before taking such a major step like the bombardment of Hiroshima and Nagasaki. But President Truman of the USA responded that this was a very sensitive and confidential subject pertaining to American security and therefore it could not be shared with any partner. Truman further widened the gulf between the Allies and USSR. Moreover, Stalin was also concerned about the potential for the United States to use nuclear weapons against the Soviet Union in the future.

Churchill and Lenin's Statement

In February 1946, Stalin declared that capitalism and communism are poles apart. In reply, Winston Churchill's '*Iron Curtain*' famous speech was delivered at Westminster College in Fulton, Missouri on March 5, 1946. In the speech, Churchill famously described the Soviet Union's actions as having drawn an 'Iron Curtain from the Baltic to Trieste' in the Adriatic across Europe, separating the Western democracies from the countries behind the curtain **(Refer Map 10.1).** He also warned of the growing divide between the Western democracies and the Soviet Union.

Map 10.1: The Cold War: The Division of Europe in Two Blocs

Points to Ponder

In this speech, Churchill warned of the Soviet Union's increasing aggression and expansionism, and he called on the United States and the other Western powers to stand firm against the threat of the spread of communism.

Churchill further stated that the defeat of communism was a prerequisite for any long-lasting peace in Europe. Thus, Churchill's *'Iron Curtain'* speech is seen as a key moment in the early stages of the Cold War, and it helped to solidify the Western alliance against the Soviet Union.

COMPREHENSIVE CAUSES OF THE COLD WAR

There were a number of causes of the Cold War, including ideological differences, mutual suspicions, and conflicting national interests.

> *The Cold War was not a traditional war between two states, but rather a struggle between two systems. It was a war between capitalism and communism, democracy and dictatorship, and freedom and oppression.*
>
> ***—David Reynolds (British Historian)***

1. **Power vacuum after the Second World War**: Every war creates a power vacuum and after that existing powers try to fill it. The same phenomenon was also visible after Second World War. In other words, after Second World War, the two superpowers USA and USSR tried to fill up the power vacuum.
2. **Ideological differences**: The United States and the Soviet Union emerged from World War II as the two dominant world powers, and they had very different ideas. The United States and the Soviet Union had fundamentally different ideologies, with the United States being a capitalist democracy and the Soviet Union being a communist dictatorship. These differences led to deep mutual suspicion and mistrust.

   Moreover, the United States and the Soviet Union had a long history of mistrust, dating back to the Russian Revolution in 1917. This mistrust was exacerbated by the fact that the two sides had very different ideologies and goals.
3. **Capitalism and Communism as state ideologies:** After the Second World War, both superpowers had divergent opinions about how to organize the political, economic, and social systems. Americans viewed the USSR and communism as enemies of the free world because they believed in capitalism and modern concepts like liberty and democracy. USSR, on the other hand, emphasized the negative aspects of capitalism and endorsed communism.
4. **British and French insecurities:** Eastern Europe like Greece and Turkey wasn't of immediate relevance to the USA. Russia tried to expand Communism in Greece and Turkey in order to dominate the Bosporus and Dardanelles Straits. However, the Bosporus and Dardanelles Straits had strategic significance for the British and France.

   Therefore, after being persuaded by Britain and France, who were apprehensive of the USSR's rise and the spread of Communism in Greece and Turkey, the United States abandoned its policy of isolation and began the policy of engagement in European politics.

   The policy of isolation was adopted by the USA in the late 19th and early 20th centuries as a way for the US to stay out of the conflicts of Europe and Asia. The policy was also intended to protect the US from the risk of foreign wars and entanglements that could potentially draw the US into conflicts its citizens did not want to be a part of **(Refer Figure 10.1).**

5. **Truman Doctrine:** The United States, led by President Truman, abandoned the USA's policy of isolation in 1947 **(Refer Figure 10.1)**. The Truman Doctrine provided military and economic aid under the Marshall Plan to several countries that were threatened by communism. The initial beneficiaries of the Truman Doctrine were Greece and Turkey, which were facing a communist insurgency and Soviet pressure, respectively. In 1948, the United States announced $400 million in military and economic aid for Greece and Turkey to help them resist communist aggression. As a result of the Marshall Plan, Western European nations recovered quickly while Eastern European countries experienced severe economic crises, which intensified hostilities.

Points to Ponder

American policy of isolationism refers to a period of time in the country's history when it sought to avoid involvement in foreign affairs and conflicts.

6. **Security of the USA**: Before the Second World War, the USA considered itself to be a secure nation that was protected by the massive coast of the Atlantic Ocean. However, a Japanese attack on Pearl Harbour exposed the vulnerability of the USA. Moreover, the advent of aircraft made it obvious that the Atlantic Ocean would no longer serve as a barrier to protection. Consequently, the USA had to discontinue its policy of isolation and begin its policy of engagement with Europe as a result.
7. **Security of Russia:** During the Second World War, Russia too had horrible memories of being invaded on both its western and eastern fronts. As a result, Russia realized that its security would always be at risk if it did not establish friendly states along its border. This was the purpose behind the establishment of communist governments in the Eastern European nations.
8. **Spread of Communism**: The Soviet Union sought to spread communism around the world, while the United States sought to prevent the spread of communism. This ideological divide further fuelled the Cold War.

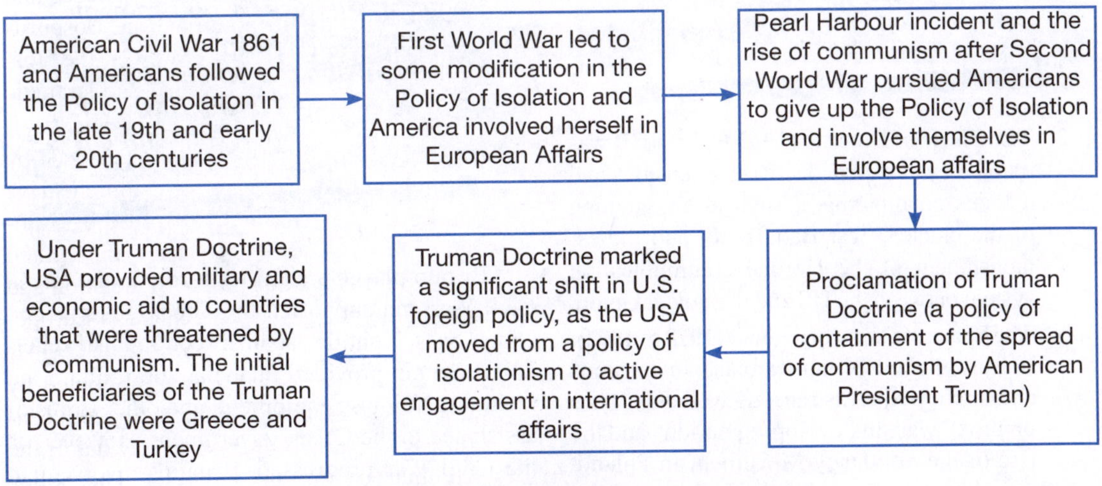

Figure 10.1: Change in USA's Foreign Policy

9. **Geo-political expansion of Capitalism and Communism**: Both the United States and the Soviet Union sought to expand their influence around the world, and they often found themselves competing for influence in various regions. This competition fuelled tensions between the two sides.

DIFFERENT PHASES OF THE COLD WAR

The Cold War can be divided into three distinct phases:

1. **The Phase of Confrontation (1948 to 1962)**: It was characterized by increased tension and hostility between the United States and the Soviet Union. The US and Soviet Union engaged in a series of proxy wars, military build-ups, and ideological confrontations that threatened to escalate into a full-scale nuclear war.

> *The Cold War was not a military confrontation between two blocs, but a complex political and ideological struggle that took different forms in different parts of the world.*
>
> ***—John Lewis Gaddis (Historian)***

2. **The Phase of Detente (1962 to 1978)**: It was marked by a relative decrease in tensions and a focus on diplomacy, such as the signing of the Nuclear Test Ban Treaty and the establishment of the Hotline communication system between the US and the Soviet Union.
3. **The Phase of Rapprochement (1978 to 1992):** It was marked by an increase in tensions and a renewed arms race, as well as a focus on proxy wars in developing nations and the rise of the Solidarity Movement in Poland. This phase ended with the collapse of the Soviet Union in 1991.

The Phase of Confrontation (1948 to 1962)

This period saw the establishment of the North Atlantic Treaty Organization (NATO), the Warsaw Pact (two of the major military alliances of the Cold War), the Civil War in Greece and the conflict of the Berlin Blockade, the Cuban Missile Crisis, and the Vietnam War.

Civil War in Greece

The Greek Civil War was fought in Greece from 1946 to 1949 between the Greek government army and the Democratic Army of Greece (DAG), which was backed by the Soviet Union. The Civil War represented a continuation of the ideological conflict between monarchists and communists. The conflict began after World War II when the economic and political differences between the right-wing governments of Greece and the left-wing forces of the DAG led to an armed struggle.

> *The Greek Civil War of 1946-1949 was the most violent chapter of the Cold War in Europe. It was a conflict between Greek communists and their allies, supported by Yugoslavia and the Soviet Union, against the Greek government forces, supported by the United Kingdom and the United States.*
>
> ***—William Hitchcock (Historian)***

Britain played a significant role in the Greek Civil War and supported the Greek government, which was fighting against communist rebels DAG. Britain provided financial and military aid including training, equipment, and other forms of assistance to the Greek government. However, as the Civil War progressed, Britain's involvement in the conflict decreased. The labour government that came to power in Britain in 1945 was more focused on domestic issues and less interested in foreign interventions **(Refer Map 10.2)**.

Although Britain decided to withdraw from the Civil War, the USA decided to get engaged. US President Truman believed that if the Soviet Union succeeded in Greece, then the USSR would topple the neighbouring nations like a series of dominoes. Therefore, US President Truman introduced the Domino Theory to prevent communists from taking over Turkey and Greece in 1946. He made an appeal to US Congress to sanction the money for military expenses in Greece. As a result, $450 million was sanctioned by the Congress for maintaining US naval force in the Mediterranean Sea.

Thus, the Civil War of Greece was further complicated by the involvement of the United States, and the Soviet Union, which both provided military aid to the opposing sides. The war ended in 1949 with the defeat of the DSE and the establishment of a pro-western government in Greece.

Truman Doctrine and Marshall Plan

The Truman Doctrine was a foreign policy initiative by President Harry S. Truman on March 12, 1947. It declared that the United States would provide economic and military assistance to Greece and Turkey in order to prevent them from falling

> *"The Truman Doctrine was a signal moment in American history. It marked the beginning of a new era, in which the United States assumed the mantle of global leadership, committing itself to the containment of communism and the promotion of democracy around the world.*
> ***—Robert Dallek (Historian)"***

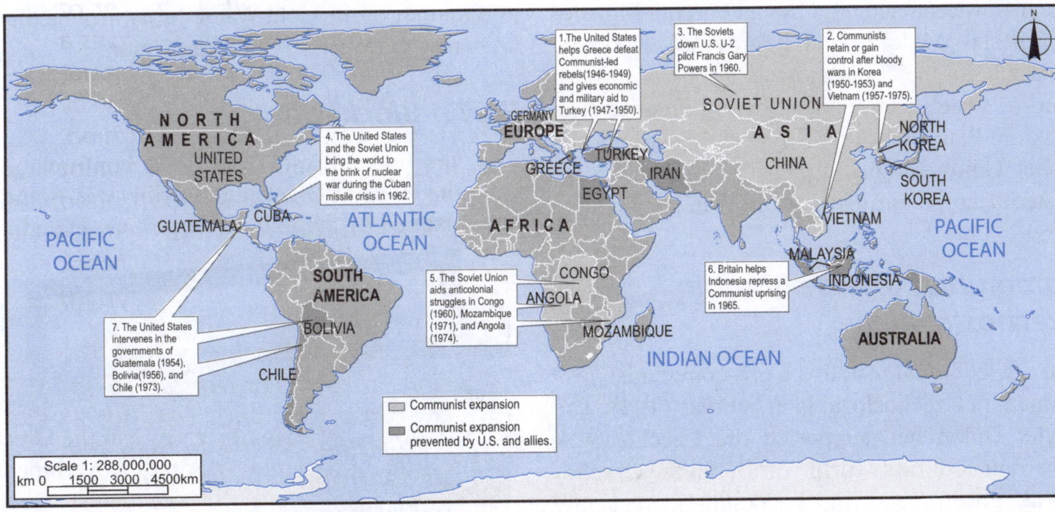

Map 10.2: Cold War Hot Spots, 1948-1975

into the sphere of influence of the Soviet Union. The policy was developed in response to the threat that the spread of Communism posed to American security and interests, as well as to the stability of the entire post-war international order. The doctrine became the cornerstone of American foreign policy for the next four decades and was used to justify U.S. involvement in the Korean War and the Vietnam War, as well as the support of anti-communist governments in countries around the world.

The Marshall Plan, also known as the European Recovery Program (ERP), was a U.S. initiative to provide economic assistance to European countries recovering from World War II and prevent the spread of Communism. The plan was announced by U.S. Secretary of State George Marshall in 1947 and provided aid to 16 European countries between 1948 and 1951. The goals of the Marshall Plan were to rebuild war-torn regions, remove trade barriers, modernize industry, make Europe prosperous again, and prevent the spread of Soviet Communism.

On the other hand, the Soviet Union's economic assistance programme known as the Molotov Plan was implemented in Eastern Europe. The plan was named after Soviet Foreign Minister Vyacheslav Molotov and it provided economic assistance to the communist countries of Eastern Europe, which were under Soviet influence. The Molotov Plan was one of the ways in which the Soviet Union sought to exert its influence over Eastern Europe during the Cold War.

Communist Government in Czechoslovakia

The Soviet Union installed a pro-communist government in Czechoslovakia in February 1948. The Soviet Union had supported the Czechoslovak government during World War II, but the Czechoslovak government was becoming increasingly independent. This displeased the Soviet Union, which feared the spread of western democratic ideals in Eastern Europe and wanted to maintain its control of the region.

Points to Ponder

The Brussels Pact, also known as the Treaty of Brussels, was a mutual defense treaty signed in Brussels on March 17, 1948 between Belgium, France, Luxembourg, the Netherlands, and the United Kingdom.

In February 1948, the Soviet Union pressured the Czechoslovak government to accept a new pro-Soviet coalition government. The new government was dominated by the Communist Party of Czechoslovakia (KSC) and its leader, Klement Gottwald. The new government pursued a pro-Soviet agenda, including nationalizing industry and eliminating democratic freedoms. The Soviet Union's actions in Czechoslovakia were condemned by western countries, who saw it as a violation of Czechoslovakia's sovereignty. The Soviet Union's actions also contributed to the development of the Cold War.

The Brussels Pact was created in 1948 in response to the Soviet Union's occupation of Czechoslovakia. It was designed to provide collective security against the threat of a Soviet invasion of Western Europe. The treaty was an important part of the Cold War security arrangement known as the Western European Union.

Berlin Blockade

The first significant Cold War confrontation was the Berlin Blockade. Berlin was jointly administered by the four victor powers, including

> “*The Berlin Blockade was the first major confrontation of the Cold War and it stands as a reminder of the human cost of confrontation between two superpowers.*
>
> **— *John Lewis Gaddis (Historian)*** ”

Britain. USA, France, and Russia. The Berlin Blockade was a political and economic blockade imposed by the Soviet Union on the western sectors of Berlin by imposing a blockade on the movement of goods and food by rail or road to West Berlin, from June 24, 1948 to May 12, 1949. It was a diplomatic standoff between the United States, the United Kingdom, and France on one side and the Soviet Union on the other.

The Soviets blocked all rail, road, and water routes leading to the western-held parts of the city of Berlin (located deep within the Soviet-controlled zone of Germany) in an attempt to gain control and force the western powers out of Berlin. The western powers responded by flying in supplies to their respective sectors, a process is known as the Berlin Airlift. Both superpowers were on the brink of war after the Berlin Airlift, but fortunately, none of them crossed the line. Americans avoided taking the land route, and the USSR did not shoot down American planes. The blockade was eventually lifted, with the Soviet Union agreeing to the Allied Powers' presence in Berlin.

Formation of NATO and Warsaw Pact

The North Atlantic Treaty Organization (NATO) was formed in 1949 as a military alliance of countries from North America and Europe. The main reason for its formation was to provide a collective defense against the Soviet Union and the threat of communist expansion in Europe following World War II. Additionally, it was intended to show the USA's serious commitment to counter any further expansion of Soviet influence.

The Warsaw Pact was created in response to the founding of NATO. It was a military alliance between the Soviet Union and several eastern European countries, signed in 1955 with a unified military command with headquarters at Moscow. The Warsaw Pact was a mutual defense agreement that provided a forum for countries in the Soviet bloc to coordinate the joint use of military forces and resources. It was disbanded in the aftermath of the collapse of the Soviet Union, and its members joined NATO.

Spread of the Cold War in other Parts of the World

The Cold War only affected Western Europe until the end of the 1940s, but it began to spread to Asia, Africa, and Latin America in the 1950s. This led to proxy wars being fought in places such as Korea, Vietnam, Cuba, Angola, Nicaragua, and Afghanistan. In Asia, the Korean War and the Vietnam War were some of the major conflicts of the Cold War. In Africa, the Cold War led to the support of authoritarian governments and proxy wars in countries such as Angola and Mozambique. In Latin America, the Cold War led to the rise of authoritarian governments and conflicts in countries such as Nicaragua and El Salvador. The Middle East saw the involvement of Cold War powers in conflicts such as the Iran-Iraq War.

The USA decided to take the following steps to check the expansion of Communism:

1. Establishment of military bases in different regions of the world, for example, in Turkey, Pakistan, and Japan.
2. Formation of military blocks like the Baghdad Pact in West Asia (1955) and SEATO (Southeast Asia Treaty Organization) in Southeast Asia in 1954 on the lines of NATO to check the expansion of communism in those areas.
3. The USA propagated the Domino theory (if one country in a region were to fall to Communism, then the surrounding countries would follow suit in a domino effect) in the context of Southeast Asia and the Eisenhower Doctrine (armed forces to assist any nation or group of nations requesting assistance against armed aggression from any country controlled by international Communism) in relation to west Asia. Furthermore, the USA revived the Munro doctrine (intended to protect Latin American countries from European interference) in order to counter Communism in Latin America.

China

The Cold War between the United States and the Soviet Union had a major impact on China. The long-running conflict in China between the nationalists supported by the United States under Chiang Kai-shek and the communists under Mao Zedong ended with a Communist victory. Thus, the Communist Party of China (CPC), under the leadership of Mao Zedong, overthrew the Nationalist government in 1949 and established the People's Republic of China.

> *The Cold War in China was a period of tension and hostility between the two superpowers, the United States and the Soviet Union. It was a period of political and economic confrontation between the two countries, but also one of tremendous economic and social change in China.*
>
> ***—Jonathan Fenby (British Historian)***

Mao Zedong sought to establish friendly relations with Moscow and signed the treaty of friendship, alliance and mutual assistance with the Soviet Union. This event shifted the balance of power in the Cold War, as the Chinese Communist Party aligned itself with the Soviet Union, and the U.S. was left without an ally in the region.

The United States disliked the change in the balance of power and the emergence of Communism in China and perceived the Chinese Revolution of 1949 as a threat to the security of Japan, a key ally of the United States. Therefore, Washington refused to recognize the Communist Party of China (CPC) in China as a legitimate government. Instead, the USA recognizes the Chiang Kai Shaikh government in Taiwan as the legitimate government of China. Moreover, the United States agreed to expand its military and financial assistance to France, Indochina, Thailand, Indonesia, and other nations in the region.

China also retaliated by increasing its military and financial assistance to Communist Northern Korea and the Democratic Republic of Vietnam. During the Korean War, China provided military and economic aid to North Korea and sent hundreds of thousands of Chinese troops to fight against the U.S.-led UN forces. Thus, the nature of the Cold War confrontation now spread beyond Europe to southeast Asia 1950 onwards and a period of proxy wars began during the Cold War.

Korean Crisis (1950–53)

The Korean War (1st hot war of the Cold War) was a conflict between North and South Korea that lasted from June 25, 1950 to July 27, 1953. The partition of Korea into two zones along the 38th parallel after the Second World War was the immediate cause of the Korean War. It began when North Korea's forces, aided by the Soviet Union and China, crossed the 38th parallel and invaded South Korea in an attempt to reunify the Korean Peninsula under Communist rule **(Refer Figure 10.2).**

> *The Korean War was the first battle in the Cold War, between the United States and the Soviet Union. It was a struggle for power and influence in Asia, and it set the stage for the proxy wars of the following decades.*
>
> ***—Henry Kissinger***

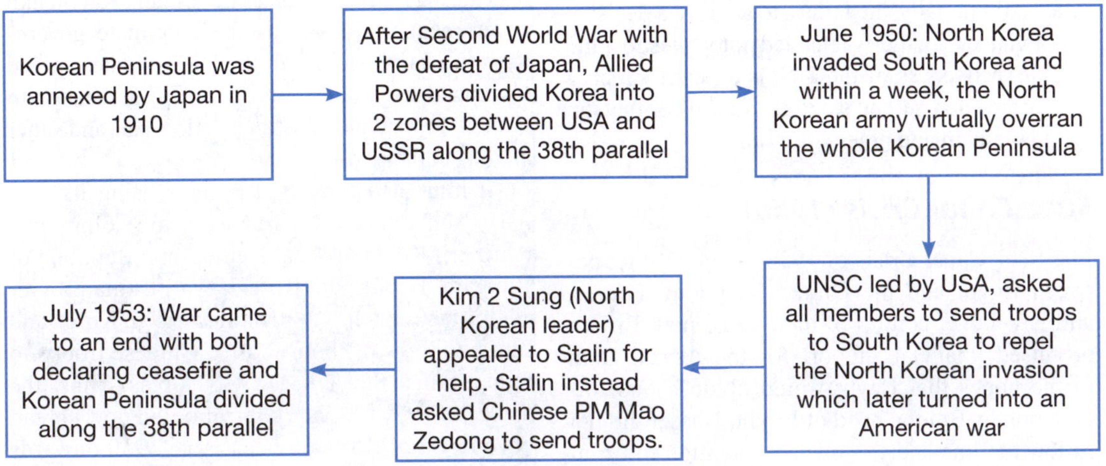

Figure 10.2: Timeline for the Korean Crisis

The United Nations, led by the United States, intervened on behalf of South Korea. A joint command was constituted under the leadership of American commander, Macarthur, with an objective to liberate South Korea. After a successful United Nations-led counterattack, the North Koreans were pushed back beyond the 38th parallel. The fighting continued until July 27th 1953, when an armistice was signed, effectively ending the war **(Refer Map 10.3)**.

Consequences of the Korean War

The Korean War had significant consequences for both superpowers and the international community as a whole.

1. Over 5 million people were killed in the war, and millions more were injured, making it one of the deadliest wars in history.
2. The Korean War left the Korean peninsula, divided into Communist North and Capitalist South Korea along the 38th Parallel and created a tense Cold War-style standoff between the two countries **(Refer Map 10.3)**.
3. The Korean War marked a shift in the US foreign policy towards greater involvement in international conflicts as a means of containing communism.
4. Korean crisis internationalized the Cold War.
5. Stalin's refusal to share the cost of the war with China caused a rift in the relations between China and the USSR.

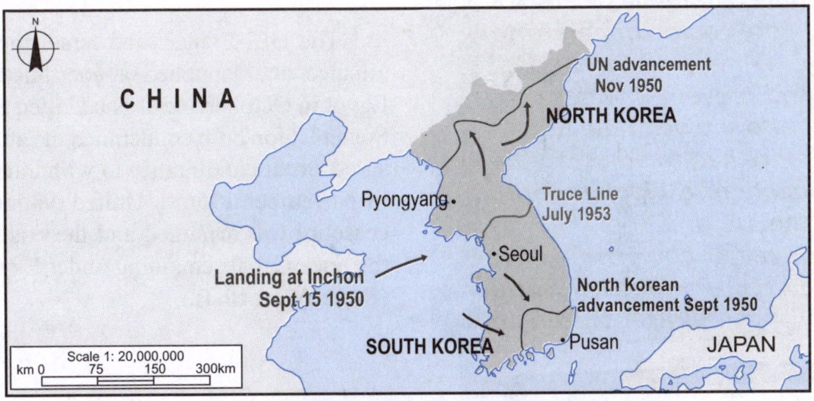

Map 10.3: Cold war in Korea and Division of Korea

6. Additionally, the failure to achieve a decisive victory in the war called into question the effectiveness of the UN as a peace keeping force and set the stage for future conflicts in Vietnam and other countries.

Suez Canal Crisis (1956)

The Suez Canal Crisis of 1956 was a conflict between Egypt and the United Kingdom, France, and Israel over control of the Suez Canal. Britain promised financial support for the Aswan Dam in the hopes that Egypt would abide by its foreign policy. But the head of Egypt, Nasser did not follow the line and extended recognition to Communist China, so in reaction, Britain withheld the amount sanctioned for Aswan Dam.

Consequently, Nasser terminated the lease of the Suez Canal and nationalized it in July 1956. This caused an international uproar due to the fact that the canal was owned by the Suez Canal Company, a French and British-led consortium. Moreover, the canal was a major strategic waterway, allowing ships to travel between Europe and Asia without having to go around Africa **(Refer Map 10.4)**.

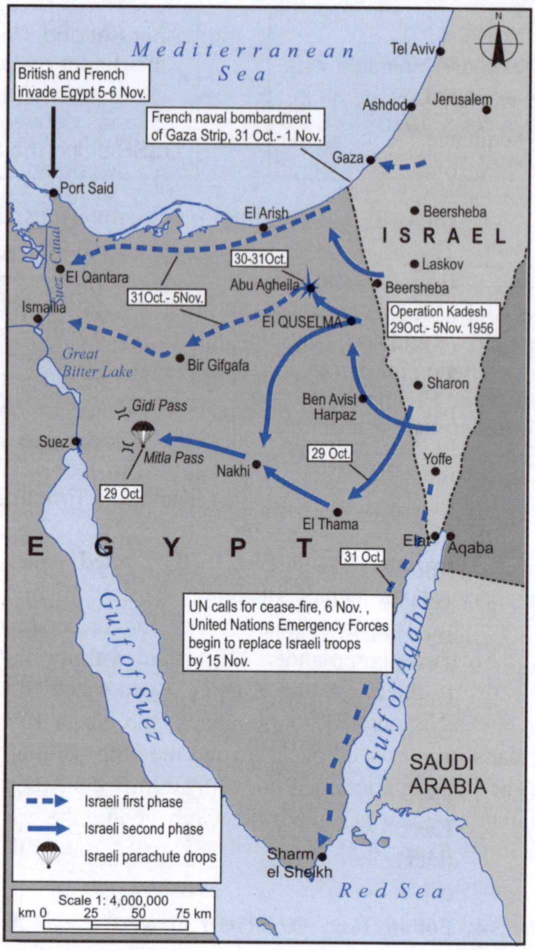

MAP 10.4: Suez Canal Crisis and British Invasion of Egypt

> *The Suez Crisis was a turning point in the world history. It showed how two superpowers, the United States and the Soviet Union, could cooperate to resolve a major international crisis and prevent a wider conflict. It also showed how Britain and France had to adjust to the new reality of a bipolar world, with the US and the USSR as the two major powers.*
>
> ***—Peter G. Boyle (British Historian)***

The UK, France, and Israel formed a secret alliance and launched a coordinated attack on Egypt in October 1956. The United States and the Soviet Union both condemned the attack and pressured Britain and France to withdraw their forces. In November 1956, a United Nations-sponsored ceasefire was arranged and the crisis ended with the Suez Canal remaining under Egyptian control **(Refer Map 10.4)**.

Consequences of the Suez Canal Crisis

The Suez Canal Crisis of 1956 had several consequences, both in the short-term and long-term. Some of the most significant consequences include:

1. **Loss of British and French imperialism**: The Suez Canal Crisis marked the end of British and French imperial power in the Middle East. The crisis contributed to the decline of British and French influence in the Middle East and the rise of Arab nationalism, particularly in Egypt. This newfound strength in the region saw the rise of Arab nationalist movements and the emergence of Arab countries such as Egypt, Syria, and Iraq.
2. **Strengthening of Soviet influence in the Middle East**: The Suez Canal crisis of 1956 saw the Soviet Union gain considerable influence in the Middle East. The crisis was seen as a victory for Soviet diplomacy, with the Soviet Union being the only major power to support Egypt in its confrontation with the United Kingdom and France.
3. **Expansion of US influence in the Middle East**: The U.S. used the crisis to assert its influence in the Middle East and to counter the expansion of Soviet influence in the region.
4. **Formation of NAM**: It also led to the strengthening of the non-aligned movement, which sought to counter the influence of the superpowers.
5. **United Nations Emergency Force:** It also led to the creation of the United Nations Emergency Force, which was established to help maintain peace in the region.

Vietnam Crisis (1954-75)

The Vietnam Crisis (1954-75) was a period of conflict between North Vietnam, supported by communist allies, and South Vietnam, supported by anti-communist forces, including the United States. After Japan left Vietnam in 1945, Ho Chi Minh, a communist leader, founded a Communist Republic in North Vietnam while the French seized control of South Vietnam.

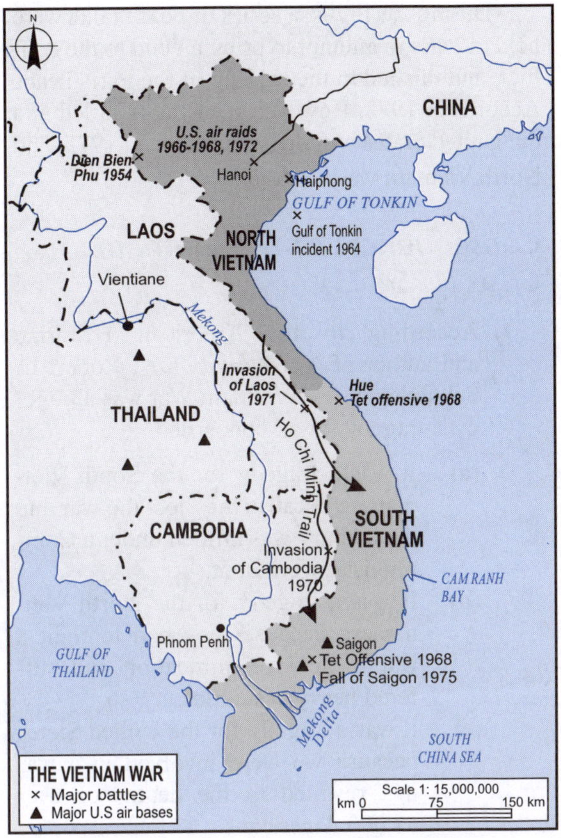

Map 10.5: The Vietnam War

The Vietnam Crisis began in 1954 when the French withdrew from their colony of Indo-China after a failed attempt to regain control of the region. This opened the door for the North Vietnamese Communist forces, known as the Viet Cong, to begin a campaign of guerrilla warfare against the South Vietnamese government in an attempt to unify the country under Communist rule **(Refer Map 10.5).**

In response, the United States provided financial, military, and political support to the South Vietnamese government, while the Soviet Union and China provided aid to the North Vietnamese. The crisis escalated in the 1960s, as the United States began to send more troops to the region in an attempt to contain the spread of Communism. This led to an increase in casualties on both sides and further alienation of the people of South Vietnam.

During the 1970s, a series of peace talks were held in Paris in attempt to bring an end to the conflict, and this led to the signing of the Paris Peace Accords in 1973. However, these talks failed and the United States withdrew its troops in 1975, and North Vietnam was victorious.

Consequences of the Vietnam Crisis (1954-75)

1. According to the American Historian and author of *'A Time for War'*, Robert D. Schulzinger 'The Vietnam War was a tragedy, a tragedy for all concerned.'
   - **(a)** It was a tragedy for the South Vietnamese because they lost the war and the country was unified under a Communist government.
   - **(b)** It was a tragedy for the North Vietnamese because they had to fight a war to achieve unification and suffered heavy casualties.
   - **(c)** It was a tragedy for the United States because we were involved in a war that resulted in the deaths of over 58,000 Americans.
2. For the United States, the war resulted in a large number of casualties, the erosion of public support for the war effort, and a significant economic cost. Vietnam War proved 'a Waterloo for the USA' as it could not prevent the reunification of Vietnam even after sacrificing 58,000 soldiers.
3. It popularised an Asian form of peasant-based communism in Asia, as opposed to a Russian or European version.
4. The war also had long-lasting environmental consequences, as the widespread use of chemical weapons and bombing left large areas of land contaminated with unexploded ordnance and toxic chemicals.
5. The war also had a significant impact on international relations, as it damaged the relationship between the United States and its allies, and led to a shift in the global balance of power towards communist countries.

Cuban Missile Crisis (1963)

The Cuban Missile Crisis was a 13-day political and military standoff between the United States and the Soviet Union in October 1962. A guerrilla leader, Fidel Castro, captured power in Cuba and started to resist American imperialism. When the USA tried to crush his government, he developed close relations with the Soviet Union **(Refer Map 10.6)**.

> "*The Cuban missile crisis was a defining moment of the Cold War, a confrontation that brought the world to the brink of nuclear disaster and forced leaders to reassess the limits and potential of diplomacy in the atomic age.*
>
> *—**Thomas Schwartz***"

Points to Ponder

The USSR wanted to install medium-range nuclear missiles in Cuba.

Cuban Missile Crisis began when the United States discovered that the Soviet Union had deployed nuclear missiles in Cuba, just 90 miles away from the US shores of Florida **(Refer Map 10.6).** USA opposed the installation of medium-range nuclear missiles in Cuba and expected USSR to withdraw missiles, on the other hand, USSR initiated to installation of more such missiles. So, there appeared the situation of direct confrontation.

Later, the US responded by imposing a naval blockade on Cuba and threatening to use military force against the Soviets if they did not remove the missiles. Eventually, after several tense days, the Soviet Union led by President Khrushchev agreed to remove the missiles in exchange for a U.S. promise not to invade Cuba and to remove U.S. missiles from Turkey. The crisis was a major turning point in the Cold War, and it demonstrated the danger of nuclear proliferation.

Map 10.6: The Threat of Cuban Missiles, 1962

Consequences of the Cuban Missile Crisis

1. **Political consequences**: The US and the Soviet Union came to the brink of nuclear conflict but ultimately avoided it through diplomatic efforts. The danger of nuclear war compelled both superpowers to think over détente (an improvement in the relationship). The crisis also had a lasting impact on US-Soviet relations, leading to increased tension and mistrust between the two superpowers.

   The Cuban Missile Crisis created differences between USA and France regarding NATO's policy. France opposed US efforts to deploy nuclear weapons in Europe, arguing that nuclear weapons should not be used as a tool of coercion. France also argued that the deployment of nuclear weapons would only increase the risk of nuclear war. The French position was based on the belief that nuclear weapons should be used as a tool of last resort.

   On the other hand, the United States argued that nuclear weapons should be used as a tool of deterrence and as a deterrent to Soviet aggression. This disagreement led to a split in NATO over how to respond to the Cuban Missile Crisis, with France taking a less aggressive stance.

2. **Diplomatic consequences**: The Cuban Missile Crisis resulted in a dramatic improvement in US-Soviet relations and became the basis for future arms control negotiations. The US and the USSR also developed a hotline for direct communication between the two governments in the event of an international crisis.

3. **Military consequences**: Moreover, both the US and the Soviet Union began to take measures to reduce the risk of war by limiting the number of nuclear weapons and delivery systems. The US and the USSR agreed to the Partial Test Ban Treaty of 1963, which prohibited the testing of nuclear weapons in the atmosphere, underwater, and in outer space. This agreement helped to reduce the threat of a nuclear war between the two countries.

Cold War Phase 2: Détente (1962–1979)

The Cold War Phase 2, also known as the period of Détente, began in 1962 with the signing of the Cuban Missile Crisis and ended in 1979 with the Soviet invasion of Afghanistan. Détente was a period of improved relations during the Cold War between the USA and USSR. During this period, both the United States and the Soviet Union sought to reduce tensions between them and prevent the outbreak of a nuclear war as both sides were fearful of a catastrophic nuclear war. This period was characterized by increased cultural, academic, and scientific exchanges between the two superpowers and the signing of numerous arms control agreements. The two sides also worked to resolve regional conflicts, such as the Arab-Israeli conflict. However, the period of Détente was marked by a continuation of the Cold War's underlying ideological rivalry, as the two sides continued to compete for global influence.

Points to Ponder

Détente was a period of improved relations between the United States and the Soviet Union during the Cold War as both recognized that the arms race and the constant threat of nuclear war were not sustainable.

> "*The era of détente marked a period of reduced tensions between the superpowers, marked by numerous arms control agreements, improved relations between the two sides, and increased dialogue and diplomatic recognition.*
>
> ***—John Lamberton Harper (Historian)***"

Key Achievements in Detente (1960s–1970s)

1. Formation of Washington-Moscow Hotline in 1963 to establish direct communication between the President of the USA and the president of Soviet Union.
2. Partial Test Ban Treaty, 1963, and Outer Space Treaty, 1967 was a treaty signed to control nuclear weapons.
3. This Nuclear Non-Proliferation treaty was signed by the United States, the USSR, the United Kingdom, and over 100 other countries. By signing the Nuclear Non-Proliferation Treaty in 1968, the nuclear-armed states committed not to share their nuclear technology with any other nations.
4. In 1971, the US decided to give up its veto and allowed communist China to join the UN. Moreover, US President Nixon visited China in 1972.
5. Nixon became the first US President to visit Moscow in May 1972. In 1972 after talks between American President Nixon and Russian head, Brezhnev led to the signing of START I (Strategic Arms Reduction Treaty).
6. The Strategic Arms Limitation Talks (SALT) I and II agreements were held between the two superpowers in 1972 and 1979 respectively. These agreements led to the limitation of the number of nuclear weapons each country could possess and marked the first time the two nations had agreed to limit their nuclear arsenals.
7. The Helsinki Accords of 1975 was signed by the two superpowers and 35 other countries and sought to improve relations between the East and West by guaranteeing basic human rights, freedom of movement, and other aspects of international cooperation.
8. The Sino-Soviet Treaty of Friendship and Cooperation in 1978 was aimed at improving relations between the two countries and included a pledge to respect each other's territorial integrity and non-interference in each other's internal affairs.

Factors leading to Détente (1960-70s)

Political Factors

1. **Cuban Missile Crisis**: The danger and fear of nuclear war during the Cuban missile crisis compelled both the superpowers to think over détente.
2. **Change in leadership**: The change in leadership in both the United States and the USSR during the 1970s was a major factor in the détente of the Cold War. Both leaders, Richard Nixon, and Leonid Brezhnev had a more conciliatory attitude towards one another and were able to negotiate more amicable terms between the two countries.
3. **Vietnam War:** High economic costs, high human costs (around the death of 58,000 soldiers), and public discontent with the Vietnam War contributed to the emergence of Vietnam Syndrome (aversion to US military involvement overseas) among American policymakers, which eventually led to Détente.

Economic Factors

Both the US and the Soviet Union were facing economic difficulties and the costs of maintaining a large military and arms race were becoming increasingly burdensome.

1. **Economic crisis**: Both USA and the USSR faced the situation of stagflation (high inflation and unemployment). The cost of the arms race was rendered unbearably expensive by the economic crisis. So, both the Superpowers decided to 'freeze' their weapons races.
2. **1973 Oil Crisis:** The 1973 Oil Crisis, caused by the Arab oil embargo in response to U.S. support for Israel during the Yom Kippur War, led to a significant increase in oil prices and a reduction in oil supplies.
   Due to an embargo imposed by its traditional Middle Eastern allies in response to the 1973 Oil Crisis, the USA was compelled to turn to the USSR for its oil needs. The 1973 Oil Crisis made it clear that the U.S. and Soviet Union were dependent on each other in certain areas, such as energy, and it created an opportunity for both sides to reduce tensions and improve relations. This led to a period of détente, or relaxation of tensions, between the U.S. and the Soviet Union during the 1970s, which included a number of arms control agreements and other measures to reduce the risk of nuclear war.

International Factors

The US was involved in the Vietnam War and the Soviet Union was involved in the Afghan War, both of which were costly and unpopular. Additionally, the threat of nuclear war and the arms race had reached a point of mutually assured destruction. Moreover, USSR had recently fallen out with China, and consequently the Cold War transformed into a '2 (USSR and China) on 1 (USA)' situation.

Limitations of Detente

1. Non-Proliferation Treaty, 1968 did not stop other countries from developing nuclear weapons such as China and Israel.
2. Neither Russia nor America kept its promises to the SALT I agreement. Moreover, neither reduced their conventional weapons.
3. America supported Israel in the Arab-Israeli War of 1973, while Russia supported Egypt and Syria.
4. Space meetings and table tennis were merely publicity stunts. Some historians argue that Nixon only visited China to stoke tensions between China and Russia.

Cold War Phase 3: Reproachment (1979–1991)

The Détente with the Soviet Union that Nixon had envisioned came to an end with the election of Ronald Reagan, who emphasized military capabilities as the key to Soviet-American relationships, and with the beginning of the Soviet war in Afghanistan in 1979. During his two terms in office, Ronald Reagan sought to end the Cold War and reduce the threat of nuclear war between the United States and the Soviet Union. He achieved this by increasing military spending and working with his Soviet counterpart, Mikhail Gorbachev, to reduce nuclear stockpiles. Reagan also sought to reduce the influence of the Soviet Union in the world by supporting anti-communist movements in Central America and Afghanistan. Reagan's aggressive foreign policy was instrumental in the ultimate collapse of the Soviet Union in 1991.

Role of Mikhail Gorbachev

Mikhail Gorbachev served as the General Secretary of the Communist Party of the Soviet Union from 1985 to 1991 and as the country's head of state from 1988 to 1991. He was responsible for initiating the democratization process in the Soviet Union and the end of the Cold War. During his tenure, Gorbachev introduced a number of policies aimed at modernizing and reforming the Soviet Union, including Perestroika (economic restructuring) and Glasnost (greater political openness).

These policies, along with Gorbachev's efforts to reduce Cold War tensions through arms control and diplomacy, played a significant role in ending the Cold War. His most notable achievement was the signing of the INF treaty with US President Ronald Reagan in 1987 which led to the destruction of thousands of intermediate-range nuclear missiles from both the US and Soviet Union, reducing the threat of a nuclear war.

Disintegration of USSR

The largest empire in the world which reached its pinnacle at the time of Russian monarch Peter the Great finally collapsed in 1991. The Soviet Union (USSR) was officially dissolved on December 26, 1991, following the signing of the Belavezha Accords by the President of the Russian Federation, Boris Yeltsin, the President of Ukraine, Leonid Kravchuk, and the President of Belarus, Stanislau Shushkevich. The process of change in the USSR became too fast in 1989 which was the bi-centenary year of the French Revolution. The collapse of the Soviet Union was a result of a combination of economic, political, and social factors, including the failure of central economic planning, the weakening of the Soviet economy, the rise of nationalist movements in the republics, and Gorbachev's reforms which had loosened the control of the Communist Party over the republics. The fall of the Berlin Wall in 1989 and the subsequent reunification of Germany also played a role in the collapse of the Soviet Union.

Causes for Disintegration of the Soviet Union

The collapse of the Soviet Union was not solely the result of external factors, but also the result of internal policies and reforms that ultimately made the system untenable. According to Historian Mark Kramer, 'The collapse of the Soviet Union was due to multiple reasons, but Mikhail Gorbachev's reforms and policies played a major role in hastening its demise. His reform policies of Glasnost and Perestroika, along with his commitment to peaceful coexistence with the West, weakened the Soviet Union and its hold on the Eastern Bloc countries.'

> “*The disintegration of the Soviet Union was not an event, but a process. It was a gradual process of disintegration, erosion, and collapse that was caused by a combination of factors, including economic decline, weak leadership, and a lack of commitment to the Soviet ideology.*
>
> ***—Michael McFaul*** ”

Economic Factors

There were several economic factors that contributed to the decline of the Soviet Union, including:

1. **Centralized control**: The Soviet economy was heavily centralized, with the government controlling all major industries and making all economic decisions. Private ownership and individual initiative were not allowed; all economic activities were under state control. The Socialist model of economy functioned well up to 1960s but after that, it stagnated due to inefficiency and a lack of innovation, as well as a lack of incentives for workers to improve productivity.
2. **Lack of technological development**: The capitalist world encouraged USSR to be converted into the energy supplier of the world. As USSR started to receive easy money through selling out hydrocarbon products its attention was diverted from improving its manufacturing sector and technology. Except in the field of defense and space, USSR lagged behind the USA in technological development. Also, USSR failed to catch up with the third industrial revolution (Information technology).
3. **Low productivity**: Soviet workers had little incentive to improve productivity, as wages and working conditions were poor. This led to low productivity and inefficiency in the economy.
4. **Inefficient agriculture**: The Soviet government collectivized agriculture in the 1920s and 1930s, which led to a decline in agricultural productivity and food shortages.
5. **High military and another spending**: Russian economy felt a heavy burden of the Cold War. The Soviet Union spent a significant portion of its budget on military spending, which left little room for investment in other areas of the economy. Apart from maintaining the armed race against the USA, it had to give economic support to many third-world nations.

All of these factors contributed to a weak and stagnant Soviet economy, which ultimately led to the collapse of the Soviet Union.

Political Factors

1. **Autocratic nature of the government**: Although Communism was supposed to be a kind of people's government, in practice it was a totalitarian regime. After the Bolshevik Revolution, Lenin established the dictatorship of the communist party. But in the era of Stalin, it was converted into the dictatorship of a particular leader. Even during the era of Nikita Khrushchev and Leonard Brezhnev, there was not any substantial change in the system. The basic freedom of the Russian people continued to be suppressed. Moreover, after the death of Stalin, there were no effective leaders control in to control the highly centralized USSR state.
2. **Racial division within Russia:** Racial division within Russia continued to be a major reason for conflict for centuries. Under the autocratic rule of the Communist government, all sorts of racial and cultural divisions remained to be suppressed. But once Gorbachev relaxed the system, different racial groups raised their heads and this led to the collapse of the system.
3. **Lack of transparency and accountability**: It led to the rise of corruption and inefficiency in the state system. Senior prominent politicians misused their position for personal gain, which deepened the crisis already present in the USSR and its satellite governments.

Role of Cold War

The Cold War played a significant role in the decline of the Soviet Union. The arms race, the space race, support for the proxies War, and competition for global influence between the Soviet Union and the United States put a strain on the Soviet economy, which was unable to keep up with the spending on military and technological development. Moreover, the economic pressure of Cold War competition pushed USSR into a deeper economic crisis. By 1970, Cold War competition started crippling the Soviet economy and by the 1980s economic crises were visible everywhere in the Soviet economy.

Role of Mikhail Gorbachev

Consciously or unconsciously, Gorbachev played a role in the demise of the USSR. Mikhail Gorbachev was the General Secretary of the Communist Party of the Soviet Union from 1985 to 1991, a period that saw the downfall of the Soviet Union and the end of the Cold War.

> *"Mikhail Gorbachev was the architect of the collapse of the Soviet Union. He was the first Soviet leader to recognize the need for political and economic reforms, and he was the first to accept that the old system no longer worked. He was the one who initiated the process that eventually led to the dissolution of the Soviet Union and the end of the Cold War.*
>
> ***—Stephen F. Cohen (Historian)"***

Being a true Communist, Gorbachev was concerned about the survival of Communism to counter prevailing challenges in the Soviet Union. Consequently, he introduced a number of policies intended to reform the Soviet economy and political system, including Perestroika (economic restructuring) and Glasnost (greater political openness and transparency). However, these policies led to increased economic instability, political dissent, and nationalist movements within the Soviet republics, ultimately contributing to the collapse of the Soviet Union **(Refer Figure 10.3).**

Renowned historian Archie Brown believes that Gorbachev played the most important role in the collapse of the Soviet Union. He wrote in his book, '*The Gorbachev Factor*' that, 'The Soviet Union was not defeated by the West, nor was it the inevitable victim of ideological or economic forces. It collapsed because the policies of Mikhail Gorbachev and the reforms he introduced made it impossible for the system to continue as it was.'

Policy of Glasnost (Openness)

Gorbachev's policy of Glasnost (a Russian word that meant 'openness') was a major political initiative taken by the Soviet leader in order to reform Soviet society in the late 1980s. Glasnost was based on the belief that public pressure would compel the Soviet Union to reform and meet public expectations. Thus, the policy of Glasnost promoted increased transparency and openness in the functioning of the Soviet government, as well as a more open dialogue between the government and the people. This was contrasted with the

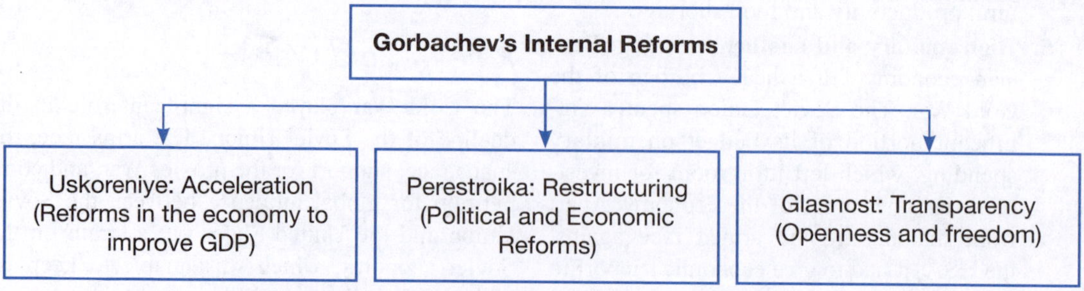

Figure 10.3: Pillars of Gorbachev's Internal Reforms

> *Glasnost was a major political and social event, a time of great change in the Soviet Union. It opened up a whole new era of openness and freedom of speech, allowing people to speak out and express their opinions without fear of persecution.*
>
> **—Mikhail Gorbachev**

previous policy of secrecy and censorship, which had restricted the freedom of speech and the flow of information in the Soviet Union. The policy of Glasnost allowed for:

1. Greater freedom of expression in the media.
2. Control of the state on television, media, and books were significantly reduced.
3. Right to criticism except for the Communist Party. For instance, the release of anti-Stalin movies.
4. The publication of previously censored material.
5. The emergence of independent political organizations.
6. A law was passed in 1988 to repeal the political exile law. Political exiles who had been barred from entering earlier arrived back in Moscow.
7. Gorbachev declared that the Soviet military would not be deployed to satellite states to put down large-scale people's protests.

Glasnost was an important step in the process of Perestroika (economic restructuring) and the eventual dissolution of the Soviet Union.

Policy of Perestroika (Restructuring)

Perestroika was a political reform program implemented in the Soviet Union during the 1980s by Soviet leader Mikhail Gorbachev. The term 'Perestroika' literally means 'restructuring' in Russian, and the policy aimed to restructure the Soviet economy and political system to make them more efficient and responsive to the needs of the people and to democratize the character of Soviet institutions **(Refer Figure 10.4)**. The majority of historians believe that Perestroika's economic reforms combined the dynamics of market capitalism with the principles of socialism rather than accepting capitalism.

> *The Perestroika reforms that began in the Soviet Union in 1985 were the boldest attempt at the sweeping economic and political change since the Bolshevik revolution. These reforms set in motion a chain of events that ultimately led to the breakup of the Soviet Union.*
>
> **—Stephen Kotkin (Historian)**

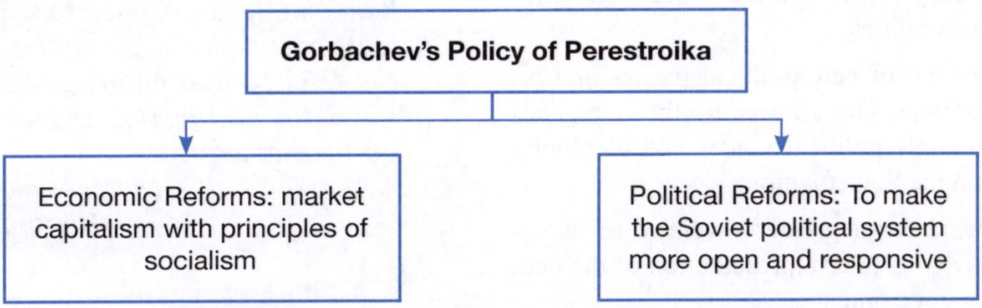

FIGURE 10.4: Gorbachev's Policy of Perestroika

The Economic Reforms of the Policy of Perestroika

1. Decentralization of economic decision-making.
2. It allowed Soviet enterprises to disengage themselves from the Soviet central planning system altogether and to become self-financing and self-managing units.
3. In June 1987, a new law—the Law on State Enterprise—was passed, freeing factories from strict state regulation. Under the new law:
   (a) factory managers were to decide on production, and
   (b) wages of workers were linked to total production in factories
4. Privately owned businesses were permitted to carry out activities like auto repair, television repair, family restaurants, etc., to provide the public with high-quality services.

The Political Reforms of the Policy of Perestroika

The political reforms under the policy of Perestroika aimed to make the Soviet political system more open, democratic, and responsive to the needs of the people. These reforms included:

1. Created a new office of the President to make the government more accountable to the people.
2. The old Soviet parliament, which had 1450 members, was replaced by the new Soviet parliament, which had 2250. This large parliament selected a smaller, 450-member parliament to carry out legislative responsibilities.
3. Formation of new political parties and organizations. This allowed for the emergence of multiple political voices and ideologies within the Soviet Union.
4. Allowed for a greater diversity of candidates and greater representation of the people in government.
5. Gorbachev introduced competitive elections for local and regional government positions.
6. In 1988 Gorbachev discarded the '*Brezhnev Doctrine*' (a policy of the Soviet Union that declared that any country in the Eastern Bloc that attempted to leave the Warsaw Pact or introduce reforms that deviated from Marxist-Leninist ideology would be subject to military intervention) in case of East European countries and recalled Russian soldiers from there.
7. Greater openness and transparency in government.

Additionally, Gorbachev sought to improve relations with the West and reduce Cold War tensions through arms control agreements and other diplomatic initiatives.

Impact of Glasnost and Perestroika

The policies of Glasnost and Perestroika were two of the major factors that led to the collapse of the Soviet Union. Though the policy was well intended but had far-reaching and negative impacts on

> *'Perestroika was a bold attempt to move the Soviet Union away from a centrally planned economy and toward a market-based system. It was an ambitious goal and, while it ultimately failed, it led to significant economic, political, and social reforms that improved living standards and helped shape the post-Soviet world.'*
>
> —***Matthew Kott (Historian)***

the Soviet Union. The implementation of these policies led to a greater sense of freedom and empowerment among Soviet citizens, as they were able to speak out more openly about the shortcomings of the Soviet system.

Unsatisfied People's Aspiration

As the Soviet Union opened up, people began to question the legitimacy of the Communist Party and the Soviet system. Gorbachev failed to manage reforms effectively and several kinds of reactions emerged.

1. The party's progressive/radical wing, led by Boris Yeltsin, demanded even more reform.
2. Peoples were not satisfied with the reforms, so they wanted more rights.
3. Bureaucracy, fearing loss of its power and privileges, obstructed much of the program under the policy.
4. Republics of the Soviet Union wanted more autonomy leading to secession.

Deepen Economic Crisis

This created economic instability, which further weakened the Soviet Union and eventually led to its collapse. The reforms also led to a surge in prices, which caused further economic hardship.

1. The Soviet economy contracted by 15% from 1988 to 1991.
2. Since wages were based on output, which was determined by the value of a product. As a result, manufacturers were tempted to focus on producing more expensive goods while reducing the production of inexpensive goods. This resulted in a basic shortage of necessary items, and queues in towns grew longer.
3. Economic crises were severe, but Glasnost gave people the right to criticize the government. Consequently, during protests and uprisings, people fill the streets.

Secession of the Republic

Political reforms led to a growing sense of nationalism among various ethnic groups within the Soviet Union, and a growing desire for independence. Additionally, the economic reforms of Perestroika led to a decline in the Soviet economy, further weakening the government's grip on power. Because the Soviet Constitutional Republic believed the communist government was to blame for political and economic crises, it advocated for more autonomy. This created an opening for nationalist and separatist movements to gain strength, leading to the eventual break-up of the Soviet Union in 1991.

In September 1991, Russia, Ukraine, and Belarus declared their separation from the Soviet Union and established the Common Wealth of Independent States. Soviet President Gorbachev agreed to the USSR's disintegration and resigned.

The Soviet Union was doomed to collapse from within by its own inherent contradictions. The Soviet system produced a crisis of legitimacy and authority, creating a major challenge to the Soviet leadership from its own people. This was compounded by the inability of the Soviet economy to keep up with the West in terms of living standards and technological innovation, creating a crisis of economic stagnation and decline. Moreover, Gorbachev's reform also assisted in the collapse of the USSR, which was hastened by the drawback of the Soviet economy, the authoritarian political system, the Soviet war in Afghanistan, and other factors. In the end, the Soviet Union simply ceased to exist.

CAUSES BEHIND THE END OF THE COLD WAR

The end of the Cold War was caused by a combination of internal and external factors. Internally, the Soviet Union was facing economic and political problems that it could not sustain. The end of the Cold War was the result of the Soviet Union's failure to keep up with the West in terms of economic and military strength. The Soviet Union's economy was unable to compete with the West's, and the arms race bankrupted the Soviet Union. Externally, the United States and its allies were able to put pressure on the Soviet Union through a combination of military, economic, and diplomatic means.

1. **Economic factors**: The Soviet Union's economy was struggling and could not keep up with the United States military spending. The Soviet economy was already in a state of decline in the late 1980s. This, coupled with its high military expenditure, led to its bankruptcy and eventual dissolution.
2. **Political factors**: The fall of the Soviet Union was the main cause of the end of the Cold War. The Soviet Union was the main power in the Eastern Bloc, and its dissolution led to the end of the Cold War. Moreover, the economic and political reforms initiated by Soviet leader Mikhail Gorbachev further contributed to its end. Gorbachev's reforms, such as perestroika and Glasnost, allowed for greater freedom of speech and consequently the weakening of the Communist Party's grip on power.

   Even the US President felt the pressure from their own people. In fact, there was already a growing anti-nuclear consciousness in America. The day after was a programme that ABC TV aired. This programme featured a portrayal of the radioactive fallout following the nuclear war. It brought people under psychological pressure.
3. **Ideological factors**: The spread of democracy and capitalism around the world, as well as the failure of Communism as a viable economic system, contributed to the decline of the Soviet Union. The fall of the Berlin Wall in 1989 marked the end of the Cold War. The Wall had been a symbol of the Cold War, and its sudden dismantling signalled a shift in the relations between the two superpowers.
4. **Strategic factors**: The arms race between the US and the Soviet Union became very expensive, and both nations began to realize that it would be more beneficial to reduce their military spending. During that period, Ronald Regan, the President of the United States, announced his infamous 'SDI Programme,' also known as the 'Star War programme.' This programme projected that Russian missiles would certainly be frozen even before they were launched. Although the program's technological viability was questionable, it nevertheless exerted significant psychological pressure on the USSR.
5. **Diplomatic factors**: The liberal policy of Russian President Gorbachev and his defense minister Eduard Shevardnadze resulted in the easing of tensions. The US and the Soviet Union began to engage in diplomacy and negotiations, which helped to reduce tensions and eventually led to the end of the Cold War.

Moreover, the Western European countries submitted a proposal for directly connecting the USSR's hydrocarbon supplies to their centres of consumption. A gas pipeline with a length of (3500 km) was required for it. However, this effort was stopped as a result of pressure from American President Ronald Regan. West European nations were greatly frustrated as a result. Therefore, even from its European allies, the USA and its President Ronald Regan felt significant pressure to reduce the tension with Soviet Russia.

In the end, it was a combination of internal and external factors that led to the collapse of the Soviet Union, and thus the end of the Cold War. The United States emerged as the sole superpower after the Cold War, taking over the role of the Soviet Union as the leader of the West.

THE HEGEMONY OF THE USA

The rise of US hegemony in 1991 refers to the United States becoming the dominant global superpower following the end of the Cold War and the collapse of the Soviet Union. As a result, the US had unparalleled influence in global affairs, leading to the rise of US hegemony. This hegemony was seen in the US's ability to shape global politics and economics, act as a global leader in promoting democracy and human rights, and become a major military power.

> *The United States has emerged as the world's only superpower in the post-Cold War era, a status that has been reinforced by the collapse of the Soviet Union in 1991.*
>
> ***—Historian Paul Kennedy in his book, 'The Rise and Fall of the Great Powers.'***

Causes Behind the Rise and Hegemony of the USA

There are several factors that contributed to the rise of the hegemony of the United States in 1991:

1. **The collapse of the Soviet Union**: The fall of the Soviet Union in 1991 marked the end of the Cold War and the emergence of the United States as the world's sole superpower. Even the largest and most powerful successor state to the USSR, the Russian Republic, decided not to take a confrontational approach against the United States after the Soviet Union fell apart.

   Following the collapse of Soviet Russia and the socialist ideology, the capitalist value system significantly grew. Additionally, as globalization progressed, American influence grew stronger. The prosperity of the capitalist system of production and the American value system are symbolized by globalization. No other country was capable of challenging the United States. Despite having the greatest economy, the European Union nevertheless looked to the USA for leadership on security issues.

2. **Economic strength**: The United States had a strong economy, which allowed it to exert influence on other countries. Under Bill Clinton, the American economy recovered at the end of the twentieth century. Therefore, the US economy once again surpassed all others nations. Moreover, the US promoted free trade policies in the 1990s, which allowed the US to gain access to foreign markets and increase its economic influence.
3. **Military dominance**: The United States had a powerful military, which it used to assert its dominance around the world. Even when the socialist bloc and the WARSA Pact disintegrated, the United States was not prepared to demobilize NATO. Instead, it chose to expand NATO by spending more on the military and keeping its military forces stationed across the world. In fact, the US significantly increased its military spending in the 1980s and early 1990s, which greatly increased the US military's might and reach.

   The United States led a coalition of countries in a successful military campaign to remove Iraq from Kuwait, which further solidified its status as a superpower. Moreover, after the 9/11 tragedy, American President George W. Bush declared that you are either with the USA or with terrorism, giving the USA a new reason to further assert its control. Consequently, Iran, Iraq, and North Korea were labelled as the 'Axis of Evils.'
4. **Political stability**: The United States had a stable political system that was seen as a model for other countries to follow.
5. **Expansion of US-led international institutions**: The US also used its influence to expand and strengthen international institutions such as the UN, NATO, and the World Trade Organization. This allowed the US to further its interests and gain a greater say in global affairs.
6. **Cultural influence**: American culture, including movies, music, and television shows, had a strong influence on people around the world, which helped to establish the United States as a dominant cultural force.

INTEGRATION OF EUROPE

The integration of Europe is the process of political, legal, economic, social, and cultural integration of states wholly or partially in Europe. This process has primarily come about through the European Union and its policies. While Europe was divided into Western and Eastern Europe, integration among the Western European nations also increased during this time. (Eastern Europe was only integrated after the 1990s). The process began with the influx of the European Coal and Steel Community (ECSC) in 1951 and has largely been led by the European Union since its foundation in 1993. The integration process has resulted in the creation of a single market, with some common policies on trade, agriculture, and regional development, as well as a common currency, the euro, which is now used by 19 of the 28 member states.

Factors Behind the Integration of Europe

Economic Factors

The formation of the European Coal and Steel Community (ECSC) in 1951 was the first step towards the integration of Europe. The main goal of this organization was to make the coal and steel industries of the six founding countries (France, Germany, Italy, Belgium, Netherlands, and Luxembourg) more efficient.

The creation of the ECSC in 1951, the European Economic Community (EEC) in 1957, and the European Union (EU) in 1993 have fostered economic integration and cooperation among European countries.

Political Factors

The devastation of World War II and the desire to prevent another war in Europe have been important drivers of political integration. After the devastation of World War II, Europe needed to rebuild. Post-World War II economic reconstruction would have been easily achievable after the integration of Europe. The European Economic Community (EEC), established in 1957, was created to promote economic integration and cooperation among European countries. This would help them to achieve economic recovery and stability.

Moreover, leaders and intellectuals in Europe realized that each generation faced a bloody, brutal, and devastating war that could only be solved by Europe's integration. France realized that only after integration would the problem and conflict with Germany be resolved. In addition, there was a general awareness of the benefits of integration among the European population.

Social Factors

The integration of Europe was also driven by the need for peace and stability in the region. The European Union (EU) was created to promote peace, security, and prosperity among European countries.

Moreover, countries in Europe are facing similar challenges such as security, migration, climate change, and economic integration, which encouraged them to work together and form a union.

External Factors

The Cold War and the influence of the United States and the Soviet Union also played a role in the integration of Europe, as Western European countries sought to strengthen their ties in the face of perceived threats from the East. Additionally, West Germany's integration into Europe was essential since it would have been swiftly accepted into the community of European nations.

Formation of European Economic Community (1958)

The European Economic Community (EEC) was an international organization that was created in 1958 by the Treaty of Rome. EEC was a loose union of different nations like the UN, established as a result of the failure to reach an agreement on the formation of an organized federation of diverse nations like the United States **(Refer Figure 10.5)**. It was the predecessor to the European Union. Its aim was to bring about economic integration, including a common market, a customs union, and a common external trade policy, among its six founding members: Belgium, France, Italy, Luxembourg, the Netherlands, and West Germany. The EEC was disbanded in 1993 when it was replaced by the European Union.

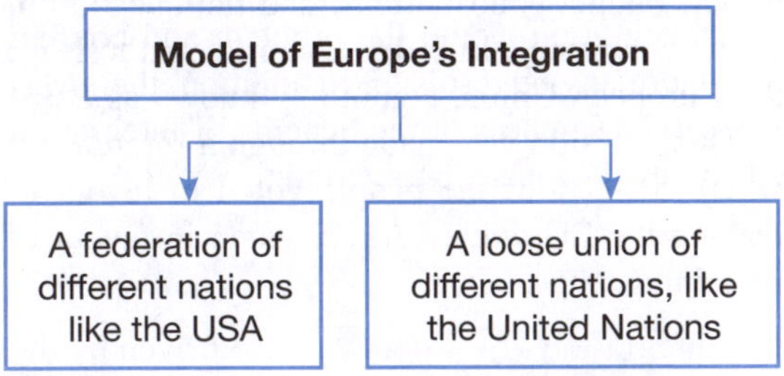

Figure 10.5: Model of Europe's Integration

Some of the Institutions of EEC

1. **The Commission**: Responsible for proposing legislation and managing the day-to-day business of the EEC.
2. **European Parliament**: Elected by citizens of the member states, it had a consultative role in the legislative process.
3. **European Council of Ministers**: Made up of the ministers from each member state, responsible for making decisions on EEC legislation.
4. **European Court of Justice**: Responsible for interpreting and enforcing EEC law.
5. **European Atomic Energy Community (EAEC or Euratom)**: A collective nuclear program of member countries.
6. **European Secretariat**

Response of Britain to the European Economic Community

Britain's response to the EEC, which was the precursor to the European Union (EU), was at best, initially one of skepticism and ambivalence. Britain did not join the EEC when it was first established in 1957 but instead decided to pursue a policy of 'splendid isolation' (a period of deliberate diplomatic non-engagement and non-intervention in European affairs) from the European continent. Instead, Britain established EFTA (European Free Trade Association) along with seven other nations.

> *"Britain's response to the European Economic Community was, at best, ambivalent. On the one hand, there was a desire to maintain sovereignty and to avoid the practical implications of membership; on the other, there was recognition of the potential advantages of closer economic and political integration with Europe.*
>
> ***—John Campbell***
> ***(British Historian)"***

Reasons for Britain not joining EEC

1. British Prime Minister Harold Macmillan had doubts about the political implications of joining and the impact it would have on the Commonwealth. He had more confidence in the Commonwealth market than in the European market.
2. Britain was concerned about the potential economic implications of joining the EEC, such as the need to harmonize tariffs and other trade regulations.
3. Some British politicians and officials felt that the EEC's focus on economic integration would dilute Britain's policy of isolation and political and military power.
4. French President De Gaulle was wary of Britain's close ties to the United States and was concerned that British membership would be detrimental to the EEC's unified economic and political goals. De Gaulle believed that Britain would be too easily in-

fluenced by American interests and would be a destabilizing force in the EEC. As a result, the French President vetoed Britain's application, leading to Britain's decision to remain outside the EEC.

5. Britain believed that its relationship with the United States would be weakened by joining EEC.

However, over the time, Britain's attitude towards the EEC began to change. Britain recognized its mistake and submitted an application to join the EEC under British Prime Minister Harold Macmillan in 1961 as a result of the rapid economic growth of France and Germany and the decline of the British economy. Despite initial resistance from other member states, particularly France, Britain eventually joined the EEC in 1973 under Prime Minister Edward Heath. After joining the EEC, Britain had a complex relationship with it, particularly in areas such as common agricultural policy, budget contributions, and the question of a single currency. In 2016, Britain voted to leave the European Union, commonly known as Brexit. This decision was made through a referendum where 51.89% of the people voted in favour of leaving the EU while 48.11% voted in favour of remaining.

LET'S REVISE

The Background to the Cold War

1. Opening of Second military front
2. Issue of the surrender of Italy
3. Percentage Agreement
4. Nuclear bombardment of Hiroshima and Nagasaki
5. Churchill and Lenin's statement

Comprehensive Causes of the Cold War

1. Power vacuum after the Second World War
2. Ideological differences
3. Capitalism and communism as state ideology
4. British and French Insecurities
5. Truman's Doctrine
6. Security of USA
7. Security of Russia
8. Spread of communism
9. Geo-Political expansion of Capitalism and communism

Different Phases of the Cold War

1. **The Phase of Confrontation** (1948 to 1962)
   (a) Civil war in Greece
   (b) Truman Doctrine and Marshall Plan
   (c) Communist government in Czechoslovakia
   (d) Berlin Blockade
   (e) Formation of NATO and Warsaw Pact
2. **The Phase of Détente (1962 to 1978)**
3. **The Phase of Rapprochement (1978 to 1992)**

Spread of the Cold War in Other Parts of the World

1. China
2. Korean Crisis (1950-53)
3. Suez Canal Crisis
4. Vietnam Crisis
5. Cuban Missile Crisis (1963)

Factors Leading to Detente (1960-70s)

1. **Political Factors**
   (a) Cuban Missile Crisis
   (b) Change in leadership
   (c) Vietnam War
2. **Economic Factors**
   (a) Economic Crisis
   (b) 1973 Oil Crisis
3. **International Factors**

Causes for Disintegration of the Soviet Union

1. **Economic Factors**
   (a) Centralized control
   (b) Lack of Technological Development
   (c) Low productivity
   (d) Inefficient agriculture
   (e) High military and other spending
2. **Political Factors**
   (a) Autocratic nature of the government
   (b) Racial division within Russia
   (c) Lack of transparency and accountability
3. **Role of the Cold War**
4. **Role of Mikhail Gorbachev**

Causes Behind the End of the Cold War

1. Economic factors
2. Political factors
3. Ideological factors
4. Strategic factors
5. Diplomatic factors

Causes Behind the Rise and Hegemony of the USA

1. The collapse of the Soviet Union
2. Economic strength
3. Military dominance
4. Political stability
5. Expansion of US-led International Institutions
6. Cultural influence

Factors Behind the Integration of Europe

1. Economic factors
2. Political factors
3. Social factors
4. External factors

UPSC PREVIOUS YEARS' QUESTION

1. What were the events that led to the Suez Crisis in 1956? How did it deal a final blow to Britain's self-image as a world power? **[2014] (10 marks)**

PROBABLE QUESTIONS

1. Outline the circumstances leading to the adoption of Marshall Plan.
2. 'After World War II, the strategy of the West towards Soviet bloc crystallized as a 'policy of containment'. Comment.
3. 'The Truman Doctrine and the Marshall Plan were considered by Russian Bloc as a weapon against Russia in order to restrict her influence.' Critically examine.
4. Critically examine the various dimensions and phases of the Cold War between 1947 and 1962.
5. Outline the circumstances leading to détente.
6. Explain the reason for Britain not joining European Economic Community (EEC).

TIMELINE (1947–1991)

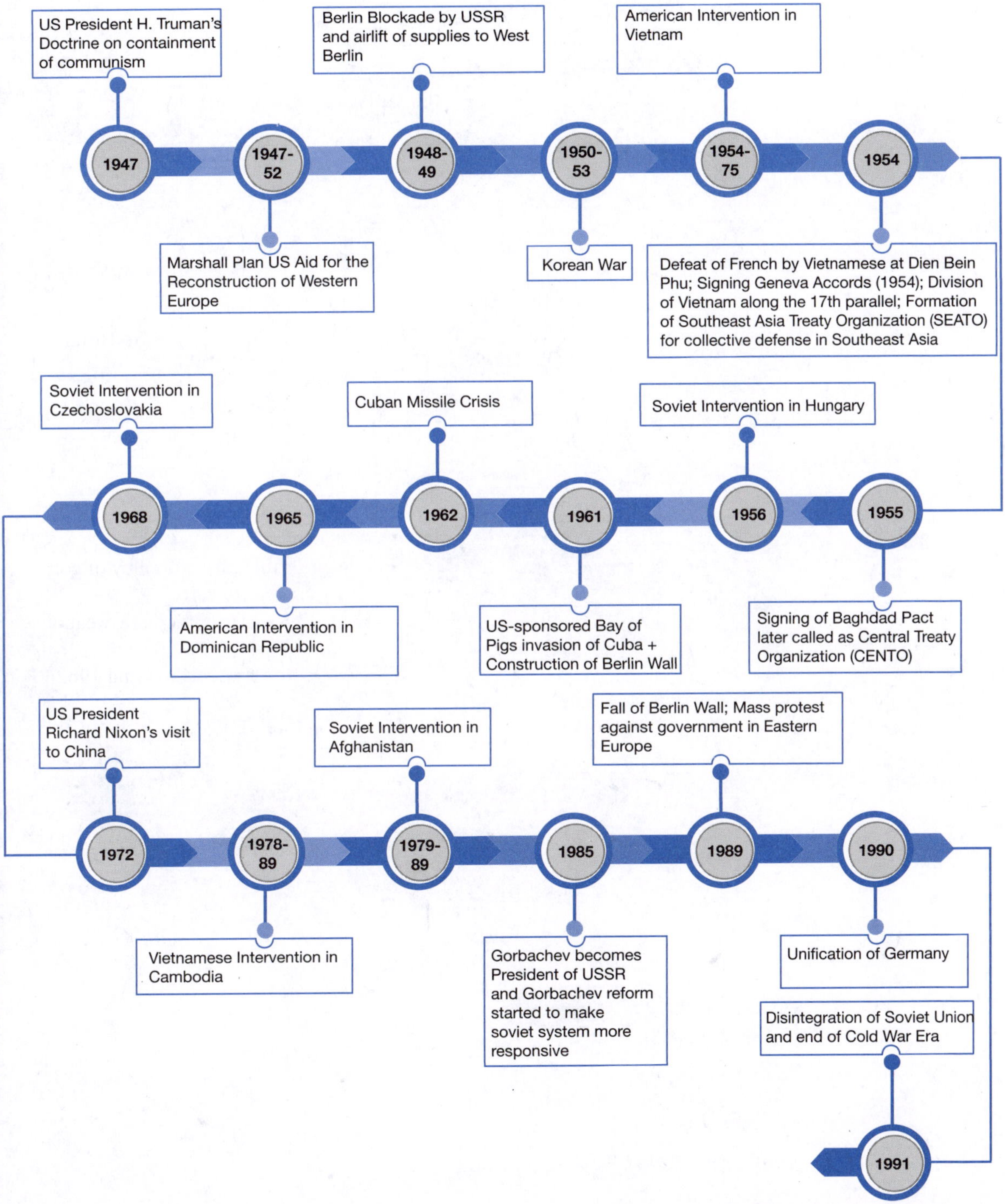

CHAPTER

11

Photo Credit: Mark Poprocki / Shutterstock; HStocks / Shutterstock

CHINESE REVOLUTION AND DECOLONIZATION OF COLONIES

> *The Chinese Revolution of 1949 was a watershed moment in world history, overthrowing a monarchy that had endured for thousands of years and replacing it with a socialist state. It not only changed the course of Chinese history but also had a lasting and far-reaching impact on the international political stage.*
>
> ***–John W. Garver (Chinese-American Historian)***

INTRODUCTION

The Chinese Revolution refers to a series of events that took place in China in the 20th century. It began with the fall of the Qing dynasty in 1911 and continued until the establishment of the People's Republic of China in 1949. The revolution was primarily a result of growing discontent among the Chinese people with the corrupt and ineffective rule of the Qing dynasty, as well as the impact of western imperialism. The revolution also included a brutal civil war and was led by the Chinese Communist Party, under the leadership of Mao Tse Tung (also known as Mao Zedong), and resulted in the defeat of the nationalist government led by Chiang Kai-shek, in a civil war **(Refer Figure 11.1).**

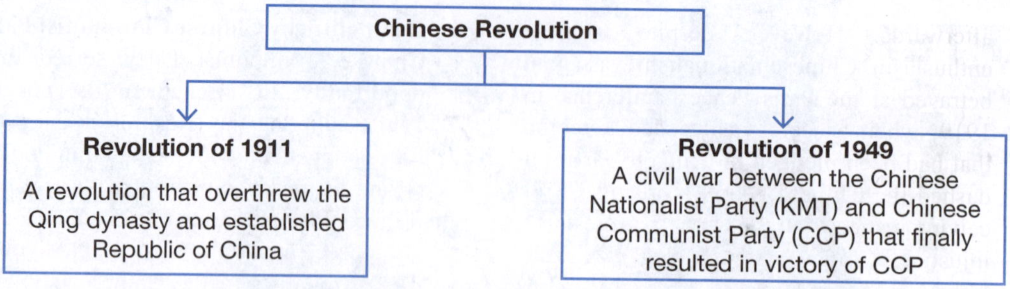

FIGURE 11.1: Chinese Revolution of 1911 and 1949

CHINESE REVOLUTION

The term 'Chinese Revolution' refers specifically to the Communist Revolution. This revolution resulted in the victory of the Chinese Communist Party (CCP) over the Nationalist Party (Kuomintang) and led to the establishment of the People's Republic of China (PRC) on October 1, 1949.

Causes for the Rise of Communism in China

1. **The legacy of imperialism:** China was a subject of European imperialist exploitation from the beginning. China was forced to open up to foreign countries for trade after two opium wars, after which its sovereignty was virtually mortgaged. Imperialism left a legacy of poverty and discontent in China, which created a fertile ground for the rise of a new ideological system in the form of Communism.
2. **Failure of Westernization of China:** The Self-Strengthening Movement was an earlier effort by China to adopt western methods for re-strengthening itself. This movement was actually a series of reforms, aimed at modernizing China's economy, military, and governance systems in order to counteract the weakening of the Qing dynasty and resist foreign domination during the late 19th and early 20th centuries. But this method didn't work. Above all, most Chinese people used to treat imperialism and capitalism as twin brothers.
3. **The failure of the nationalist government:** Before embracing communism, China experimented with a variety of anti-imperialist protest strategies, but nearly all of them were unsuccessful. When Dr. Sun-Yat-Sen and the Kuomintang party created the Chinese Republic in 1911, the Chinese people had high expectations for it. But Chiang Kai-Chinese Shek's republic also proved to be a failed system. The failure of the nationalist government to address the needs of the people (such as land reforms), helped to create a climate of discontent that the Communists were able to capitalize on.
4. **Disappointment during the Paris Peace Conference:** In the First World War, the Chinese Republic cooperated with the Allies (Britain, France, USA and Italy) in the hopes of gaining some sort of benefit

> *"The rise of communism in China was due to a combination of several factors, including a long history of foreign imperialism, the failure of the Chinese Nationalist Party to bring about economic and social reforms, and a desire among the Chinese people for a better life.*
> ***–Richard H. Immerman"***

afterwards. However, despite Chinese enthusiasm, Chinese nationalism was again betrayed at the Paris Peace Conference in 1919, when a secret deal ceded a region that had been pledged to China to Japan. It dashed the Chinese people's dreams of receiving justice from the west. To protest this injustice, Chinese citizens organized the '4th May Movement.'

The '4th May Movement' was a political and cultural movement in China that took place on May 4, 1919. It was a response to the Paris Peace Conference, which awarded territories in Shandong, China to Japan following World War-I. Encouraged by the success of the Russian Revolution, the movement was characterized by student protests and demonstrations calling for an end to foreign imperialism, a boycott of Japanese goods, and a push for political and cultural modernization. The movement was a key turning point, considered a precursor to the Chinese Revolution of 1949, and helped to lay the foundation for the Chinese Communist Party's rise to power in 1949.

5. **The success of the Soviet Union:** The success of the Soviet Union in transforming itself into a powerful communist state encouraged the Chinese people to believe that Communism could do the same for them.
6. **The spread of Marxist ideology:** Communist rule was successfully established in the neighbouring region of Russia. So, naturally Marxist ideas gradually percolated to China and there was formation of the Communist Party of China by Mao Tse Tung in 1919. The spread of Marxist ideology in the 1920s and 1930s helped to fuel the rise of Communism in China.

Causes for the Success of the Chinese Communist Party in 1949

The success of the Chinese Communist Party (CCP) in 1949 was due to several key factors, including:

1. **Realpolitik by Chinese Communist Party:** Chinese Communist Party seized every opportunity to strengthen its position. While adopting the 'Realpolitik', it sometimes cooperated with the Kuomintang Party and formed a joint front with it. Then it utilized this time frame to expand its area of influence. Later, the CCP was able to defeat the Nationalists in the Chinese Civil War through a combination of guerrilla tactics and conventional warfare.

> "*The Chinese Communist victory in 1949 was due to a combination of circumstances including a weak and divided Nationalist government, Japanese imperialism, and peasant discontent.*
> ***—Roderick MacFarquhar (Historian)***"

2. **Support from the Soviet Union:** The Soviet Union provided financial and military aid to the Chinese Communist Party. This allowed the CCP to gain a significant advantage in the civil war which ultimately led to its victory.
3. **Support from the peasantry:** Mao Tse Tung adopted a pragmatic strategy even towards private properties. While slightly neglecting the rigid and aggressive Marxist strategy, Mao preferred to redistribute the land among the peasantry after seizing the land of the landlords in Kiangsi province.

The CCP gained widespread support from the rural population by implementing land reforms and alleviating poverty. The Chinese peasantry was the backbone of the CCP's success. They provided the manpower and resources needed to fight the Civil War, as well as provided support for the party, once it was in power.

4. **Ideological appeal:** Mao Tse Tung was an effective leader who was able to inspire and motivate the Chinese people to join the Communist Party. Mao's ideology of Communism and his focus on national self-reliance resonated with the Chinese people, particularly in the aftermath of World War-II.

   Moreover, in China, Mao Tse Tung adopted a very pragmatic policy course. He devised a new revolution strategy and redefined communism to meet China's specific circumstances. He predicted that the revolution in China would move from rural to urban areas, not the other way around. The proletariat class would include Chinese peasants. Above all, the peasant force would be the foundation for the Communist Revolution in China in the future.
5. **Japanese invasion of China:** Communist Party of China benefitted even from the Japanese invasion. The Japanese invasion of China weakened the Chinese Nationalist Party (Kuomintang) and created conditions that helped the Chinese Communist Party (CCP) gain control of mainland China in 1949. China's invasion caused widespread destruction and led to the breakdown of the Kuomintang's rule, allowing the CCP to gain popular support and promote their anti-Japanese nationalistic message. Due to the invasion from Japan, the area of the Kuomintang government shrunk. At this moment, the CCP rushed to fill up the vacuum and expanded its base in the region. The CCP's victory in the Chinese Civil War, which followed the Japanese invasion, was largely due to Japanese invasion of China.
6. **Nationalist weaknesses:** The nationalist government was plagued by corruption, ineffective leadership, and economic problems, which weakened its support among the population.
7. **Poor economic conditions:** The Chinese economy was in a state of decline and the people were desperate for a change. This created a perfect opportunity for the CCP to take power and implement its own policies.

Overall, the success of the CCP in 1949 can be attributed to a combination of effective military strategy, popular support, ideological appeal, nationalist weaknesses, international support, and control over information.

Impact of the Foundation of the Chinese Communist Republic

The foundation of the Chinese Communist Republic had a major impact on China and the world.

1. Due to the CPC's (Communist Party of China) victory in 1949, the Communist Revolution became significant in Asia as Mao Tse Tung redefined Marxist ideology to suit Asia's unique circumstances.
2. In contrast to the Russian communist model, the Chinese Communist Republic offered a new development model. While rejecting the heavy industry-based Russian model, the Chinese model put an emphasis on the development of agriculture.
3. It led to significant social and economic reforms, including land reforms, collectivization of agriculture, and rapid industrialization in China.
4. The establishment of a communist government in China in 1949, gave an alternative model of protest to colonies. Thus, the Chinese Republic accelerated the process of decolonization of Asia.
5. After the establishment of the Chinese Republic in Asia, a strong nation called China emerged that may represent a threat to western imperialism.

Limitations of the Chinese Revolution

1. **One-Party rule:** The CCP's monopoly (One-Party Rule) on power had restricted prospects for democratic political and social advancement. The Chinese Communist Party maintained tight control over the government and society, suppressing political opposition and dissent.

2. **Cultural suppression:** The CCP's drive to modernize and control the nation resulted in the suppression of traditional Chinese culture, religion, and local customs.
3. **Agricultural reforms:** The CCP's collectivization of agriculture initially led to increased food production but later resulted in decreased efficiency and food shortages.
4. **Promoted violence:** The Chinese revolution's offspring, Maoism, came to be associated with violence. It has now led to a law-and-order problem in several Asian countries such as Nexalism in India.

DECOLONIZATION

Decolonization refers to the process of dismantling colonial systems of governance and liberation of colonies that were previously under the rule of a foreign power. Decolonization often occurs as a result of a combination of internal resistance and external pressure from other countries and international organizations. But, the liberation process turned out to be a complex, long drawn-out process rather than being smooth. It is argued that the Second World War had a similar effect on the colonies of Britain, France, Holland, etc. in Asia and Africa as the Napoleonic War had on the Spanish colony of Latin America under Simon Bolivar.

> *"The winds of change were blowing across the continent. The rigid and unequal colonial structures could no longer be sustained in a rapidly changing world where national independence movements and anti-colonial sentiment were growing stronger.*
> ***—David Killing Ray (Historian)"***

Debate on Decolonization

Colonial historians argued that colonial rule was a positive force, bringing peace, stability, and a break from violence to the people living there and that it operated via the consent of the colonists rather than through coercion. By constructing railways, roads, bridges, telegraphs, and irrigation projects, they built the foundation for progress and a modern nation in the colonies.

On the other hand, nationalist historians argue that colonial rule was a negative force. Although colonial rule caused the colonies to integrate into the world capitalist system, it did not result in the growth of an industrialized capitalist economy in the colonies. The colonies were subordinately incorporated into the global economy. Additionally, they contend that the colonial state's policy of divide and rule, which was implemented everywhere, intensified ethnic and religious conflicts in colonies.

Causes of Decolonization

In the latter half of the 18th century, the process of decolonization began to spread throughout Latin America and the world. It continued on for more than 200 years and culminated in the independence of the colonies. This process of decolonization was triggered, intensified and sustained by a number of cultural, intellectual, political and economic factors.

> *"The Second World War was a major impetus for decolonization throughout the world. It weakened the colonial powers and provided an opportunity for their former colonies to challenge the legitimacy of colonial rule and to assert their independence.*
> ***–John McNeill (Historian)"***

Second World War

The Second World War had a major impact on the process of decolonization. The war weakened the European colonial powers and provided an opportunity for the colonies to fight for their independence. According to scholar Adekeye Adebajo, the Second World War was a major factor in the decolonization process. After the end of the war, the defeated powers—Germany, Italy, Japan, and colonial powers such as France and Britain—could no longer maintain their overseas empires. In addition, the war weakened both the will and the capacity of the colonial powers to maintain their control. Moreover, the Second World War also changed the global balance of power, leading to the rise of new powers and the emergence of the United Nations, which also helped to facilitate the process of decolonization. Thus, the Second World War had a major impact on the process of decolonization in the following manner:

1. Since the Second World War had been both militarily and economically costly, the European powers agreed to grant independence to the colonies after the Second World War.
2. The rise of the US and the Soviet Union as superpowers after the war altered the global balance of power and made it more difficult for the European powers to maintain their empires as both superpowers were against colonialism.
3. Colonial powers faced difficulty in justifying their colonial rule to their own citizens and to the international community. This loss of legitimacy was an important factor in the decolonization process.

> *The Second World War was a major factor in decolonization, as it destroyed the European empires and weakened their economic and political power. This enabled the colonized people to gain their freedom and self-determination, and for the process of decolonization to begin.*
>
> **—David Killing Ray**

Economic Factors

The high cost of maintaining and administering large colonial empires put a strain on the resources of the imperial powers. The Second World War was expensive and the European countries were in no position to bear the financial burden of their colonies. Moreover, the colonies were no longer as profitable as before.

European powers also found the European market more lucrative than the colonial market. The German example led European powers to realize that colonization had a negative impact on their domestic economies.

Political Factors

The nature of the colonial regime was exploitative. Native people revolted against colonial control due to the extreme suffering as well as the growing discontent caused by economic exploitation. People defied the colonial rule which ultimately resulted in decolonization.

Additionally, the idea of nationalism and anti-colonial movements, such as the Indian National Congress was gaining strength in the colonies and people were increasingly demanding political freedom and self-rule. Many colonies saw the emergence of national movements against the colony, including the 'Quit India Movement' in India, the 'Mao Movement' in Kenya, and the 'Bloody Conflict' in Vietnam and Algeria.

Intellectual Factors

The spread of ideas of enlightenment had resulted in the growth of awakening among the natives which led to demand for political and administrative reforms. The reforms initiated by colonial masters also helped in the growth of a further awakening. The spread of modern western education and growing contact with the West instilled an awakening among the people of colonies. They realized the differences between western society and colonial society apprehending the true nature of the colonial empire. This awakening triggered national movements in colonies for independence which resulted in the fall of colonial empires.

New Power Equation and Cold War

All three colonial powers, the British, French, and Dutch declined after the Second World War and were involved in post-war economic reconstruction. The new power equation created by World War II and the Cold War was also very significant for decolonization. The rise of the two superpowers, the United States and the Soviet Union, had a major influence on decolonization. Both countries supported the idea of self-determination and opposed colonialism.

> *The Cold War had a profound impact on the process of decolonization as it created a power vacuum in which newly independent nations could assert their independence and influence. The competition between the US and the USSR for global influence often put pressure on colonial powers to grant independence to their colonies, as each side sought to gain allies in the developing world.*
>
> ***—John Lewis Gaddis (Cold War Historian)***

Moreover, Cold War's beginning prompted the US to persuade western colonial powers to surrender control of their colonies because the culmination of colonial rule was facilitating Communist expansion. Colonies became closer to the USSR and communism gained popularity as a result of the Soviet Union's support for colonial countries' national independence movements.

Additionally, both the capitalist and communist models formed the basis for the decolonization movement. The majority of the countries in Asia and Africa achieved freedom based on a capitalist model, but in some, like China and Vietnam, the Communist Party took the initiative. Thus, the Cold War quickly integrated these countries' liberation movements.

Role of United Nations

International pressure from the United Nations and other world organizations also played an important role in the decolonization process.

> *The United Nations played a crucial role in the decolonization process by providing a platform for colonized peoples to voice their demands, and by supporting the transition to independence through diplomatic and financial means.*
>
> ***—Stephen Schlesinger***

UN supported the quest of people for their independence from the colonial rule when disputes were brought to it. In addition, the UN has organized regional conferences, such as the Conference on Decolonization in 1960, which led to the granting of independence to many countries. The UN has also established a special committee on decolonization in 1962, which works to promote the right to self-determination and to provide technical assistance to non-self-governing and trust territories.

Points to Ponder

The UN Charter, which was signed by all the then-existing members, enshrined the right to self-determination.

Nature of Decolonization

The nature of decolonization varied, ranging from peaceful negotiations to violent uprisings, and was influenced by factors such as the strength of anti-colonial movements, the willingness of colonial powers to relinquish control, and Cold War politics. The process of decolonization varied from one power to another power and region to region.

1. **Hardliner in approach:** France's approach to decolonization was shaped by its desire to maintain its global influence, as well as its political, economic, and strategic interests in its former colonies.

   In its approach, France was a bit more conservative; it did not let its colonies easily elude its control. This approach included the use of military force to suppress independence movements, the refusal to recognize independence until it was absolutely necessary, and the refusal to negotiate with independence movements unless they agreed to remain within the French Union. France undertook harsh and violent retaliations in its colonies, such as Algeria and Vietnam. France also had a policy of assimilation, which aimed to make the colonized population more French in culture and language. This policy was largely unsuccessful and France faced increasing pressure from anti-colonial movements and the international community, eventually leading to the gradual granting of independence to its colonies.
2. **Softline approach:** Britain adopted a softline approach towards decolonization. This involved negotiations and peaceful means of transfer, and a willingness to consider the demands of independence movements. Britain also sought to maintain political, economic, and cultural ties with its former colonies through measures such as granting independence with continued ties to the Commonwealth, providing aid and development assistance, and preserving cultural and language links.

   Nevertheless, the character of decolonization was dependent on how engaged certain colonial powers were in the region in question. A colonial power was not prepared to leave an area peacefully if the interests were higher, notably if there was a greater settled population and greater investment in the region. For instance, the British resisted the Liberation Movement in nations like Egypt and Kenya for a longer period of time.

   Even the word 'decolonization' is misleading. Although it may have appeared that colonial powers willingly liberated colonies, the reality was rather contrary. The imperialist powers liberated the colonies only then it became almost impossible for them to hold the colonies. For instance, Britain liberated Egypt and Kenya only after intense nationalist pressure.

Decolonization of Latin America

Decolonization of Latin America refers to the political and social process by which Latin American countries achieved independence from European colonial rule in the 19th and early 20th centuries. The process of decolonization was influenced by the American Revolution and French Revolution in 1789 and was characterized by military struggles, nationalistic movements, and negotiations between colonial powers and their former colonies. The end of Spanish rule in the Americas was the first step towards decolonization, with countries such as Mexico and Haiti gaining independence in the early 1820's. It was a result of the Spanish-American wars of independence (1808-1826) which saw Spain lose control of its colonies in the new world. Later, countries such as Brazil, Argentina, and Chile declared independence from Portugal and Spain, respectively.

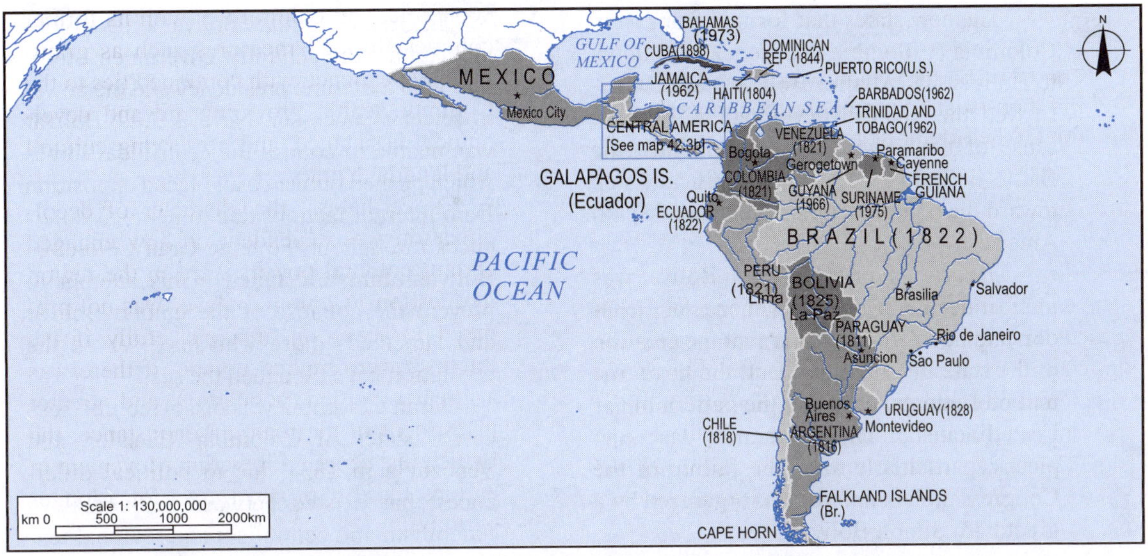

MAP 11.1: Decolonisation of Latin America

Causes behind the Liberation of Latin America

1. **Role of Napoleon Bonaparte:** Napoleon's invasion of Spain in 1808 led to a wave of independence movements in Latin America. He established the puppet state of New Granada in 1810, and he provided military and financial support to other pro-French governments. However, these efforts were ultimately unsuccessful, and the Latin American countries eventually regained their independence.
2. **Role of Simon Bolivar:** Simon Bolivar was a Venezuelan military and political leader who played a key role in the independence of several countries in Latin America, including Venezuela, Colombia, Ecuador, Peru, and Bolivia **(Refer Map 11.1)**.

   Simon Bolivar led the Liberation Movement by launching a war against Spain with covert British support. Simon Bolivar, himself a Creole, started a war of liberation after having been inspired by the episode of British Americans. Bolivar led several successful military campaigns against Spanish colonial rule in the early 19th century, and his ideas about nationalism and independence greatly influenced other independence leaders throughout the region. Bolivar is often referred to as 'The Liberator' and is considered one of the most important figures in Latin American history.

Points to Ponder

Most of Latin America achieved its independence by 1825.

At the Battle of Carabobo on June 24, 1821, Simón Bolivar, the great Liberator, commanded his troops against the Spanish Army. Although the Spanish monarchy no longer had the desire to fight back, the Spanish had not yet been driven out of South America. The next conflicts, such as the Battle of Pichincha on May 24, 1822, completed what Carabobo had begun: the desire for independence among South America's several republics.

Points to Ponder

More than just a battle, Carabobo 'was a geopolitical war.'

The new states that formed from Gran Colombia (Colombia and Venezuela) down to Bolivia (1825) after Bolivar's armies destroyed the Spanish developed a dynamic sense of their own sovereignty. Thus, the Battle of Carabobo was a significant step toward the complete independence of South America.

The original plan of Simon Bolivar was to liberate the region of Venezuela, Ecuador, and new Grenade after that the creation of the state of Columbia. But, the hope of a unified Latin America, on the pattern of the United States of America, simply dashed to pieces, particularly after the failure of the Congress at Panama in 1826 organized by a great hero Simon Bolivar.

3. **Bolivar and idea of Gran Colombia (1819 to 1831):** Simon Bolivar suggested ideas for South American independence in the Jamaica Letter of September 6, 1815, and said that South America should 'not adopt the best system of government, but the one that is most likely to succeed.' He hoped to unite some countries of South America, similar to the United States to be known as Gran Colombia.

   Gran Colombia was a republic in South America that existed from 1819 to 1831. It was founded by Simon Bolivar, who led successful military campaigns to achieve independence from the Spanish Empire. It included territories that now belong to several modern-day countries, including Colombia, Ecuador, Panama, Venezuela, and parts of northern Peru and north-western Brazil. The capital of Gran Colombia was Bogotá. Simon Bolivar envisioned a united Spanish America, and in order to bring Peru and Bolivia together with the aforementioned countries, he not only founded Gran Colombia but also the Confederation of the Andes. Thus, in order to keep the newly freed South American countries united, he established a system of treaties.

   In Gran Colombia, Bolivar aimed to implement a more centralist government structure with a lifetime presidency and the power to select a successor. Nevertheless, Bolivar was unable to control the centrifugal forces which pushed outwards and faced opposition from internal factions due to regional differences throughout the huge Gran Colombia. Bolivar ultimately failed in his attempt to prevent the collapse of the uniono Bolivar and lamented 'those who have served the revolution have ploughed the sea.'

   Gran Colombia was dissolved into successor states of Colombia, Ecuador, and Venezuela in 1831 due to political differences that existed between supporters of federalism and centralism and regional tensions among the peoples that made up the republic.

Causes Behind the Failure of Gran Colombia

1. The disparity between the geographic boundary and the community is comparable to that in Africa. Urban minority leaders and their followers were divided during the freedom movement.
2. Racial division
3. Economic dependency
4. Growing role of the Church in politics.
5. The affairs of the republics were usurped by Caudillos (Military aristocracy).
6. Civil wars ensued between different states.

Impediments in the Development of Latin America

1. As former European colonies that subsequently became United States' semi-colonies, Latin American republics found independence to be meaningless.
2. Dominance of an alliance between landed elites and military elements - Banana Republic (means politically unstable country with an economy dependent upon the export of natural resources).

3. Control of Church on the education system

Decolonization of Asian Countries

Decolonization of Asian countries refers to the process of transition from a colonial state to an independent nation. This process began in the mid-20th century, with most Asian countries gaining independence from European colonial powers. The process of decolonization involved multiple steps, such as the withdrawal of foreign troops, the establishment of a new government and the adoption of a new constitution, and the recognition of the newly independent nation by the international community.

The process of decolonization in Asia was a long and turbulent process, with several nations experiencing armed rebellion and civil wars. In some cases, the decolonization process was peaceful, with countries such as India, Pakistan, and Indonesia achieving independence through negotiations with the former colonial powers. In others, however, the process was more violent and involved armed conflicts, such as in Vietnam, Laos, and Cambodia.

In the post-world war era, India was the first country to attain independence. An English educated middle-class leadership, which was the product of English education, emerged in India and led the premier nationalist organization, Indian National Congress. It worked as an umbrella organization in the national movement under Gandhi. It was in 1947 British negotiated the transfer of power to India. Some other notable examples include:

1. Indonesia: declared independence from the Netherlands in 1945.
2. Vietnam: declared independence from France in 1945, but only fully achieved it in 1975.
3. Philippines: gained independence from the US in 1946
4. Malaysia: gained independence from Britain in 1957.

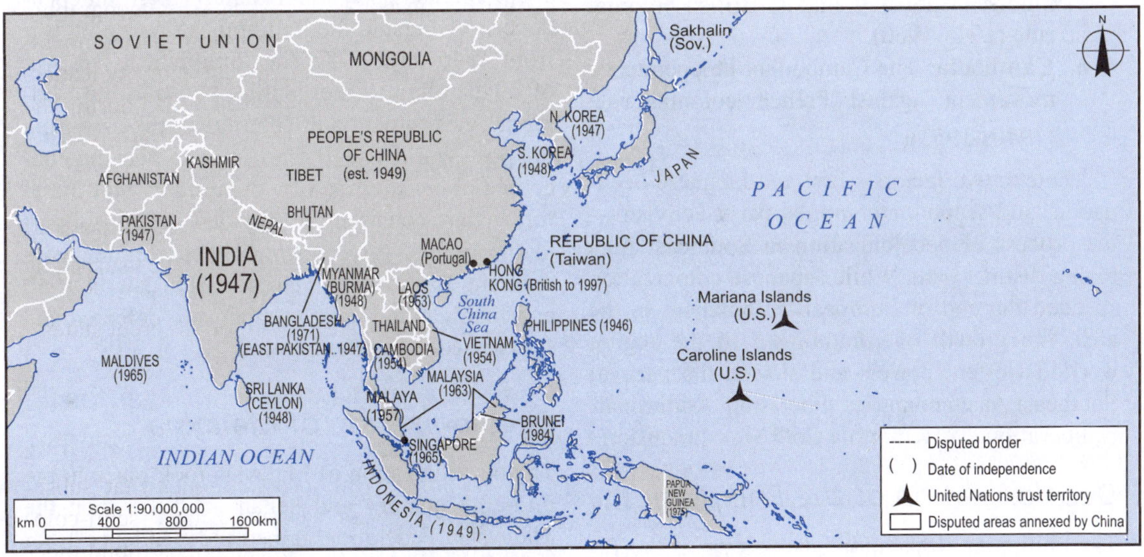

Map 11.2: Liberation of Asian Countries

Liberation Movement in Southeast Asia

The liberation movements in Southeast Asia refer to various political and social movements in the 20th century aimed at achieving independence and freedom from colonial rule for Southeast Asian countries, including **(Refer Map 11.2)**:

1. **Philippines:** The Philippine Revolution against Spanish rule in 1896, followed by the Philippine-American War against American colonial rule in 1899-1902.
2. **Vietnam:** The Indochina Wars, with the First Indochina War against the French (1946-1954) and the Second Indo-China War, also known as the Vietnam War, against the United States and South Vietnam (1955-1975).
3. **Indonesia:** The Indonesian National Revolution against Dutch colonial rule (1945-1949).
4. **Myanmar (Burma):** The Burmese independence movement against British colonial rule (1930s-1948).
5. **Malaysia:** The Malayan Emergency, a communist insurgency against British colonial rule (1948-1960).
6. **Cambodia:** The Cambodian independence movement against French colonial rule (1940s-1953).

Due to two factors—first, the Japanese occupation, and second, communist party activism—the process of decolonization in Southeast Asia took a distinct path. While Japanese colonization speeded the end of European colonialism in the area, the growth of communism in the region worried western powers and slowed the pace of Southeast Asian countries' liberation. Additionally, liberation evolved into a Cold War dimension.

Decolonization of the Philippines

The Philippine Revolution, also known as the Tagalog War was a military conflict fought between nationalists and the Spanish colonial authorities. It is regarded as the first successful revolution in southeast Asia against a European colonial power. It was led by the Katipunan (an anti-colonial secret organization) movement, which was founded by Andrés Bonifacio and Emilio Jacinto in 1892 and was later led by Emilio Aguinaldo.

The Philippine Revolution began in 1896 when the Spanish authorities discovered the Katipunan. The revolution ended in 1902, with the signing of the Treaty of Biak-na-Bato, which marked the beginning of the short-lived First Philippine Republic.

After being seized from Spain in 1898, the Philippines later became an American colony and was the first territory in which the USA could experiment with its neo-colonialism policy. During the Second World War, Japan invaded and colonized the Philippines. The demand to liberate the Philippines from its semi-colonial position under the USA extend back to the 1930s, but it wasn't until the Second World War that Japan was defeated and left the Philippines. In 1946, after World War II, the United States granted the Philippines independence.

However, the conservative Philippine government had to deal with a serious challenge from a communist party immediately after independence. As a result, the Philippines saw a civil war from 1946 until 1957.The Philippine Civil War of 1946 refers to the conflict between the Philippine government and communist rebels during the post-World War II era. America became concerned about the rise of Communism and therefore it has consistently provided covert support to the rightist government. The Philippine government eventually declared martial law in 1950 and finally communist groups were defeated and suppressed in the Philippines.

Decolonization of Malaysia

The decolonization of Malaysia took place in the mid-20th century and began in 1957 when the Malaysian Federation gained independence from the British Empire, ending more than 144 years of British rule. There were three main ethnic groups in Malaysia: Chinese, Malayans, who made up the majority, and others, including immigrants from India. British separated Singapore from Malaya and united the whole Malaya region. Due to economic reasons, Britain chose to remain in Malaysia even after 1945 due to the export of tin and rubber. However, Britain ultimately decided to withdraw as a result of nationalist pressure.

The decolonization process was driven by a combination of internal pressure from nationalist and anti-colonial movements, and external pressure from the United Nations, United States, and other countries. The decolonization process was peaceful and orderly and involved negotiations between the British and Malaysian governments.

Following Malaysia's independence, a situation similar to the post-Second World War Philippines was posed to Great Britain. The British were concerned about spread of communism when Chinese communists became extremely active in Malaysia. Chinese Communist guerrillas (Malayan Communist Party) led by Chin Peng, who played a leading role in the resistance to the Japanese, now began to stir up strikes and violence against the British in support of an independent communist state.

As a result, the British, Malays, and non-communist Chinese were all united in their opposition to communists and the British decided to impose a state of emergency in 1948. Malays remained firmly pro-British and gave very little help to the communists, who were Chinese. Consequently, communists were ultimately defeated.

Then, Malay Party under leader Tunku Abdul Rahman formed the Alliance Party, which won 51 out of the 52 seats in the 1955 elections andthe British were persuaded to grant full independence in 1957 through peaceful talks and negotiations. The British eventually left in 1957 and the Federation of Malaysia was set up in 1963.

Decolonization of Vietnam

Vietnam was an independent country till 1869, but was gradually colonized by France. The decolonization of Vietnam refers to the process by which Vietnam gained independence from French colonial rule. Vietnam's decolonization took place after the Second World War when the French colonial empire was disbanded and the Indochina Union was dissolved.

Beginning of the 19th century, a nationalist movement commenced in Vietnam under the leadership of Ho Chi Minh against French control. However, the entry of Japan in the Second World War changed the geopolitical situation in Vietnam. Vietnamese people were left at Japan's mercy after the French fled Vietnam. Vietnamese were exploited to the greatest potential by the Japanese, which contributed to the sustained strength of the nationalist movement. When the Japanese surrendered in August 1945, Ho Chi Minh declared Vietnam independent, called the Democratic Republic of Vietnam. However, after the Second World War, the French decided to re-establish their control over Indo-China and Africa. Ho Chi Minh expected support from the United States in 1945 but instead, the US decided to help the French in restoring their rule in Indochina.

Points to Ponder

When Japan left Vietnam in 1946 following the Second World War, French forces re-established colonial rule.

The process of decolonization in Vietnam was a long and difficult one, marked by several wars. The First Indo-China War (1946-1954) was between the communist Viet Minh and the French colonial government. In 1950, both Moscow and Beijing recognized the Democratic Republic of Vietnam under Ho Chi Minh as the sole legitimate government.

However, France underestimated the skill, resourcefulness, and determination of the Vietnamese to succeed. The Vietnamese played havoc with the French defense. The French garrison at Dien Bien Phu surrendered on May 7, 1954 which resulted in the Geneva Accords of 1954. The Geneva Accords divided Vietnam into two: communist North Vietnam under the leadership of Ho Chi Minh and the non-communist South Vietnam under puppet emperor Bao-dai. The USA did not sign the accord but pledged to abide by them.

The apprehension that Vietnam would fall into the lap of communism under the leadership of communist leaders like Ho Chi Minh pushed the USA into the conflict. The USA view Vietnam as the first Domino' whose fall could result in the emergence of Communist regimes from Singapore to the Philippines, prompting the USA to proclaim the Domino theory. Thus, the USA decided to get engaged in the Vietnam War by aiding France in keeping control of Vietnam.

However, later a struggle commenced between the USA and its allies on the one side and the Vietnamese people on the other. The two sides fought a long and bitter conflict, known as the Vietnam War. The Vietnam War, also known as the Second Indo-China War, was a conflict fought between North Vietnam and South Vietnam from 1954 to 1975. North Vietnam was supported by the Soviet Union, China, and other communist allies; South Vietnam was supported by the United States, South Korea, the Philippines, Australia, Thailand, and other anti-communist allies. The war began in 1954 (though the conflict in the region stretches back to the mid-1940s) and continued against the backdrop of an intense Cold War. In addition, the USA officially recognized Bao Dai as the Emperor of Vietnam in 1950.

In August 1964, America claimed that northern Vietnamese forces had attacked American troops in the Gulf of Tonkin. Consequently, President Johnson dispatched troops and began Operation Rolling Thunder, an aircraft bombardment of northern Vietnam, in March 1965.The North Vietnamese government sent regular army troops to southern Vietnam to conduct guerrilla and conventional military operations. In January 1968, the national liberation front (NLF) organized general apprising in southern Vietnam known as the Tet offensive against America to fight for the Republic of Vietnam. US Embassy was attacked and was shown live on TV across the United States.

Growing opposition to the war in the United States led to bitter divisions among the Americans. President Richard Nixon ordered the withdrawal of U.S. forces in 1973. Consequently, in 1973, the Paris Peace Accords were signed, ending the war and leading to the reunification of Vietnam. The Accords allowed for the withdrawal of all foreign troops, the formation of a coalition government in the north, and the holding of free elections in the South. On April 30, 1975, the Viet Cong and North Vietnamese armies captured Saigon, marking the end of the war and the establishment of the Socialist Republic of Vietnam.

Decolonization of Indonesia

In Southeast Asia, Indonesia's liberation movement largely adopted the same trajectory as Korea and Vietnam. Indonesia was colonized by the Netherlands East Indies Company (VOC) in 1619 and by the Dutch government in the 19th century. The decolonization of Indonesia refers to the process of ending Dutch colonial rule over Indonesia, which started in the late 1940s and ended in 1949.

In course of the Second World War, Indonesia also fell prey to Japanese occupation by Dutch. In August 1945, as the Japanese surrendered, Indonesia once again became a colony of the Dutch. However, since Dutch was preoccupied with domestic issues, the British government of India arrived and took over Indonesia on behalf of Holland. But in the meantime, a nationalist party led by Dr. Sukarno, which had strengthened its position under the Japanese government, fought back fiercely against the decolonization of Indonesia. Consequently, the Indonesian National Revolution begins in 1945, when Sukarno and Mohammad Hatta declared Indonesian independence from Dutch colonial rule.

It was also at that time even communist spread resurfaced in Indonesia but Dr. Sukarno's party countered it. Dr. Sukarno gained the support of western nations due to his anti-communist position. Then, colonial power Dutch had to face the burden of external pressure.

The process of decolonization began in 1947 when the Dutch recognized Indonesia's right to self-determination. This was followed by the 1949 Round Table Conference, which was held due to the intervention of the UN to discuss the transfer of sovereignty from the Dutch to Indonesia.

Even Jawaharlal Nehru, the Indian Prime Minister, was essential in influencing world diplomacy in Indonesia's favour. In 1949, he arranged a meeting of Asian nations to discuss the topic of liberating Indonesia. During the Round table conference, the Indonesian government and the Dutch government agreed on the transfer of sovereignty. The agreement was ratified in the 1950 Renville Agreement, which officially ended more than 300 years of Dutch colonial rule and declared Indonesia's independence.

The Liberation Movement in Africa

The African Liberation Movement is a term used to describe the struggle of African peoples to end colonialism and white minority rule in Africa in order to achieve self-determination.

> *"The liberation movements in Africa were the last great wave of anti-colonial struggle in the world, and their achievements rank among the greatest in human history.*
>
> ***—Walter Rodney"***

The African Liberation Movement has a long history, beginning in the 19th century and continuing to the present day. It has taken many forms, from armed struggle to diplomatic negotiations and civil disobedience. The movements, led by African nationalist and anti-colonial leaders, sought to assert their independence and establish autonomous, democratic states. Key events and figures include Ghana's independence in 1957, led by Kwame Nkrumah, the Algerian War of Independence (1954-1962), and Nelson Mandela's leadership in the struggle against apartheid in South Africa.

Indian Contribution to the Liberation of Africa

India was one of the first countries to recognize the newly independent African nations and provide them with diplomatic support. India also contributed to the liberation of many African states through its military and diplomatic aid. India made significant contributions to the liberation of African countries from colonial rule through various means including:

1. **Diplomatic support:** India provided diplomatic support to African countries in their struggle for independence, particularly in the United Nations. Gold Coast, Tunisia, and Morocco all made demands for independence, but colonial powers consistently rejected them. However, after India attained independence in 1947, the demand for their liberation could no longer be put off for as long, and in 1956 Tunisia and Morocco did so, while the Gold Coast became an independent country under the name of Ghana in 1958.
2. **Ideological support:** India, as a former colony and a newly independent nation, served as a model and inspiration for African countries seeking independence. Nkrumah of Ghana and Kenneth Kaunda of Zambia were at least two African leaders who made it clear in their autobiographies that they were greatly influenced by Indian independence.
3. **Inspiration from Gandhi:** South Africa's African National Congress was enlightened to a novel method of protest through the Gandhian Satyagraha. Albert Luthuli, the ANC's leader, and later Nelson Mandela inspired by Gandhi's influence.

Decolonization in Africa

Decolonization in West and East Africa followed different paths and time lines. In West Africa, the process began in the mid-twentieth century with the emergence of nationalist movements, which gained momentum and resulted in the attainment of independence by many countries in the region by the 1960s. For example, Ghana became the first African colony to gain independence in 1957 **(Refer Map 11.3)**.

In contrast, decolonization in East Africa was a slower process, with the first country to gain independence being Kenya in 1963. This was due to a number of factors including the existence of white settler communities in the region who had established themselves as a political and economic force, and the fact that East Africa was a strategic location for the colonial powers during the Cold War. Ultimately, the differences in the paths to decolonization in West and East Africa were shaped by the unique historical, political, and economic conditions of each region.

If we evaluate the entire decolonization process in West Africa, with the exception of Algeria, all other West African countries had reasonably peaceful negotiations for the transfer of power. The pioneer of decolonization in western Africa was to be Ghana's, Kwame Nkrumah. In Eastern Africa the process of liberation appeared to be a bit more difficult than in countries like Egypt, Sudan, Kenya, etc. British were having a greater stake in these colonies. If Ghana prepared the model of the liberation of colonies in West Africa, Kenya prepared its model in east Africa.

Factors Supported the Growth of Imperialism in Africa

1. **Role of explorers:** Explorers and adventurers further helped in discovering and opening up new areas to be colonized.

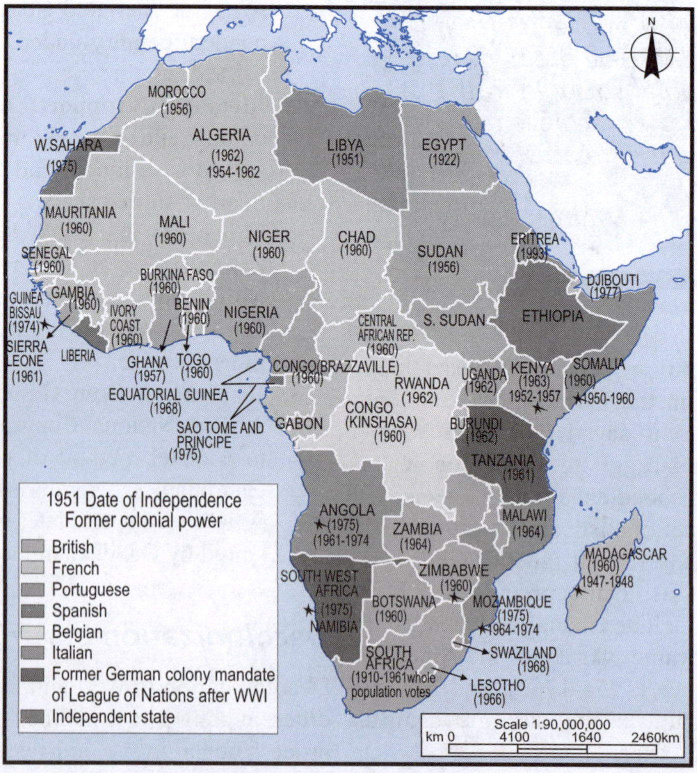

MAP 11.3: Liberation movements in Africa

2. **Political weakness:** The governments of the countries of Africa were very weak. The old ways of governing were still followed. Strong nation-states in the modern sense had not developed. The people's loyalties were still to local princes as in feudal times, or to tribal chieftains. These rulers cared little for the welfare of the people.
3. **Lack of industrial growth in Africa:** The most important condition was that the Industrial Revolution had not come to this part of the world.
4. **Military failure:** Africa was politically and militarily unable to stand up to the armed might and power of Europe.
5. **Huge size of the African continent:** The huge size of this continent was very difficult to control by a strong centre as there were no proper means of transport, communications, etc.

Reasons for Delay in African Decolonization

The process of decolonization began in Asia in 1945 after Japan surrendered before the allied forces 1945. However, the decolonization process in Africa stretched over a much longer period than in Asia, lasting up till 1990. Between 1950 to 1959, six African countries were liberated with the sacrifice of over 2,00,000 African lives. The 1960s saw the dismantling of the British, French, and Belgian colonial empires with mass support. In the mid-1970s, the Portuguese empire in Africa collapsed. The process of decolonization ended only in the early 1990s with the independence of Rhodesia and Namibia.

1. **European needs of raw materials:** As compared to Asia, the African continent was endowed more with raw materials, mineral resources, labour, and territory for future settlement. As a result, the colonial powers tried to stay there for as long a time as possible.
2. **Delay in the rise of Nationalist movement:** The nationalist movements for freedom started early in Asia, while in many African countries such movements could start only after the Second World War. Asian continent saw the advent of modern education early, which ignited the intelligentsia to demand civil and political liberties, starting with the beginning of 19th century. As a result, the colonial powers deliberately delayed the introduction of modern education into the African continent.
3. **Diverse ethnicity and lack of trust:** European powers carved up Africa with very little regard for the identity of the people living there resulting in tribal division and hatred. They lacked mutual trust and did not witness pan-African unity against the common enemy- colonialism.
4. **Cold War politics:** It was this fear of Soviet influence in Africa, particularly on the part of the United States, that created such a major problem for African nations. Western powers viewed African independence through the lens of the Cold War, which rendered African leaders as either pro-West or pro-East. Hence, there was little scope for an acceptable middle ground.
5. **Presence of racism:** Because of centuries-old slave-trade of African people by the white colonialists, the racist repression was very intense (in the form of apartheid) which could be dismantled only after a prolonged battle.

Decolonization of Africa

Decolonization in Ghana

Decolonization in Ghana (formerly known as the Gold Coast) refers to the process of ending British colonial rule in the country, which began in the late 1940s and ended on March 6, 1957, when Ghana became the first African colony to gain independence. The movement was led by political leaders such as Kwame Nkrumah and marked by peaceful negotiations due to the absence apartheid system of racial segregation and discrimination.

Decolonization in Ghana, began in 1947 when the UK granted the colony limited self-rule under the chairmanship of Dr. Kwame Nkrumah. This limited self-rule was extended in 1951, when

Nkrumah and his Convention People's Party (CPP) were elected to form the first democratically elected government in the Gold Coast. In March 1957, the Gold Coast achieved full independence from the UK and changed its name to Ghana in honour of the ancient Ghana Empire. The Ghana process followed in other countries of West Africa such as Senegal, Zambia, Guinea Bissau, Sierra Leon, Mauritania, etc. The case of Algeria seems to be exceptional where France was having a greater stake in the colony. So, it took the form of a military conflict.

Decolonization in Kenya

Decolonization in Kenya was a long and often violent process, marked by resistance from colonial authorities and the white settler community, as well as struggles for independence led by Kenyan nationalist movements. The Suez Canal crisis in 1956 put a death knell on British colonialism in Africa. Still British resisted the liberation of Kenya.

The Mau Mau Uprising of 1952-1960 in which Kenyan nationalists used armed resistance, and guerrilla tactics to attack British targets and demand independence, was a significant turning point in the country's decolonization journey. The uprising was led by the militant group, the Mau Mau, and was largely a response to the oppressive labour policies and land dispossession of the British.

The British government responded with a brutal crackdown on the Mau Mau and other independence movements, but the tide was turning in favour of independence. The pressure for decolonization continued to grow, and in 1963 Kenya gained independence from Britain, with Jomo Kenyatta becoming the country's first president.

However, the transition to independence was not easy. White settlers, who had established a significant political and economic presence in the country, were concerned about losing their privileged status, and there were also tensions between different ethnic groups within Kenya. These challenges, along with others, have continued to shape the country's political and social landscape in the decades since independence.

Decolonization in South Africa

A new kind of colonization may be observed in South Africa. The worst form of colonization, known as apartheid, was then imposed on the Black majority, the Bantus, in South Africa by White settlers. It is more than just racial policy; rather, it is the most severe form of racial discrimination based on the total social segregation of the Black population.

Decolonization in South Africa was a long and difficult process marked by decades of resistance against apartheid, a system of racial segregation and oppression implemented by the white minority government. The African National Congress (ANC) and other anti-apartheid organizations led a nonviolent struggle for equality and freedom, which was met with violence and repression by the government.

Apartheid System

1. **Homeland system:** The government attempted to divide South Africa into a number of separate states, each of which was supposed to develop into a separate nation-state for a different ethnic group. Under the 'Population Registration Act of 1950' the white and black populations had to be settled in different regions.
2. Separate areas were earmarked for black residents known as Bantustan. A Pass Permit System was introduced according to which movement of black citizens were monitored.' The black could come to the white region to work as a labour only after attaining a pass.
3. Black and brown people's political representation was restricted, and they were prohibited from participating in political activities.
4. Every person was given a racial classification and an identity card.
5. Separate transport systems were started for blacks.
6. Blacks and whites were not allowed to be married or have sexual intercourse. According to 'Mixed Marriage Act of 1949', whites were prohibited to marry blacks.

7. Black children went to separate schools and were given a much inferior education.

Transformation of Apartheid System to Democracy in Africa

Britain conquered South Africa in 1795. British colonial sovereignty over South Africa was recognized by the Vienna Congress of 1815. South Africa was still a British colony up until 1910, at which point it gained independence. After independence, South Africa came under white rule. The increasing demands for racial equality in South Africa following the Second World War alarmed the white population. They started fearing that their traditional privileges based on racial distinction might disappear. Elections were held in South Africa in 1948, and Dr. DF Malan's African National Party triumphed. He promised to establish white supremacy in South Africa and established the Apartheid system.

> *Apartheid was a system of institutionalized racial segregation and discrimination in South Africa between 1948 and the early 1990s. It was a destructive and deeply flawed policy that left deep scars on South African society and the legacy of its legacy continues to this day.*
>
> **—Ibram X. Kendi**

Apartheid was a system of institutionalized racial segregation and political discrimination that was enforced in South Africa from 1948 to 1994 to preserve the dominance of the white race. Thus, apartheid laws divided South Africa's population based on race. The apartheid government classified citizens into different racial groups (such as white, black, coloured, and Indian) and imposed various forms of discrimination and segregation on them, including restrictions on movement, education, and political participation. The most pathetic aspect of the policy of apartheid is that it was enforced in South Africa at the time when the policy of decolonization was being followed in the rest of the world.

Factors which Encouraged Apartheid in South Africa

1. An official census was conducted in 1946, and it was established from its findings that blacks outnumbered whites even in metropolitan areas. Therefore, it raised some concerns in white people's minds. In 1946 itself 'The Fagan commission' was formed to view the issue. According to its recommendations, blacks should be gradually assimilated into common public life. Such a recommendation created a larger concern among the white people and members of the Nationalist Party (1912) who were inclined to maintain the purity of white blood.
2. In 1948, the Nationalist party won the election and it formed the government under Malan. This government introduced the policy of apartheid. Decolonization began in the 1940s, leading to the independence of nations like Pakistan and India. After that, non-white nations were also allowed to join the British Commonwealth. The majority of black Commonwealth nations would put pressure on the South African government to adopt black rights, which caused fear among South Africa's white racists. The Nationalist party, therefore implemented a strict system of racial discrimination earlier on as a counter measure.

Reaction Against Apartheid

The apartheid system of racial segregation and discrimination in South Africa faced widespread opposition and protest both domestically and internationally. The resistance against apartheid system include both Internal and external reaction against apartheid.

Internal Reaction Against Apartheid

Anti-apartheid leaders such as Albert Luthuli, Nelson Mandela, Walter Sisulu, and Steve Biko led peaceful protests, marches, and demonstrations against the apartheid government.

In 1913, African National Congress (ANC) was formed under Albert Luthuli and he started to break apartheid laws peacefully and demonstrations started against apartheid. The blacks were asked to boycott work. In 1955, All Black and Brown organizations came together and issued a 'freedom charter' demanding the removal of apartheid. South African government reacted sharply and it cracked down on the movement in the name of suppression of communism. ANC leader Albert Luthuli was found dead in a mysterious condition.

Later, the Sharpeville massacre was a pivotal event in the anti-apartheid struggle in South Africa. It took place on March 21, 1960, in the township of Sharpeville, near Johannesburg. On that day, a peaceful demonstration was organized by the Pan Africanist Congress (PAC) to protest against the apartheid government's pass laws, which required black South Africans to carry passbooks at all times and restricted their freedom of movement.

During the demonstration, the police opened fire on the peaceful protesters, killing 69 people and injuring 180 others. The Sharpeville massacre shocked the world and brought international attention to the brutality of the apartheid regime. Nelson Mandela was a leader in the anti-apartheid movement and a member of the African National Congress (ANC) at the time of the Sharpeville massacre. In the aftermath of the massacre, the ANC was banned and Mandela was arrested and sentenced to life in prison for sabotage and conspiracy to overthrow the government.

External Reactions Against Apartheid

After the Sharpeville incident, international pressure on South Africa increased to abandon apartheid.

1. British prime minister Harold McMillan visited cape town and advised the government of South Africa to abandon apartheid in 1960.
2. Commonwealth condemned apartheid; the South Africa government led by white left it in protest in 1961. At the initiative of Indian PM Rajiv Gandhi, British Commonwealth was compelled to bring an economic embargo against the government of South Africa.
3. After the liberation of African countries, African League also started the protest against apartheid.
4. The United Nations General Assembly adopted its first resolution against apartheid in 1962, condemning the country's racial policies. Thus, over the next two decades, the UN passed numerous resolutions against South Africa's apartheid policies and imposed mandatory economic and political sanctions on the country.
5. The United Nations led a global sporting boycott of South Africa, which prevented the country's teams and athletes from participating in international competitions.
6. 1970s and 80s internal and external pressure on the South African government to abandon apartheid increased significantly.
7. USA and Western countries were having very ambivalent approaches to the issue. As the Cold War was going on so they took the white government of South Africa as a bulwark against communism. That's why they remained to be soft towards the South African government. But later due to excessive democratic pressure they had to break their relationship with the South African government. The USA imposed economic sanctions on South Africa in 1986.

Abandonment of Apartheid

Under the pressure of world public opinion, for the first time, at the end of 1970s the government of both took some initiatives in relaxing the system.

1. Pass permit system was abolished in 1966
2. The 'mixed marriage act' was abolished
3. Bantus (native blacks) were given the right to fight elections and cast their votes in the elections of municipal corporations.

But it did not satisfy the blacks (Bantus) in South Africa and they continued the protest.

(a) Apartheid regulations were gradually abandoned in 1979. Blacks were given the right to form trade unions and go on strikes.

(b) A bicameral parliament was constituted in 1984. One house included black people, whereas the other house contained white people.

(c) Matrimonial relations between blacks and whites were permitted in 1985.

However, the partial withdrawal of apartheid provisions didn't satisfy the aspirations of the South African coloured people which led to further intensified struggles.

(d) In the meantime, the economy of South Africa fell to its lowest ebb due to an economic embargo which forced the government of W.D. Clark to take initiative and released Nelson Mandela from jail in 1990. In the same year, the last colony in Africa, Namibia was liberated by South Africa.

In the 1980s and early 1990s, the international community increased pressure on South Africa to end apartheid, with economic sanctions and cultural boycotts playing a significant role in bringing about change. In 1990, the government released Nelson Mandela from prison after 27 years, and negotiations for a transition to a democratic system began.

Nelson Mandela adopted a conciliatory approach toward the South African government and in order to dispel the fear of whites he gave two promises. First, the white oppressors would not be punished and second, the industries (mostly owned by white) would not be nationalized. With whites, negotiations started in 1991 and were finished in 1993. A new constitution was written having democracy and racial equality as its principles.

The first democratic elections in South Africa were held in 1994, and the ANC, with Nelson Mandela as its leader, won a decisive victory. The country's first black president, Mandela, took office, and the process of rebuilding and reconciliation began. The end of apartheid and the establishment of a democratic government in South Africa marked a significant turning point in the country's history and was celebrated as a triumph of the human spirit over oppression and prejudice.

Constraints in the Development of Africa

1. Mismatch between geography and ethnic community.
2. Lack of a binding force as a nation.
3. Lack of proper industrialization and economic backwardness due to inadequate infrastructure.
4. Lack of quality human resources and technology.
5. Dependence over the export of one or two items.
6. Even the economic liberalization strategy backfired on African economies.

Change in Colonization Form After the Liberation of the Asian-African Colonies

Colonialism did not end; rather it changed its form and it manifested itself in a non-formal way. After the liberation of Asian and African colonies, the form of colonization changed from direct political control to indirect control through economic and cultural means. The former colonial powers continued to exert influence over their former colonies through trade agreements, aid programs, and cultural exchange programs. This new form of colonialism was referred to as neo-colonialism and was characterized by the continued economic dependence of the former colonies on the developed world. Its manifestation can be seen as follows-

1. **In the Economic sector:**
   - (a) Just after decolonization, institutions like the IMF, World Bank, and GATT were established in order to maintain western economic hegemony.
   - (b) To encourage capital investment and open the service sector in developing nations in the name of economic liberalization.
2. **In the Social sector:**
   - (a) A programme of racial discrimination against non-Europeans and the labelling of them as 'Orientals'.
3. **In the Cultural sector:**
   - (a) Western intellectuals divided the world into a core region (West) and a peripheral region (East), attempting to show that all significant and forward-thinking concepts started in the core region (West) and spread from there to the peripheral region (East).
   - (b) Michel Foucault, a postmodernist philosopher, has given the concept of power and argued that 'knowledge is superimposed by the higher authority.' Consequently, Western scholars maintained their hegemony over subjects like history, sociology, political science, anthropology, and other after making research on them, and their analysis was inclined to prove the superiority of the West. This is probably the most dangerous form of colonialism.

The Rise of Third World

The phrase 'Third World' has two distinct meanings: political and economic. The capitalist nations of western Europe are referred to as the 'First World' in a political context, whereas the communist nations of eastern Europe are referred to as the 'Second World.' On the other hand, the newly independent nations of Asia, Africa, and Latin America are referred to as being in the Third World. Similarly, in an economic sense, the phrase 'Third World' refers to nations that share certain socioeconomic problems, such as large birth rates, low per capita incomes, weak sections of the health and education sectors, etc.

Achievements of the Third World

1. **Formation of Third World Organisation:** Third World nations started taking the initiative to form several associations in the late 1940s. For instance, Nehru's advocacy led to the convening of the Asian Relations Conference in New Delhi in March 1947. A similar conference concerning the independence of Indonesia was held in New Delhi in 1949. The Bandung Conference, which featured 29 Asian-African nations, was organized later in 1955. Particularly after the Bandung Conference, there was a considerable improvement in Third-World nation consolidation.

Points to Ponder

The Third World nations organized NAM at Belgrade in 1961.

2. **Common opinion on important international issues:** At the international forum, they could form a common opinion on important international issues like colonialism, imperialism, racialism, etc. Later, even western powers were compelled to accept their importance in these forums.

Challenges Before Third World Nations

1. Following their independence, the majority of the third-world countries adopted a capitalist form of governance, and as a result, their economies naturally became dependent on the developed economies of the western world. Their economic dependence on western nations naturally rendered their economic freedom ineffective. Additionally,

multinational corporations and multilateral organizations like the IMF, World Bank, and GATT frequently interfered with the economies of Third World nations.

2. Following the Berlin Blockade in 1949, peace and stability returned to the First World (Western Europe) during the Cold War. Similarly, even Second World (eastern Europe) stabilized after the initial disturbance. However, the Third World has continued to be disturbed and damaged as a result of being the main theatre of the proxy wars between both superpowers (USA and USSR), such as the Vietnam War and the Afghanistan Crisis.
3. Above all, in the 1990s, economic liberalization policy was enforced on third-world countries based on the Washington Consensus, and on that basis, their market was forcefully opened. The Washington Consensus is a set of economic policy recommendations, which emphasized market-oriented policies such as fiscal discipline, monetary stability, trade liberalization, and private property rights for developing countries by international financial institutions like the IMF.

NON-ALIGNED MOVEMENT

The Non-Aligned Movement (NAM) is an international movement of countries that are not formally aligned with or against any major power bloc. It was started in 1961, in Belgrade by Yugoslavia's President Josip Broz Tito, India's first Prime Minister Jawaharlal Nehru, Egypt's second President Gamal Abdel Nasser, Ghana's first President Kwame Nkrumah, Indonesia's first President Sukarno, and other leaders from countries in Asia, Africa, and Latin America. The purpose of the organization was to promote solidarity among these countries, to promote mutual respect and understanding, and to prevent the world from being divided into two hostile blocs of the Cold War.

> *"The Non-Aligned Movement played an important role in international politics during the Cold War, representing the interests of the developing world, and helping to shape the outcome of the Cold War in ways that often went beyond the expectations of its founders.*
> ***—Dr. Erika Harris (Historian)"***

Nevertheless, non-alignment does not imply a neutral policy like the policy of isolation which had been followed by the USA from the era of the Munro Doctrine to the Second World War. In fact, the non-alignment strategy was adopted by Austria and Switzerland in international politics. On the contrary, non-alignment requires active engagement in global politics. It involves making independent decisions about significant global issues without being influenced by any superpower **(Refer Map 11.4).**

Causes Behind the Formation of Non-aligned Movement

The Non-Aligned Movement (NAM) was formed in the mid-20th century in response to the Cold War between the two superpowers, the United States and the Soviet Union. The main causes behind the formation of NAM include:

1. **Cold War:** The formation of the NAM was a direct result of the Cold War between the United States and the Soviet Union. The Cold War saw the two superpowers divide the world into two camps, the capitalist West and the communist East. The countries that were part of the NAM wanted to remain independent and neutral, rejecting both of the superpowers' ideologies. Additionally, Third-world countries

would expect economic help for their reconstruction programmes from both blocks simultaneously under the policy of non-alignment.

> *The Non-Aligned Movement was a reaction to the Cold War, and its chief architects were Jawaharlal Nehru of India, Gamal Abdel Nasser of Egypt, and Josip Broz Tito of Yugoslavia. It was a means for these states to express solidarity with the developing world and to reject the bipolar power structure of the Cold War.*
>
> ***—James Bell (Historian)***

2. **Peace and economic development:** Economic development was given first priority by newly independent Asia-African countries. Thus, joining any block involved using up of limited resources on military spending instead of development initiatives. Moreover, the NAM also sought to promote peace and economic development among its members and to provide a forum for discussing international issues.
3. **Sovereignty:** They came to realize that to join any military block meant to get their foreign policy mortgaged and, in that eventuality, their hard-earned freedom would be meaningless.
4. **A counterbalance organization:** The NAM also served as a counterbalance to the two superpowers' power. The desire of countries in the global south was to assert their independence and avoid domination by the superpowers. Moreover, it acted as a unifying force for countries in the Third World and was a significant factor at the end of colonialism and apartheid.

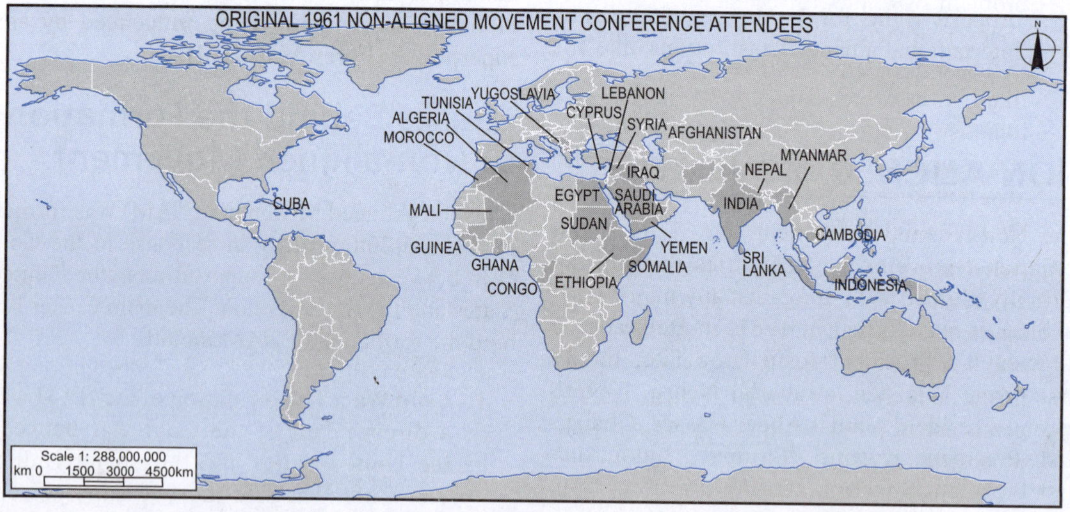

MAP 11.4: Original 1961 Non-Aligned Movement Conference Attendees

- The external boundaries and coastlines of India agree with the Record/Master Copy certified by Survey of India.
- The spellings of names in this map, have been taken from various sources.
- The administrative boundaries of J&K UT and Ladākh UT shown here are yet to be authenticated by concerned authorities

Contribution of Non-aligned Movement

NAM was established in 1961 as a response to the Cold War and aimed to promote peace, equality, and economic development among its members. Some of the key contributions of NAM include:

1. **Providing a platform for dialogue:** NAM has provided a platform for its member countries to engage in open and constructive dialogue on a range of global issues, including peace and security, economic development, and human rights. Moreover, non-alignment worked as a strong pressure group against the imperialist powers in UNO.
2. **Impact on world politics:** The non-alignment doctrine has had an impact on world politics ever since it was first established in Belgrade. The key global issues have always been addressed by the NAM. For instance, during its first meeting, it brought up the problem of a nuclear test by France while concurrently demanding that China be admitted to the UN and the Security Council. In addition, it brought up the subject of colonialism from the outset as well as the issue of apartheid in South Africa. Additionally, non-alignment worked on the front for the liberation of colonies.
3. **Advocating for global disarmament:** NAM has been a strong advocate for disarmament and arms control and has held several international conferences to promote this agenda. Non-alignment also carried the persistent demand for the democratization of economic relations at the international level.
4. **Supporting economic development:** NAM has also played a role in promoting economic development among its member countries, especially in areas such as trade, technology transfer, and investment.

Limitations of Non-aligned Movement

1. **Ideological differences:** The member countries had different ideologies and this resulted in ideological differences within the movement. Moreover, some NAM members frequently attach themselves to either superpower, casting doubt on the concept 'non-alignment.'
2. **Lack of common security policy:** The member countries had different views on security matters, making it difficult to develop a common security policy.
3. **Limited resources:** The Non-Aligned Movement had limited resources and this made it difficult to mount effective diplomatic and economic pressure on the world powers. Even the apartheid regime of South Africa could not take the NAM seriously.
4. **Cold War influence:** The movement was greatly influenced by the Cold War and this limited its ability to effectively challenge the policies of the major powers. NAM persistently failed to stop any major international war like the Iran-Iraq war.

Relevance of Non-aligned Movement

Since the 1990s, the issue of whether NAM is still relevant in the post Cold War world has been raised frequently. However, the relevance of the Non-Aligned Movement lies in its role as a voice for the developing world and its efforts to promote peace, equality, and economic cooperation among its member states.

1. The original objective of NAM was to protect the basic interest of the Third World, as at that time Cold War and block politics worked as a major threat to the interest of the Third World nations. However, even now, after the Cold War, the nations' fundamental interests are not only in danger, but they are also more open to imperialist powers' intervention. Here NAM can work as an important forum for protecting their interest.

2. In addition, a multilateral strategy is required to resolve many important worldwide problems in the globalized era, such as terrorism, environmental difficulties, etc. Therefore, it is only conceivable after extensive international cooperation. We should keep in mind that since NAM is the second-largest organization after UNO, it can serve as an effective forum here.
3. Third-world countries are also concerned and alarmed by the arm-twisting tactics used by the developed countries against them on such important international issues. Even in that circumstance, NAM can function as a potent bulwark against such strategies. However, we should restructure NAM with new initiatives and objectives if we want to increase its effectiveness.
4. NAM has played a significant role in promoting a more balanced and multipolar world and promoting South-South cooperation, particularly in the fields of development, trade, and technology.

In conclusion, the Non-Aligned Movement remains relevant in the contemporary international system as a voice for the developing world and a platform for promoting cooperation, peace, and development.

UNITED NATIONS ORGANIZATION (UNO)

The United Nations (UN) was established on October 24, 1945, after World War II, with the aim of preventing another global conflict by promoting international cooperation and security. The UN's objectives are to foster international relations, promote economic, social, and cultural development, and provide humanitarian aid.

Factors for the Formation of UNO

The main factors leading to the formation of the United Nations (UN) were:

1. The tragedy of the Second World War, in which nearly 4 million people died and more than 2 million were left homeless. Thus, the need for international cooperation in the aftermath of World War II, with the aim of preventing another global conflict led to the formation of the UN.

> *The United Nations represents not a final stage in the development of world order, but only a primitive stage. Therefore, its primary task is to create the conditions which will make possible a more highly developed organization.*
>
> ***—Arnold J. Toynbee (British Historian)***

2. The desire to establish a new international order based on principles of peace, justice, and respect for human rights as perceived by the Atlantic Charter of 1941. The Atlantic Charter was a joint statement issued by British Prime Minister Winston Churchill and US President Franklin D. Roosevelt on August 14, 1941, during the Second World War. It set forth their vision for a post-war world, including the principles of national self-determination (the right of all people to choose their own form of government) and the promotion of economic cooperation and social welfare. The Atlantic Charter provided the foundation for the United Nations.
3. The recognition of the need to promote economic and social development, and to address issues such as poverty, disease, and hunger.
4. The desire to address issues related to decolonization and the creation of new nation-states in the aftermath of World War II.
5. The need for a platform for dialogue and diplomacy between nations to address global challenges and promote peace and stability.

These factors came together in the signing of the United Nations Charter on June 26, 1945, which established the UN as a successor to the League of Nations, and laid the foundation for the organization's work in promoting peace, security, and development.

Differences between the League of Nations and the United Nation

After the failure of the League of Nations, UN was established, and efforts were made to improve and strengthen it. However, the League of Nations and the United Nations (UN) differ in several ways in terms of their structure and functions.

1. **Membership:** Compared to the League of Nations, the UN is more representative. The League had a smaller membership, with only 42 member states at its height. The UN has 193 member states and a more complex structure, including a General Assembly, where all member states are represented, a Security Council with 5 permanent members and 10 non-permanent members, an International Court of Justice, and various specialized agencies.

> *The League of Nations was the first attempt to build a world organization to protect peace and stability. It was largely a failure, but it inspired the creation of the United Nations, an organization that has been much more successful in maintaining international peace.*
>
> ***—Kofi Annan (Former Secretary-General of the UN)***

2. **Power of security council:** The failure of the League of Nations was attributed mostly to the equal power of the Assembly and Council. Thus, UN Security Council acquired more authority than the UN General Assembly.
3. **Structure:** The structure of the League of Nations was much simpler than the United Nations. The League of Nations had only four main organs – the Assembly, the Council, the Permanent Court of International Justice, and the Secretariat. The UN, on the other hand, is composed of six main organs – the General Assembly, the Security Council, the Economic and Social Council, the Trusteeship Council, the International Court of Justice, and the Secretariat.
4. **Function:** The League's primary aim was to prevent another world war and it had limited powers to enforce its decisions. It could not act unless a dispute was referred to it by a member state, and it had no military force to enforce its decisions. The UN has a wider range of responsibilities and powers, including maintaining international peace and security, promoting economic and social development, protecting human rights, and providing humanitarian assistance. It has a peacekeeping force and the power to take collective military action to enforce its decisions.
5. **Special power to permanent members:** Powerful nations have no special rights within the League of Nations. As a result, they lacked the enthusiasm to fight for world peace. Thus, at the UN, there is a concept of special status for powerful countries in addition to the equality of all nations. This is in the form of the 'Veto' power granted to the Security Council's five permanent members.
6. **Enforcement power:** The League of Nations was largely ineffective due to the lack of enforcement power. The League was only able to make recommendations to its member countries, and it had no way to enforce its decisions. The UN, on the other hand, has the authority to impose sanctions on countries that violate international law.

7. **Military system:** When compared to the UN, the League of Nations lacked any kind of military system. The UN may employ force against countries that are obstructing international peace.

   Overall, the UN has a more comprehensive and complex structure and a broader range of responsibilities and powers compared to the League of Nations.

Achievements of the United Nations

The United Nations (UN) has achieved many significant political, economic, social, and cultural accomplishments since its creation in 1945, including:

1. **Political contribution:** The UN has successfully prevented and resolved numerous international conflicts and maintained peace through its peacekeeping missions. The UN was significant in resolving numerous international disputes such as the Suez Canal Crisis of 1956, the Congo Crisis of 1961, the Gulf Crisis of 1990-1991, the Cambodia Crisis of 1993, and others. Additionally, the UN has been a major force in strengthening international cooperation. It has established various organizations and committees to promote dialogue and cooperation between nations and has helped to create a more peaceful and prosperous world.
2. **Economic contribution:** The UN has made significant progress in reducing poverty and hunger worldwide through its development programs, including the Millennium Development Goals. UN promotes innovative research through its specialized organizations like the IMF, ILO, etc. to improve the global economic condition.
3. **Social contribution:** The UN provides humanitarian assistance to those affected by natural disasters, armed conflicts, and other crises. Additionally, it made a significant advancement in the realm of health. Polio and smallpox are now under control. The UN has played a key role in promoting gender equality and women's empowerment, including through the creation of UN women.
4. **Cultural contribution:** It is admirable that United Nations is working to restore the remnants of ancient cultures. The UN has made significant contributions to the advancement of human rights globally, including the Universal Declaration of Human Rights and the establishment of the office of the High Commissioner for Human Rights.

   The UN has also played a key role in shaping international norms and laws, such as the Universal Declaration of Human Rights, the Convention on the Rights of the Child, and the Paris Agreement on climate change.

Limitations of United Nation

According to Samantha Power, former US Ambassador to the United Nations and historian, 'The United Nations has proven to be an effective tool in dealing with international conflicts, but its limitations have become increasingly clear. It is hampered by the lack of enforcement power, the difficulty in reaching consensus among its members, and the slow pace of decision-making.'

1. **Failing to prevent some war:** In the political sphere, it has had little success. The veto system prevented the system from operating effectively during the Cold War. It was ineffective even after the end of the Cold War. For instance, the UN failed to effectively stop or manage the US invasion of Iraq in 2003, the Libyan conflict in 2011, and the military conflict in Syria.
2. **Outdated structure:** Since the organization's founding in 1945, its structure has essentially not changed even though many things have changed since then. The UN's current structure does not accurately reflect the global power balance, leading to unequal representation and decision-making. Therefore, this structure should be changed, and emerging powers like India, Brazil, Japan, and Nigeria should be given new positions.

3. **Limited funding:** UN has no suitable financing structure. The UN relies on member states to fund its operations and programs, which can lead to financial constraints and limited resources. Moreover, due to the organization's reliance on US funding, the US has an excessive influence over it.
4. **Lack of enforcement power:** The United Nations does not have its own military force and therefore, relies on member countries to enforce its resolutions and mandates. This is a major limitation as member countries may be unwilling or unable to commit their own resources to the cause.
5. **Ineffective decision-making:** The UN's decision-making process is often slow and ineffective due to the need for consensus among member states and the influence of major powers. Additionally, the UN is subjected to the political divisions of its member states. Decisions are often blocked by the veto power of the five permanent members of the Security Council, leading to inaction in critical areas.

LET'S REVISE

Causes for the Rise of Communism in China

1. The Legacy of Imperialism
2. Failure of Westernization of China
3. The Failure of the Nationalist government
4. Disappointment during the Paris Peace Conference
5. The Success of the Soviet Union
6. The Spread of Marxist ideology

Causes for the Success of the Chinese Communist Party in 1949

1. Realpolitik by the Chinese Communist Party
2. Support from the Soviet Union
3. Support from the peasantry
4. Ideological appeal
5. Japanese invasion of China
6. Nationalist weaknesses
7. Poor economic conditions

Limitations of the Chinese Revolution

1. One-Party rule
2. Cultural suppression
3. Agricultural reforms
4. Promoted violence

Causes of Decolonization

1. Second World War
2. Economic factors
3. Political factors
4. Intellectual factors
5. New power equation and Cold War
6. Role of United Nations

Indian Contribution to the liberation of Africa

1. Diplomatic support
2. Ideological support
3. Inspiration from Gandhi

Factors that Supported the Growth of the Imperialism in Africa

1. Role of explorers
2. Political weakness
3. Lack of industrial growth in Africa
4. Military failure
5. Huge size of the African continent

Reasons for Delay in African Decolonization

1. European needs for raw materials
2. Delay in the rise of the Nationalist movement
3. Diverse ethnicity and lack of trust
4. Cold War politics
5. Presence of Racism

Causes behind Formation of Non-aligned Movement

1. Cold War
2. Peace and economic development
3. Sovereignty
4. A counterbalance organization

Contribution of Non-aligned Movement

1. Providing a platform for dialogue
2. Impact on world politics
3. Advocating for global disarmament
4. Supporting economic development

Limitations of Non-aligned Movement

1. Ideological differences
2. Lack of common security policy
3. Limited resources
4. Cold War influence

Differences between the League of Nations and United Nations

1. Membership
2. Power of the Security Council
3. Structure
4. Function
5. Special power to permanent members
6. Enforcement power
7. Military system

Achievements of the United Nations

1. Political contribution
2. Economic contribution
3. Social contribution
4. Cultural contribution

UPSC PREVIOUS YEARS' QUESTIONS

1. What problems were germane to the decolonization process in the Malay Peninsula? **[2017] (10 marks)**
2. The anti-colonial struggles in West Africa were led by the new elite of Western-educated Africans. Examine. **[2016] (12.5 marks)**

PROBABLE QUESTIONS

1. The most far-reaching consequence of Second World War was the decolonization of 19th-century empires. Discuss.
2. Explain the circumstances that favoured European imperialism in Africa. In the process of decolonization, why Africa was decolonised later than Asia?
3. Discuss the factors constraining development of Africa after decolonization.
4. Write a critical note on the process of decolonization accelerated by the Second World War.
5. Trace the significant role played by Ho Chi Minh in Vietnam's struggle for freedom.
6. Why did Vietnam go through thirty years of war after the Second World War?
7. Explain the features of Apartheid in South Africa.
8. Explain why Bolivar's efforts failed to fructify in bringing about united stand of the Latin Americans.

TIMELINE OF CHINESE HISTORY (1644–1992)

1644-1912 CE
Qing dynasty: The Qing dynasty was the last imperial dynasty of China, founded by the Manchu people.

1912-1949 CE
Republic of China: The Republic of China was established after the fall of the Qing dynasty and was marked by political instability, social unrest, and foreign invasions.

1919
May Fourth Movement: This student-led movement was called for cultural and political reforms in China and marked the beginning of the Chinese intellectual movement.

1926-1928
Northern Expedition: This military campaign led by the Nationalist Party (Kuomintang) was aimed at unifying China and defeating the warlords who controlled various regions.

1927-1949
Chinese Civil War: This was a political and military struggle between the Nationalist Party and the Communist Party of China for controlling China. The war was interrupted by the Second Sino-Japanese War (1937-1945), during which China fought against Japan.

1934-1935
Long March: This was a military retreat by the Communist Party from their base in Jiangxi to Shaanxi, covering a distance of about 9,000 kilometres.

1936
Xian Incident (1936): This was a political crisis in which General Zhang Xueliang and Yang Hucheng kidnapped Chiang Kai-shek, the leader of the Nationalist Party, and forced him to form a united front with the Communist Party against Japan.

1937-1945
Second United Front: This was a temporary alliance between the Nationalist Party and the Communist Party to fight against Japan during the Second Sino-Japanese War.

1945-1949
Chinese Communist Revolution (1945-1949): After Japan's surrender in 1945, the Chinese Civil War resumed. The Communist Party emerged victorious in 1949, establishing the People's Republic of China, while the Nationalist Party retreated to Taiwan.

1958-1962
Great Leap Forward: An economic and social campaign initiated by Mao Tse Tung, which aimed to transform China from an agrarian economy to a modern industrialized society. It resulted in widespread famine and economic disaster.

1966-1976
Cultural Revolution: This was a political and social movement initiated by Mao Tse Tung, which aimed to purify the Communist Party and eliminate perceived enemies. It led to widespread violence, persecution, and disruption of Chinese society.

1978-1992
Deng Xiaoping's reforms: After Mao's death, Deng Xiaoping initiated a series of economic and political reforms that opened up China to the world and led to significant economic growth.

TIMELINE OF DECOLONIZATION IN SOUTH EAST ASIA (1945–1999)

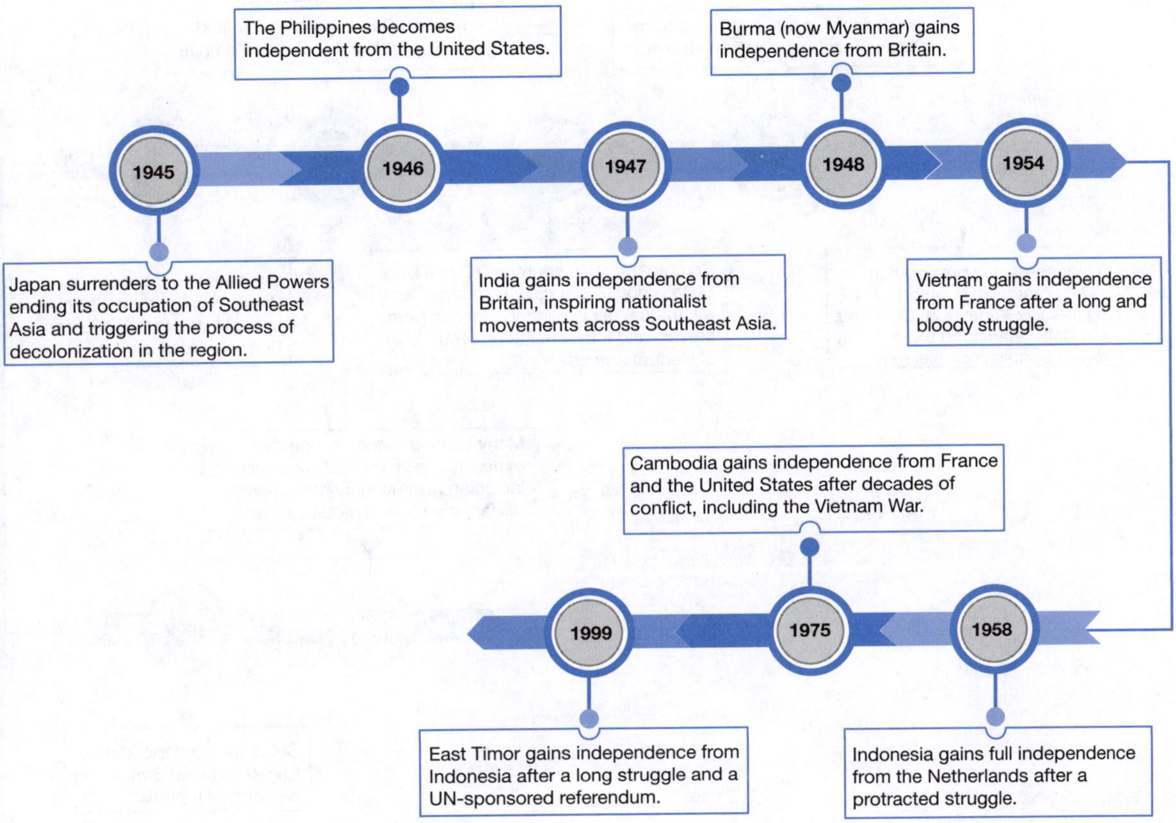

TIMELINE OF DECOLONIZATION IN LATIN AMERICA (1810–1970s)

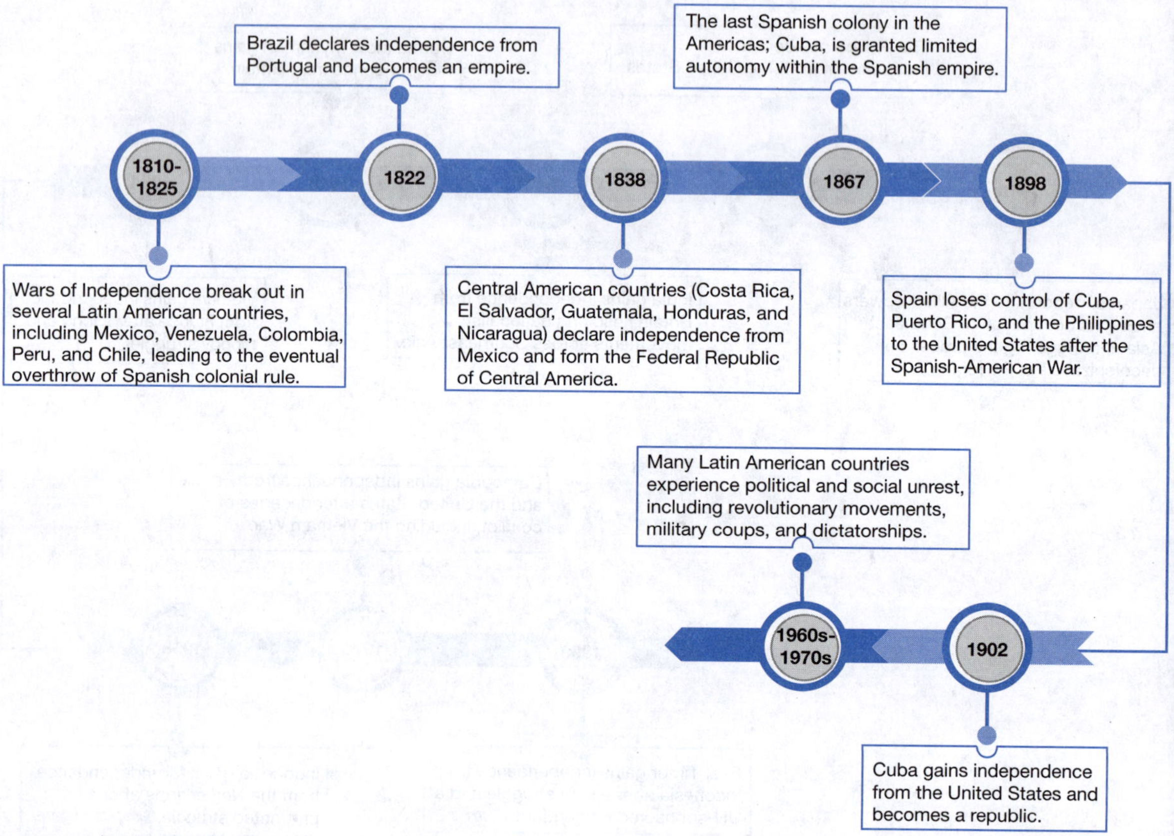

TIMELINE OF DECOLONIZATION IN AFRICA (1884–1990s)

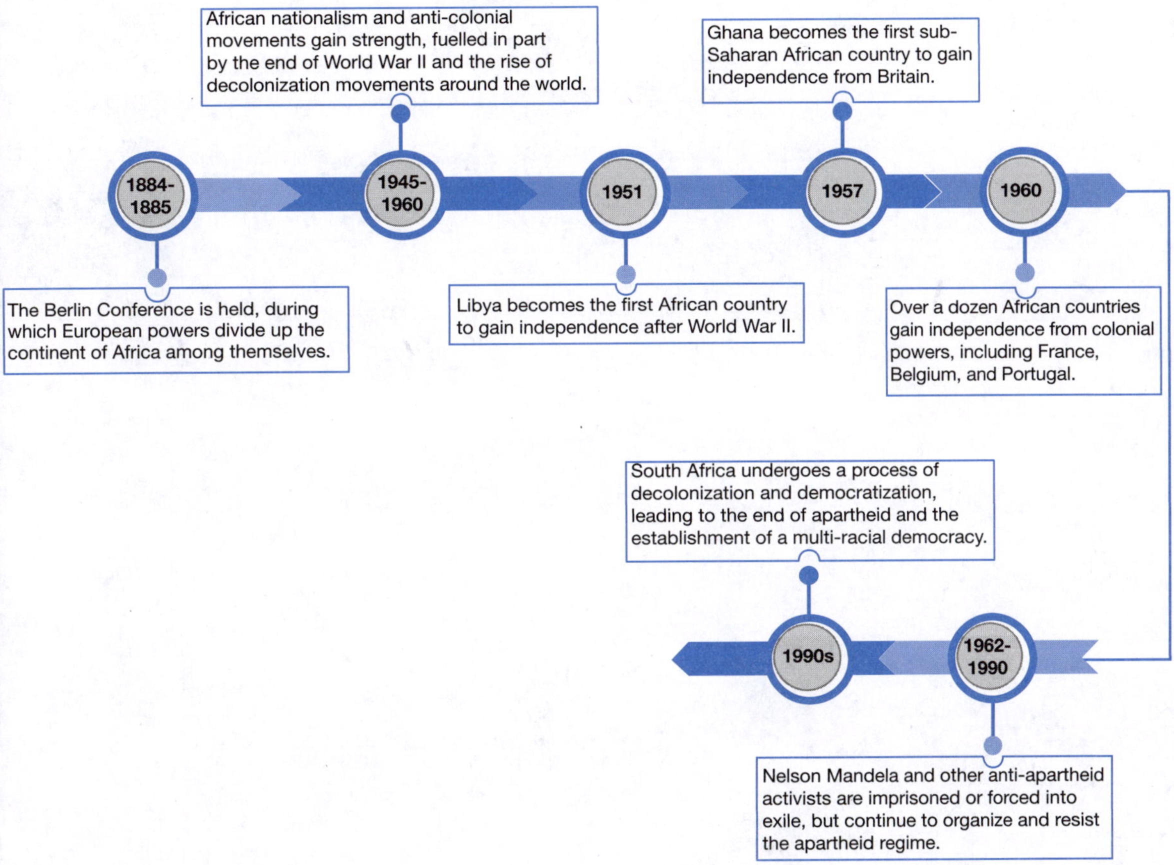

1 American Revolution and Civil War

AMERICAN HISTORY FROM REVOLUTION TO CIVIL WAR

- **1756-1763**: The Seven Years' War happens between (Austria, Prussia, Great Britain, France, and Russia) and the Treaty of Paris ended this Seven Years' War
- **Oct. 1765**: The Stamp Act was one of the first acts of the taxation imposed by the British government on the American colonies without their consent, and it sparked outrage in the colonies.
- **1770**: Boston Massacre was a confrontation between British soldiers and American colonists in 1770 which resulted in the deaths of five colonists
- **1773**: Boston Tea Party occurs, in which colonists disguised as Native Americans dump British tea into Boston harbour in protest of the Tea Act
- **April 1775**: The American Revolutionary War begins with the Battle of Lexington and Concord
- **July 4, 1776**: The Continental Congress adopts the Declaration of Independence, officially declaring independence from Britain
- **Aug. Dec 1776**: The Battle of Long Island, (the largest battle of the Revolutionary War) and the Battle of Trenton takes place
- **Oct. 1777**: The Battle of Saratoga, a major turning point in the war, takes place in upstate New York
- **Feb. 1778**: The Treaty of Alliance with France is signed, giving America crucial support from the French government and military
- **March 1781**: The Articles of Confederation, the first constitution of the United States, are ratified
- **Sept. 1781**: The Battle of Yorktown, the last major battle of the Revolutionary War, takes place in Virginia
- **Sept. 1783**: The Treaty of Paris is signed, officially ending the American Revolutionary War and recognizing the independence of the United States.
- **1860**: Abraham Lincoln is elected President of the United States
- **1861**: The Confederate States of America is formed, and the Confederate forces fire on Fort Sumter, starting the Civil War.
- **1863**: The Emancipation Proclamation is issued, and the Battle of Gettysburg, takes place in Pennsylvania, in July 1-3
- **Dec. 6, 1865**: The 13th Amendment to the U.S. Constitution, which abolished slavery, is ratified.
- **April 9, 1865**: Confederate General Robert E. Lee surrenders to Union General Ulysses S. Grant at Appomattox Courthouse in Virginia, effectively ending the war.

1. American Revolution was an economic revolt against mercantilism. Substantiate.

Model Answer

1. American Revolution was an economic revolt against mercantilism. Substantiate.

Approach

- Explain how the American Revolt was an economic revolt.
- Explain other factors for American Revolution.

The American Revolution or the American War of Independence was caused by a number of long-term as well short-term factors, including the Seven Years' War, the Crown's Proclamation of 1763, the imposition of multiple taxes, the conflict between American and British capitalism, nature of American population, the revolution in the realm of ideas and many other factors.

The American Revolution was an economic revolt against mercantilism. Mercantilism was an economic system that was used by the British to control the colonies' economy and to benefit from their natural resources. British mercantilism was inclined to bring the American economy under strict British colonial control. For this purpose following steps were taken-

(a) **Navigation Acts** – It was introduced in the 17th century to promote the British shipping industry at the cost of American shipping. It had a provision that all sorts of exports to and imports from American colonies could have been done or carried on only in British ships, or in the ships in which at least 75 % of employees should have been British.

(b) **Enumerated Commodities Act 1660** – Colonies were compelled to export sugar, tobacco, cotton, and indigo only to England.

(c) British tried to bring monetary policy and export-import policy of American colonies under British control. Furthermore, on the purchase of two products, tobacco and maize, from American colonies, there was a complete British monopoly. Not simply that, the British even discouraged industrialization in American colonies.

The American economy was a fast-growing economy. American industry in general and the shipping industry in particular, could not thrive if the British control could not been relaxed. Americans realized that they could not go for industrialization in British presence.

However, apart from economic factors, other factors like the Seven Years' War, the Crown's Proclamation of 1763, the imposition of multiple taxes, the nature of the American population, and the revolution in the realm of ideas caused the American Revolution.

2. 'The American War of Independence transformed Europe as well as America.' Critically examine.

Model Answer

2. 'The American War of Independence transformed Europe as well as America.' Critically examine.

Approach

- Explain how the American War of Independence transformed Europe.
- Explain how the American War of Independence transformed America.

The American Revolution had significant and widespread repercussions on both America and Europe.

EFFECTS ON WORLD

Inspired the European and Other Non European Freedom Movements

American Revolution led to three major events which had significant and far-reaching consequences on Europe and the Liberation Movement. These were documents of the Declaration of Independence, the implementation of ideas of enlightenment and liberal and constitutional values in the US Constitution.

The significance of the American Revolution lies in the fact that it was the:

1. First successful revolution against an European empire.
2. First time a colony had rebelled successfully.
3. First republican form of democratically elected government.

The above facts inspired many European nations and colonies to revolt against the colonial empire and free the mother country from the clutches of colonial imperialism. American Revolution inspired

1. Ireland to pursue armed rebellion against Britain.
2. Liberation movement from Spanish and Portuguese colonial rule in South America under Simon Bolivar in 1820s.
3. French Revolution and French Declaration of Rights of man and citizen of 1789.

EFFECTS ON AMERICA

Some historians criticized the American Revolution as it did not lead to radical consequences as in French Revolution or revolutionary Russia. Some other historians criticize the American Revolution as it did not lead to the empowerment of women and slavery. They argue:

1. American Revolution did not abolish slavery and empowerment of women.
2. American Revolution did not significantly change the structure of American society; rather, reinforced the political, economic, and social status quo.
3. American Revolution did not establish a truly democratic government. Nevertheless, no truly democratic nations existed in the late 18th century.
4. American Revolution did not create a new economic structure; rather kept capitalism to speed up the process of industrialization.

Nevertheless, some other historians argue that American Revolution and revolutionary spirit impacted nearly every aspect of the American life. The attitude of Americans changed forever. Some changes in society were carried out immediately and while some later like abolition of slavery and empowerment of Women. Slavery was not abolished for another 100 years but the revolutionary spirit led to organization of the Abolitionist Movement. Moreover, these historians argue that and revolutionary spirit and ideas produced a new outlook among Americans which had huge ramifications into future.

2 French Revolution and Rise of Napoleon

FRENCH HISTORY FROM STORMING OF THE BASTILLE TO BATTLE OF WATERLOO

- **1769** — Napoleon Bonaparte is born on Corsica Island.
- **1778** — The French entered the war on the side of the American Revolutionaries.
- **July 14, 1789** — Storming of the Bastille, a prison in Paris, is seen as the start of the French Revolution.
- **Sep. 21, 1791** — The Declaration of the Rights of Man and Citizen is adopted, outlining the rights and freedoms of the French people.
- **Sep. 20, 1792** — The French monarchy is abolished, and France is declared a republic.
- **Jan. 21, 1793** — King Louis XVI is executed by guillotine.
- **Sep. 5, 1793** — The Reign of Terror begins, as the committee of public safety cracks down on those seen as enemies of the Revolution.
- **July 27, 1794** — The Reign of Terror ends and Maximilien Robespierre, a key leader of the Revolution, is arrested and executed.
- **1795** — Napoleon leads the successful defense of the national convention against an insurrection.
- **1796** — Napoleon leads the French army in Italy, successfully defeating the Austrians.
- **1797** — Napoleon signs the Treaty of Campo Formio, ending the War of the First Coalition.
- **Nov. 9,1799** — Napoleon Bonaparte seizes power in a coup, marking the end of the French Revolution and the start of the Napoleonic era.
- **1804** — Napoleon is crowned Emperor of France.
- **1805** — Napoleon wins the Battle of Austerlitz against a coalition of Austrian and Russian forces, becoming the most powerful man in Europe.
- **1812** — Napoleon invades Russia, but his grand army is defeated and forced to retreat due to the brutal winter.
- **1814** — Napoleon abdicates the throne and is exiled to the island of Elba.
- **1815** — Napoleon escapes from Elba and returns to France, but is defeated at the Battle of Waterloo.
- **1815** — Napoleon is exiled to the island of Saint Helena, where he dies in 1821.

1. 'The causes of the French Revolution of 1789 included both long-term and structural factors, as well as more immediate events.' Critically examine.

Model Answer

1. 'The causes of the French Revolution of 1789 included both long-term and structural factors, as well as more immediate events.' Critically examine.

Approach

- Explain the immediate cause of the French Revolution.
- Explain long-term and structural causes.

The causes of the French Revolution are complex and are still debated among historians. The foundation for the revolution has been attributed to a number of political, economic and social factors, which among other things included growing social inequality, new political ideologies from the enlightenment, economic mismanagement, environmental factors that led to agricultural failure, an unmanageable national debt, and political mismanagement on the part of King Louis XVI.

Immediate Cause: Financial Crisis

After Louis XIV's several wars, the Seven Years' War, the corrupt extravagance of Louis XV and Louis XVI, and the American Revolutionary War, the French government was heavily in debt and tried to improve its financial situation through controversial taxation methods.

The French government's financial crisis and its desperate efforts to find a solution led to the summoning of the Estate General (which had been in an animated state for the previous 175 years) as the 1st and 2nd estates argued that only the Estate General had the authority to impose new taxes and not the French monarch. But it was in the Estate General on the issue of voting those differences among different classes took the form of a political crisis.

Finally, the representatives of the third estate boycotted the assembly of the Estate General and moved to the Tennis Court Assembly. It is here they were joined by artisans of Paris and peasants of France, popularly known as the 'Mob of Paris'. Thus, the revolution started.

Long Term and Structural Causes

1. **Feudal Social Division:** French society was based on an ancient regime, divided into the privileged and the unprivileged class. The first estate (clergy) and the second estate (nobility) made up the privileged class, while the third estate (middle and lower class) made up the unprivileged class.
2. **Economic Causes:** The French economy had significant growth between the 1730s and 1760s, but from the 1770s onward, a depressive scenario predominated. Moreover, the French Industrial Revolution did not begin until the 1780s and the bulk of industry suffered from poor production while agriculture remained mired in the medieval era with most of the land controlled by feudal lords and minimal infrastructure development.
3. **Political Causes:** Louis XIV fought many wars which became one of the factors for financial bankruptcy. Nevertheless, he was a capable king. But Louis XV and Louis XVI were weak kings. Anybody could be imprisoned by warrants, called 'letters de cachet'. Therefore, French government became corrupt, oppressive and arbitrary which led to widespread discontent among the French people.
4. **Ideological Factors:** The influence of enlightenment philosophers, such as Rousseau, Voltaire, and Montesquieu, and their ideas on human rights and government played a very important role in the French Revolution. Deglorification of the institution of absolute monarchy was based on the concept of Divine Theory. It led to the hostility of royal absolutism, criticism of the policy of Louise XVI, hate of Queen Marie-Antoinette, and anger towards the oppressive and corrupt administration. Moreover, recommends the creation of a modern society based on the 'rule of law', 'equality', and 'reason' instead of traditions. It encouraged the French people to strive for social, political, and economic equality as well as republicanism.

2. 'Napoleon showed himself at once, the heir of the revolution and the product of the reaction against it.' Comment.

Model Answer

2. 'Napoleon showed himself at once, the heir of the revolution and the product of the reaction against it.' Comment.

Approach

- Explain how Napoleon was a child of the revolution.
- Explain how Napoleon worked against revolution.

Napoleon adopted the principle of fraternity and equality in social and financial affairs but rejected the 'principle of liberty, which was one of the founding ideas of the French Revolution. By proclaiming, 'I am the Revolution,' Napoleon referred to himself as a child of the revolution.

However, historians differ about whether or not, Napoleon was a child of the French Revolution. Napoleon Bonaparte is viewed by some historians as a child of the French Revolution, while other historians consider him as the product of the reaction against it.

Napoleon was a Child of the Revolution

(a) Napoleon positioned himself as the 'Representative for Revolution' and the 'Architect of Modern Europe' based on revolution's principles. Therefore, he welcomed and promoted revolutionary ideals even in conquered territory.
(b) The French Revolution opened the gate for the rise of talent and merit against the pre-revolutionary birth-based privilege system.
(c) Napoleon was able to preserve certain revolutionary ideas in the religious sphere. He ended the excess of the Revolution (Reign of Terror) by signing the concordat with the Pope, which healed division in the church and among the people.
(d) Napoleon's Code of 1804 was based on revolutionary ideals of equality and religious toleration. It also abolished the feudal privilege structure, based on birth.
(e) In pre-revolutionary France, all government posts were opened only to the 1st and 2nd estate and not to the third estate. Napoleon also abolished aristocratic privilege and opened all government posts to all on the basis of merit and principle of equality.

Napoleon Worked Against Revolution

(a) Napoleon undermined the republican ideals of the French Revolution by restoring the monarchy in a modified form in 1804 and even tying his legacy to earlier Bourbon kings.
(b) He favoured using his secret police to eliminate his opponents and carried out his work through plebiscite while ignoring the legislative body which was against the ideals of democracy.
(c) Napoleon viewed liberty as a disruptive force that prohibited a state from functioning effectively.
(d) Napoleon removed the autonomy of local departments and imposed centralization via a prefect and a sub-prefect.
(e) Napoleon, especially outside of France, tended to represent the misguided and distorted ideas of the revolution.

Due to the centralized government, the curtailment of political freedom, the expansion of the empire, opposition to the ideals of nationality, mercantilist continental policy, and the return to Louis XIV's methods, some historians view Napoleon Bonaparte as a 'Destroyer of Revolution' rather than its 'child.'

Napoleon nevertheless encouraged the idea of equality by eliminating privileges and social barriers and by opening up jobs to merit. He established a centralized administration and was against the idea of liberty. Therefore, it was correctly remarked that historically Napoleon represented a period of transition. He was among the last of a series of benevolent despots, and was at the same time one of the first of great modern statesmen.

3 British Democratic Politics

BRITISH HISTORY FROM MAGNA CARTA TO VOTING RIGHT TO ALL BRITISH CITIZEN

- **1215** — The signing of the Magna Carta, which established the principle of rule by law and limited the power of the monarch.
- **1642-1651** — The English Civil War, in which parliamentary forces defeated the monarchy, leading to the establishment of the commonwealth under Oliver Cromwell.
- **1653** — Oliver Cromwell becomes Lord Protector of England, establishing a period of military rule.
- **1688** — The Glorious Revolution, in which King James II was replaced by William of Orange and Mary II, establishing parliamentary supremacy over the monarch.
- **1707** — The Act of Union unites England and Scotland, creating the Kingdom of Great Britain.
- **1832** — The Reform Act, which expanded the franchise and redistributed seats in the House of Commons, marked the beginning of a series of reforms that gradually increased the political power of the middle class.
- **1837** — Queen Victoria comes to the throne and begins a long period of stability and prosperity known as the Victorian era.
- **1838** — The Chartist movement is founded in Britain, with the aim of securing political and social rights for working-class people through parliamentary reform.
- **1839** — The Chartist petition, signed by over 1.5 million people, is presented to Parliament but rejected.
- **1848** — The Chartists hold another mass rally in London, but it is also dispersed by the authorities.
- **1850** — The Chartist movement begins to decline as some of its demands are incorporated into government policy and other working-class organizations emerge.
- **1854-1856** — The Crimean War is fought between Britain, France, and the Ottoman Empire against Russia.
- **1867** — The Second Reform Act is passed, extending the vote to all male householders over the age of 21.
- **1872** — The last major Chartist gathering takes place in London, marking the end of the movement's political activism.
- **1914** — World War-I begins with Britain joining forces with France and Russia against the Central Powers.
- **1918** — The Representation of the People Act, which granted suffrage to women over the age of 30 and to all men over the age of 21.
- **1928** — The Representation of the People (Equal Franchise) Act, which granted equal suffrage to men and women over the age of 21.
- **1997** — The devolution of power to Scotland, Wales, and Northern Ireland establishing semi-autonomous governments in these countries.

1. 'The Reform Act of 1832 was criticized for a variety of reasons, yet it was nonetheless significant for what it was and why it started.' Explain.

Model Answer

1. 'The Reform Act of 1832 was criticized for a variety of reasons, yet it was nonetheless significant for what it was and why it started,' Explain.

Approach

- Explain criticism of the Reform Act of 1832.
- Explain the significance of the Reform Act of 1832.

The representation of People Act of 1832, often known as the first Reform Act, was a law passed by the British parliament that made significant reforms to the British parliamentary election process and electoral system. It was an outcome of changes brought by the Industrial Revolution in the British sociocultural, political, and economic spheres.

Criticism of Reform Act 1832

Although the Reform Act of 1832 brought about significant and far-reaching change, it still had a number of fundamental issues.

1. **Unfranchised working-class:** The property qualifications of £10 meant that the majority of working men still could not vote. This led to a breach in the working class's alliance with the middle class, which in turn gave rise to the Chartist Movement. Additionally, the number of voters went from approximately 400,000 to just 650,000, therefore the overall number of franchises was still quite low.
2. **Exclusion of women from voting right:** Since a voter was defined in the 1832 Reform Act to be a male individual, another change made by the Act was the explicit prohibition of women from voting in legislative elections. Instances of women voting existed before 1832, albeit rare and infrequently.
3. **Influence of Feudal Lords continued:** Voter bribery continued to be an important issue. Even though the Reform Act of 1832 eliminated the majority of Pocket Boroughs, tenants who paid a £50 annual rent were still granted the right to vote. Most tenants-at-will followed their landlords' instructions when casting their ballots. Additionally, even if the Act did disenfranchise Rotten Boroughs, a small number of them still existed.
4. **Influence of the House of Lords remained:** By lowering the number of Nomination Boroughs under feudal lord rule, the Reform Act strengthened the House of Commons. Nevertheless, the House of Lords and feudal lord's interests 'suffered very little' from the Reform Act of 1832. The House of Lords maintained its power and even forced the House of Commons to approve significant amendments to several bills. In contrast, the second Reform Act of 1867 significantly reduced the legislative authority of the House of Lords.

Significance of Reform Act 1832

1. **Eliminated threat to the British Government:** The Reform Act of 1832, which was a compromise, disappointed a sizable majority, especially the working class. However, from the perspective of the British government, it achieved its main goal and eliminated a direct threat to national security, like the French Revolution in France.
2. **Creation of a modern political system in Britain:** One of the most significant pieces of legislation in modern Britain's history, the Reform Act of 1832, played a key role in the country's transition to representative democracy and the creation of a modern political system in Britain. At the local level, voter registration lists were created for the first time. For the purpose of registering their supporters, political parties formed registration committees.

3. **Transferred sovereignty from the feudal class to the middle class:** It paved the way for the entry of the middle class into the British parliament. Additionally, it was the first effort to redefine the franchise right and redraw the political map. It was rightly referred to as the first parliamentary reform that effectively transferred sovereignty from the feudal class to the middle class because it reduced the influence of the House of Lords and elevated the status of the House of Commons, which had a greater proportion of middle-class MPs.
4. **Representation of newly created urban area:** Moreover, the British parliament also represented several newly developed urban districts. In addition, based on their eligibility for property ownership, the middle class were given franchise rights.
5. **Opened a door to new reforms and political order in Britain:** The Reform Act of 1832 is rightly said to have 'opened a door to a new political world.' It was never going to be 'the final solution of a great constitutional question.' It was the first in a string of events where the public protested for the expansion of voting rights and parliamentary reforms.

Even though the Reform Act of 1832 extended the feudal class's hold on British parliament by about 50 years, it paved the way for further parliamentary reforms in 1867, 1884, or 1918, which were crucial in establishing representative democracy in Britain.

2. The roots of the Chartist Movement in Britain were partly political and partly economic. Comment.

Model Answer

2. The roots of the Chartist Movement in Britain were partly political and partly economic. Comment.

Approach

- Explain the political causes for the Chartist Movement.
- Explain the economic causes for the Chartist Movement.

In contrast to the Reform Act of 1832, the aim of the 'Chartist Movement' was to secure political rights mainly for the working class. The Chartist Movement was primarily caused by political and economic reasons however, social factors also played a part.

Political Causes of the Chartist Movement

1. **Dissatisfaction from the 1832 Reform Act:** The working-class felt that parliamentary changes and political rights, like the right to vote would solve all of their social and economic problems. However, the Reform Act of 1832 did not grant the right to vote to the working class, because the property requirement of £10 still prevented them from doing so. This led to the breach in the working class's alliance with the middle class as a result of the feeling of betrayal, which gave rise to the Chartist Movement.
2. **Several Discriminatory Acts of the British government:** British government's discriminatory and unpopular acts, such as the Factory Act of 1833 and New Poor Law in 1834, deprived the working class of a number of rights, sparked a major wave of protest in England and helped to catapult the Chartist Movement into a large-scale mass movement.
3. **Failure of trade unions:** The Combination Acts of 1799 and 1800, which prohibited trade unions and strikes were abolished by legislation in 1825. As a result, trade unions were once more permitted, and numerous unions were formed after 1825, but none were successful in securing workers' interests or engaging in productive negotiations with the employers.

Economic Causes of the Chartist Movement

1. **Industrial Revolution and exploitation of workers:** Industrial Revolution led to the migration of a large number of workers to industrial towns. However, working class was discontent due to exploitation, poor working environment, long working hour, low wages, periodic unemployment and high prices of necessary goods. The working class started the Chartist Movement because they felt that political rights would resolve all of their social and economic issues.
2. **Corn Laws and a protectionist economy:** In Britain, the 1815 Corn Laws and a protectionist economy were still in effect. Since domestic markets for manufactured goods were weak due to the Corn Laws (which kept food prices artificially high), employment was also weak. Exports and industrial output both fell, as a result of undercutting foreign markets.
3. **Financial crisis of 1830's:** The 1830s were characterized by a number of financial crises. Between 1830 and 1841, the Whigs held the reins of the government and had a poor economic plan, and left a huge deficit behind them. Moreover, about 63 English banks failed between 1836 and 1838. As a result of the lack of investment and the high cost of food, there was unemployment.

4. **Problem of taxation and poor harvest:** By 1941, fiscal, banking, and taxation reforms were also required. The working classes were mostly subjected to indirect taxation which affected the poor more than the rich. The tax burden accounted for at least 16% of their actual wages. The circumstance became worse by the repeal of income tax in 1816 which reduced the real value of wages. Additionally, a number of poor harvests worsened the situation.

Therefore, speaking in 1938 in favour of the Chartist Movement, Joseph Stephens called Chartism a 'knife and fork, a bread and cheese question' thereby, highlighting the significance of the economic factors in the inception of Chartist Movement.

4 Mercantilism and Industrial Revolution

INDUSTRIAL INNOVATION IN BRITAIN AND EUROPE

- **1700** – The invention of the flying shuttle by John Kay increased the speed of weaving by hand.
- **1712** – Thomas Newcomen patents the first practical steam engine.
- **1733** – John Kay invents the spinning frame, which mechanizes the spinning of yarn.
- **1760** – James Watt patents the modern steam engine.
- **1760s-1780** – The Industrial Revolution begins in Britain, characterized by the introduction of new machinery and technology in the textile industry.
- **1769** – James Hargreaves invents the spinning jenny, which allows for the production of multiple threads at once.
- **1784** – Edmund Cartwright invents the power loom, improving the efficiency of textile production.
- **1769-1843** – The steam engine is developed and improved by James Watt and others, leading to its widespread use in factories, mines, and transportation.
- **1793** – Henry Cort invents the puddling process for refining the iron, leading to an increase in iron production.
- **1800s** – The Industrial Revolution spreads to other industries, including coal mining, ceramics, and chemicals.
- **1806** – George Stephenson builds the first steam locomotive, revolutionizing transportation and leading to the development of the railway system.
- **1851** – The Great Exhibition is held in London's Crystal Palace, showcasing the achievements of British industry and technology.
- **1860-1870s** – The Second Industrial Revolution takes place, characterized by the introduction of new technologies such as the telegraph and telephone, as well as the growth of heavy industry.
- **1876** – Alexander Graham Bell patents the telephone, revolutionizing communication.
- **1870-1890s** – The steel industry experiences rapid growth, leading to the development of new construction techniques and the expansion of rail networks.

1. Explain why England became the harbinger of the Industrial Revolution. Also, throw light on its social consequences.

Model Answer **1. Explain why England became the harbinger of the Industrial Revolution. Also, throw light on its social consequences.**

Approach

- Explain the economic, social, political, and geographical factors for Industrial Revolution in Britain.
- Explain the social consequences of the Industrial Revolution.

The term 'Industrial Revolution' refers to the changes brought in the mode of the production process from using hand tools to machine tools. The first country to experience the Industrial Revolution was Britain, where mechanized manufacturing began in the 1760s and continued to gather momentum with the passage of time. Renowned historian Phyllis Deane in his book 'The First Industrial Revolution' mentions four factors for British industrialization. These were demographic, agricultural, commercial, and transport. Nevertheless, these factors could be divided down into political, economic, cultural, geographical, and ecological factors.

Economic Factors

1. **Agricultural Revolution:** Famous historians W.J. Ashley and Robert Brenner highlighted the contribution of Agricultural Revolution to the British Industrial Revolution.
2. **Enclosure Movement:** Enclosure Movement meant the enclosure of the common village fields and unproductive land holdings into private landholdings. It made it possible for the application of technology and improved farming techniques on a wider scale and made a large number of peasants landless thereby forcing the migration of unemployed peasants into urban areas. Consequently, it provided both skilled and unskilled labour needed for the Industrial Revolution.
3. **Financial innovations and risk-taking private sector:** The Industrial Revolution occurred in Britain because of the presence of financial institutions including central banks, stock markets, and joint stock corporations.
4. **Availability of coal and iron mines:** Britain possessed the most abundant coal and iron reserves and the cheapest energy source in the world. It became vital to the growth of textile mills, locomotives, and other industries, driven by coal-fired machinery.

Political Factors

1. **Stable political situation:** Liberal-progressive character of the British political system played an important role in the commencement of the Industrial Revolution. After the Glorious Revolution of 1668, British society was more open to change and the governmental system was more stable than it was in other European nations' fragmented political order, which later became the significant determinant of the Industrial Revolution.
2. **Napoleonic wars:** The continental system of Napoleon was hostile to the British trade and banned continental European trade for Britain. However, it encouraged Britain to innovate further and become independent.
3. **Imperialist policy and expansion of British empire:** Britain had an extensive colonial empire that provided it with cheap raw materials, labour, and a monopolized market for finished goods.

Social Factors

1. **Population growth and British empire:** Britain's population grew very rapidly from the 15th to the 18th century. Moreover, increased trade with British colonies like America and India caused Britain's population to rise further.
2. **High socio-cultural stability in Britain:** While social upheavals like the French Revolution were occurring in continental Europe for liberty, equality, and fraternity, there was high socio-cultural stability in Britain at the same time. It provided a stable environment for the growth of the economy.

Geographical Factors

1. **Separation of the British Island:** Britain's island was isolated from the rest of continental Europe. As a result, Britain had a number of advantages over other European countries.

Social Impact of the Industrial Revolution

1. **Widening social Gap between rich and poor:** Due to the Industrial Revolution, those with money profited and amassed enormous wealth, while others who were workers merely continued to fall into poverty. As a result, the Industrial Revolution widened the wealth inequality and income disparity. Additionally, the Industrial Revolution divided the societies into the proletariat and the bourgeois, which later led to the rise of socialism.
2. **Poor working conditions:** Because there were no regulations governing them in the early stages of the Industrial Revolution, it resulted in a high unemployment rate for workers and bad working conditions (from 1790 to 1840).
3. **Joint family system into nuclear families:** The traditional joint family system was transformed into nuclear families. It became challenging for these family institutions to function because most migrants were men, which resulted in tension and pressure within the family.
4. **Urban overcrowding and diseases:** Low diets, bad sanitation, and densely populated, poorly built working-class neighbourhoods all contributed to extremely poor public health of the workers. In the first half of the 19th century, new industrial cities were attacked by cholera, tuberculosis, typhus, typhoid, and influenza, which had a terrible impact on the average life expectancy of British people.
5. **Emergence of the middle class:** Towards the end of the 19th century, in particular, a middle class started to gradually emerge in industrial centres. Earlier aristocrats and low-income commoners had been the only two primary social classes but the Industrial Revolution led to rise of the middle class.

2. 'Latecomer' Industrial Revolution in Japan involved certain factors that were markedly different from what the West had experienced. Analyse.

Model Answer

2. 'Latecomer' Industrial Revolution in Japan involved certain factors that were markedly different from what the West had experienced. Analyse.

Approach

- Explain the similarities between Japan industrial development and West industrialisation.
- Explain the dissimilarities between Japan industrial development and West industrialisation.

Between 1870 and 1980, modern industrialization began in Japan, the first nation in Asia. The policy of isolation was maintained until 1853 when the Japanese government forbade the entry of European traders out of concern that it might come under the colonial rule of Europe. A revolution in Japan in 1868 led to the restoration of the Meiji Dynasty. This dynasty was renowned for its fervent nationalism. The Meiji emperors pushed Japan towards industrialization so that Japan could transform into an industrial nation and Japanese prestige could be restored. Certain features of Japan's industrialization resembled and differed from those of Europe. These were:

Similarities with West Industrialisation

1. Capitalist nature based on mass production
2. Laissez-faire principal and profit emerged as dominant forces
3. Primacy to white goods

Dissimilarities with West Industrialization

1. **Role of State:** The role of the state was important as it provided the capital to entrepreneurs to set up factories. Since the Japanese rich class invested its capital in real estate and had no capital, so, the state pushed for industrial growth.
2. **Forced process:** When the Japanese markets were forced to open due to pressure, the local markets were swamped with foreign goods because there was no demand for Japanese goods in the global markets up until that point.
3. **Fast pace of industrialisation:** Japan's industrialization progressed at an incredibly fast rate, reaching levels, comparable to those attained by Europe in more than a century in just three decades. Japan had established itself as a great power at the start of the 20th century, thanks to its win over Russia in 1905. Japan was significantly more powerful than most of the Europe by 1930.
4. **Less emphasis in quality:** Initially, Japanese manufacturers lacked quality concerns because their primary goal was to produce inexpensive products in large quantities so that domestic requirements could be met for less money, with the target market being the common people.
5. **Lack of Japanese invention:** Japanese invention played a minor role because they adopted a reverse engineering policy.
6. **Less exploitation of working class:** Because Japanese nationalism inspired people to work hard to gain national prestige, there was less working-class exploitation than in Europe.

5 Rise of Nation States and Unification of Italy

RISE OF NATIONALISM AND UNIFICATION IN ITALY

- **1796-1797**: Napoleon's forces conquer Northern Italy.
- **1805**: Napoleon creates the Kingdom of Italy.
- **1815**: The Congress of Vienna creates the Kingdom of Sardinia, which becomes the main force for Italian unification.
- **1815-1848**: The Italian states are ruled by Austria.
- **1820**: Carbonari secret society is formed to promote Italian unification.
- **1831**: Giuseppe Mazzini finds Young Italy, a secret society to promote Italian unification.
- **1848-1849**: Revolutions break out across Europe, including in Italy, but are quickly suppressed. The First War of Italian Independence is fought, but Piedmont Sardinia was defeated.
- **1852**: Count Camillo di Cavour becomes the Prime Minister of Sardinia and begins implementing reforms to modernize the economy and strengthen the state.
- **1859**: Sardinia and France defeat Austria in the Second Italian War of Independence, leading to the creation of the Kingdom of Lombardy-Venetia.
- **1860**: Garibaldi leads the expedition of the thousand, unifying the kingdom of the Two Sicilies with Sardinia.
- **1861**: Victor Emmanuel II is proclaimed king of Italy, and the country is officially unified as the Kingdom of Italy.
- **1866**: Italy defeats Austria in the Third Italian War of Independence, leading to the acquisition of Venetia.
- **1870**: Rome is captured by Italian forces, and the city becomes the capital of the newly unified kingdom.

1. 'Mazzini's conception of Italian nationality was not exclusive, and his dominant ideal was the recreation of the moral unity of mankind.' Critically examine.

Model Answer

1. 'Mazzini's conception of Italian nationality was not exclusive, and his dominant ideal was the recreation of the moral unity of mankind.' Critically examine.

Approach

- Explain Mazzini's conception of Italian nationality.

Mazzini was a great visionary and soul of Italian unification who ignited the concept of united Italy and turned united Italy into a popular movement. Mazzini's speeches and writings sparked an intellectual revolution in Italy.

In Mazzini's view, the three pillars of Italian national identity—Independence, Unity, and Liberty—would be attained through the establishment of a republic. Mazzini's conception of Italian nationality was not exclusive to just Italy but a recreation of the moral unity of mankind. Mazzini believed that a free nation should help others to get freedom and to create moral 'Unity of Mankind'. In fact, Mazzini was one of the early proponents of European unification and the idea of a 'United States of Europe.' He asserted that Italian unification was a logical step towards the European Union.

Mazzini also gave the concept of three-fold unity–

1. **Unity of man–** Unity of all men to overcome the isolation of modern man in an industrialized mass civilization.
2. **Unity of nation–** Unity of nation to bind all free individuals and a community of liberty and equality.
3. **Unity of mankind–** Unity of mankind for peace and collaboration of all nations.

However, Mazzini's strategy was overly idealistic. Republicanism was his first priority and unification was the second one.

2. Though Garibaldi and Cavour disagreed, both made significant contributions to the movement for Italian unification. Explain the statements.

Model Answer **2. Though Garibaldi and Cavour disagreed, both made significant contributions to the movement for Italian unification. Explain the Statements.**

Approach

- Explain the comparison between Cavour and Garibaldi.
- Explain the contribution of both Cavour and Garibaldi.

While Mazzini spiritually attempted to unite the nation and disseminate nationalism throughout the country, Garibaldi militarily defended Rome and occupied Naples and Sicily in the South. On the other hand, Cavour logically planned each step of Italian unification.

Comparison between Cavour and Garibaldi

1. Cavour was a wise politician who carefully evaluated all choices before acting, in contrast to Garibaldi, who was more extreme and a proponent of revolutionary ideas.
2. Cavour was a politician and a proponent of constitutional monarchy, whereas Garibaldi was a republican, a warrior, and an opponent of catholicism.
3. When it was essential, Cavour partnered with France because he exploited international influence to further his domestic objectives. In contrast, Garibaldi relied on the grassroots strength, helped by young Italian Republicans.
4. While Garibaldi used his military prowess to protect Rome and capture Southern Italy, Cavour used his political acumen to organize every move Piedmont would make.

Contribution of both Cavour and Garibaldi

1. **Role of Cavour:** He was a shrewd politician and the Prime Minister of Piedmont. His judgment was clear, when, in 1861 he sent Victor Immanuel II to curb Garibaldi's zeal in order to avert a conflict between France and an Italian revolutionary. Moreover, Cavour's internal reforms and establishment of Piedmont Sardinia, as a model state, aided in the unification of Italy.

   Being a monarchist and having a mind for Italian unification, Cavour's initial goal was to create a constitutional monarchy under the leadership of Piedmont-Sardinia. He had previously not favoured the union of Italy, and his primary goal was to enlarge Piedmont-Sardinia by annexing the regions of Lombardy and Venetia.

   Cavour's vision of Italian unification was limited to Northern Italy, therefore, he did not favour annexing Southern Italy following the unification of Northern Italy. However, when Garibaldi opted for an independent course of action, Cavour interfered and sent Victor Immanuel II to acquire the southern states out of concern that they would turn Republican. Therefore, Cavour did not envision the Italy that eventually came to exist in 1870.

2. **Role of Garibaldi:** Garibaldi was a student of Mazzini and was known as the 'Sword of Italian unification'.
   A skilled soldier, Garibaldi organized revolutions with the Red Shirt (Guerrilla Group).
   Even though he was a Republican, he prioritized unification over Republican ideas, always choosing the path of unification wherever there was a conflict between the two. Thus, he loved his country more than he loved his Republican principles. He had a heart of a lion but the mind of a fox.

> Count Cavour once said in anguish, 'Aah! what have you done, we have expelled Bourbon from Naples and Sicily but brought another dynasty of Immanuel II, we have removed a corpse from the throne but restored on that his sick brother'.

Though Garibaldi and Count Cavour disagreed, both made some significant contributions to the movement for Italian unification. Scholars have, therefore, correctly argued that the unification of Italy was neither entirely in the vision of Count Cavour nor in the vision of Garibaldi, and that both had to make a great deal of compromises.

6 Unification of Germany

RISE OF NATIONALISM AND UNIFICATION IN GERMANY

- **1815** — The Congress of Vienna redraws the map of Europe and creates the German Confederation, a loose union of 39 states.
- **1848** — The Revolutions of 1848 break out in Germany, leading to a failed attempt to establish a constitutional monarchy and a strong, centralized government.
- **1850** — Austrian forces compelled the Prussian King to sign the Olmutz Convention after defeating Frederick William IV at the battle of Olmutz
- **1857-1861** — After suffering a stroke king Frederick William IV was unable to continue to reign of Prussia; as a result, Prince Wilhelm I became king.
- **1860-1862** — Deadlock between Wilhelm I and Prussian Diet over Army Reforms
- **1864** — Prussian-Austrian soldiers jointly defeated Denmark in German-Danish War.
- **1866** — Austria was shocked by how brutally Prussia defeated them in the battle of Sadowa during the Austro-Prussian war.
- **1870-1871** — France was defeated in Franco-Prussian War and Germany and France signed the Treaty of Frankfurt.
- **1871** — The German Empire is established, with Wilhelm I as its first emperor and Otto von Bismarck as its chancellor.
- **1871-1890** — Bismarck implements a series of domestic and foreign policies that would strengthen the empire and make Germany a major European power.
- **1888** — Wilhelm II becomes German Emperor, Bismarck is dismissed and the era of 'New Course' begins, marked by a shift away from Bismarck's policies.
- **1890** — The German Empire begins a period of rapid industrialization.
- **1890-1914s** — Germany becomes increasingly assertive in foreign affairs, leading to tensions with other European powers and contributing to the outbreak of World War I in 1914.

1. Was German unification achieved more by 'coal and iron' than by 'blood and iron'?

Model Answer

1. Was German unification achieved more by 'coal and iron' than by 'blood and iron'?

Approach

- Explain German unification by 'coal and iron'.
- Explain German unification achieved by 'blood and iron'.

John Maynard Keynes, a notable British economist of the 20th century, believed that the German empire was not built on 'blood and iron,' but rather on 'coal and iron.' 'Blood and iron' refer to the unification of Germany through war, while 'coal and iron' refer to the unification through economic linkages and economic power.

Unification of Germany by Coal and Iron

According to John Maynard Keynes, Prussia became strong economically because of fast industrialization. It laid the foundation for unification, which was subsequently expanded by Bismarck's skillful diplomacy. The policy of coal and iron created the foundation by:

1. **Weaken regionalism among German states:** Members of the Prussian-led Zollverein (Customs Union) enacted uniform economic policies and tariffs towards non-members, which promoted collaboration and dependence among the German states. Consequently, the regional barriers and rivalry between the German states were broken down by economic unification, which eventually resulted in political unification among German states.
2. **Established leadership of Prussia:** With the help of Zollverein, Prussia became the country's economic leader. Many German states, therefore, saw Prussia as the obvious choice to lead united Germany. By 1851, all the German states had joined Zollverein, with Austria being the only exception. This demonstrated that Prussian dominance was established in the economic arena even before the appointment of Bismarck in the 1860s.
3. **Coal and iron created the foundation for blood and iron policy:** Without Prussia's economic dominance, which supplied the resources and technology for the military, Bismarck's blood and iron policy would not have been feasible.

Unification of Germany by Coal and Iron

Other scholars, however, suggest that 'blood and iron' rather than 'coal and iron' was responsible for the unification of Germany. They argue that:

1. Bismarck's contribution to the unification of Germany was the most important factor. Before Germany was united, Bismarck followed a policy of 'blood and iron' and fought three wars against Denmark, Austria, and France for the unification of Germany.
2. Although Zollverein (Customs Union) was established in 1834, attempts to unify Germany in the revolution of 1848 were unsuccessful, highlighting the fact that coal and iron were not the primary factors in the unification.
3. The majority of the German states still looked to Austria for the political affairs, despite the economic unification of Germany brought about by Zollverein (Customs Union).

It is true that Austria was economically isolated from the rest of Germany while Prussia was integrated due to Zollverein. But it is also true that the political integration was not conceivable until Austria's decline as a major political force, notwithstanding the economic integration. Therefore, according to the modern scholars, the 'coal and iron' foundation for German unification was laid, upon which Bismarck's 'blood and iron' policy was built. As a result, both had an impact on the unification, albeit to varying degrees and at different times.

2. Compare and contrast the history of the unification of Germany and Italy.

Model Answer

2. Compare and contrast the history of the unification of Germany and Italy.

Approach

- Explain similarity between the unification of Germany and Italy.
- Explain dissimilarity between the unification of Germany and Italy.

Similarity between the Unification of Germany and Italy

1. **Role of Napoleon:** Napoleon was responsible of the initial attempt to unite both Germany and Italy. Efforts of Napoleon in the form of Rhine federation and propagation of the ideals of French Revolution laid the basis for rise of the German nationalism. Similarly, Napoleonic measures of establishing Swiss Alpine Republic and reforms in accordance with the ideals of French Revolution triggered growth of awakening in Italy.
2. **Vienna Congress:** The Vienna Congress of 1815 attempted to reverse the changes made by Napoleon in both Germany and Italy, but they were partially successful.
3. **Revolution of 1848:** The 1848 Revolution failed to bring liberty or unity to Germany, as it had failed in Italy. However, the 1848 Revolution, made it obvious that under Prussian leadership, the German unification would be realised, whereas the Italian Unification would be under Piedmont Sardinia.

Dissimilarity between the Unification of Germany and Italy

1. **Role of the leader:** Unlike Italy, where Garibaldi and Mazzini aided Cavour in his efforts to unify Italy, Bismarck single handedly brought German unification.
2. **Foreign assistance:** Cavour was successful in gaining the support of France and Britain for the cause of Italian unification through diplomatic tactics, such as offering support in the Crimean War. Unlike Cavour, Bismarck was able to unite Germany using military force rather than foreign assistance.
3. **Zollverein:** No Customs Union equivalent to Prussia's Zollverein helped Italy move towards unification, which played a role in making Prussia the most economically advanced German state.
4. **Parliamentary politics:** The deliberate combination of military diplomacy, parliamentary politics, and a popular movement led to the unification of Italy. However, there was less scope for popular agitation and parliamentary politics during the unification of Germany. In his speech, Bismarck expressed his contempt for parliamentary politics by saying, 'Germany is not looking to your liberalism, but to your strength.'
5. **Nature of merger of the states:** The unification of Italy was influenced by several factors. The Piedmont-Sardinian monarchy had to accept the liberal constitution's limitations on its power since it had made a compromise to liberal ideology. However, Prussia proceeded on with its own terms for German unification. That is why some scholars have remarked that the Piedmont-Sardinia state merged with the Italian states; the German states just vanished into Prussia.

7 Rise of Nationalism and World War I

VARIOUS EVENT OF WORLD WAR I

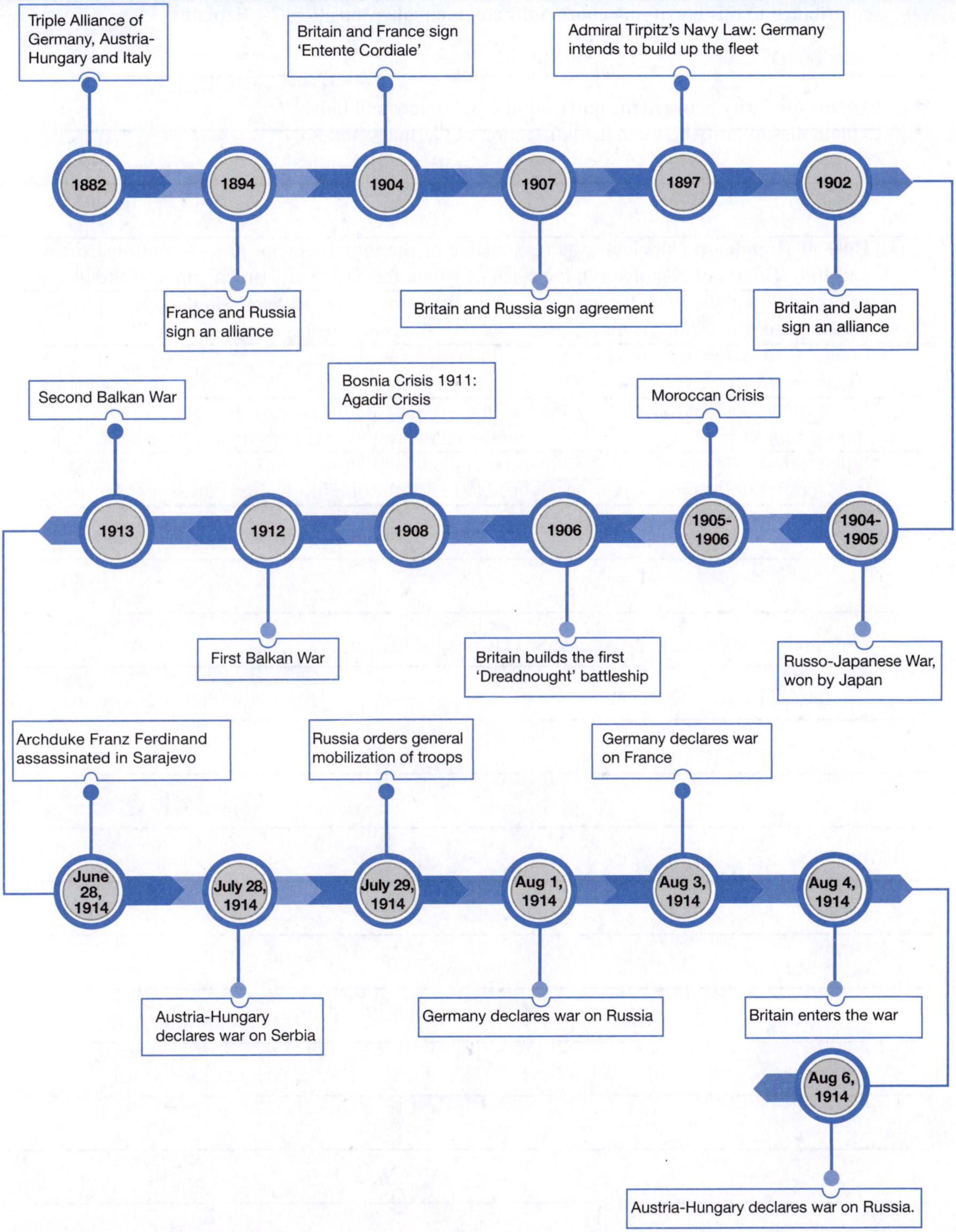

1. 'Any single explanation for the outbreak of the First World War likely to be too simple. An amalgam of factors such as intellectual, social, economic as well as political and diplomatic contributed to this horrifying conflict of monumental propositions.' – Explain.

Model Answer

1. 'Any single explanation for the outbreak of the First World War likely to be too simple. An amalgam of factors such as intellectual, social, economic as well as political and diplomatic contributed to this horrifying conflict of monumental propositions' – Explain.

Approach

- Explain various intellectual, social, economic as well as political factors responsible for the war.

The assassination of Ferdinand was the immediate cause of the First World War , but there were also long-term causes such as extreme nationalism, the alliance system, competitive militarism, Anglo-German naval competition, economic rivalry, and imperialist strategy.

Although the assassination of Archduke Ferdinand is commonly quoted as having started the First World War, its outbreak was actually the outcome of a prolonged sequence of circumstances brought on by economic, political, and social factors that began in 1871.

The assassination of a king and a prince was actually not such a significant moment that it could have triggered a war. Before this incident, in 1900 and 1909, respectively, the kings of Italy and Portugal were assassinated. However, these events failed to spark a war. The fundamental reasons for the ignition of war were:

1. **Policy of imperialism by the European Nations:** The Industrial Revolution played an important economic role during the First World War. Multipolar centres were developed in Europe during the Industrial Revolution. In other words, after the Industrial Revolution, the search for a market and imperialistic rivalry commenced. Moreover, greatness of the European nations is dependent on their power position in Europe as well as non-European possessions in Asia and Africa. Large colonial empires and Non-European possessions were held by Russia, France, and England. Germany, however, possessed very few colonies inside and outside of Europe. Hence, Wilhelm II and Germany desired 'Weltpolitik,' or 'the place in the sun.' Moreover, Bernhard von Bulow, the chancellor of Germany, stated in 1897, 'We do not want to put anyone into the shade, but we demand a position for ourselves in the sun.' Therefore, the unfulfilled imperialist ambitions of Germany and other European nations were the major cause of the international tensions and crisis that culminated in the outbreak of the First World War.
2. **Ultra-nationalism in Europe and incipient nationalism in Balkan:** Ultra-nationalism in Italy, France, Serbia, and Germany inflamed cultural and national pride among Europeans and ignited the First World War. With the rise of feeling of ultra-nationalism in Europe along with the imperialist policy, various European nations created imperialist rivalries, such as those between Austria and Serbia in the Balkan and Germany and Great Britain in naval and military competition.
3. **Alliance system or 'armed camps':** The creation of the alliance system was credited to Bismarck's diplomacy when he realized that France would not easily forget its humiliation and loss of Alsace-Lorraine and to maintain peace. However, Bismarck was also mindful that France was not a threat if it had no allies. As a result, he created a system of military alliances, which prompted counter-alliances and caused Europe to become divided into two hostile armed camps.
4. **Competitive militarism and armament race:** Rising ultra-nationalism and the establishment of alliance structures developed a feeling of apprehension and fear that prompted military preparations for a potential invasion.
   (a) Germany's standing army and navy were both expanded.
   (b) France increased the length of the compulsory two-year military service requirement to three years.

(c) Russia began a new initiative for modernizing its military.
(d) Great Britain further increased her already high naval expenditures.

All nations became fearful and hostile as a result of this competitive arms race. Each declaration by European nations increased their spending on arms and armaments.

5. **Economic rivalry among the European nation:** Marxist historians argue that during the late 19th and early 20th centuries, the economic competition brought on by the Industrial Revolution provided the major cause of the global crisis and was marked by a struggle for markets, sources of raw materials and investment of surplus capital.

2. Do you agree with the view that the Treaty of Versailles was a bad compromise between a treaty based upon force and a treaty based on ideas?

Model Answer

2. Do you agree with the view that the Treaty of Versailles was a bad compromise between a treaty based upon force and a treaty based on ideas?

Approach

- Treaty of Versailles was a bad compromise between a treaty based upon force and a treaty based on ideas.

  The First World War came to an end on November 11, 1918, and on January 18, 1919, a conference was held in Paris which came to be called as Paris Peace Conference. The Council of Four, sometimes referred to as the 'Big Four'—Prime Ministers, Lloyd George of Great Britain, Georges Clemenceau of France, Vittorio Orlando of Italy, and U.S. President Woodrow Wilson—acted as the major decision-makers throughout the peace-making process.

  However, the victors of the Paris Peace Conference had different objectives. While, France sought to protect its empire and punish Germany, Britain wanted to defend its financial interests, and the United States intended to establish a new international order based on Woodrow Wilson's fourteen points.

  A harsh treaty was imposed on Germany during the Paris Peace Conference. The Treaty of Versailles was harsh due to the following reasons:

1. It was a peace treaty without peace and an imposed peace treaty because all of its terms were determined by the victors. Even German representatives were prohibited from speaking or participating in conferences. There would have been two beneficial outcomes if the German representatives had been allowed to express their opinions.
   (a) The Treaty of Versailles could have been more lenient and acceptable.
   (b) The treaty would have gained legitimacy, and the German government might have worked to get its provisions put into effect.
2. It was a humiliating and retaliatory treaty that France enacted in retaliation for the revenge of the Franco-Prussian War of 1871 and the Treaty of Frankfurt. In fact, Germans were made to sign the Treaty of Versailles in the same Hall of Mirrors where the German king was crowned following the unification of Germany in 1870–1871.
3. The treaty was economically devastating to Germany. The German economy might have been severely wrecked if this pact had been completely enforced. John Menard Keynes, a British delegation member, and economist, resigned from his position on account of this.
4. Only Germany alone was blamed for the creation of the First World War.

Practical and Moral Defects under the Treaty of Versailles

1. It was a peace treaty without the peace and an imposed treaty.
2. The fourteen points proposed by Woodrow Wilson were not the basis of the Treaty of Versailles.
3. The self-determination principle was only applied to and exploited against Germany.
4. Principle of self determination was not allowed for the unification of Germany and Austria.
5. The pact severely damaged the German economy, but it also forced Germany to pay a massive war indemnity.
6. A large country like Germany could not possibly have a smaller army than Belgium.

8 Europe between Two World Wars (1919-39)

RUSSIAN REVOLUTION

- **1703** – Peter the Great finds the city of Saint Petersburg, which becomes the capital of Russia.
- **1721** – Peter the Great declares himself Emperor of Russia.
- **1762** – Catherine II seizes power from her husband, Peter III.
- **1773** – Catherine II creates the first state-sponsored educational system in Russia.
- **1812** – Napoleon's invasion of Russia leads to the retreat of his army.
- **1861** – Tsar Alexander II abolishes serfdom in Russia.
- **1881** – Tsar Alexander II is assassinated by a group of revolutionaries.
- **1905** – The Bloody Sunday Massacre sets off a series of protests and strikes across Russia, prompting the creation of the first Russian Parliament.
- **1917** – The February Revolution overthrows Tsar Nicholas II and establishes a provisional government.
- **1918** – The Bolsheviks, led by Vladimir Lenin, seize power in the October Revolution by overthrowing the provisional government and establishing the Soviet Union.
- **1918** – The Russian Civil War begins between the Red Army and White Russian forces.
- **1921** – The Soviet Union is established and the New Economic Policy is introduced.
- **1992** – The Union of Soviet Socialist Republics (USSR) is formed.
- **1924** – Lenin dies and Joseph Stalin succeeds him as leader of the USSR.
- **1939** – The Soviet Union invades Poland, beginning World War II.
- **1941** – World War II begins; the Soviet Union is invaded by Nazi Germany.
- **1945** – The Soviet Union defeats Nazi Germany and Japan in World War II and emerges as one of the two major powers of the post war world.
- **1953** – Stalin dies and Nikita Khrushchev becomes the leader of the USSR.
- **1991** – The Soviet Union is dissolved and the Commonwealth of Independent States is created.

NAZISM

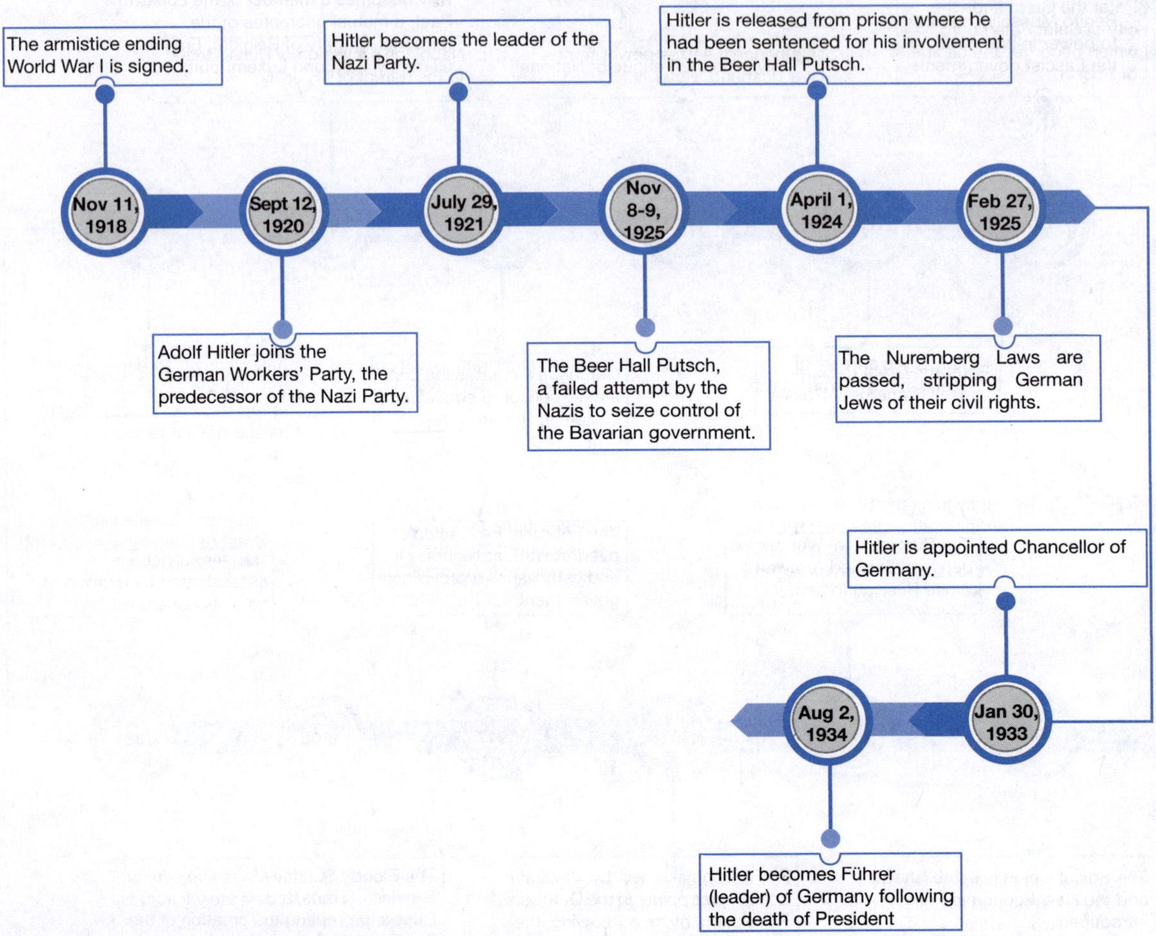
Nov 11, 1918
The armistice ending World War I is signed.
Sept 12, 1920
Adolf Hitler joins the German Workers' Party, the predecessor of the Nazi Party.
July 29, 1921
Hitler becomes the leader of the Nazi Party.
Nov 8-9, 1925
The Beer Hall Putsch, a failed attempt by the Nazis to seize control of the Bavarian government.
April 1, 1924
Hitler is released from prison where he had been sentenced for his involvement in the Beer Hall Putsch.
Feb 27, 1925
The Nuremberg Laws are passed, stripping German Jews of their civil rights.
Jan 30, 1933
Hitler is appointed Chancellor of Germany.
Aug 2, 1934
Hitler becomes Führer (leader) of Germany following the death of President

ITALY

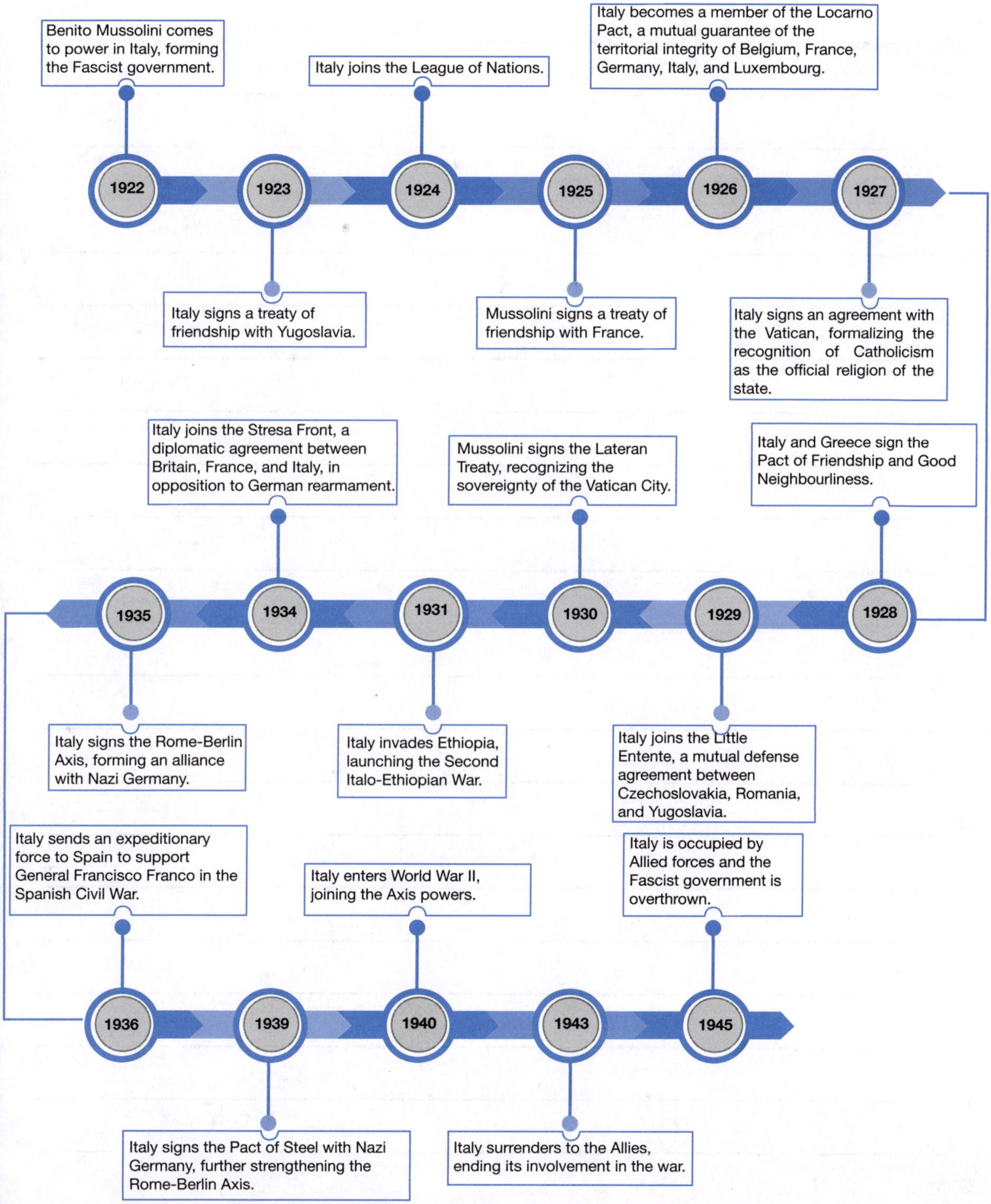
1922
Benito Mussolini comes to power in Italy, forming the Fascist government.
1923
Italy signs a treaty of friendship with Yugoslavia.
1924
Italy joins the League of Nations.
1925
Mussolini signs a treaty of friendship with France.
1926
Italy becomes a member of the Locarno Pact, a mutual guarantee of the territorial integrity of Belgium, France, Germany, Italy, and Luxembourg.
1927
Italy signs an agreement with the Vatican, formalizing the recognition of Catholicism as the official religion of the state.
1928
Italy and Greece sign the Pact of Friendship and Good Neighbourliness.
1929
Italy joins the Little Entente, a mutual defense agreement between Czechoslovakia, Romania, and Yugoslavia.
1930
Mussolini signs the Lateran Treaty, recognizing the sovereignty of the Vatican City.
1931
Italy invades Ethiopia, launching the Second Italo-Ethiopian War.
1934
Italy joins the Stresa Front, a diplomatic agreement between Britain, France, and Italy, in opposition to German rearmament.
1935
Italy signs the Rome-Berlin Axis, forming an alliance with Nazi Germany.
1936
Italy sends an expeditionary force to Spain to support General Francisco Franco in the Spanish Civil War.
1939
Italy signs the Pact of Steel with Nazi Germany, further strengthening the Rome-Berlin Axis.
1940
Italy enters World War II, joining the Axis powers.
1943
Italy surrenders to the Allies, ending its involvement in the war.
1945
Italy is occupied by Allied forces and the Fascist government is overthrown.

1. Examine the causes of the Russian Revolution of 1917 and indicate its significance in world history.

Model Answer

1. Examine the causes of the Russian Revolution of 1917 and indicate its significance in world history.

Approach

- Explain the causes of the Russian Revolution of 1917.
- Explain the significance of the Russian Revolution of 1917.

The Russian Revolution of 1917 was a major event in world history and had a profound impact on the course of modern history. The revolution was the result of many factors, both long-term and short-term causes including economic hardship, government corruption, and a long-standing sense of frustration among the working class. Economic hardship was caused by the First World War, which left the country in a state of economic crisis. The government was plagued by corruption and inefficiency, leading to poor decision-making and a lack of trust in the government by the people. This sense of frustration was further compounded by the Tsar's refusal to grant basic civil liberties and freedom of expression, leading to a sense of powerlessness among the people.

Political Causes of the Russian Revolution

1. **Tsar's incompetence:** Tsar, or the ruling monarch, had absolute power over the people and the government. Tsarist rule was autocratic and oppressive, with no real representation of the people or their interests.

   Tsar Nicholas II was a weak and ineffective leader who was unable to respond effectively to the problems facing Russia, such as poverty and social unrest.

   Moreover, the ideas of Tsar Nicholas II, which included royal absolutism, semi-divine monarchy, aristocratic privileges, exploitative feudal institutions, and an arbitrary legal system, resulted in a great deal of suffering and dissatisfaction among the Russian people.

2. **The Russian Revolution of 1905:** The Russian Revolution of 1905 was caused by Japan's defeat of Russia in 1905. It was a major uprising in the Russian empire against the autocratic rule of Tsar Nicholas II. It began with a peaceful protest of workers in St. Petersburg on January 9, 1905, and soon escalated into a series of massive strikes, demonstrations, and riots that would spread throughout the empire.

   Tsar responded with harsh repression, including military intervention, but the movement was too powerful to be stopped. The revolution ended with the Tsar's October Manifesto of 1906, which promised a number of reforms, including the formation of a legislative assembly, universal suffrage, freedom of speech, and freedom from arbitrary arrest.

   Tsar Nicholas II, however, breached his promises in the following years. Additionally, the murder of Prime Minister Stolypin, whose limited land reforms helped a lot of peasants, caused further delays in the reforms, which further intensified mistrust and dissatisfaction against the Tsarist authority. Therefore, it is rightly regarded by historian Richard Pipes that, 'Seeds of the Russian Revolution were sown in the 19th century with the oppressive policies of the Tsar and their refusal to share power with the people.' Thus, the revolution of 1905 was a watershed moment in the Russian history and laid the groundwork for the subsequent revolutions of 1917.

Economic Causes of the Russian Revolution

Russia had experienced a number of economic problems leading up to the revolution. Russia's economy was in a state of turmoil, heavily burdened by debt, with sharply rising prices, shortages of food, and growing unemployment. The Russian government was unable to address the economic issues, and the suffering of the lower classes only increased. This further fuelled the fire of revolution.

1. **Peasant uprisings:** The Russian peasants, who constituted the majority of the population, were discontented with the oppressive and unjust taxation policies of Tsar and the aristocrats. Moreover, most of the land was owned by feudal lords, who in turn further exploited the peasantry. This led to several peasant uprisings, which were brutally suppressed by the Tsarist government.
2. **An excessive reliance on agriculture:** Russia's economy was largely dependent on agriculture, much like France before the French Revolution. While some modern industries did emerge in Russia, the Industrial Revolution had not yet started in Russia, while other European countries reaped immense prosperity as a consequence of the Industrial Revolution. In the words of some critics, industries in Russia were an island in the vast sea.

Social Causes of the Russian Revolution

1. **Social inequality:** Russian society was divided into two distinct classes – the privileged upper class and the oppressed lower class. This social inequality was one of the major causes of the revolution.
2. **Poverty:** The majority of the population was living in poverty and lacked the basic necessities of life. The workers were paid very low wages, while the few feudal lords enjoyed the luxuries of life.
3. **Non-Implementation of reforms:** Tsar had refused to implement any meaningful reforms like land reforms to help improve the lives of the people. This caused further unrest and resentment among the people, which eventually led to revolution.

Significance of the Russian Revolution

1. **First successful communist revolution:** With the first serious attempt at a communist revolution, the 1917 Bolshevik Revolution transformed Marx's theory of communism into reality.
2. **Impact on the political landscape:** The revolution had a huge impact on the political landscape of the world. For the first time, a communist government had come to power. This was a major challenge to the capitalist world order and it sparked a wave of revolutions in other countries, such as Germany, Hungary, and China. The revolution also inspired other movements, such as the Civil Rights Movement in the United States.
3. **Impact on the economy:** The Soviet Union established a centrally planned economy, with the goal of achieving economic equality. This system of economic planning was adopted by many other countries, including China and Cuba.
4. **Policy of Appeasement:** The rise of communism in Russia forced western democracies like Britain and France to follow the Policy of Appeasement which led to the rise of Fascism and Nazism. The Policy of Appeasement was the idea of giving in to the demands of a potentially

aggressive nation in order to avoid war. This policy was most famously employed by the British Prime Minister Neville Chamberlain in 1938 when he allowed Nazi Germany to annex the Sudetenland, a region of Czechoslovakia, in order to avoid conflict. The Policy of Appeasement ultimately failed to prevent the Second World War and has since been widely criticized.

5. **Profound effect on international relations:** The Soviet Union and the United States became adversaries in the Cold War, a struggle that lasted nearly fifty years. The revolution also led to the formation of the United Nations; an organization dedicated for maintaining world peace.

In conclusion, the Russian Revolution of 1917 was a major event in world history. It had profound effect on politics, economics, culture, and international relations. It helped to shape the world we live in today and it is a reminder of the power of collective action.

2. Critically examine the main features of the foreign policy of Nazi Germany.

Model Answer

2. Critically examine the main features of the foreign policy of Nazi Germany.

Approach

- Explain the main features of the foreign policy of Nazi Germany.

  The rise of Adolf Hitler and his appointment as German chancellor in January 1933, marked the start of a new era in the history of Europe, since his foreign policy brought about a number of changes worldwide. He destroyed the Paris Peace Agreement, which ultimately led to the outbreak of the Second World War.

Main Features of the Foreign Policy of Nazi Germany

1. Hitler's foreign policy was driven by his desire to achieve power and glory for Germany and himself. He sought to expand German borders, claiming more 'Lebensraum' (living space) for the German people. This involved invading and occupying neighbouring countries and forcing them to accept German rule.
2. Most of Hitler's policies were aimed at undermining the Treaty of Versailles and his foreign policy was opposed to the system established by the Paris Peace Conference.
3. It was guided by German national interest and Hitler also sought to restore Germany as a powerful world power, and to gain international recognition of this status.
4. Militarism and Expansionism were dominant features in Hitler's foreign policy.
5. Idea of the Tird Reichstag also inspired Hitler's foreign policy. He wanted to create the third German empire on the lines of the empire created by Frederick the Great and Bismarck.
6. Hitler built a large army using conscription, as desired by the Germans. His industrial policy resulted in the large-scale production of weapons. This powerful German army persuaded him to pursue an aggressive foreign policy. His foreign policy had a systematic step-by-step approach.
7. Hitler's systematic step-by-step approach to achieve his goals was the so-called 'Führerprinzip,' or the 'Leader Principle.' This system was based on a top-down hierarchy, where Hitler was the supreme leader and all decisions were made by him. Under the Führerprinzip, Hitler and his inner circle had absolute control over the Nazi Party and its policies. Hitler's goal was to create a totalitarian state where he could rule by decree, and the Führerprinzip allowed him to establish his dictatorship.
8. Idea of pan-Germanism was also dominant in Hitler's foreign policy. He wanted to bring all Germans together as a part of one unit.
9. His foreign policy was guided even by racism. For example, in his text, '*The Secret Book*', he mentioned that Germans were pure Aryans so they deserve to possess a larger chunk of the region. However, although being of a lesser race Slabs (Russia), they had more land than they were supposed to. Therefore, it was necessary to remove the Slab people from the additional area.

9 Second World War (1939–1945)

VARIOUS EVENT OF SECOND WORLD WAR

Date	Event
Sep-Dec, 1939	Germany and Soviet Union invades Poland, beginning World War II in Europe; and Japanese attack on Pearl Harbour marks the US entry into World War II.
May 10, 1940	Germany invades France, Belgium, Netherlands and Luxembourg.
June 22, 1940	France signs an armistice with Germany, effectively ending the war in Western Europe.
Sep-Dec 1940	Germany, Italy and Japan sign the Tripartite Pact, forming the Axis Powers and Japan invades British-controlled Hong Kong.
June-Dec 1941	Germany invades the Soviet Union. Japan declares war on the US and the British Empire and attacks the US naval base at Pearl Harbour, Hawaii.
Dec 1941- Feb 1942	Japan captures the British colony of Singapore along with Dutch East Indies.
June -Aug 1942	US and its allies, along with US Marines launch their first major offensive in the Pacific, the Battle of Midway and Guadalcanal, respectively; Soviet forces launch a counteroffensive against the Germans at Stalingrad.
Feb 2, 1943	The Germans surrender at the Battle of Stalingrad, ending the German advance into the Soviet Union.
July 7, 1943	US and British forces launch their invasion of Sicily, beginning the liberation of Europe.
Sep-Oct 1943	Italy surrenders to the Allies and Soviet forces launch a massive counteroffensive against the Germans at the Battle of Kursk.
June 6, 1944	The Allies launch their invasion of Normandy, beginning the liberation of Western Europe.
June 22, 1944	The Soviet Union launches a massive summer offensive against the Germans, pushing them out of the Soviet Union.
Sep 17, 1944	The Allies launch their invasion of the Netherlands, beginning the liberation of the Netherlands.
Dec 17, 1944	U.S. forces launch their invasion of the Philippines, beginning the liberation of the Philippines.
Mar 6, 1945	U.S. forces launch their invasion of Iwo Jima, beginning the liberation of Japan.
April 25, 1945	The Allies launch their invasion of Italy, beginning the liberation of Italy and accept Germany's unconditional surrender, ending the war in Europe.
Aug 6 & 9, 1945	The U.S. drops an atomic bomb on Hiroshima and Nagasaki, Japan.
Aug 15, 1945	Japan officially surrendered, ending World War II.

1. Explain the causes of the Second World War.

Model Answer

1. Explain the causes of the Second World War.

Approach

- Explain the various factors responsible for the Second World War.

According to Historian Erick Hobsbawm, the Second World War was a war of 31 years which ended on August 15, 1945. A number of fundamental and immediate factors caused the Second World War including the Treaty of Versailles, the Great Depression of 1929, the development of Fascism, the establishment of the Rome-Berlin-Tokyo axis, and the failure of the League of Nations.

Immediate Causes of the Second World War

Following the signing of the German-Soviet Non-Aggression Pact (a Non-Aggression pact signed between Nazi Germany and the Soviet Union), Germany's invasion of Poland in 1939 was the final straw for Britain and France that led to the outbreak of the Second World War. This was the result of a series of diplomatic manoeuvres between Germany, Britain, France, and other countries in Europe in the 1930s, as Hitler sought to expand German territories.

Even though the Second World War began with Hitler's invasion of Poland, according to professor Alan Bullock (British Historian), 'It was caused by the political and economic disorders of the inter-war years, the failure of collective security, and the rise of militarism and totalitarianism in Europe and Asia.'

1. **Limitations of the Treaty of Versailles:** The Treaty of Versailles is widely regarded by historians as one of the primary causes of the Second World War. After the First World War, the Allies imposed a harsh Treaty of Versailles on Germany which required it to pay heavy reparations and accept full responsibility for the war. This caused a great deal of resentment in Germany, which was further compounded by the Great Depression of the 1930s.

   People blamed the Treaty of Versailles for the social, economic, and political ills of Germany which led to a revival of German nationalism. This resentment provided fertile ground for the rise of Adolf Hitler and his Nazi Party, which promised to undo the harsh conditions of the Treaty of Versailles and restore Germany's former glory. Hitler's aggressive expansionism and refusal to abide by the terms of the treaty led to the outbreak of the Second World War in 1939.
2. **Emergence of ideology of Fascism and Nazism:** The rise of Fascism (an extreme version of nationalism) in Europe in the 1930s was a major factor in the outbreak of the Second World War. The rise of Hitler's Nazi party in Germany and Mussolini's Fascist party in Italy created two powerful regimes that sought to expand their territories and influence. The aggressive expansionist policies of the Fascists (for example, Hitler's Kebensraum– Living Space Policy), were combined with their militaristic rhetoric and propaganda. When the Allies did not resist these moves (for example, Munich Agreement), it encouraged the Axis Powers (Germany, Japan, and Italy) to continue their aggression. But later, as a consequence of Fascist policies that combined authoritarianism, militarism, and racism, diplomatic tension and conflicts in Europe escalated. This, in turn, led to a series of diplomatic crises after the Munich Agreement. Moreover, by 1939, the two Fascist powers had formed an alliance, called the Axis Powers, which ultimately led to the outbreak of the Second World War.

3. **Failure of the League of Nations:** The League's powers were also limited by its lack of an army of its own, and its failure to respond effectively to the aggressive actions of Japan, Italy, and Germany such as–
   (a) Japanese attack on Manchuria & Italian Abyssinian attack tarnished the image of the League of Nations.
   (b) Failure of the League to act against the aggressive foreign policy of Hitler aimed at creating living space for Germany.
   (c) No action was taken by the League in the Spanish Civil War to restrict Franco's rise as a dictator against the elected government in Spain which practically marked the end of the League of Nations.

   This led to a build-up of tensions which was not resolved by the League, culminating in the outbreak of the Second World War in 1939.
4. **The Appeasement Policy:** Appeasement is a policy of making concessions to an aggressive power to avoid conflict. It is usually pursued through diplomatic negotiations and is designed to satisfy the demands of the aggressive power in order to prevent war. Appeasement is generally viewed as a failed foreign policy due to its inability to prevent war and its encouragement of further aggression.

   The Appeasement Policy, adopted by the British Prime Minister Neville Chamberlain and France in the 1930s, was an attempt to avoid war by allowing Adolf Hitler to annex parts of Czechoslovakia and other territories without offering any resistance. Chamberlain's Policy of Appeasement was rooted in his belief that it was possible to negotiate with Hitler and the Nazi regime in order to preserve peace in Europe.
5. **Economic Crisis and Economic Depression of 1929:** The economic depression of the 1930s played a major role in creating the conditions for the outbreak of the Second World War. The Great Depression, sparked by the stock market crash of 1929, caused widespread economic hardship throughout the world. The economic collapse of the 1920s and 1930s had a devastating impact on the global economy, leading to rampant unemployment, poverty, and economic instability. This economic instability, combined with the rise of authoritarian regimes and the spread of militaristic ideologies, created a volatile global situation.

   Moreover, the rising levels of unemployment and a collapse in international trade, caused countries to pursue increasingly protectionist policies. This in turn caused a further decline in global trade, further exacerbating the economic crisis.
6. **Role of Hitler and Hitler's foreign policy:** Adolf Hitler was the dictator of Nazi Germany and was the main driving force behind the Second World War. Hitler was an Austrian-born German politician who was the leader of the Nazi Party. He rose to power in Germany during the 1930s and became chancellor in 1933. He quickly established an authoritarian regime, under which he pursued an aggressive foreign policy with the aim of expanding German Lebensraum ('Living Space') at the expense of other European nations.

2. Hitler did not want a World War but rather a limited war in Poland. Critically examine.

Model Answer

2. Hitler did not want a World War but rather a limited war in Poland. Critically examine.

Approach

- Explain the responsibility of Hitler for the Second World War.

Recent historiography on the responsibility of the Second World War has largely focused on the role of the major powers in the conflict. Historians have argued whether the war was the result of conscious decisions made by leaders, or if it was the result of more complex factors.

According to renowned Historian A.P.J. Taylor, Hitler did not desire a World War but rather a limited war in Poland. A.P.J. Taylor believed that Allied Powers followed an inconsistent policy towards Hitler which led to the Second World War. Whereas, on one hand, on the issue of Czechoslovakia, they remained to be much soft with Hitler but on the other hand, on the issue of Poland they quickly launched the war so, Hitler was caught unaware.

The majority of recent of historians also agree with A.P.J. Taylor's view that it is true that Hitler did not seek out the World War because he understood the risk and devastation involved. On August 22, 1939, just 9 days before the attack on Poland, Hitler in his conversation with his military generals, made this point clear that Allied Powers could not take any risk of war with us. Nevertheless, it is also true that Hitler's relentless desire for territory made the Second World War inevitable even though he did not want it. Hitler was having his ambition to move further east of Poland and this desire has been proved by Hitler's invasion of Soviet Russia.

Finally, it is difficult to say with certainty who is responsible for the Second World War. The war was a complex international event with many contributing factors, and the history of the war is still being debated by scholars today. It is difficult to definitely assign responsibility for the outbreak of the Second World War. Historians have debated the issue for decades, and no single answer has emerged yet.

10 Cold War

COLD WAR IN EUROPE AND OUTSIDE EUROPE

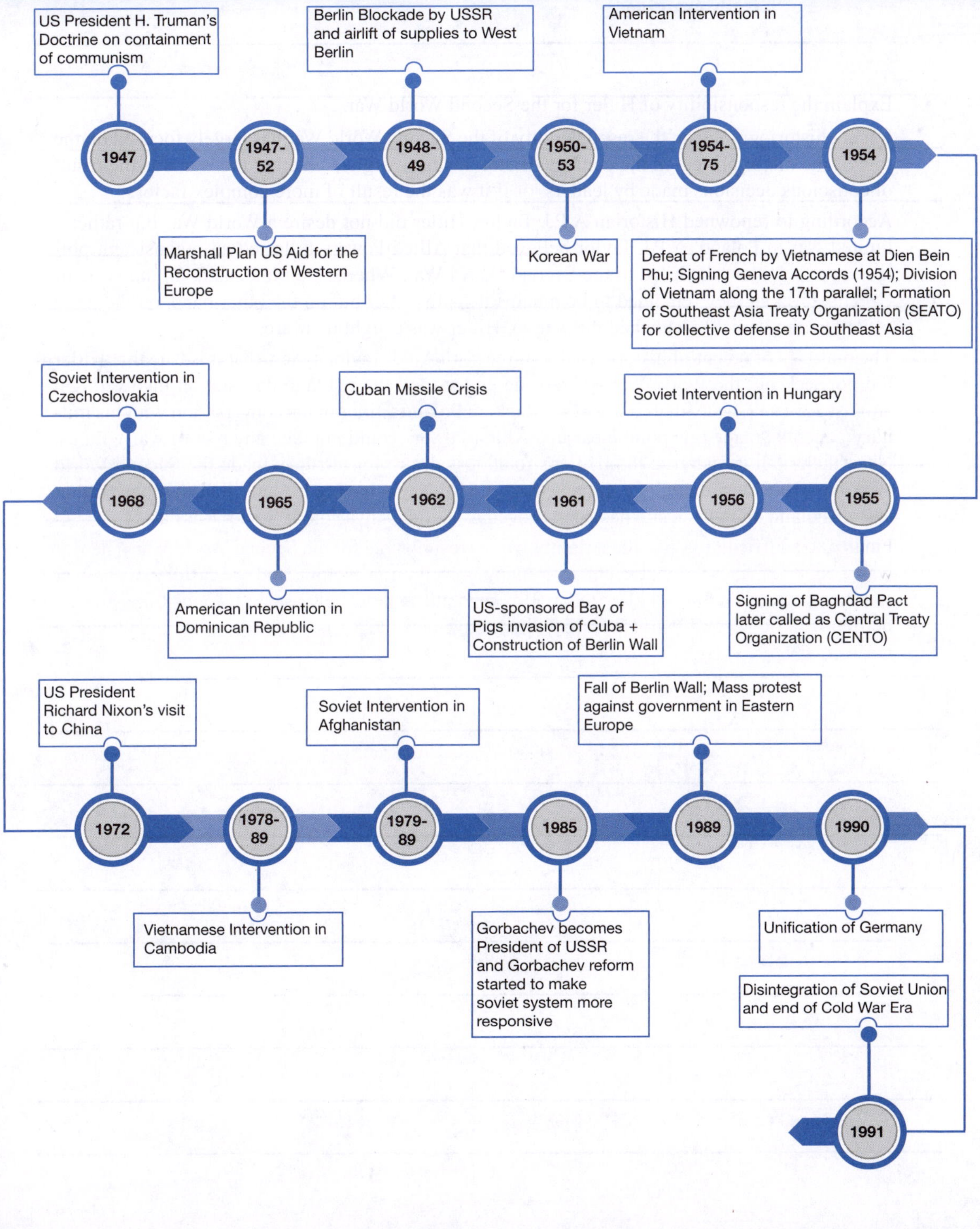

1. What were the events that led to the Suez Crisis in 1956? How did it deal a final blow to Britain's self-image as a world power?

Model Answer

1. What were the events that led to the Suez Crisis in 1956? How did it deal a final blow to Britain's self-image as a world power?

Approach

- Explain the events that led to the Suez Crisis in 1956.
- Explain how it deals a final blow to Britain's self-image as a world power.

The Suez Canal Crisis of 1956 was a conflict between Egypt and the United Kingdom, France, and Israel over control of the Suez Canal. Britain promised financial support for the Aswan Dam in the hopes that Egypt would abide by its foreign policy. But, the head of Egypt, Nasser did not follow the line and extended recognition to Communist China, so in reaction, Britain withheld the amount sanctioned for Aswan Dam.

Consequently, Nasser terminated the lease of the Suez Canal and nationalized it in July 1956. This caused an international uproar due to the fact that the canal was owned by the Suez Canal Company, a French and British-led consortium. Moreover, the canal was a major strategic waterway, allowing ships to travel between Europe and Asia without having to go around Africa.

The UK, France, and Israel formed a secret alliance and launched a coordinated attack on Egypt in October 1956. The United States and the Soviet Union both condemned the attack and pressurized Britain and France to withdraw their forces. In November 1956, a United Nations-sponsored ceasefire was arranged and the crisis ended with the Suez Canal remaining under Egyptian control.

Consequences of the Suez Canal Crisis

The Suez Canal Crisis of 1956 had several consequences, both in the short term and long term.

- **Loss of British and French imperialism:** The Suez Canal Crisis marked the end of British and French imperial power in the Middle East. The crisis contributed to the decline of British and French influence in the Middle East and the rise of Arab nationalism, particularly in Egypt. This newfound strength in the region saw the rise of Arab nationalist movements and the emergence of Arab countries such as Egypt, Syria, and Iraq.

2. Critically examine the various dimensions and phases of the Cold War between 1947 and 1962.

Model Answer

2. Critically examine the various dimensions and phases of the Cold War between 1947 and 1962.

Approach

- Examine the various dimensions and phases of the Cold War.
- Explain the phases of the Cold War between 1947 and 1962.

The Cold War was not a military confrontation between two blocs, but a complex political and ideological struggle that took different forms in different parts of the world.

The Cold War can be divided into Three Distinct Phases

1. **The Phase of Confrontation (1948 to 1962):** It was characterized by increased tension and hostility between the United States and the Soviet Union. The U.S. and Soviet Union engaged in a series of proxy wars, military build-ups, and ideological confrontations that threatened to escalate into a full-scale nuclear war.
2. **The Phase of Détente (1962 to 1978):** It was marked by a relative decrease in tensions and a focus on diplomacy, such as the signing of the Nuclear Test Ban Treaty and the establishment of the hotline communication system between the U.S. and the Soviet Union.
3. **The Phase of Rapprochement (1978 to 1992):** It was marked by an increase in tensions and a renewed arms race, as well as a focus on proxy wars in developing nations and the rise of the Solidarity Movement in Poland. This phase ended with the collapse of the Soviet Union in 1991.

The Phase of Confrontation (1948 to 1962)

This period saw the establishment of the North Atlantic Treaty Organization (NATO) and the Warsaw Pact (two of the major military alliances of the Cold War), the Civil War in Greece, the conflict of the Berlin Blockade, the Cuban Missile Crisis, and the Vietnam War.

1. **Civil War in Greece:** The Greek Civil War was fought in Greece from 1946 to 1949 between the Greek government army and the Democratic Army of Greece (DAG), which was backed by the Soviet Union. The Civil War represented a continuation of the ideological conflict between monarchists and communists. The conflict began after the Second World War when the economic and political differences between the right-wing governments of Greece and the left-wing forces of the DAG led to an armed struggle.

   Although Britain decided to withdraw from the Civil War, the US decided to get engaged. US President Truman believed that if the Soviet Union succeeded in Greece, then the USSR would topple the neighbouring nations like a series of dominoes. Therefore, US President Truman introduced the Domino Theory to prevent communists from taking over Turkey and Greece in 1946. He made an appeal to the U.S. Congress to sanction the money for military expenses in Greece. As a result, $450 million was sanctioned by the Congress for maintaining U.S. naval force in the Mediterranean Sea.

   Thus, the Civil War of Greece was further complicated by the involvement of the United States, and the Soviet Union, which both provided military aid to the opposing sides. The war ended in 1949 with the defeat of the DSE and the establishment of a pro-western government in Greece.

2. **Truman Doctrine and Marshall Plan:** The Truman Doctrine was a foreign policy initiative by President Harry S. Truman on March 12, 1947. It declared that the United States would provide economic and military assistance to Greece and Turkey in order to prevent them from falling into the sphere of influence of the Soviet Union. The policy was developed in response to the threat that the spread of Communism posed to American security and interests, as well as to the stability of the entire post-war international order. The doctrine became the cornerstone of American foreign policy for the next four decades and was used to justify U.S. involvement in the Korean War and the Vietnam War, as well as the support of anti-communist governments in countries around the world.
3. **Berlin Blockade:** The first significant Cold War confrontation was the Berlin Blockade. Berlin was jointly administered by the four victor powers, including Britain, USA, France, and Russia. The Berlin Blockade was a political and economic blockade imposed by the Soviet Union on the western sectors of Berlin by imposing a blockade on the movement of goods and food by rail or road to West Berlin, from June 24, 1948 to May 12, 1949. It was a diplomatic standoff between the United States, the United Kingdom, and France on one side, and the Soviet Union on the other.

   The Soviets blocked all rail, road, and water routes leading to the western-held parts of the city of Berlin (located deep within the Soviet-controlled zone of Germany) in an attempt to gain control and force the Western powers out of Berlin. The Western powers responded by flying in supplies to their respective sectors, a process is known as the Berlin Airlift. Both superpowers were on the brink of war after the Berlin Airlift, but fortunately, none of them crossed the line. Americans avoided taking the land route, and the USSR did not shoot down American planes. The blockade was eventually lifted, with the Soviet Union agreeing to the Allied Powers' presence in Berlin.
4. **Korean Crisis (1950-53):** The Korean War (1st Hot War of the Cold War) was a conflict between North and South Korea that lasted from June 25, 1950 to July 27, 1953. The partition of Korea into two zones along the 38th parallel after the Second World War was the immediate cause of the Korean War. It began when North Korea's forces, aided by the Soviet Union and China, crossed the 38th parallel and invaded South Korea in an attempt to reunify the Korean Peninsula under the Communist rule.
5. **Suez Canal Crisis (1956):** The Suez Canal Crisis of 1956 was a conflict between Egypt and the United Kingdom, France, and Israel over control of the Suez Canal. Britain promised financial support for the Aswan Dam in the hopes that Egypt would abide by its foreign policy. But, the head of Egypt, Nasser did not follow the line and extended recognition to Communist China, so in reaction, Britain withheld the amount sanctioned for Aswan Dam.

   Consequently, Nasser terminated the lease of the Suez Canal and nationalized it in July 1956. This caused an international uproar due to the fact that the canal was owned by the Suez Canal Company, a French and British-led consortium. Moreover, the canal was a major strategic waterway, allowing ships to travel between Europe and Asia without having to go around Africa.

   The UK, France, and Israel formed a secret alliance and launched a coordinated attack on Egypt in October 1956. The United States and the Soviet Union both condemned the attack and pressured Britain and France to withdraw their forces. In November 1956, a United Nations-sponsored ceasefire was arranged and the crisis ended with the Suez Canal remaining under Egyptian control.

6. **Vietnam Crisis (1954-75):** The Vietnam Crisis (1954-75) was a period of conflict between North Vietnam, supported by communist allies, and South Vietnam, supported by anti-communist forces, including the United States. After Japan left Vietnam in 1945, Ho Chi Minh, a communist leader, founded a Communist Republic in North Vietnam while the French seized control of South Vietnam.

   The Vietnam Crisis began in 1954 when the French withdrew from their colony of Indo-China after a failed attempt to regain control of the region. This opened the door for the North Vietnamese communist forces, known as the Viet Cong, to begin a campaign of guerrilla warfare against the South Vietnamese government in an attempt to unify the country under Communist rule.

7. **Cuban Missile Crisis (1963):** The Cuban Missile Crisis began when the United States discovered that the Soviet Union had deployed nuclear missiles in Cuba, just 90 miles away from the U.S. shores of Florida. The USA opposed the installation of medium-range nuclear missiles in Cuba and expected USSR to withdraw missiles. On the other hand, USSR initiated to install more such missiles. So, there appeared the situation of direct confrontation.

   Later, the U.S. responded by imposing a naval blockade on Cuba and threatening to use military force against the Soviets if they did not remove the missiles. Eventually, after several tense days, the Soviet Union led by President Khrushchev agreed to remove the missiles in exchange for a U.S. promise not to invade Cuba and to remove U.S. missiles from Turkey. The crisis was a major turning point in the Cold War, and it demonstrated the danger of nuclear proliferation.

11 Chinese Revolution and Decolonization of Colonies

CHINESE HISTORY

1644-1912 CE — Qing Dynasty: The Qing Dynasty was the last imperial dynasty of China, founded by the Manchu people.

1912-1949 CE — Republic of China: The Republic of China was established after the fall of the Qing Dynasty and was marked by political instability, social unrest, and foreign invasions.

1919 — May Fourth Movement: This student-led movement was called for cultural and political reforms in China and marked the beginning of the Chinese intellectual movement.

1926-1928 — Northern Expedition: This military campaign led by the Nationalist Party (Kuomintang) was aimed at unifying China and defeating the warlords who controlled various regions.

1927-1949 — Chinese Civil War: This was a political and military struggle between the Nationalist Party and the Communist Party of China for controlling China. The war was interrupted by the Second Sino-Japanese War (1937-1945), during which China fought against Japan.

1934-1935 — Long March: This was a military retreat by the Communist Party from their base in Jiangxi to Shaanxi, covering a distance of about 9,000 kilometres.

1936 — Xian Incident (1936): This was a political crisis in which General Zhang Xueliang and Yang Hucheng kidnapped Chiang Kai-shek, the leader of the Nationalist Party, and forced him to form a united front with the Communist Party against Japan.

1937-1945 — Second United Front: This was a temporary alliance between the Nationalist Party and the Communist Party to fight against Japan during the Second Sino-Japanese War.

1945-1949 — Chinese Communist Revolution (1945-1949): After Japan's surrender in 1945, the Chinese Civil War resumed. The Communist Party emerged victorious in 1949, establishing the People's Republic of China, while the Nationalist Party retreated to Taiwan.

1958-1962 — Great Leap Forward: An economic and social campaign initiated by Mao Zedong, which aimed to transform China from an agrarian economy to a modern industrialized society. It resulted in widespread famine and economic disaster.

1966-1976 — Cultural Revolution: This was a political and social movement initiated by Mao Zedong, which aimed to purify the Communist Party and eliminate perceived enemies. It led to widespread violence, persecution, and disruption of Chinese society.

1978-1992 — Deng Xiaoping's reforms: After Mao's death, Deng Xiaoping initiated a series of economic and political reforms that opened up China to the world and led to significant economic growth.

DECOLONIZATION IN SOUTH EAST ASIA

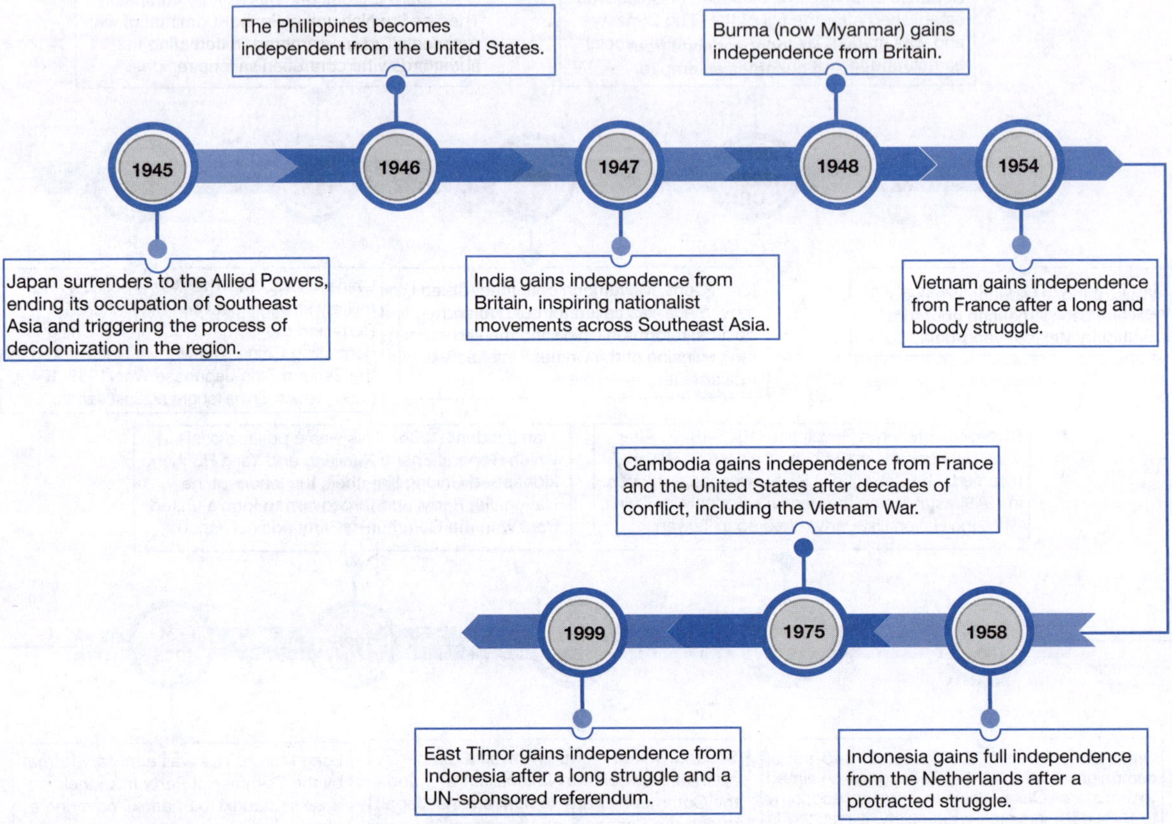

DECOLONIZATION IN LATIN AMERICA

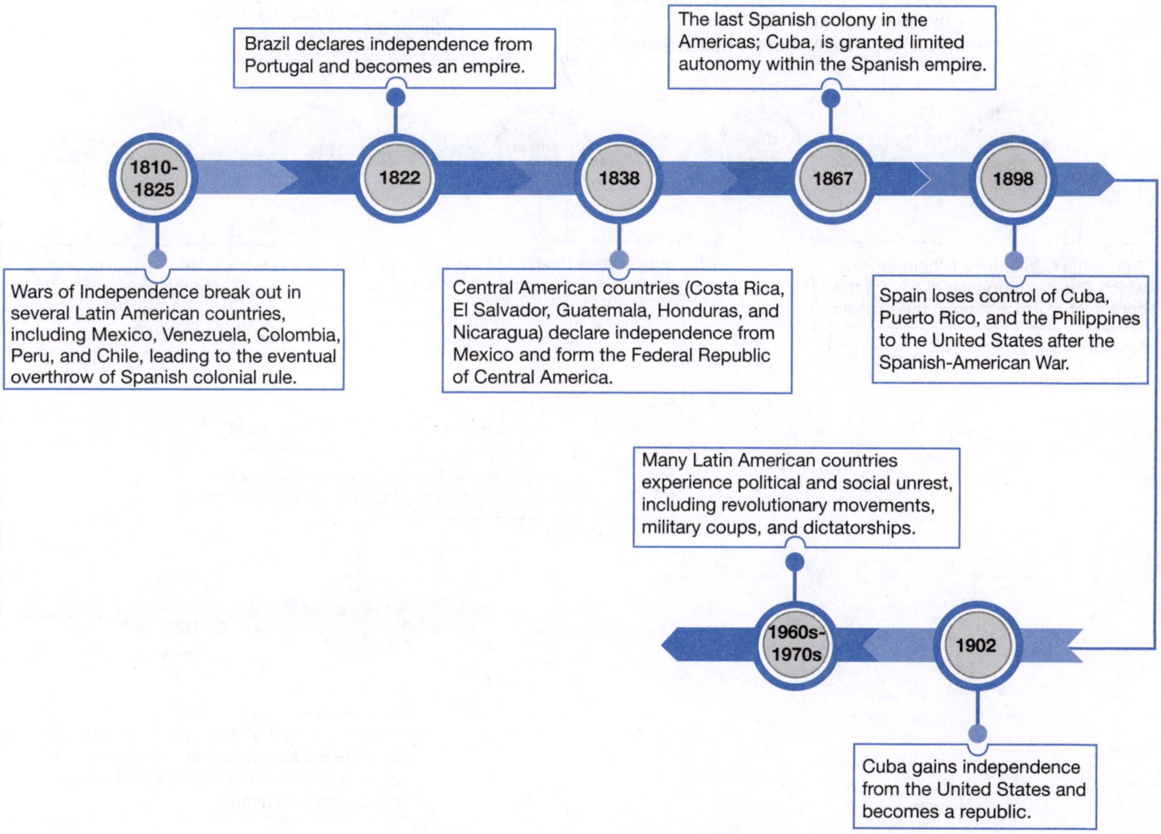

DECOLONIZATION IN AFRICA (1884–1990s)

1884-1885
The Berlin Conference is held, during which European powers divide up the continent of Africa among themselves.

1945-1960
African nationalism and anti-colonial movements gain strength, fuelled in part by the end of World War II and the rise of decolonization movements around the world.

1951
Libya becomes the first African country to gain independence after World War II.

1957
Ghana becomes the first sub-Saharan African country to gain independence from Britain.

1960
Over a dozen African countries gain independence from colonial powers, including France, Belgium, and Portugal.

1962-1990
Nelson Mandela and other anti-apartheid activists are imprisoned or forced into exile, but continue to organize and resist the apartheid regime.

1990s
South Africa undergoes a process of decolonization and democratization, leading to the end of apartheid and the establishment of a multi-racial democracy.

1. Explain the circumstances that favoured European imperialism in Africa. In the process of decolonization, why Africa was de-colonized later than Asia?

Model Answer

1. Explain the circumstances that favoured European imperialism in Africa. In the process of decolonization, why Africa was de-colonized later than Asia?

Approach

- Explain the circumstances that favoured European imperialism in Africa.
- Explain the causes why Africa was de-colonized later than Asia.

The African Liberation Movement is a term used to describe the struggle of the African people to end colonialism and white minority rule in Africa, in order to achieve self-determination. The African Liberation Movement has a long history, beginning in the 19th century and continuing to the present day. It has taken many forms, from armed struggle to diplomatic negotiations and civil disobedience. The movement, led by African nationalist and anti-colonial leaders, sought to assert their independence and establish autonomous, democratic states. Key events and figures include Ghana's independence in 1957 led by Kwame Nkrumah, the Algerian War of Independence (1954-1962), and Nelson Mandela's leadership in the struggle against apartheid in South Africa.

Factors Supporting the Growth of Imperialism in Africa

1. **Role of explorers:** Explorers and adventurers further helped in discovering and opening up of new areas to be colonized.
2. **Political weakness:** The governments of the countries of Africa were very weak. The old ways of governing were still followed. Strong nation-states in the modern sense had not developed. The people's loyalties were still to local princes (as in feudal times) or to tribal chieftains. These rulers cared little for the welfare of the people.
3. **Lack of industrial growth in Africa:** The most important condition was that the Industrial Revolution had not come to this part of the world.
4. **Military failure:** Africa was politically and militarily unable to stand up to the armed might and power of Europe.
5. **Huge size of African continent:** The huge size of this continent was very difficult to control by a strong centre as there were no proper means of transport, communications, etc.

Reasons for Delay in African Decolonization

The process of decolonization began in Asia in 1945, after Japan surrendered before the Allied forces in 1945. However, the decolonization process in Africa stretched over a much longer period than in Asia, lasting up till 1990. Between 1950 to 1959, six African countries were liberated with the sacrifice of over 2,00,000 African lives. The 1960s saw the dismantling of the British, French and Belgian colonial empires with the mass support. In the mid-1970s, the Portuguese empire in Africa collapsed. The process of decolonization ended only in the early 1990s with the independence of Rhodesia and Namibia.

1. **European needs of raw materials:** As compared to Asia, the African continent was endowed more with raw materials, mineral resources, labour, and territory for future settlement. As a result, the colonial powers tried to stay there for as long a time as possible.

2. **Delay in the rise of nationalist movements:** The nationalist movements for freedom started early in Asia, while in many African countries such movements could start only after the Second World War. Asian continent saw the advent of modern education early, which ignited the intelligentsia to demand civil and political liberties. As a result, the colonial powers deliberately delayed the introduction of modern education into the African continent.
3. **Diverse ethnicity and lack of trust:** European powers carved up Africa with very little regard to the identity of the people living there, resulting in tribal division and hatred. They lacked mutual trust and did not witness pan-African unity against the common enemy-colonialism.
4. **Cold War politics:** It was the fear of Soviet influence in Africa, particularly on the part of the United States, that created such a major problem for African nations. Western powers viewed African independence through the lens of the Cold War, which rendered African leaders as either Pro-West or Pro-East. Hence, there was little scope for an acceptable middle ground.
5. **Presence of racism:** Because of centuries-old slave-trade of African people by the white colonialists, the racist repression was very intense (in the form of apartheid) which could be dismantled only after a prolonged battle.

2. Explain the features of Apartheid in South Africa.

Model Answer

2. Explain the features of Apartheid in South Africa.

Approach

- Explain the features of Apartheid in South Africa.

Apartheid was a system of institutionalized racial segregation and political discrimination that was enforced in South Africa from 1948 to 1994 to preserve the dominance of the white race. Thus apartheid laws divided South Africa's population based on race. The apartheid government classified citizens into different racial groups and imposed various forms of discrimination and segregation on them, including restrictions on movement, education, and political participation. The most pathetic aspect of the policy of apartheid is that it was enforced in South Africa at the time when the policy of decolonization was being followed in the rest of the world.

Features of the Apartheid System

1. **Homeland System**: The government attempted to divide South Africa into a number of separate states, each of which was supposed to develop into a separate nation-state for a different ethnic group. Under the 'Population Registration Act of 1950' the white and black populations had to be settled in different regions.
2. Separate areas were earmarked for black residents known as Bantustan. A Pass Permit System was introduced according to which movement of black citizens were monitored. The black could come to the white region to work as labour only after attaining a pass.
3. Black and brown people's political representation was restricted, and they were prohibited from participating in political activities.
4. Every person was given a racial classification and an identity card.
5. Separate transport systems were started for blacks.
6. Blacks and whites were not allowed to be married or have sexual intercourse. According to 'Mixed Marriage Act of 1949', whites were prohibited to marry blacks.
7. Black children went to separate schools and were given a much inferior education.